D1321846

Fatal Path

*British Government and Irish
Revolution 1910–1922*

RONAN FANNING

FABER & FABER

First published in 2013
by Faber and Faber Ltd
Bloomsbury House
74–77 Great Russell Street
London WC1B 3DA

This paperback edition first
published in 2013

Typeset by Agnesi Text
Printed and bound in the UK by
CPI Group (UK) Ltd, Croydon CRO 4YY

A CIP record for this book
is available from the British Library

ISBN 978-0-571-29740-5

FSC
www.fsc.org
MIX
Paper from
responsible sources
FSC® C101712

2 4 6 8 10 9 7 5 3 1

In memory of
my English mother, Margaret Ella Bristow (1911–1996),
and my Irish father, Patrick Ronan Fanning (1901–1975)

Contents

Illustrations

There is a path of fatality which pursues the relations between the two countries and makes them eternally at cross purposes.

David Lloyd George
House of Commons
22 December 1919

Chronology

1906
January Liberals win overall majority in general election.

1907
29 January Augustine Birrell appointed chief secretary for Ireland.
21 April Inaugural meeting of Sinn Féin.
3 June Collapse of Irish Council Bill in House of Commons.

1908
8 April Herbert Henry Asquith appointed prime minister.

1909
30 November House of Lords rejects David Lloyd George's budget.
10 December Asquith's Albert Hall speech promising Irish home rule.

1910
January– General election: nationalists hold balance
February   in House of Commons.
21 February Edward Carson elected leader of Irish Unionist MPs.
6 May Death of Edward VII; accession of George V.
17 June Constitutional Conference on powers of House
    of Lords.
10 November Collapse of Constitutional Conference.
December General election: nationalists retain balance
    in Commons.

1911
18 August Parliament Act: Lords' power to reject bills cut to
    two years.

23 September	Carson reveals plans for a provisional Ulster government.
13 November	Andrew Bonar Law succeeds Arthur Balfour as leader of Conservative and Unionist Party.

1912

6 February	Lloyd George and Winston Churchill propose Ulster's exclusion from Home Rule Bill at cabinet.
9 April	Bonar Law pledges British unionists' support for resistance of Ulster unionists to Home Rule Bill at mass rally in Belfast.
11 April	Asquith introduces Home Rule Bill in House of Commons.
11 June	Liberal rebel MP moves amendment (defeated 18 June) excluding four north-eastern counties from Home Rule Bill.
29 July	Bonar Law's inflammatory speech at Blenheim Palace.
28 September	'Ulster Day': unionists sign Covenant to resist home rule.

1913

16 January	Third reading of Home Rule Bill carried in Commons.
30 January	Bill defeated in Lords.
31 January	Formation of Ulster Volunteer Force (UVF).
7 July	Home Rule Bill again passes Commons.
15 July	Home Rule Bill again rejected by Lords.
11 August	George V urges Asquith to exclude Ulster.
24 September	Ulster Unionist Council (UUC) approves plan for seizure of power by provisional government if Home Rule Bill enacted.
14 October, 6 November, 10 December	Asquith's and Bonar Law's secret meetings on exclusion.
19 November	Inaugural meeting of Irish Citizen Army in Dublin.
25 November	Inaugural meeting of Irish Volunteers in Dublin.
4 December	Proclamation prohibiting arms importation into Ireland.
16 December, 2 January 1914	Asquith's secret meetings on exclusion with Carson.

1914

22 *January*	Asquith informs cabinet of secret meetings.
2 *February*	Asquith tells Redmond that he must offer exclusion.
9 *February*	Cabinet defers decision on when offer will be made public.
6 *March*	Asquith offers exclusion of Ulster for six years on moving second reading of Home Rule Bill for third time; Carson rejects.
20 *March*	Curragh 'mutiny': 57 of 70 officers in 3rd Cavalry Brigade prefer dismissal to moving north to enforce home rule.
24–25 *April*	Ulster gun-running: 25,000 rifles for UVF landed without hindrance at Larne, Bangor and Donaghdee.
12 *May*	Asquith announces amending bill to Home Rule Bill.
16 *June*	John Redmond secures leadership of Irish Volunteers.
23 *June*	Government of Ireland (Amendment) Bill providing for temporary exclusion by county option introduced in Lords.
28 *June*	Archduke Franz Ferdinand assassinated at Sarajevo.
8 *July*	Amendment Bill amended in Lords to provide for permanent exclusion of all Ulster.
10 *July*	Ulster provisional government meets in Belfast.
21–24 *July*	Buckingham Palace conference fails to agree on terms of Ulster's exclusion.
23 *July*	Austria-Hungary declares war on Serbia.
26 *July*	Irish Volunteers land rifles at Howth, Co. Dublin; British troops fire on crowd in Dublin: 4 killed, 30 wounded.
1–2 *August*	Irish Volunteers land rifles at Kilcoole, Co. Wicklow.
3 *August*	Germany declares war on France. Redmond pledges Irish support if UK enters war.
4 *August*	Germany invades Belgium; UK declares war on Germany.
15 *September*	Bill to suspend operation of home rule passes all three readings.
18 *September*	Third Home Rule Bill and suspensory bill enacted; Government of Ireland (Amendment Bill) abandoned.
20 *September*	Redmond calls on Irish Volunteers to join British army.

1915

7 May   *Lusitania* torpedoed off south-west coast of Ireland.
25 May   Asquith forms coalition government that includes
           Carson.

1916

24 April   Easter rebellion in Dublin: proclamation of 'Irish
           Republic'.
29 April   Unconditional surrender ends rebellion: 450 dead.
3 May   Birrell resigns as chief secretary.
3–12 May   Thirteen leading rebels court-martialled and executed.
23 May   Asquith asks Lloyd George to negotiate Irish settlement.
12 June   Ulster Unionist Council accepts Lloyd George's
           proposal for immediate implementation of home
           rule with temporary exclusion of six counties.
1 July   Somme offensive begins: 20,000 British deaths.
24 July   Failure of Lloyd George's negotiations evident.
3 August   Roger Casement hanged in Pentonville gaol.
           Henry Duke becomes chief secretary for Ireland.
7 December Lloyd George appointed coalition prime minister.

1917

1 February   Germany begins unrestricted submarine warfare.
5 February   Sinn Féin wins North Roscommon by-election.
8–15 March   Revolution in Russia: abdication of Tsar Nicholas II.
6 April   USA declares war on Germany.
9 May   Sinn Féin wins South Longford by-election.
21 May   Lloyd George announces Irish Convention to prepare
             scheme of Irish self-government.
16 June   All Irish prisoners gaoled since 1916 rebellion released.
10 July   Éamon de Valera wins East Clare by-election for
             Sinn Féin.
25 July   First meeting of Irish Convention; Sinn Féin abstains.
25 October   De Valera elected president of Sinn Féin.
27 October   De Valera elected president of Irish Volunteers.
6–7 November Lenin and Bolsheviks seize power in Russia.
5 December   Russia signs armistice with Germany at Brest-Litovsk.

1918

8 January	President Woodrow Wilson sets out 14 points for peace.
6 March	Death of John Redmond.
12 March	John Dillon elected leader of Irish Parliamentary Party.
21 March	Last great German offensive on western front.
5 April	Final meeting of Irish Convention ends in failure.
9 April	Lloyd George proposes extending conscription to Ireland.
16 April	John Dillon leads Irish Parliamentary Party out of Commons.
18 April	Sinn Féin and Irish Parliamentary Party unite against conscription; delegation meets Catholic bishops.
23 April	Anti-conscription general strike in Ireland (outside Ulster).
4 May	Edward Shortt appointed chief secretary for Ireland.
5 May	Viscount French sworn in as Lord Lieutenant of Ireland.
10 May	War cabinet abandons plans to extend conscription, coupled with immediate introduction of home rule.
17–18 May	'German plot': arrest of many Sinn Féin leaders.
4–9 November	Revolution in Germany, which becomes a republic.
11 November	Armistice ends First World War.
14–28 December	General election: 478 coalition candidates returned but Conservative Party (358) gains overall majority; Sinn Féin win 73 of the 105 Irish seats.

1919

12 January	Paris peace conference begins.
13 January	Ian Macpherson appointed chief secretary.
21 January	Sinn Féin MPs abandon Westminster and hold first meeting of Dáil Éireann ('Irish parliament') in Dublin.
	War of independence begins when Irish Volunteers – Irish Republican Army (IRA) – kill two policemen at Soloheadbeg, County Tipperary.
3 February	De Valera escapes from Lincoln gaol.
1 April	De Valera elected president of Dáil Éireann.

1 June	De Valera leaves Ireland for New York.
15 June	First non-stop transatlantic flight by Alcock and Brown.
28 June	Versailles Treaty between Germany and Allied powers.
29 June	Lloyd George returns from Paris.
12 September	Dáil Éireann declared illegal.
7 October	Cabinet committee on Irish self-government appointed.
4 November	Cabinet committee proposes two parliaments: one for all nine Ulster counties, and one for 'Southern Ireland'.
15 December	Cabinet informed that Ulster Unionists want the scheme 'applied only to the six Protestant counties'.
19 December	IRA's attempted assassination of Lord French.
22 December	Lloyd George outlines two-parliament policy to Commons.

1920

2 January	Royal Irish Constabulary (RIC) enrols first British recruits, later notorious as the 'Black and Tans'.
25 February	Government of Ireland Bill, providing that Northern Ireland consist of only six counties, introduced in Commons.
20 March	Ulster Unionist Council accepts Government of Ireland Bill.
23 March	General Nevil Macready appointed GOC in Ireland.
12 April	Hamar Greenwood appointed chief secretary.
12 May	Warren Fisher's critical report triggers new appointments in Dublin Castle headed by John Anderson.
27 July	Auxiliary Division of RIC, recruited from British ex-officers.
23–31 August	Sectarian violence in Belfast: 30 deaths.
20 September	Black and Tans sack Balbriggan, Co. Dublin.
1 November	Recruitment begins for Ulster Special Constabulary.
3 November	Lloyd George's 'we have murder by the throat' speech.
21 November	'Bloody Sunday' in Dublin: IRA kills 14 suspected secret service agents; Auxiliaries kill 2 IRA commandants; Black and Tans fire on football crowd in Croke Park and kill 12.
28 November	IRA kill 18 Auxiliaries at Kilmichael, Co. Cork.

10 December	Martial law proclaimed in Cork and three adjoining counties.
11–12 December	Auxiliaries and Black and Tans sack Cork city.
23 December	Government of Ireland Act, 1920 becomes law. De Valera returns to Ireland from USA.

1921

4 February	Edward Carson resigns as Ulster Unionist leader; James Craig elected to succeed him.
13 February	Walter Long resigns from government.
17 March	Bonar Law resigns from government; succeeded as Conservative Party leader by Austen Chamberlain.
2 May	Viscount Fitzalan sworn in as Lord Lieutenant of Ireland.
5 May	De Valera meets Craig in Dublin.
24 May	Northern Ireland election: Unionists win 40 of the 52 seats.
25 May	IRA destroys Custom House in Dublin but suffers 100 arrests.
7 June	Craig appointed prime minister of Northern Ireland.
22 June	George V opens Northern Ireland parliament.
9 July	British army and IRA representatives agree terms of truce.
14 July	Lloyd George and de Valera meet in Downing Street.
7 September	Lloyd George holds cabinet meeting in Inverness Town Hall.
29–30 September	Lloyd George and de Valera agree terms for conference.
11 October	Anglo-Irish conference begins in London.
6 December	Anglo-Irish treaty provides for establishing Irish Free State (IFS) as self-governing dominion.

1922

7 January	Dáil Éireann approves Anglo-Irish treaty by 64 votes to 57.
9 January	De Valera resigns as president of Dáil Éireann.
14 January	Provisional Government for IFS established.

16 January	Lord Lieutenant formally transfers power at Dublin Castle to Michael Collins as chairman of provisional government.
21 January	Craig–Collins pact includes guarantees for Belfast Catholics.
2 February	Publication of James Joyce's *Ulysses* in Paris.
12–15 February	Violence in Belfast: 27 killed, 68 wounded.
30 March	Second Craig–Collins peace pact.
14 April	Anti-treaty elements in IRA occupy Four Courts in Dublin.
20 May	Collins–de Valera pact provides for pro- and anti-Sinn Féin candidates at IFS election proportionate to current strength.
16 June	IFS election: Sinn Féin – pro-treaty 58, anti-treaty 36.
22 June	IRA assassinates Henry Wilson in London.
28 June	Pro-treaty forces attack Four Courts: start of civil war.
22 August	Michael Collins killed in ambush in County Cork.
25 August	William T. Cosgrave appointed chairman of provisional government.
23 October	Andrew Bonar Law appointed prime minister.
25 October	Irish Constitution approved by Dáil.
5 December	Irish Free State Constitution Act [UK] ratifies Treaty.
6 December	Cosgrave appointed president of executive council of IFS; Timothy Healy sworn in as first governor general of IFS.
7 December	Northern Ireland opts out of IFS.

1923

27 April	End of Irish civil war.
20 May	Resignation of Andrew Bonar Law.
23 May	Stanley Baldwin appointed prime minister.
20 July	IFS appoints Eoin MacNeill to boundary commission.

1924

22 January	Ramsay MacDonald becomes first Labour prime minister.
5 June	Richard Feetham chosen to chair boundary commission.
6 November	First meeting of boundary commission.

1925

7 November	*Morning Post* leaks findings of boundary commission.
20 November	Eoin MacNeill resigns from boundary commission.
3 December	Tripartite agreement between British, Irish and Northern Irish governments suppresses boundary commission report and maintains existing border of Northern Ireland.

Introduction

Violence, or, more specifically, the British government's response to violence, determined the course of the fatal path
spoken of by David Lloyd George when, as prime minister,
he introduced the bill that partitioned Ireland.

Fear of Ulster Unionist violence so paralysed British policy
from 1912 to 1914 that it prevented the implementation of
home rule and corroded the faith of Ireland's constitutional
nationalists in parliamentary democracy; the clear majority of
Irish seats in the House of Commons held by the Irish Parliamentary Party for forty years disintegrated at the next election.

The apocalyptic violence of the Great War of 1914–18
brought the tentacles of death into most houses in Britain, including 10 Downing Street, and ensured that for its duration
the British sought not to solve but to shelve the problem of
Ireland. Although the republican rebellion of 1916 registered
as no more than a blip against such a cataclysmic backdrop,
its legacy – the Irish Republican Army's guerrilla war for
independence – was the key determinant of British policy
between 1920 and 1922.

The role of violence in British–Irish relations has always
been among the most contentious of historical subjects. It is
now a hundred years since the beginning of a decade, 1912–
22, when this was especially true: a decade that began with

the introduction of the third Home Rule Bill in 1912 and ended with the establishment in 1922 of the Irish Free State as a self-governing dominion from which the six counties of Northern Ireland were excluded.

This was a decade of revolution, yet even that simple statement is a matter of contention. Some may take issue with the title of this book because the term 'revolution' is rarely ascribed to the Ulster Unionists' successful resistance to the third Home Rule Bill. Yet, given their rejection of British parliamentary authority as expressed between 1910 and 1914 through the government's democratic mandate in the House of Commons, in the creation and arming of the 90,000-strong Ulster Volunteer Force, in the establishment of a provisional government in Belfast in September 1913, and in the mutiny threatened by an elite corps of British army officers at the Curragh and endorsed by the British Conservative Party in March 1914, a revolution it undoubtedly was. It was among the most successful of bloodless revolutions: the mere threat of force, sustained and carefully coordinated, sufficed to achieve the Unionist revolution.

The Irish republican revolution was neither bloodless nor initially successful. Indeed, the very fact that a large minority of republicans so vehemently rejected the Anglo-Irish Treaty of December 1921 explains the otherwise inexplicable republican reluctance to claim the title of revolution for what happened between 1916 and 1922. The civil war's impact on Irish historiography endured because its combatants continued to demand competing interpretations of the revolution and the government that took office in 1932, like that in 1922, still had to overcome the challenge of armed resistance to its authority.

Events in Northern Ireland after 1969, much the most significant eruption of violence in Ireland since the civil war, compounded the difficulties of writing impartial and dispassionate history. To give weight to the revolutionary nature of what happened between 1912 and 1922, so the argument ran, was to give comfort and support to the Provisional IRA in its bloody and ultimately futile war in Northern Ireland. Political imperatives prevailed, as they invariably do, over historical truth in the revisionist debate that then ensued.

Few historians would dispute that 'we are all revisionists now',[1] although professional historians use the term sparingly: for them it means no more than revising our knowledge of the past in accordance with new evidence unearthed or old evidence revisited. But revisionism as practised by some historians, as well as by politicians, publicists and polemicists, is a different matter. They have been well described by Bernard Lewis, the eminent historian of the Middle East, as those who

> . . . would rewrite history not as it was, or as they have been taught it was but as they would prefer it to have been . . . [Their] purpose of changing the past is not to seek some abstract truth, but to achieve a new vision of the past better suited to their needs in the present and their aspirations for the future. Their aim is to amend, to restate, to replace, or even to recreate the past in a more satisfactory form.[2]

And Lewis also writes of how 'those who are in power control to a very large extent the presentation of the past and seek to make sure that it is presented in such a way as to buttress and legitimise their own authority'.[3]

There is no better description of how and why throughout Northern Ireland's long war the British and Irish political establishments sought to control the presentation of the history of 1912–22 in order to buttress and legitimise their own authority while at the same time denying legitimacy and authority to the Provisional IRA and other paramilitary forces.

This inherent problem for historians of Britain's Irish policy was compounded by the timetable of archival releases. The Public Records Act of 1967, which made British cabinet and departmental records available after thirty years, meant, in effect, that the release of the papers for the Anglo-Irish War of 1919–21 coincided with the beginning of the Northern Ireland crisis. This induced historians to shrink from the realities of the republican revolution and to question, for example, 'whether the bloody catalogue of assassinations and war from 1919–21 was necessary to negotiate [the treaty]'.[4]

This book argues that it was indeed necessary: that there is no shred of evidence that Lloyd George's Tory-dominated government would have moved beyond the 1914-style limitations of the Government of Ireland Act of 1920 unless impelled to do so by the campaign of the IRA. Indeed, as Charles Townshend has argued in his seminal work on the British campaign in Ireland, 'on the British side some form of military struggle was inevitable before Irish demands would be taken seriously'.[5]

History, as the teacher reminds the narrator in Julian Barnes's novel *The Sense of an Ending*, is more than 'the lies of the victors . . . it is also the self-delusions of the defeated'. One of the more unfortunate by-products of the revisionist debate about twentieth-century Irish history is that it legitimised the self-delusions of the intellectual heirs to the constitutional nationalists who had been so resoundingly defeated by the republican revolutionaries.

Although much of the heat has ebbed from the revisionist controversy since peace came to Northern Ireland, the preoccupation with commemoration now poses a comparable threat to intellectual honesty. For the likely focus during the coming decade will not be to establish a value-free history of 1912–22 but with massaging that history and forcing it into moulds designed to persuade the people of Ireland, North and South, Protestant and Catholic, to prefer forms of commemoration that will avoid exacerbating the latent tensions between divided communities. Commemoration is an entirely laudable if somewhat utopian political objective. But it is not history. The danger is that its practitioners will propagate a bland, bloodless and bowdlerised hybrid of history, designed to offend no one, in the pious hope that it may command unanimous acquiescence. Theirs is but another variant of the phenomenon branded by Bernard Lewis as 'history not as it was . . . but as they would prefer it to have been'.

This book neither sympathises nor identifies with the political uses of violence then or now. It is simply a case study in the high politics of how physical force can prevail over democracy. It explains rather than condemns the behaviour of ministers in the governments led by Herbert Henry Asquith and Lloyd George as they sought a solution to Irish demands, unionist as well as nationalist, for self-determination – behaviour for the most part neither better nor worse than that of politicians in other parliamentary democracies. Vacillation, indecision, and a predilection for postponing intractable political problems are features of parliamentary democracies. The subordination of framing legislative policy to the imperative of never jeopardising a parliamentary majority is another.

The story of how and why power changed hands on a scale not witnessed in Ireland since the seventeenth century cannot be ignored because the methods used to persuade a British government to surrender power to a native Irish government offend the sensitivities of revisionists or commemorators. Those who insist that it is better to write nothing about how the threat of physical force triumphed in Ireland between 1912 and 1922 might instead reflect on an alternative proposition: that a candid account of how British parliamentary democracy crumpled when confronted by the threat of violence in the past might make it less likely that it will again do so in the future.

I
Gladstone's Legacy

When the Act of Union created the United Kingdom of Great Britain and Ireland, it conferred on 1801 a significance rarely attained by the first year of a new century. No such significance can be assigned to 1900. So tranquil was the dawn of the twentieth century that it was in this year, the last of her long life, that Queen Victoria paid her first visit to Ireland for forty years. By 1900 the course of British–Irish relations resembled a stagnant pond, encircled by banks deposited by the greatest upheaval since 1800: the crisis over William Ewart Gladstone's first Home Rule Bill in 1886.

On the morning after Gladstone had introduced his revolutionary Bill for the Government of Ireland in the House of Commons, he went to Westminster Abbey for the funeral service of William Edward 'Buckshot' Forster, his former chief secretary for Ireland – an occasion symbolic of the burial of the coercive policies epitomised by the nickname of the deceased. Gladstone there remarked to Lord Rosebery, his successor as Liberal prime minister in 1894, that 'this Home Rule question will control and put aside all other political questions in England till it is settled'.[1]

Gladstone's prophecy came to pass. In Ireland, the Union had been the cause of the great political divide even before Daniel O'Connell, the founding father of Irish constitutional nationalism, proposed its repeal to the House of Commons in 1834. But not until 1886 did the Union achieve the same status in British politics. Although home rule split Gladstone's party asunder when an alliance of Conservatives and Liberal Unionists threw out his 1886 bill on its second reading in the Commons, the next three decades saw the Irish question polarise British political parties as it had not done before and as it has never done since. Only in 1914, when the Great War compelled both Liberals and Conservatives to abandon partisan Irish policies in favour of the bipartisanship embodied in the coalition governments of 1915–22, was the shape of the division thrown up by the cataclysm of 1886 finally blurred.

Bipartisanship had also informed Britain's Irish policy in the eighty-five years between the enactment of the Union and Gladstone's fateful conversion to home rule. There were, of course, differences between Whigs and Tories, between Liberals and Conservatives, on Irish as on other policies. But consensus reigned on the core of the Irish issue: the immutability of that constitutional relationship between the two islands explicitly declared irrevocable and indissoluble under the terms of the Act of Union.

Until Gladstone concluded 'that the Act of Union was "a gigantic though excusable mistake"'[2] and shattered the bipartisan consensus on the governance of Ireland, both great parties were Unionist and neither, therefore, needed to be so described. 'Unionist' became a commonplace description of supporters of the Act of Union, in Britain and in Ireland, only when the Union was first imperilled, in 1886. That the Tories swiftly renamed themselves 'the Conservative and Unionist Party' testified to what they had gained and what the Liberals had lost by the abandonment of bipartisanship.

Yet few were as conscious as Gladstone of the hazards of abandoning bipartisanship, for he knew that, whatever happened in the Commons, the inbuilt Conservative majority in the upper house meant that he could never get his home-rule bill through the Lords. As late as 20 December 1885 – some days after the news of his conversion to home rule, and a month after the election that gave the Irish Parliamentary Party, led by Charles Stewart Parnell, control of the balance of power in the Commons and the ability to replace Lord Salisbury's Conservative government with a Liberal government – Gladstone wrote to Arthur Balfour, Salisbury's nephew and confidant, warning against the calamity of the Irish question becoming a matter of party conflict and urging that Salisbury settle it, with Parnellite support and Liberal acquiescence. 'He be damned!'[3] responded Randolph Churchill, catching the Tory mood as it became evident that if a home-rule government were formed it would be under Gladstone's leadership.

Gladstone's credentials for such a role seemed impeccable. 'My mission', he had declared when invited to form his first government in 1868, 'is to pacify Ireland.'[4] He had disestablished the Church of Ireland in 1869 and, in 1870, launched the programme of land reform that won Tory support from 1885 and began to tilt the balance of power away from the landlords (who were often British and absentees) and in favour of their Irish tenants. But Gladstone's home-rule policy was fatally flawed because, although he had indelibly branded his party with the home-rule stamp, too many Liberals – right wing and left wing alike – fled from the brand. The defection of Lord Hartington's Whig faction was unsurprising; they had already grown restive with Gladstone's leadership, particularly on Irish land reform. But the loss of the radical wing, led by the Birmingham-based, energetic and popular Joseph

Chamberlain, was traumatic. Indeed it might be said, after Oscar Wilde, that to lose one wing of a party may be regarded as a misfortune; to lose both looks like carelessness.

At best, then, Gladstone's conduct of Irish policy in 1885–6 was 'problematic'; at worst, it was riddled with 'strategic errors'. Moreover, what Alvin Jackson has well described as Gladstone's 'evangelical self-assurance'[5] prompted him to reject the Commons' verdict on home rule. Rather than resign, he dissolved parliament and carried his crusade to the people. The overwhelming popular rejection of home rule in the British constituencies in the 1886 general election hardened the lines of the new party divide. 'I decided some time ago', Randolph Churchill wrote in mid-February 1886, 'that if the GOM [Grand Old Man] went for Home Rule, the Orange card would be the one to play. Please God it may turn out the ace of trumps and not the two.'[6] The impact of the 1886 crisis on the political climate that shaped the Irish policy of successive British governments in the decades ahead flowed from the voters granting this Tory prayer.

In six of the seven general elections in the thirty years before 1886 the Liberals had won over 300 seats and formed the government; the Conservatives only once topped 300 seats in the same period, under Disraeli in 1874. The enormity of the electoral catastrophe that now overwhelmed the Liberals may be as simply stated. After three of the four elections in the next twenty years (when it was the Conservatives who won at least 300 seats and formed the government) the number of Liberal MPs sank below 200 – an ignominy that had never befallen their opponents between 1857 and 1885. And even in 1892, when Gladstone formed his last government with the support of the Irish Parliamentary Party, the Liberals fell far short of 300 seats. The contrast wrought by 1886, painted in terms of political power, was correspondingly stark. The Liberals were in office for almost twenty of the thirty years before 1886 and they were out of office for all but three of the next twenty years.

Such, for the Liberals, were the stigmata of Gladstone's conversion. Such, for the Conservatives, were the blessings bestowed by the Orange card. For the Conservatives, 1886 inaugurated those rare circumstances dear to all democratic politicians when the quest for electoral advantage dovetails with the celebration of party ideology. The Tory ideology, in so far as the Tories had an ideology, was the ideology of empire. To urge the wisdom of cherishing ties with more far-flung outposts of empire made little sense if Ireland (the country with which Britain had geographically the closest, and historically the longest, connection) broke the Union. 'On Tory principles,' as Salisbury had written in 1872, 'the case presents much that is painful, but no perplexity whatever. Ireland must be kept, like India, at all hazards: by persuasion, if possible; if not, by force.'[7]

In 1886 the arguments took on a cast coloured by the racial and religious prejudice that had perennially characterised English attitudes to Ireland at moments of crisis. 'We are to have confidence in the Irish people,' Salisbury exclaimed to a public meeting in May. 'Confidence depends on the people in whom you are to confide. You would not confide free representative institutions to the Hottentots for example', and he insisted that 'this which is called self-government, but which is really government by the majority, works admirably well when it is confided to people who are of Teutonic race, but it does not work so well when people of other races are called upon to join in it'.[8] The 'Protestants of Ireland', declared Randolph Churchill in February, 'are at one with England, with the English people . . . in race and religion. They are essentially like the English people, a dominant and imperial caste'; Gladstone intended 'to effect the dissolution of the unity of the United Kingdom . . . It is a policy of civil war.'[9]

The comprehensive defeat of Gladstone's bill glossed over the greatest obstacle to the enactment of home rule: the strength of Ulster Unionist opposition centred on the Protestant majorities in the counties of Antrim, Down, Londonderry and Armagh. But that the defeat of the bill was so swiftly accomplished by the normal workings of the House of Commons rendered almost invisible the phenomenon of Ulster Unionist resistance. When in 1893 Gladstone's second Home Rule Bill was likewise defeated by conventional parliamentary procedures, albeit in the House of Lords, Ulster Unionists again had no need to embrace the extra-parliamentary and revolutionary methods that characterised their opposition to the third Home Rule Bill from 1912 until 1914. In 1886 and 1893, concludes Alvin Jackson, the foremost historian of Unionism, 'local agitation on behalf of the Union varied little from the types of pressure politics adopted in contemporary Britain: there was certainly much talk of an armed struggle, but no evidence has survived to suggest that such talk was ever seriously translated into action'.[10] Ulster Unionists were content to confine their efforts to the parliamentary arena because, before 1911, they knew they would win there.

These circumstances created a conspiracy of silence about the reality: that no British government had addressed the right of Ulster's Unionist majority to political self-determination comparable to that accorded Ireland's Nationalist majority under the terms of the home-rule bills. Although the ultimate fate of home rule would hinge on the demand of separate treatment for Unionist Ulster, all the major parties – Liberals and Conservatives, Irish Nationalists and Unionists – had a vested interest in preserving what was to become a twenty-five-year silence. Silence suited the Liberals and Nationalists because it was the best climate for nourishing their always uneasy entente; they clung to the wobbly crutch of Ulster having returned 18 Nationalists, as opposed to 17 Unionists, in the 1885 general election. Silence suited the Conservatives and Unionists because they wanted to defeat home rule not only for Ulster but for all Ireland. Most Unionists used Ulster's opposition as 'the argument to block any form of Home Rule, rather than providing an incentive for thought about how the Irish minority should be catered for'; Joseph Chamberlain, the radical Liberal leader who led the Liberal Unionists after he split with Gladstone over the 1886 Home Rule Bill, was then 'almost alone' in grappling 'with the idea of separate assemblies for Dublin and Belfast, the Irish "solution" into which politicians stumbled by default in the years 1914–22'.[11]

The parliamentary defeat of both Gladstone's home-rule bills obscured a fundamental truth about the Irish question in British politics that became glaringly obvious in 1912: that it would be difficult – even, perhaps, impossible – to amend the Act of Union and devolve government to Ireland through the normal workings of British parliamentary democracy. The heart of the difficulty had been identified by Chamberlain during his celebrated Commons speech on the 1886 bill when, to cries of 'No, no!' from the more passionate home-rulers in the House, he insisted that 'Ireland is not a homogeneous community – that it consists of two nations – that it is a nation that comprises two nations and two religions.'[12] John Bright, a staunch friend of earlier Gladstonian reforms in Ireland but also the Nonconformist conscience of the Liberal

Party and no friend of Roman Catholicism, likewise denounced the bill because it was 'so offensive to the whole Protestant population of Ireland, and to the whole sentiment of the province of Ulster so far as its loyal and Protestant people are concerned'.[13]

Bright's attitude well illustrates how antipathy to subjecting the 'loyal Protestants' in a majority in north-east Ulster to the dominance of the huge Catholic majority in the island of Ireland characterised Liberal as well as Conservative attitudes to home rule. For the next twenty-five years this mattered little: the realities of parliamentary politics (the Conservatives' near-monopoly of government coupled with their permanent inbuilt majority in the House of Lords) presented insurmountable obstacles to the passage of home rule. But the risk of loyal Protestants falling under the sway of nationalist Catholics in Ireland became real when the Parliament Act of 1911 emasculated the House of Lords and triggered the demand, among Liberals as well as Conservatives, that Ulster Unionist aspirations be separately satisfied.

The circumstances of the defeat of the second Home Rule Bill compounded dissatisfaction among leading Liberals with Gladstone's Irish policy, not least because, in 1893 as in 1886, he kept his cabinet colleagues in the dark about the terms of his bill. The 1892 general election had produced a small majority for home rule in the House of Commons because, although 273 Liberals barely outnumbered 269 Conservatives, 81 Irish home-rulers outnumbered 46 Liberal Unionists and the bill was passed by 34 votes on 1 September 1893. But, only a week later, the unassailable Conservative majority in the House of Lords predictably destroyed it by 419 votes to 41. Although Gladstone wanted to lead his troops to the country yet again, his cabinet colleagues had had a bellyful of his Irish crusading. 'He proposes an immediate dissolution – pretext being action of H. of Lords on our Bills; we all agreed that this is madness,'[14] wrote Henry Asquith, the brilliant young home secretary and future prime minister, in his diary for 7 February 1894. In 1910 those words came to haunt him when he twice dissolved parliament on the very issue he had indicted as insane sixteen years before. The consensus among Gladstone's cabinet colleagues was that he was no longer mentally or physically fit to continue in office and he formally resigned on 3 March 1894.

The tragedy of Gladstone's Irish crusade was that it excited Irish nationalist appetites that neither he nor any other leader of a Liberal government could satisfy while also ignoring Ulster Unionist demands for a comparable right of self-determination. That he was 'put out'[15] on Ireland prompted a decisive shift in his party's Irish policy, which was disguised because a Liberal government would not again frame a bill for the government of Ireland until 1912.

The significance of this shift in the Liberals' Irish policy was personified by Gladstone's successor as prime minister: Archibald Philip Primrose, fifth Earl of Rosebery. Rosebery shared neither Gladstone's austere temperament nor his messianic vision. Worldliness instead characterised the three ambitions invariably linked with his name in London society: to marry an heiress, to own a Derby winner, to be prime minister of England. He had married a Rothschild in 1878, and in 1894, when at the age of forty-six he became prime minister, he had already won the first of three Derbies. Rosebery laid bare the difference between his Irish policy and Gladstone's in his very first parliamentary speech as prime minister: he endorsed Salisbury's statement 'that before Irish Home Rule is conceded by the Imperial Parliament, England as the predominant partner of the Three Kingdoms will have to be convinced of its justice and equity'.[16]

Rosebery's speech achieved instant notoriety. It stupefied his cabinet colleagues, angered Gladstonian Liberals and out-raged the Irish Parliamentary Party. Rosebery wanted to re-capture the bipartisan consensus on Ireland ruptured in 1886 and his 'predominant partner' doctrine provided the ideo-logical underpinning for the Liberal imperialist retreat from Gladstonian home rule. Reopening the debate about the Liberal commitment to home rule for Ireland further diverted attention from the issue of Ulster. If and when it did again become an issue, English MPs (the elected representatives of the 'predominant partner') would scarcely agree that the claims of Irish nationalism should be satisfied at the expense of the claims of Ulster Unionism. Although Rosebery pooh-poohed the furore triggered by his 'predominant partner' speech, he never withdrew it and his growing appetite for Lib-eral imperialism etched the contrast with Gladstone's Irish policy. He 'remained unmindful, or more probably indiffer-ent, to the need for discretion in the handling of Irish issues'. Given his indifference to Irish nationalist sentiment, it was richly appropriate that his government, 'dependent upon the Irish vote, lurched to final and deserved disaster on a proposal to erect a statue of Oliver Cromwell [reviled in the demon-ology of Catholic Ireland] in Parliament Square'.[17] That Rose-bery's government was so ill starred and so short-lived, and that he resigned as leader of the Liberal Party in 1899 and was never again in government, are among the reasons why historians have failed to recognise the lasting significance of his U-turn on Irish policy.

Rosebery was succeeded as leader of the Liberal Party by Henry Campbell-Bannerman, a partner in his family's drapery business in Glasgow until he entered parliament in 1868 as MP for the Stirling Burghs, which he represented for the next forty years. Although his brief term as Irish chief secretary in 1884–5 and his generally warm relations with Parnell's party suggested he was less antipathetic to Irish nationalist aspirations, Campbell-Bannerman had also been pessimistic about the prospects of home rule since January 1886. But, while he defended home rule in a major speech in 1899, he simultaneously repudiated 'the necessity, the expediency, aye, and the possibility' of making it the first item on the agenda of a Liberal government. [18]

The likelihood of a Liberal government remained remote, however, when war in South Africa widened the rift between Gladstonians and Liberal imperialists. The Boer war also heightened tension between the Liberals and their Irish allies by challenging assumptions about the compatibility of Irish nationalism and British imperialism. Following pro-Boer riots in Dublin on 17 December 1899, 'in effect, the Irish pro-Boer movement and the Irish nationalist movement were, for a period of thirty months, indistinguishable'.[19] It was not simply that the Liberals used 'the war as a mere excuse to "drop" Home Rule from the head of their list of priorities. They were outraged at the attitude adopted and the language used in the House of Commons by the Irish pro-Boers.'[20] All this compounded Liberal alienation from their Irish allies. Ironically, it was Gladstone's son, Herbert, the new Liberal chief whip, who sought Campbell-Bannerman's authority to relieve prospective Liberal candidates of any obligation to support another home-rule bill in the next parliament in order to win back that 'not inconsiderable number of Unionists who are real Liberals apart from the Irish question'. Herbert Gladstone's proposals were circulated to all members of the last

Liberal cabinet still active in politics and their replies showed 'the leaders of the party in virtually complete agreement on a policy of withdrawal and detachment'[21] – a policy, in Herbert Gladstone's words, of 'stand and wait', of marking time.

But the Liberal imperialists wanted more than this mealy-mouthed compromise. Rosebery threw down the gauntlet in an eagerly anticipated speech at Chesterfield on 16 December 1901: the Liberal Party would not again hold power while its leaders were 'men who sit still with the fly-blown phylacteries of obsolete policies bound round their foreheads, who do not remember that while they have been mumbling their incantations to themselves, the world has been marching and revolving'.[22] A new century demanded new policies and a 'clean slate'. Rosebery 'left no doubt in the minds of those who heard or read him that in his opinion Home Rule was dead, and that it was high time for Liberals to unchain themselves from the corpse'.[23] In February 1902 he disavowed Campbell-Bannerman's leadership and established the Liberal League (in place of the Liberal Imperialist League) under his own presidency and the vice-presidency of Henry Asquith, Edward Grey and Henry Fowler (subsequently joined by Richard Haldane). The strength of this imperialist bloc in the Liberal governments that held office from December 1905 until May 1915 was reflected in the cabinet ministries held by all four vice-presidents: Asquith, chancellor of the exchequer until 1908 and prime minister thereafter; Grey, foreign secretary, 1905–16; Haldane, secretary of state for war, 1905–12, and Lord Chancellor, 1912–15; and Fowler, Chancellor of the Duchy of Lancaster, 1905–8, and Lord President of the Council, 1908–10.

Although the end of the Boer war and Rosebery's small appetite for public life reduced the League's importance, many Liberal leaders 'had become convinced that Home Rule was an election-losing policy, though they were not above keeping the policy sufficiently alive to secure the Irish vote, while sufficiently inert to avoid alarming the rest of the electorate'.[24] Asquith spelt out the message to his constituents in East Fife on 1 March 1902 in an open letter that sought to endorse the message of Rosebery without spurning the memory of Gladstone: it should be no 'part of the policy and programme of our party that, if returned to power, it will introduce into the House of Commons a bill for Irish Home Rule'. He argued that home rule could be achieved only 'by methods which will carry with them, step by step, the sanction and sympathy of British opinion. To recognise facts like these is not apostasy; it is common sense.'[25] Asquith's prescription, which soothed the nerves of a party plagued by dissent on Ireland since 1886, became more addictive in 1904 and 1905 with the imminence of an election. Rosebery, however, remained immune to its charms: in a speech nicely calculated to tap the Nonconformist springs of anti-Catholicism, he denounced 'any middle policy – that of placing Home Rule in the position of a reliquary, and only exhibiting it at great moments of public stress, as Roman Catholics are accustomed to exhibit relics of a saint'.[26]

Campbell-Bannerman, however, hugged the middle ground bordered by the realisation that a renewed commitment to home rule would be a godsend enabling the Tories, who had split asunder on tariff reform in 1903, to reunite, and the recognition that the Liberals might need the votes of the Irish nationalist MPs to form a government, just as they had done after the general elections of 1885 and 1892. He accordingly assured John Redmond (the leader of the reunited Irish Parliamentary Party since 1900) that 'he was stronger than ever for Home Rule'. While he believed 'it would not be possible to pass full Home Rule' in the next parliament, 'he hoped to be able to pass some serious measure which would be consistent with and would lead up to the other. He would say nothing, however, to withdraw the larger measure from the electors.'[27]

This was the party line spelled out by Campbell-Bannerman on 23 November 1905 and endorsed by such leading Liberal imperialists as Asquith, the Marquess of Crewe (Rosebery's son-in-law and the Liberal leader in the House of Lords from 1908), and Grey: 'a continued commitment to Home Rule but a gradualist approach – the "step by step" policy'.[28] When Campbell-Bannerman formed his government a fortnight later, Rosebery alone stood out; none of his followers in the Commons – Asquith, Grey, Haldane and Fowler – could afford the luxury of his aristocratic indifference to the fruits of office. Conservative dreams that the Liberals might yet again split on Ireland were dashed, but they still clung to the Orange card in the hope that Liberal government would again be impossible without Irish support and even leading Liberal Unionist tariff reformers, such as Joseph Chamberlain and his son Austen, put Ireland rather than tariff reform in the forefront of their election manifestos.

The Liberals had never enjoyed a majority independent of the Irish Parliamentary Party since Gladstone had embraced home rule, and they were never to do so again. Throughout the life of the 1906–9 parliament their huge majority empowered them to do what the Liberal leaders had wanted to do for so long: to wipe the slate clean of Gladstone's legacy. Home rule was put on ice in a classic demonstration of the Cooke and Vincent axiom that 'the Irish policies of British governments at Westminster cannot be explained in terms of Irish circumstances. They must be explained in terms of parliamentary combinations.'[29]

Two combinations were critical. The first hinged on the conflict between the two Houses of Parliament as the Conservatives, powerless to form combinations in the Commons, resorted to their hereditary majority in the House of Lords to veto Liberal legislation and to ensure that 'the Conservative Party would come into its own again' and that what Tory diehard Lord Willoughby de Broke described as 'the hideous abnormality of a Liberal Government independent of the Irish [that] would go the way of all flesh'.[30] Normality returned when the two general elections of 1910, precipitated by the constitutional crisis caused by the Lords' rejection of Lloyd George's 'People's Budget' of 1909, reduced the Liberals to dependence on the Irish Parliamentary Party and again put Ireland centre stage in British politics.

The second critical parliamentary combination between 1906 and 1909 hinged on the shifting balance of power within the Liberal cabinet. Lord Rosebery's virtual disappearance from political life disguised the triumph of his thinking personified by the starring ministerial roles of his Liberal imperialist acolytes. First among these was Herbert Henry Asquith, chancellor of the exchequer and heir apparent to a prime minister already in failing health. Nicholas Mansergh's assessment cannot be bettered:

Mr Asquith was grave. He was a man of the highest intellectual attainments. To an unimpeachable integrity of mind he added the sagacious scepticism of an Oxford humanist. Yet he made no personal contribution to the solution of the Irish question. To a degree surprising in one 'who was a master of so many of the arts of government, he was without initiative in ideas and policy . . . It was not his mission to find the raw materials of policy, but rather to shape and direct them, when the course of events brought them within his reach' . . . In Irish affairs this lack of intellectual initiative was reinforced by the history of Home Rule . . . He had lived with the Irish question all through his political life and had sat in Cabinet when Gladstone made his last great effort in 1893. He knew . . . the Irish controversy by heart. That may well have been his greatest liability. All his thoughts were second thoughts.[31]

Asquith had quoted Herodotus when he became the youngest minister in Gladstone's last cabinet: 'Of all human troubles the most hateful is to feel that you have the capacity of power yet you have no field to exercise it.'[32] A barrister by profession, he had inherited neither wealth nor patronage and he lost more than most from another decade in the political wilderness; he never forgot that, 'except for the three years between 1892 and 1895, when a Liberal Government lived almost from day to day on a composite and precarious majority, it may be said that the Irish controversy kept the Liberal Party out of power for the best part of twenty years'.[33] Thereafter, he determined that Ireland should never deny him power again and this instinct governed his Irish policy from the moment he succeeded the dying Campbell-Bannerman as prime minister until his departure from 10 Downing Street in December 1916.

Almost as eminently placed at the foreign office, at Asquith's insistence, was Edward Grey, who had come closest to following Rosebery into self-imposed exile over Ireland. The third of a triumvirate of friends who had sat and acted together in the Commons since 1886 was R. B. Haldane, at the war office. The Asquith–Grey–Haldane troika was bolstered in cabinet by such other Liberal imperialists as Crewe and Fowler. Only John Morley was still imbued with any of Gladstone's messianic instincts and he was isolated at the India office, safely sequestered from Dublin Castle from where, as chief secretary, he had steered the first and second home-rule bills.

Campbell-Bannerman's choice as chief secretary of James Bryce – an Ulsterman by birth and a jurist, educationalist and historian by profession – reflected his step-by-step approach to Irish policy. Such, indeed, was the new Liberal government's abhorrence of home rule that the Irish Parliamentary Party leaders at first feared there might be no reference whatever to Ireland in the King's Speech; it eventually included an anodyne assurance about 'effecting economies in the system of government in Ireland and for introducing into it means for associating the people with the conduct of Irish affairs'.[34] Bryce was putty in the hands of Antony MacDonnell, the permanent under-secretary of state at the Irish office. Although personally sympathetic to home rule, MacDonnell recognised 'that England will not give Home Rule (as defined by Mr Redmond) . . . within any period that can be foreseen, and that proceeding by any other method than Devolution means postponing Administrative Reforms as well as Home Rule to the Greek Kalends'.[35] MacDonnell's devolutionary instincts owed little to Gladstone but much to his long experience in the Indian civil service and the Bryce–MacDonnell minimalist devolution schemes drew sustained criticism from nationalists until, at the end of 1906, an unhappy Bryce escaped to the sanctuary of the British Embassy in Washington.

Bryce was succeeded by the amiable but indolent Augustine Birrell – professor of law, distinguished essayist and critic, and president of the Board of Education since 1905 – who became much the longest-serving chief secretary under the Act of Union and whose tenure of Dublin Castle was terminated only in 1916. Birrell never wanted the job and his reaction when offered it well illustrates how generations of politicians have struggled vainly against prime ministerial will in their efforts to evade exile to Dublin and, after 1972, to Belfast. Why had 'I crossed that odious Irish Channel in February 1907 to become the fifty-fourth Chief Secretary to the Lord Lieutenant?' asked Birrell years later. 'I went because the Prime Minister of the day asked me to do so. I expect most, if not all my predecessors, would have given the same answer.'[36]

Birrell has had a bad press, partly because of his reputation as a dilettante and partly because his acceptance of responsibility for Dublin Castle's failure to anticipate the Easter rebellion made him a scapegoat in 1916. But until then, from the perspective of 10 Downing Street, Birrell's chief secretaryship was a resounding success. His primary objective was to improve relations with the Irish Parliamentary Party – in particular with Redmond and John Dillon – to whose wishes he so skilfully tailored the presentation of the government's Irish policy that, throughout 1910–14, Asquith's parliamentary majority remained secure. By 1908 Charles Hobhouse, who as financial secretary to the Treasury worked closely with the Irish chief secretary, had recognised that Birrell was 'the most cynical man in public business it is possible to conceive. He cares nothing about the rights or wrongs of a public matter – his sole concern is whether the Irish party will accept it or not.'[37]

But not even Birrell's blandishments could avert the fate of the Irish Council Bill of 1907, an exercise in diluted devolution that sought to give expression to the Liberals' 'step-by-step' Irish policy. Its timidity was dictated by government determination to prevent the issue of Ireland blurring the already looming and electorally advantageous issue of the Peers against the People; even the Gladstonian John Morley warned that Irish self-government 'would be "an ugly and dangerous issue" on which to try conclusions with the House of Lords'.[38] And when the bill was introduced (on 7 May, after protracted negotiations about every clause and comma between Birrell and the Irish leaders) government speakers highlighted its limitations, as F. S. L. Lyons has put it, 'for the tactical reason that they wanted it to pass the House of Commons with the minimum of trouble so that it could be offered to the House of Lords as an innocent lamb for the slaughter'.[39]

Birrell set the tone. Recalling the great occasions when the House had listened to Gladstone unfolding his Home Rule Bills, he explained that his task was of 'far humbler dimensions' and that his measure did 'not contain a touch or a trace, a hint or suggestion, of any new legislative power or authority'. That the prime minister had not troubled to introduce the bill underscored the point, and the leader of the opposition, Arthur Balfour (Tory prime minister from 1902 to 1905 and chief secretary for Ireland in 1887–91) witheringly responded that Birrell 'has not left upon my mind the impression that the plan he has laid before the House is one that even he himself takes seriously'.[40] Worse was to come in the prime minister's cringing description of the bill when he did break silence: a 'little, modest, shy, humble effort to give administrative powers to the Irish people'.[41]

The 'Irish people', mindful of Gladstone's heroic effort twenty-one years before, were inevitably unimpressed. So much so that the Irish National Convention, numbering some three thousand delegates, meeting in an electric atmosphere in Dublin's Mansion House on 21 May 1907, unanimously endorsed Redmond's resolution rejecting the Irish Council Bill as 'utterly inadequate in its scope, and unsatisfactory in its details', and reiterated the conviction that 'any attempt to settle the Irish problem by half-measures would be entirely unsuccessful'.[42] On 7 June, Campbell-Bannerman told the House that, since Redmond had already declared that 'he would abide by the decision of the Convention', ministers felt they had 'no choice but to conclude that the entire influence of the Irish Members, speaking for the Irish people, would be thrown against the measure; and in those circumstances, which are a source of regret and disappointment to us, we cannot of course go further with it'.[43] After one faltering step, the Liberals' gradualist policy had dissolved in a torrent of crocodile tears. Winston Churchill, who had deserted the Tories for the Liberals when he crossed the floor of the House of Commons in 1904 and was enjoying the perquisites of his first ministerial appointment as under-secretary of state for the colonies on the banks of the Nile, put it in a nutshell: 'that stupid Bill . . . has been our one disaster. But it is a big one; for it leaves us without an Irish policy . . . Ireland at the moment is utterly pigged.'[44]

The episode boosted the fortunes of Sinn Féin, the radical Irish nationalist umbrella movement inaugurated in May 1907. At this stage Sinn Féin, meaning 'Ourselves', embodied the idea of an Anglo-Irish dual monarchy as enunciated in 1904 in Arthur Griffith's *The Resurrection of Hungary: A Parallel for Ireland*. Griffith argued that Ireland, like Hungary, should reject the right of the imperial parliament to legislate for her and should refuse to send members to Westminster. The Sinn Féin blend of national self-respect and self-reliance appealed to the physical-force separatists of the Irish Republican Brotherhood and to the cultural nationalists of the

Gaelic League as well as to smaller radical groups such as feminists and pacifists. In the summer of 1907 it also attracted a handful of Irish Party MPs disillusioned by the Irish Council Bill fiasco. One MP, Charles Dolan, precipitated a trial of strength between the two parties when he resigned his North Leitrim seat and stood for Sinn Féin in the ensuing by-election. The Irish Party beat off the challenge by a comfortable margin of almost three to one, but it was the first ominous test of the patience of Irish nationalists, frustrated by over twenty years of waiting in vain for Gladstone's promised land.

The omen, inevitably, went unheeded: the Liberals were too preoccupied with the succession to a terminally ill Campbell-Bannerman – Asquith became prime minister on 5 April 1908 – and with their intensifying war with the House of Lords. Some of the battles in that war, moreover, did nothing to improve ministerial relations with the Irish Party. The Irish had especially offended Liberal sensibilities by championing Catholic opposition in Britain to the ill-fated Education Bill for England and Wales, which legislated for compulsory non-denominational teaching and which was thrown out by the House of Lords in December 1906. The episode was doubly unfortunate for the Liberal–Irish alliance. First, it reminded Liberals that, on education, as on issues such as free trade and the licensing laws, Irish nationalists were more in tune with the Tories. Second, the thanks proffered Redmond by English Catholics (including Francis Bourne, Cardinal Archbishop of Westminster, and the Duke of Norfolk[45]) and the 1907 papal decree *Ne temere* (enforcing Catholic upbringing on the children of marriages between Catholics and Protestants) fed the anti-Catholic sentiment found 'in any gathering of elderly English gentlemen'.[46] Such sentiment was not, moreover, confined to gentlemen but reflected what Daniel

Jackson has recently identified as 'the important position that anti-Catholicism still held in the matrix of British national identity'.[47]

Anti-Catholicism was no less characteristic of Liberals than of Conservatives. The depth of Asquith's anti-Catholicism was revealed only months after he became prime minister by his reaction to the Eucharistic Congress, held in London in September 1908, when the announcement of a eucharistic procession in the streets around Westminster Cathedral roused certain Protestant societies to obtain counsel's opinion that carrying the host and wearing vestments in the streets was illegal under the 1829 Catholic Emancipation Act. A sympathetic and incensed King Edward VII bombarded his prime minister with telegrams to intervene but the home secretary, Herbert Gladstone, mindful of similar if smaller processions that had taken place without official interference in 1898 and 1901, declined to act. Asquith turned instead to the only Catholic in his cabinet, a humiliated Lord Ripon, whom he persuaded to make a last-minute appeal to the Cardinal Archbishop to abandon the ceremonial elements of the procession. Cardinal Bourne agreed, but only after he was authorised to say publicly that he was acting at the prime minister's behest.[48]

The blandness of the prime ministerial telegraphic request revealed none of the venom of Asquith's private reaction. 'Such a procession appears to be clearly illegal,' he had fumed to Lord Crewe, then bearing the brunt of royal wrath at a house party with the king, 'and there is a good deal of quite respectable Protestant sentiment which is offended by this gang of foreign Cardinals taking advantage of our hospitality to parade their idolatries through the streets of London: a thing without precedent since the days of Bloody Mary.'[49] Asquith was again bland but unrelenting when asked in the

Commons by William Redmond and Lord Edmund Talbot on 14 October whether he would introduce a bill repealing Catholic disabilities, saying only that his government 'cannot give facilities to any measure which is not of a wholly non-controversial character'.[50] Although Gladstone resisted ferocious royal pressure to resign and refused the first prime ministerial offer of a sinecure, he was exiled, a year later, to South Africa as the first governor general – a symbol that there was no place at Westminster for Gladstonian sentiment in the age of Asquith.

David Lloyd George, whose antennae were finely attuned to every shift in the ministerial balance of power, was in no doubt that the new premiership heralded a 'great weakening' of the radical element in the cabinet in which he had become the most powerful minister with his elevation from the presidency of the Board of Trade to the chancellorship of the exchequer. 'Besides the substitution of Asquith for Campbell-Bannerman', Bryce, Elgin, Ripon and Gladstone had all been lost. 'In their places Churchill (unstable), Pease (a nobody), Runciman and Samuel (men owing promotion to and dependent on Asquith and Runciman an avowed Liberal Leaguer) – altogether an almost purely Liberal League Cabinet.'[51] This mattered little so long as Ireland could be ignored, but that the government confronted by the great Irish crisis of 1912–14 was a government not of Gladstonians but of Liberal imperialists then became a factor of the first importance.

2

The Constitutional Crisis of 1910–11

The first decade of the twentieth century is best seen as a coda to the political history of Britain in the nineteenth century. In this sense, 1910 was the first year of a new and very different period. This is especially true of British–Irish relations: 1910 was the year in which the seeds of change were sown, when the collapse of the constitutional framework that had paralysed the British government's Irish policy since 1886 became inevitable.

The year began with a general election in January that destroyed the last overall majority the Liberal Party was ever to enjoy in the House of Commons. In Britain, the Liberals won 274 seats as opposed to the 252 Unionist seats (Conservative and Unionist Party and Liberal Unionist Party combined) and the 40 seats of the Labour Party. In Ireland, the nationalists won 81 and the Unionists 21. The upshot was that the Irish Parliamentary Party held the balance of power in the House of Commons.

Pre-electoral tension had been mounting throughout 1909 with the unprecedented prospect that the House of Lords would precipitate an election by rejecting the first budget introduced by Asquith's new chancellor of the exchequer, David Lloyd George. This caused Asquith's government to reconsider its relations with John Redmond's Irish Parliamentary Party. The veto, exercised so devastatingly by the House of Lords since 1906, had been the largest single obstacle thwarting Irish nationalist aspirations since the upper house threw out Gladstone's second home rule bill in 1893; if it were removed, the Liberals would lose their best excuse for postponing a third home rule bill. Asquith's government was assured of the Irish Party's unwavering support in an election fought on the issue of 'the People against the Peers' *if* – and this was the rub – it stopped prevaricating about its commitment to home rule. The evidence of by-elections, much more numerous before 1918 because ministers had to stand for re-election on appointment, and the best guide to the mood of the voters in the days before opinion polling indicated that the electoral pendulum had swung back from the heady heights of the 1906 general election. In 1906–9, the Liberals lost 18 of the 20 seats that changed hands – 12 to the Conservatives, 6 to Labour; by the end of 1908 one minister reported that the cabinet was already 'infected with a view that we are bound to look forward to defeat at the next election'.[1]

Redmond seized the chance to extract renewed commitments to home rule from increasingly anxious ministers. After the Liberal chief whip met Lloyd George on 17 February 1909, a telegram from him to a by-election candidate authorised him on behalf of 'Asquith, Lloyd George, Churchill, Harcourt and the Whips . . . to say that . . . he was "strongly of opinion that Home Rule should be a leading issue at the next General Election"',[2] a major advance on Campbell-Bannerman's gradualism before the 1906 election. The Liberals lost four more by-elections between May and the end of October, and, as ministerial pre-election jitters intensified, Redmond demanded 'an official declaration on the question of Home Rule'. Otherwise he would ask Irish voters in Britain to vote against Liberal candidates, threatening that 'the opposition of Irish voters in Lancashire, Yorkshire, and other places, including Scotland, would most certainly mean the loss of many seats'.[3]

On 30 November the Lords finally threw out the budget and a general election became inevitable. When the cabinet discussed Redmond's terms the next day, Birrell scribbled him a report of the outcome: 'It is to be made plain that Home Rule is the *live policy of the party, without limitation or restriction other than the old tag about the supreme control of the Imperial Parliament*.' The right of Ulster's Unionists to any comparable measure of self-determination was again ignored because any proposal of separate treatment for Ulster would be like a red rag to a bull to Redmond's party. When Asquith opened his election campaign at the Royal Albert Hall on 10 December, he dutifully described Ireland as 'the one undeniable failure of British statesmanship' and declared 'that the solution of the problem can be found only in one way [cries of "Home Rule" and loud cheers], by a policy which, while explicitly safeguarding the supremacy and inde-fectible authority of the Imperial Parliament, will set up in Ireland a system of full self-government in regard to purely Irish affairs'. He then abandoned the 'step-by-step' policy: 'For reasons which I believe to have been adequate the pres-ent Parliament was disabled in advance from proposing any such solution, but in the new House of Commons the hands of a Liberal Government and of a Liberal majority will, in this matter, be entirely free.'[4]

The general election of January 1910 catapulted Ireland to the top of the cabinet agenda. 'Parnell's dream of the balance of power at Westminster had once again come true . . . The Liberals must either do [Redmond's] bidding or allow the

Unionists to come back to power.'⁵ T. P. O'Connor (who sat for a Liverpool constituency and whose personal friendship with Lloyd George and other leading Liberals gave him a key role as the Irish Party's go-between, especially when Redmond and Dillon were in Ireland) outlined the Irish terms (which Redmond made public in a speech in Dublin the next day): that the government proceed immediately with a bill to abolish the Lords' veto; that they promise to seek guarantees from the king to create the number of peers needed to overcome the Lords' continued resistance, and that they take these steps *before* reintroducing the 1909 budget.⁶

The Irish dream was the Liberal nightmare and Redmond's *démarche* caused a major cabinet crisis. 'The Irish have declared their intention of voting against the budget unless quite impossible pledges are given,' wrote Winston Churchill. 'This probably terminates the government in a fortnight.'⁷ Asquith, too, was pessimistic and, after the cabinet meeting on 10 February, advised the king that no such pledges 'could or should be given'⁸ and warning that, 'upon the question of the enactment of last year's budget', the government might be defeated in the Commons.

The vehemence of the government's reaction to terms already effectively conceded by the prime minister in his Albert Hall speech reflected Liberal imperialist resentment at again being shackled by the Irish yoke. The absence of both Asquith and Lloyd George in the south of France and the fact that the cabinet never even bothered to meet after the election before Asquith's return to London on 9 February created a temporary power vacuum, which Edward Grey filled by default. Grey's distaste for the Irish alliance was intense and of long standing; he had argued since 1901 that, while he wanted to be able to co-operate on Ireland, there was 'a difference

between co-operation and dependence, and Redmond's attitude and tone have been so overbearing that it is necessary to
repudiate dependence'. After the cabinet meeting on 10 February, Lord Hardinge, his permanent under-secretary at the
foreign office, observed that Grey was 'very pleased with himself' and had told Hardinge 'that the Cabinet would tell the
Irish to go and be damned'.[9] Hardinge's assessment was more
perceptive: 'The difference is that Asquith wants to remain in
office and Grey does not care whether he does or not.'[10]

Now Asquith had cause again to recall his Herodotus and
to fear the loss of power for this was the only time before the
Curragh mutiny of 1914 when his position as prime minister
was in jeopardy.[11] Although the cabinet met almost daily during the week beginning 14 February, it failed to resolve its differences. Lloyd George felt they were 'blundering into a great
catastrophe through lack of nerve'[12] and claimed that only his
and Churchill's efforts averted the government's craven resignation on 18 February. Lloyd George and Churchill shared
with Asquith a determination not to lose office, but their
strategies on how best to achieve that objective differed. Where
Asquith temperamentally favoured masterly inactivity, Lloyd
George and Churchill were instinctively interventionist and,
as this was but the first of their many critical interventions, it
is worth looking more closely at their respective attitudes
towards the governance of Ireland.

What divided Lloyd George and Churchill from the Liberal
imperialists was that they were more pragmatic, not more
idealistic, about Ireland. The man 'closest to L. G. politically
and mentally', explained his mistress, Frances Stevenson, was
Churchill. 'Both were born politicians, and interested in politics on the grand scale . . . their ideas were uninhibited by convention or creed.'[13] Their common disdain for the conventions

of party politics informed their sporadic joint endeavours to break the mould of Irish policy from 1910 until 1922.

Lloyd George was repelled by the 'narrow tribalism' of Irish nationalism, for, although proud of his Welshness, he never suggested that Wales 'become a separate nation-state . . . and saw no good reason why what was good enough for Wales should not be good enough for Ireland'.[14] He was among those Welsh Liberals 'who opposed Irish home rule, in large part on religious grounds'. He argued that 'the case for national recognition was stronger for Wales', because its language and culture were 'more vigorous'; because its industrial base prevented mass emigration, and, above all, because 'Wales had no Ulster'. That the few Irish migrants in Wales 'were regarded as virtual outcasts, socially isolated, technically unskilled and, of course, Papists in one of the most vehemently Protestant societies in Europe'[15] was also significant. 'Wales had no Ulster': the racial and religious resonances must never be forgotten when assessing Lloyd George's attitude to the campaign of Ulster's Protestants. For Lloyd George had no time for Papists: 'While not a religious man at all in the conventional sense – he veered between a deistic worship of nature and a stern rationalism worthy of his Unitarian father . . . he once told a Welsh friend, "I hate a priest, Daniel, whenever I find him".'[16] Lucy Masterman, the wife of one of his cabinet colleagues, well described Lloyd George's attitude to home rule as 'not very keen. He admits it as an abstract proposition but he has a good deal of the Protestant in him.'[17] Professor W. G. S. Adams, who worked for Lloyd George between 1916 and 1918, later wrote of feeling as he talked to him that 'below the surface of his mind there was this deep primitive "No Pope here" of Ulster'.[18]

Although widely travelled – he had visited the United States twice as a backbencher, had cruised in the Mediterranean, and went often to the south of France – Lloyd George visited Ireland only twice. The first visit, a brief motoring trip to Galway in April 1905, had no political purpose. But on the second, when he went to Belfast as president of the Board of Trade in February 1907, he had faithfully followed the 'step-by-step' line on home rule and waxed eloquent about the dangers of Irish separatism. Ireland's schism from the Empire was, he insisted, 'unthinkable', and, 'to ringing Protestant cheers', he declared that 'the supremacy of the Imperial Parliament must be maintained'.[19]

Winston Churchill's case was different. A Unionist by birth, he was a boy of eleven when his father, Randolph, played the Orange card in 1886. Winston's first political speech, in 1897 (only three years after his father suffered a lingering and 'terrible public death'[20] from syphilitic paralysis), deplored the decline of the 'great Liberal party . . . around whose necks is bound the millstone of Home Rule'[21] and his first election address as a Conservative candidate, in 1899, declared that 'all true Unionists must . . . be prepared to greet the reappearance of that odious measure with the most strenuous opposition'.[22] His 1906 election address, albeit as a Liberal who had left the Conservative Party over tariff reform, declared in not dissimilar vein that he would 'support no Irish legislation . . . likely to injure the effective integrity of the United Kingdom, or to lead, however indirectly, to separation'. But by 1908, when Asquith put him in the cabinet, he trimmed his sails in bidding for the Irish vote in North-West Manchester in the consequent by-election:

My opinion on the Irish question has ripened during the last 2 years when I have lived in the inner . . . councils of Liberalism. I have become convinced that a national

settlement of the Irish difficulty on broad and generous
lines is indispensable to any harmonious conception of
Liberalism . . . At the next election . . . the Liberal party
should claim full authority and a free hand to deal with
the problem of Irish self-government without being
restricted to measures of administrative devolution of
the character of the Irish Council Bill.[23]

But it was not enough. When the Tories, after a vengeful campaign against their renegade, won by 429 votes, Churchill
knew whom to blame. 'But for those sulky Irish Catholics
changing sides at the last moment under priestly pressure, the
result would have been different,' he confided to his future
wife. 'Now I have to begin all over again.'[24]

Churchill's hostility to Catholicism, unlike Lloyd George's,
derived from his imperialist instincts. 'I know that . . . super-
stitious faith in nations rarely promotes their industry,' he
wrote from India in 1899; Catholicism was 'a delicious nar-
cotic . . . [that] checks our growth and saps our strength',
vitiating 'the improvement of the British breed . . . my political aim in life'.[25] 'The Catholic Church has ruined every country in wh[ich] it has been supreme & worked the downfall of
every dynasty that ruled in its name,' he wrote in similar vein
to his wife in 1911 in a letter published by his biographer son
fifty years later under the instructive page-heading 'THE
CURSE OF CATHOLICISM'.[26]

By 1910 Churchill had learned enough of 'the language of
radicalism'[27] from Lloyd George for Redmond to agree that,
while Asquith, Grey and Haldane were not 'really in earnest
about Home Rule',[28] Churchill and Lloyd George were. Indeed, Asquith felt Churchill had trimmed his sails so adroitly
that he invited him 'to take what is bound to be one of our

most delicate & difficult posts – the Irish Office'.[29] The offer was guilefully declined and Churchill instead held out for the plum of the home office, becoming, at the age of thirty-five, the youngest home secretary since Robert Peel.

Asquith's Liberal imperialism, his ties of friendship with Grey, Haldane and Crewe, and his personal distaste for depending on the Irish all contributed to his reluctance to come to grips with Redmond after the first election of 1910. Asquith himself 'personally dislikes the Irish', wrote one minister's wife, in describing the 'anti-Irish prejudice'[30] of his cabinet; Redmond 'hates Henry',[31] fulminated Asquith's wife when the crisis was at its height. The relationship between the two party leaders was, at best, one of mutual mistrust. In February 1910 Redmond 'believed in Asquith to the extent that he would trust him if he made a promise in so many words, but he had not quite done so about Ireland'.[32] Ireland exacerbated Asquith's predilection for procrastination. 'Driven to bay he would act with vigour; but the habit, which grows on most prime ministers, of postponing decisions and trusting that time will untie the knots, obtained an altogether excessive hold on him.' His 'attitude behind the scenes towards Redmond' was 'one of complete unreliability', wrote R. C. K. Ensor in his *Oxford History of England*. 'It shows Asquith, whose career elsewhere exhibited so many features of greatness, at his weakest and worst.'[33] 'Wait and see,' responded Asquith when questioned in the Commons about his government's legislative programme on 3 March 1910. The phrase had yet to become the byword for indolence with which opponents later pilloried his premiership, but Asquith repeated it at least three times in the next month and it epitomised the inertia of his Irish policy.

On 25 March Grey offered his resignation in writing to Asquith and it seemed likely that Crewe, Haldane, Runciman and McKenna might go with him. The crisis moved into its final phase at cabinet on 8 April, when Lloyd George's intention to drop the whisky tax – to which the Irish had always objected – from the budget provoked 'a general outburst of refusal'; now it was Lloyd George's turn to threaten resignation, and he and Churchill 'took an almost formal leave of the Cabinet'. The Master of Elibank, the chief whip and then Lloyd George's only close friend on the Liberal front bench apart from Churchill, intervened and the three men met just before the decisive cabinet meeting of 12 April when Lloyd George surprised his colleagues by announcing that he would retain the whisky tax and would 'tell the Irish so quite plainly'.[34] Lloyd George's volte-face on whisky allowed Asquith to tell the king, then in Biarritz, that the government was 'strongly and unanimously of opinion that to purchase the Irish vote by such a concession would be a discreditable transaction which they could not defend', and that it was 'possible and not improbable' – a classic Asquithian circumlocution – that the Irish Party would consequently vote against the budget and create 'a crisis of extreme urgency'.[35]

The rhetoric belied the reality. The government was not creating a crisis by standing up to the Irish, but ending a crisis by giving in to them. Lloyd George's U-turn flattered the self-esteem of his cabinet opponents by allowing them to represent defeat as victory; he had 'realised more and more that it was the whisky tax and the giving way to the Irish upon it that stuck in Grey's throat'.[36] What finally resolved the crisis was Lloyd George's insistence at the same meeting that, unless the government immediately decided to approach 'the Sovereign in respect of guarantees, he would leave the Cabinet and join the Irish'. Lloyd George got his way and Asquith informed the king that the government had decided to seek contingent guarantees for the creation of peers to ensure that the will of the Commons would prevail against the Lords.

'I never saw a set of men more relieved than the members of that Cabinet on its break-up,' observed Elibank. 'Why in heaven's name they could not have come to this decision two months earlier and saved all this pother, I for one cannot understand.'[37] Yet the pother makes sense, given Liberal divisions over Irish policy since 1886. It marked a triumph for the Lloyd George–Churchill axis – the new men of substance in the cabinet – aided and abetted by the new chief whip: these three alone went to congratulate the prime minister when he announced the new policy – *their* policy – in the Commons on 14 April when the Parliament Bill received its first reading.

The Irish were satisfied. There was no more talk of their voting against the government. The budget, duly reintroduced on 18 April, went smoothly and was passed by the Commons on the 27th and by the Lords on the 28th, the day before parliament adjourned for the Easter recess. That the logic of the Irish alliance was resisted by the cabinet to the point where it was able to accept Irish demands only by pretending to reject them ensured that the alliance was always poisoned by suspicion. Gladstone's enthusiasm for his Irish alliances had made a virtue of necessity. Asquith was always an unwilling ally, a resentful partner in a loveless marriage. Although Redmond was under no illusions to the contrary, he had to hide the miseries of the marriage bed from the outside world because divorce would dash his hopes of ultimate bliss: the enactment of home rule. Hence the Irish Party's fears about the misalliance were marginal in the sense that their only alternative was the impotence of parliamentary isolation.

Opposition perceptions, however, were very different and of the highest political significance. They saw Redmond as the bartered bride whose bride-price was the destruction of the Union. From now on, as Robert Blake, the doyen of historians of the Conservative Party has written:

> It was the normal Conservative Party line to declare that the Government's actions were wholly dominated by an immoral bargain with Redmond, whereby the latter contrary to his true convictions agreed to support the budget in return for a promise by Asquith to destroy the veto of the House of Lords and to carry Home Rule. This belief was sincerely held and it goes far to explain the extraordinary bitterness which soon began to mark party politics.[38]

That there was in fact no formal agreement or understanding between Redmond and the government was irrelevant. Unionists saw only that the government had made a U-turn at the behest of the Irish. But it was not simply that the opposition regarded Asquith's policy as, in Balfour's words, 'nothing short of the destruction of the Constitution':[39] they also knew it was a policy that the prime minister and several of his senior cabinet colleagues disliked and had resisted until threatened with the loss of office. Opposition leaders were well informed about cabinet dissension on Ireland; this was due partly to information gleaned from friends at court (notably Lord Esher) and partly to ministerial indiscretion. Indeed this was a political culture that set small store on secrecy. Government and opposition frontbenchers mingled freely regardless of party affiliation, which was no barrier to friendship. Asquith's cabinet leaked like a sieve.

The point is fundamental to understanding the dynamic of Tory outrage about the corrupt bargain. It was not merely political rhetoric prompted by hunch or suspicion. The Tory leaders *knew* that Asquith 'was probably one of the least enthusiastic Home Rulers in his party',[40] just as they *knew* of his personal dislike for Redmond and of ministerial repugnance at depending on the Irish. They *knew* that the government's commitment to home rule was, at most, lukewarm. They also *knew* that many Liberals shared the instinctive Anglo-Saxon aversion for all the works and pomps of Irish nationalism, especially in their Roman Catholic manifestations. For, as Gary Peatling has pointed out, there were 'intrinsic similarities [between] the assumptions of British home rulers and Unionists. Both groups . . . shared many ideals, aims and points of reference, imperial and domestic. Even British home rulers such as [John] Morley presupposed the superiority of Anglo-Saxon Protestant institutions.'[41]

Such shared and largely unspoken assumptions about Ireland privately united leading Liberals and Conservatives and explains why the Tories were so certain that the Irish policy that emerged from the 1910 cabinet crisis was riddled with hypocrisy and humbug, and also why it was so destructive of their inhibitions about adopting the extraordinary and extreme extra-parliamentary policies of 1912–14. The Liberals, the Tory argument ran, had been the first to break the rules of the constitutional game.

The conviction that the government had little stomach for home rule had another consequence: it made the opposition suspect that the government's commitment to the third Home Rule Bill was no more than a gigantic bluff. This suspicion fuelled the violence of Unionist policies in opposition for, in order to call that bluff, Unionists felt justified in adopting almost any policy, however anarchic or unprecedented. But, before the Parliament Act finally cleared the way for the introduction of the third Home Rule Bill, there was a last chance for the British parties to pull back from the brink of confrontation over Ireland: the Constitutional Conference of 1910.

The sudden death of Edward VII, on 6 May 1910 in the middle of a constitutional crisis, confronted the new king, George V, 'with an unprecedented constitutional problem of which he had little previous knowledge and in which he was accorded no consistent guidance'.[42] Deference to royal wishes, together with Asquith's Fabian temperament and the Tories' instinct to defer the castration of the House of Lords, prompted both parties to accept the new king's request to seek a constitutional compromise that would at least postpone the crown being sucked into party strife. The Constitutional Conference first met on 17 June; it broke for the summer recess between 28 July and 11 October and concluded, after twenty-two sittings, on 10 November. The government delegates at the conference were Asquith, Lloyd George, Crewe and Birrell; the opposition delegates were Balfour, Austen Chamberlain and two peers, Lansdowne and Cawdor; neither of the minority parties was represented.

Redmond's exclusion was yet another reflection of government resentment at dependence on the Irish and he realised that the conference was 'largely inspired by a desire to destroy his own dominating position'.[43] If the two major parties acted in unison, the concept of the parliamentary balance of power on which Redmond's leverage was utterly dependent became meaningless. Making common cause with the Tories enabled Asquith to shed the shackles binding him to Redmond and offered an opportunity to restore the bipartisan consensus on Irish policy shattered by Gladstone in 1886. Indeed the first phase of the conference is best understood, in John Fair's phrase, 'as a wilful act of sublimation by both parties to avoid direct confrontation over the only issue on which no rational agreement was possible': Ireland.[44]

The Unionists argued that legislative measures embodying fundamental or – as they came to be called – 'organic' changes 'must be subjected to special safeguards, ensuring that, if the two Houses disagreed, the nation should be consulted before they became irrevocable'.[45] At the last meeting before the summer recess, they realised that the government was determined 'that questions like Home Rule, Disestablishment and franchise can have no special safeguards . . . this is an ultimatum – give up Home Rule or we break off'.[46] Although they agreed to resume in October, the Unionists were already seeking the best electoral grounds on which to engineer the collapse of the conference.

But the most significant effort to put Irish policy on a bipartisan plane occurred on the fringes of the conference. It arose from Lloyd George's revolutionary secret memorandum of 17 August 1910 proposing a coalition of the two major parties. Although the thrust of the memorandum was socioeconomic, the penultimate paragraph referred to the Irish question: 'The advantages of a non-party treatment of this vexed subject are obvious. Parties might deal with it without being subject to the embarrassing dictation of extreme partisans, whether from Nationalists or Orangemen.'[47]

The exploratory talks about coalition between Lloyd George and Balfour were highly secret and wholly distinct from the Constitutional Conference. Yet the conference was the catalyst, for it was there that the two men – who had never before grappled at close quarters but who later worked hand in glove in Lloyd George's coalition governments of 1916–22 – first hit it off. 'Both were consummate artists in the exercise of charm,' observed Asquith's daughter, 'and each proved susceptible to the other's mastery of the instrument . . . Both had an element of flexibility almost amounting to fluidity.'[48] Lloyd George was 'absolutely hypnotised' by Balfour who was 'the only person on the opposite side with whom he could deal' – he dismissed Lansdowne as 'an ineffectual echo' of Balfour, Cawdor as contributing 'nothing whatever', and Austen Chamberlain as 'such a slow and commonplace mind that he did not count'. The attraction was mutual, for Balfour 'addressed almost all his remarks personally to George'.[49]

But mutual fascination did not seduce Balfour from fidelity to the Union and, by the first week in November, when it became clear that 'Home Rule in some form' was a prerequisite to their success, Balfour's secret talks with Lloyd George were doomed to failure. By 10 November it was also clear that the conference had failed and Asquith advised the king that 'the point of divergence' was 'whether organic and constitutional changes (such . . . as Home Rule, the franchise, redistribution) should be excepted from the procedure of joint session'.[50] 'The organic change which provided the main text of these discussions was Home Rule,'[51] Balfour told the king. Chamberlain, writing privately to his wife a month earlier, had been more blunt: 'Neither side can get over the Home Rule fence or (to speak more frankly) the Government cannot quarrel outright with the Irish.'[52]

Balfour found Lloyd George's plan intellectually attractive but politically impossible: to compromise on home rule would split his Conservative and Unionist Party asunder. The new leader of the Irish Unionist MPs, elected on 21 February 1910, was Edward Carson – a Southern Unionist educated at Trinity College Dublin who hoped to use Ulster Unionist resistance to prevent home rule coming into effect in any part of Ireland – and he had already written to Balfour of his fears of betrayal.[53] The reaction of Ulster's Unionists, fearful of the imminent collapse of their strongest bulwark against the enactment of home rule, was more extreme: the Ulster Unionist Council established 'a secret committee which was to oversee approaches to arms dealers, and to select weapons for an Ulster army'. On 22 November 1910 the gun-runner F. H. Crawford, 'acting apparently under the instructions of this Committee, wrote to five munitions works in England, Austria, and Germany, and invited a quotation for 20,000 rifles and one million rounds of ammunition'[54] and within three weeks the committee had received sample weapons.

A party split worried Balfour more than the danger of civil war in Ulster. For seven years he had struggled to hold together a party disintegrating on the economic policy of tariff reform. Defence of the Union was the one issue on which Tory unity was assured, while Liberal disunity seemed almost certain. Lord Salisbury put it most succinctly: the 'great object is to get the present Government out of power. When we fight them on the Veto [of the House of Lords] we are fighting them on the point which unites them most. When we fight them on Home Rule, we are fighting them on the point which divides them most.'[55] Balfour himself admitted that 'his whole history' – not least his coercive regime as Irish chief secretary from 1887 to 1891, when nationalists nicknamed him Bloody Balfour – 'forbade his being a party to any form of Home Rule, though younger men less involved in the controversies of '86 and '93 might be free to contemplate what he could not accept'.[56] Those free to contemplate what Balfour could not accept included Lloyd George, Churchill and Elibank, the same triumvirate that had lost patience with the paralysis of Irish policy during the post-election cabinet crisis, and F. E.

Smith (Lloyd George's go-between with the Tory leadership). They found the trappings of party an encumbrance to political achievement. Their 1910 overture was but an early, muted manifestation of bipartisan instincts, which found later expression in coalition under Lloyd George, and of which the partition of Ireland, set in stone by the Anglo-Irish Treaty of December 1921 (to which all but Elibank were British signatories), was the final flowering.

Asquith, who had learned of Lloyd George's secret plan only *after* the approach to Balfour,[57] had always remained sceptical, but no one stood to gain more than the prime minister by the removal of the Irish issue from the arena of party conflict, especially after Lloyd George and Churchill had won over Edward Grey at a dinner on 25 October.[58] Although, as Asquith's biographer Roy Jenkins has argued, 'it was Balfour's caution and not Asquith's scepticism which wrecked the plan',[59] the consequences were comparable for both party leaders: the last pre-war opportunity for a bipartisan Irish initiative had been lost. Both men were forced back into the lists as the respective champions of the Orange and the Green. But whereas Balfour was comfortable in his champion's armour because jousting again in defence of the Union offered his party its best prospect of regaining power, Asquith remained home rule's most reluctant champion.

The collapse of the Constitutional Conference was swiftly followed by the second general election of 1910. The December results (Liberals, 272; Unionists, 272; Irish Nationalists, 84; Labour, 42) uncannily mirrored those of January. The Liberals had no more appetite for Ireland than before: 188 of the 272 successful Liberal candidates, including Asquith and Lloyd George, omitted all mention of home rule from their election addresses.[60] But Irish control of the parliamentary balance of power had been reaffirmed and the fetters on the Liberals' Irish policy forged anew: constitutionally at least, the way was clear for the enactment of the Parliament Bill, and then for home rule.

Parliament assembled on 6 February 1911, and on 21 February the Parliament Bill was again introduced. It passed the Commons on 15 May and there followed another truce in party politics because of the celebrations for the coronation of George V. The two Houses reached deadlock when the government rejected the Lords' amendments (deleting organic or constitutional legislative changes from the bill). Only then, on 19 July, were the Tory leaders outraged by the revelation that, before the second election of 1910, the government had already sought and obtained secret guarantees from the king to create as many new peers as might be necessary to overcome the Lords' opposition to the bill. The Tories also discovered that the government had not interpreted the pledge of secrecy as extending to their Irish allies. On 21 December 1910, when the election results were complete, Elibank told T. P. O'Connor of Asquith's interview with the king. 'All good news for us,'[61] reported O'Connor to Redmond. The electoral reaffirmation of Redmond's hold on the balance of power brought home to ministers the futility of chafing against their Irish marriage of convenience. This time there was no post-election cabinet crisis. If the Irish had not known of the secret guarantees, they might have jeopardised the government's parliamentary strategy. Instead, and in distinct contrast with their behaviour during the early months of 1910, they proved the most amenable of allies.

The Tories, outraged at being kept in the dark, accused Asquith of again acting unconstitutionally at Redmond's command in pressing the king for guarantees *before* the second election and they shouted him down on his next appearance in the Commons: 'The whole thing depends on the Irish vote – let us have Redmond'; 'Cannot we have the "Dictator" first?'; 'Leave out the King: who killed him?'; 'What about England?'; 'England is against you'; 'American dollars' (Unionists had branded Redmond the 'Dollar-Dictator' when, on his return on 12 November 1910 from an election fundraising visit to America, he was greeted by bonfires along the coast of Cork), and a final chorus of 'Redmond, Redmond'.[62]

Once the guarantees became public knowledge, the Unionist leaders recognised that the destruction of the Lords' permanent veto was inevitable. Government and opposition both accepted that the first great crisis to be resolved under the Parliament Bill would be the Irish crisis. The capacity of an emasculated House of Lords to resist Irish legislation lay at the heart of the dissension, about how best to conduct the final phase of resistance to the bill, which now consumed the Conservative Party and toppled Balfour. Preserving the Lords' ability at least to delay the destruction of the Union had weighed heavily with Balfour since the end of 1910 when he had argued against provoking a wholesale creation of peers, which would ease the passage of home rule. He was supported by most Irish Unionist leaders – Lansdowne, Walter Long, Londonderry, Midleton and Ashbourne – in shadow cabinet on 21 July. Ulster Unionists, however, were beginning to part company with their Southern Unionist brethren and Edward Carson reflected the Ulster Unionist perspective, notwithstanding his own Southern Unionist background. Carson was concerned less with the efficacy of Tory opposition to the Parliament Bill than with its character. What Balfour most despised about the diehard peers, their military metaphors and essential theatricality, was what Carson most cherished:

their extremism and their hatred of compromise. The diehard mentality mirrored Carson's mood as he laid the ground for revolution. 'What I am very anxious about', he told James Craig, his leading lieutenant in Ulster, 'is to satisfy myself that the people over there really mean to resist. I am not for a mere game of bluff & unless men are prepared to make great sacrifices which they clearly understand the talk of resistance is no use.'[63]

The Parliament Bill was enacted on 18 August 1911 after the diehards were narrowly defeated in the dramatic division of 10 August. Thereafter the House of Lords had no power over money bills and its power over all other bills was limited to a suspensive veto, a deferment of two years. Their defeat notwithstanding, Carson identified the diehards as an ideal power base to incite Tory revolution against the coming Home Rule Bill. 'We must not disband,' he urged Lord Willoughby de Broke, the leader of the diehard peers. 'I know you will help us in the pitched battle over Home Rule and we must find out where the party stands and to what extent they will go. I fear more private council tactics over this and we cannot afford it. There is a splendid fighting spirit in the north of Ireland only waiting for a lead.'[64]

On Saturday, 23 September 1911, Carson gave that lead when he addressed fifty thousand representatives of Orange lodges and Unionist clubs from all over Ulster who had marched from Belfast to meet him at Craigavon, the seat of James Craig, whose grounds on Belfast Lough offered a natural amphitheatre:

We must be prepared, in the possible event of a Home Rule Bill passing, with such measures as will carry on for ourselves the government of those districts of which we have control. We must be prepared – and time is precious in these things – the morning Home Rule passes, ourselves to become responsible for the Government of the Protestant Province of Ulster.[65]

Alvin Jackson's conclusion is indisputable: 'There can be no doubt . . . that the groundwork for civil war was being laid in the winter of 1910–11, with the first attempts at arming and drilling.' The Craigavon rally was the moment when 'the movement for weapons was made public: even the menu cards at Craig's luncheon party on this occasion bore an illustration of crossed rifles and the motto – "The Arming of Ulster"'.[66] Two days later, four hundred delegates of the Ulster Unionist Council met in Belfast and appointed a Commission of Five (headed by Craig and in consultation with Carson) immediately 'to frame and submit a Constitution for a Provisional Government for Ulster, having due regard to the interests of Loyalists in other parts of Ireland', which would 'come into operation on the day of the passage of any Home Rule Bill'.[67]

On 8 November 1911 Balfour announced his resignation as leader of the Conservative and Unionist Party; his resignation was prompted by the diehards' contempt for the rules and conventions on which his approach to politics reposed, a contempt that found cogent and extreme public expression in Carson's revolutionary demagoguery. He was succeeded by Andrew Bonar Law who shared none of Balfour's disgust at the diehards. Under Bonar Law's leadership rules would be broken, conventions abandoned, revolution encouraged. In Bonar Law the party had now a man ready to supply the demand for forceful leadership that had created him: his speeches would not be qualified; moderation would hold no appeal for him, and under him the Conservative and Unionist Party would embrace a policy of revolution without parallel in modern British history.

3

A 'Prickly Hedge': The Charades of 1912–13

John Bull's Other Island, George Bernard Shaw's first play set in Ireland, had its premiere at London's Royal Court Theatre on 1 November 1904. Commissioned by William Butler Yeats as the inaugural production of Dublin's Abbey Theatre a month later, it was too long and its caricatures of English and Irish national stereotypes too controversial for that occasion. But it made Shaw's name as a playwright: its commercial success was assured when the corpulent King Edward VII won the play priceless publicity when he laughed so convulsively during the royal command performance that he broke his chair. Arthur Balfour, the prime minister and leader of the Conservative and Unionist Party, also enjoyed the play, so much so that he saw it five times. On one occasion he brought as his guest Henry Campbell-Bannerman, the then leader of the Liberal Party, who, a year later, was to succeed him as prime minister; on another he brought Henry Asquith, the Liberal prime minister from 1908 until 1916, who presided over the fate of the third Home Rule Bill.

Balfour's Irish experience was rooted in his years as chief secretary for Ireland from 1887 to 1891 when his repressive policies had earned him the nickname of 'Bloody Balfour' among Irish nationalists. His deep-seated Unionism was the rock on which the efforts to establish a bipartisan policy on the Irish problem had foundered in 1910. In 1920 Balfour was the cabinet minister arguing most forcefully for Ulster's right to remain a fully integrated part of the United Kingdom. In November 1921 he remained so sceptical of negotiating with Irish republicans in the aftermath of the truce that ended the Irish war of independence that Lloyd George sent him to head the British delegation at the Washington Naval Conference lest his presence in London disrupt the negotiations that led to the establishment of the Irish Free State. Arthur Balfour was at once the most cultivated, the most cynical and the most cerebral of prime ministers. The trouble with Arthur, a colleague observed, is that he knows there has been one Ice Age and he thinks there's going to be another. Who better, then, to share Balfour's enjoyment at Shaw's lampooning of the conduct of well-meaning English liberals in Ireland than the two Liberal leaders who were to follow him into 10 Downing Street?

That shared enjoyment neatly illustrates those unspoken assumptions about Ireland that privately united leading Liberals and Conservatives and lays bare the gulf between the political reality and the charades in the House of Commons in 1912–13 over the third Home Rule Bill. It also explains why the Conservatives in opposition understood that the Liberal government's Irish policy was riddled with hypocrisy and humbug, a by-product of the parliamentary arithmetic determined by the two general elections of 1910.

As Edward Carson himself admitted to a Tory backbencher in July 1913, 'he had known for a long time that the government would not force Home Rule on Ulster. So it is all play acting.'[1] And so it was. The 'Big Beasts' in Asquith's cabinet had none of Gladstone's messianic fervour for Irish home rule. Some – the prime minister himself, his foreign secretary,

Edward Grey, and his secretary of state for war, Richard Haldane – were Liberal imperialists; they were former acolytes not of Gladstone but of Lord Rosebery, Gladstone's successor as prime minister in 1894. Other senior ministers were pragmatists, of whom the most formidable were the chancellor of the exchequer, David Lloyd George, and the home secretary and, later, First Lord of the Admiralty, Winston Churchill, a former member and future leader of the Conservative and Unionist Party, whose father, Randolph, first coined the phrase 'Ulster will fight, Ulster will be right.' None of these men envisaged that the third Home Rule Bill could be or should be enacted until the issue of Ulster's exclusion was first addressed. Neither did the cabinet minister with direct responsibility for Irish policy: Augustine Birrell, the chief secretary for Ireland from 1908 until 1916. The Liberal government, in short, never intended that the third Home Rule Bill should be enacted in the form in which it was introduced.

Some days before the parliament of 1911–18 first met, Augustine Birrell wrote that 'it was almost inconceivable to him that Home Rule shd [should] be got through without another dissolution, that people did not realise what a "prickly hedge" was set up by the Parliament Bill with its two years delay and necessity for tripple [*sic*] passage of a Bill *substantially unaltered*.'[2] As he saw it, Birrell's role as chief secretary for Ireland was to do nothing to upset the government's Irish allies, so he never said publicly what he already thought privately. Yet he understated the case, for on closer examination his 'prickly hedge' assumes the appearance of a parliamentary Becher's Brook.

Historians have underestimated this aspect of the Parliament Act, perhaps because both its supporters and opponents preferred to ignore it. After such a titanic struggle, ministers had a vested interest in protecting the currency of their victory against devaluation. This compounded the perennial tendency of legislators to exaggerate the benefits of their legislation, which, in this instance, assumed particular significance because of the government's dependence on the Irish Parliamentary Party for its majority in the House of Commons. The assumption that the Parliament Act smoothed the way for the passage of home rule cemented the Liberal–Irish alliance. Neither ally saw profit in acknowledging that its triumph contained the seeds of disaster or in dwelling on the uniquely corrosive feature of the act: that, while it removed the largest obstruction to the resurrection of home rule, it effectively postponed the day of resurrection for at least three years. For, although it destroyed the permanent veto of the House of Lords, it sanctioned a new two-year veto. What this meant in practice was that, although a home-rule bill could be *introduced* in 1912, it could not be *enacted* before the high summer of 1914.

Parliamentary politics were more than ever reduced to the level of charades since all the leading actors understood that, under the new rules, their performances could have no legislative effect in 1912 or in 1913. The impact on the conduct and the prestige of parliament was as devastating as the opportunity offered to Ulster's extra-parliamentary opponents of home rule was immense. That the Home Rule Bill could be enacted neither in 1912 nor in 1913 diminished the authority of ministers in parliament. The government surrendered control of the political timetable to the opposition because the Parliament Act effectively made sure that the crisis must suppurate until 1914. Although the act curbed the powers of the House of Lords, its *immediate* effect was to give the Tories 'a licence to delay Liberal legislation for more than two years, while in the process wasting an immense amount of Parliamentary time'.[3] That the act also reduced the life of parliaments from seven to five years gave them an added incentive to play the Orange card because the opposition's greater freedom to obstruct could be indulged with the prospect of a relatively early general election. Asquith had in effect designed a procedure that, in John Grigg's phrase, 'institutionalised the principle of "wait and see"'.[4]

The conflict over the Parliament Act prompted the opposition to exaggerate the significance of its defeat just as it induced ministers to exaggerate the dimensions of their victory. 'We should always remember that we are now for the first time given a chance of resisting the Parliament Act in operation,' F. E. Smith reminded Carson in September 1913, when the Irish storm was about to break. 'That Act was revolutionary; perhaps we have our one and only chance of defeating it by counter-revolutionary means.'[5] Birrell's 'prickly hedge' offered an ideal environment for sedition because it gave the Ulster Unionists three years to plot and to plan their extra-parliamentary campaign. The Craigavon demonstration was but the first example of Carson's appetite for opposing the government's Irish policy by taking to the streets. The 'prickly hedge' put a premium on such diehard stratagems while reducing parliamentary politics to the level of a Punch and Judy show.

Indeed Bonar Law admitted as much in his celebrated aside on the traditional walk as leader of the opposition side by side with the prime minister from the House of Lords after listening to the King's Speech in February 1912: 'I am afraid I shall have to show myself very vicious, Mr Asquith, this session. I hope you will understand.'[6] Posturing and role-playing was, of course, nothing new in that British parliamentary tradition of party games sustained by the nurseries of the Oxford and Cambridge Unions where so many politicians learned the rudiments of their trade. What *was* new, however, was Bonar Law's admission of role-playing, and Asquith cast him as Mephistopheles because he understood they were acting in different traditions.

The tradition into which Andrew Bonar Law was born and bred was Ulster Presbyterian. His father, James, was born in Coleraine where he was a Presbyterian minister before emigrating to Canada in 1845 to become a minister of the Free Church of Scotland in New Brunswick. Andrew was born there in 1858, but his mother died when he was only two; he left New Brunswick at the age of twelve (when his father remarried) and he was reared and educated by more affluent relations in Glasgow. The Ulster connection did not end there: in 1877 ill health forced Bonar Law's father to return to Ulster, where he died five years later. During those five formative years, from the age of nineteen to twenty-four, Bonar Law travelled from Glasgow to see his father almost every weekend. 'When I got to Belfast from the Clyde,' he wrote at a key moment in the treaty negotiations of 1921, 'I found a community less different from Glasgow probably than Edinburgh is. When I went to Dublin I was obviously in a foreign atmosphere. My real conviction is that . . . you have no right to ask Belfast to submit to something that Edinburgh or Glasgow would not submit to.'[7] The emotive circumstances under which Bonar Law 'came both to know and love the land of his ancestors' have been well charted by Robert Blake, as has how his 'distress at his father's death . . . intense, almost excessive in its expression'[8] sowed the seeds of that conviction. Although unmoved by 'the mere decline of aristocratic power, lacking the romantic reverence for things past . . . which so often goes with Tory beliefs . . . the least sentimental, most unromantic Conservative that ever lived',[9] Bonar Law 'felt with genuine passion' about home rule:

> Upon Irish Home Rule there is no need to suppose that his violence was in any way artificial or affected. On that topic he meant every word he said . . .
>
> He was after all himself the son of a Presbyterian minister who had been born in Ulster and had died in Ulster . . . He deeply sympathised with his compatriots' aversion to being ruled by Roman Catholics. He recognised . . . the profound mistrust which the average Englishman and Scotsman [and Welshman?] entertained for Roman Catholicism. Moreover it seemed to him morally outrageous that his fellow countrymen, who claimed merely to remain under their traditional allegiance to the crown, should be forced to submit to their hereditary enemies in the southern provinces of Ireland.[10]

Passion set Bonar Law apart from his protagonist, Asquith, as much as from his predecessor, Balfour. Asquith's antipathy for emotion was rooted in the traditions of Balliol and the bar. The Balliol influence on his Irish policy was pervasive. Asquith, wrote the famous radical journalist, A. G. Gardiner,

> . . . creates confidence and carries conviction but he does not inspire men with great passions . . . The Balliol mind distrusts 'great thoughts' even if it thinks them . . . Balliol, in fact, is really atrophy of the heart. It is exhaustion of the emotions . . . If he [Asquith] is wanting in any essential of statesmanship, it is a strong impulse to action. He has patience rather than momentum.[11]

It also bred intellectual contempt for Bonar Law instead of the respect and affection in which he held Balfour. Asquith christened Bonar Law 'the gilded tradesman' and dismissed him as having 'the mind of a Glasgow Bailie' (a municipal magistrate); perhaps, as Robert Blake has suggested, 'he found it impossible to believe that someone, lacking his own wide intellectual background of Bar and University, and brought up in the narrower world of the counting house and the iron market, could ever really be his equal in politics'.[12]

Asquith's antipathy for Bonar Law stiffened the new Tory leader's sense of being an outsider whose instinct of alienation was reinforced by his inferiority complex about Arthur Balfour. Bonar Law, who did not enter the House of Commons until 1900 (when Balfour had already sat there for quarter of a century and was about to become prime minister) and who was innocent of any cabinet experience when he became leader, was in awe of his predecessor: 'He goes in holy terror of A.J.B.,'[13] observed Walter Long. Balfour's cerebral attitude towards politics rendered him immune to the emotional pressures to which other politicians were prone.

Churchill touched on this in a conversation with Lloyd George on the strength of character of another cabinet colleague, Edward Grey. Lloyd George facetiously suggested that – in the event of a German invasion during the Great War – Grey, an enthusiastic naturalist, could be made to yield by an opponent who threatened to exterminate the squirrels around his home at Fallodon. 'Arthur Balfour', Churchill observed, 'had no squirrels.'[14]

Andrew Bonar Law's squirrel was Ulster.

When Bonar Law made his first major speech as party leader on 26 January 1912 at the Albert Hall he referred to 'a strange reticence' among ministers as to the principles on which the Home Rule Bill would be framed; they 'are finding it difficult – they may find it impossible – to frame any Bill which is acceptable to Ireland and possible in England'.[15] Their fundamental difficulty was an inability to agree about how and when Unionist Ulster should be excluded from the terms of the bill.

The pragmatists in the cabinet, Lloyd George and Churchill, wanted to grasp the Ulster nettle immediately and their concern about Ulster Unionist resistance should be placed in the context of a remarkable letter that Augustine Birrell wrote to Churchill on 25 August 1911 (only a week after the enactment of the Parliament Bill had cleared the way for the introduction of the Home Rule Bill) and which he asked him to show Lloyd George; all three were members of the cabinet's committee established in January 1911 to draft the Home Rule Bill.[16] Although Birrell declined to forecast the scale of resistance, he argued that:

Ulster has cried 'Wolf' so often and so absurdly that one is inclined to ridicule her rodomontade, but we are cutting very deep this time and her yells are genuine . . . Great ferment and perturbation of spirit exists – mainly fed among the poor folk by hatred of Roman Catholicism and amongst the better to do by the belief that under a Home Rule regime Ireland will become a miserable, one-horsed poverty stricken, priest ridden, corrupt oligarchy.

 . . . Were the question referred to Ulster county by county, it is probable that all Ulster save Antrim and Down would by a majority support Home Rule and it might then be suggested and agreed to that for the transitional period, say five years, Antrim and Down might stand out and that at the end of that time there should be a fresh referendum to settle their fate. If this was done, there could be no Civil War.[17]

The significance of the fact that, more than seven months before the Home Rule Bill was introduced, the minister with cabinet responsibility for Irish policy anticipated civil war unless at least part of Ulster was excluded from its terms of reference can scarcely be exaggerated. But equally significant was the yawning gulf between Birrell's private fears and his self-appointed role as the Irish Party's cabinet spokesman. 'I had seen my own policy clearly from the first,' he later explained in his autobiography. 'It was to pave the way for Home Rule (on more or less Gladstonian lines), and to do all that in me lay to make any other solution of the problem *impossible*.'[18] Political expediency therefore demanded that Birrell conceal his conviction that the exclusion of Ulster was essential. So he did nothing in cabinet to acquiesce in, let alone to advance, the exclusion policy he secretly urged on Lloyd George and Churchill because, as Patricia Jalland has observed, for him to do so, as chief secretary for Ireland, 'would have been regarded as the worst kind of treachery by the Nationalists; it might well have entirely destroyed their confidence in the Liberal party's good faith'.[19] And that might in turn have destroyed the government's parliamentary majority which Asquith relied on Birrell to sustain.

The proceedings of the cabinet committee on Ireland dragged aimlessly on throughout 1911. Such was the lack of realism about Ulster that two successive drafts of the allegedly new bill, dated June and August 1911, included schedules that failed to take account of Queen Victoria's death since the bill had last been drafted in 1893. Ministerial procrastination was more blatantly advertised by the admission (in a confidential cabinet memorandum dated 29 January 1912, twelve months after the Irish committee had been set up) that it 'was not the result of serious consideration, but had been hurriedly thrown together, and was not to be regarded as expressing the settled view of the Cabinet'. The next day Lloyd George, lunching with two Liberal colleagues, agreed 'that Home Rule was neither popular nor unpopular in Great Britain and that it could not be imposed upon Ulster by force and that if possible the Protestant counties in Ulster should be exempted'.[20]

Lloyd George, backed by Churchill, formally proposed Ulster's exclusion at a cabinet meeting on 6 February 1912. The substance of their proposal was 'that every county should be given the option of "contracting out" – really to apply to Ulster, but nominally for every part'. They were backed by Haldane, Charles Hobhouse and – according to Hobhouse – initially by Asquith. But, continued Hobhouse, 'Birrell vowed he would not touch any Bill different to that of '86 and '93. He had made no inquiry into the real condition or intentions of Ulster, and roundly declared such to be useless.'[21] Birrell was supported by Loreburn (the Lord Chancellor Lloyd George and Churchill independently recalled as 'most violent' and 'most blood thirsty' in his opposition to Ulster's exclusion); he was also supported by Lord Crewe, Rosebery's son-in-law and the leader of the Liberals in the House of Lords, whose judgement, as ever, weighed heavily with Asquith – when the prime minister drew up a class list of his cabinet colleagues for the delectation of his confidante, Venetia Stanley, 'like a Tripos at Cambridge',[22] he placed Crewe first. Asquith then 'followed the mood of the meeting'[23] and gave what, according to Hobhouse, was a classic example of his style of chairing the cabinet:

The Prime Minister carries naturally great weight, and everybody likes him, and has great admiration for his intellect and for the ease and rapidity of transacting business, and extraordinary quickness in seizing the right point in any case. On the other hand he has little courage; he will adopt the views of A with apparent conviction and enthusiasm, but if the drift of opinion is against A he will find an easy method of throwing him over. He is nearly always in favour of the last speaker, and I have never seen him put his back to the wall.[24]

The prime minister reported next day to the king on his government's first serious discussion of Irish policy, arguably the most significant such discussion since Gladstone's commitment to home rule in 1886.

The subject was debated at great length and from a number of diverse points of view. In the end the Cabinet acquiesced in the conclusions suggested by Lord Crewe and strongly recommended by the Prime Minister, *viz*:
(a) that the Bill as introduced should apply to the whole of Ireland;
(b) that the Irish leaders should from the first be given clearly to understand that the Government held themselves free to make such changes in the Bill as fresh evidence of facts, or the pressure of British opinion, may render expedient;
(c) that if, in the light of such evidence or indication of public opinion, it becomes clear as the Bill proceeds that some special treatment must be provided for the Ulster counties, the Government will be ready to recognise the necessity either by amendment of the Bill, or by not

pressing it on under the provisions of the Parliament Act. In the meantime, careful and confidential inquiry is to be made as to the real extent and character of the Ulster resistance.[25]

In the event that inquiry was stillborn, largely because of Birrell's hostility, which dated back to August 1911 when he had refused Churchill's offer, in his capacity as home secretary, of 'his secret service machinery'. Although the Irish chief secretary circulated to the cabinet 'conflicting and inadequate' reports on probable resistance to home rule and on drilling in Ulster (the Unionists were drilling in all Ulster counties except Donegal and Monaghan) on 14 and 28 February respectively, his senior officials at Dublin Castle disputed that 'platform speeches will materialise into deliberate and armed resistance to authority'.[26] Neither the Royal Irish Constabulary (RIC) nor any other police or intelligence agency ever attempted 'to make a systematic appraisal of the opposition's strength, let alone to spy on or to penetrate its leadership'.[27] Nearly two years were wasted before Birrell began circulating statistics on 'the escalation in the importation of arms and ammunition' in November 1913 and he then did so reluctantly only in response to ministerial complaints 'about the inadequacy of Cabinet information on the "goings-on" in Ulster'.[28]

Birrell's inertia was compounded by his domestic circumstances after 1911 when his wife became insane as a result of an inoperable brain tumour; she was permanently hospitalised in England from the autumn of 1913 until her death in March 1915 while her miserably unhappy husband trailed backwards and forwards across the Irish Sea. The consequences of Birrell's refusal to support Lloyd George and Churchill on the exclusion of Ulster at the fateful cabinet meeting on 6 February 1912, notwithstanding his telling them privately of the need for exclusion to avoid civil war six months before, were profound and enduring. The cabinet never again discussed Ulster exclusion until 31 December 1912 and never after that until mid-October 1913; in the meantime the Ulster Unionist revolution gained momentum.

Although Birrell may be blamed for defects in the cabinet's Irish intelligence, ultimate responsibility for Irish policy rested, as always, not in the Irish office but in Downing Street. Yet again a Liberal government had decided nothing. Instead it had merely acquiesced (Asquith's own word) in the institutionalisation of their 'strange reticence', the policy of 'wait and see'. And for what were they waiting? To see 'fresh evidence' or 'indication of public opinion . . . that some special treatment must be provided for the Ulster counties'. It was tantamount to a tacit invitation to revolution: the more seditious the Ulster Unionists became, the more persuasive the 'fresh evidence' and the more strident the 'public opinion' compelling Asquith's government to give them the special treatment demanded by a clear majority in north-east Ulster.

The primary responsibility rested with the prime minister, who favoured exclusion but could not or would not decide on the timing or the manner of its implementation. 'I have always thought (and said) that, in the end, we should probably have to make some sort of bargain about Ulster as the price of Home Rule,' he reminded Churchill, the most persistent advocate in cabinet of Ulster's exclusion, when the Irish crisis was coming to a head in September 1913. 'But I have never doubted that, as a matter of tactics and policy, we were right to launch our Bill on its present lines.'[29] No one was better acquainted than Asquith with the unique characteristics of the Parliament Act: no one knew better that, even after three years, a home-rule bill that provided separately for Ulster could not be automatically enacted under its terms unless such Ulster provisions were inserted *before* the bill had completed its first parliamentary circuit. And that would bring the government close to the five-year deadline when, again under the terms of the Parliament Act, the life of the hung parliament elected in December 1910 must end.

Asquith's 'tactics and policy', in short, were designed to postpone rather than to resolve the Irish crisis. One of his biographers, Roy Jenkins, has argued, 'The whole technique of his statesmanship was to watch events calmly until he saw an opportunity for effective intervention. "A sudden curve developed of which I took immediate advantage", was his typical description.' But such exercises in political Micawberism were ill suited to Ireland where they had a cumulatively devastating effect on the power base of the Irish Parliamentary Party whose supporters ultimately deserted them in droves when the third Home Rule Bill never came into effect. An advantageous curve, moreover, was unlikely when, as Roy Jenkins acknowledges, 'the Parliament Act procedure put a premium on delay. The first two circuits were dummy runs. Why should anyone settle until they saw what the disposition of forces was likely to be when it came to the final confrontation?'[30] Why indeed, when the only curve in sight was that vicious spiral from faction to sedition, which Bonar Law had sketched for Asquith when parliament assembled on 14 February.

The shape of the spiral was more clearly delineated at Balmoral, in south Belfast, on Easter Tuesday, 9 April 1912, when a hundred thousand Irish Unionists marched in military formation past Bonar Law, Carson and some seventy other MPs standing on a saluting base over which was unfurled a gigantic Union Jack of 1,200 square feet at the moment the resolution against home rule was passed. Protestant prayers were offered by the Primate of All Ireland and the Moderator of the Presbyterian Church followed by the singing of the 90th Psalm. The crescendo came with Bonar Law's imperial homily to the faithful: 'Once again you hold the pass for the Empire.'[31] Once again Ulster's Unionists had seized the emotional high ground. When, two days later, home rule came at last before the House of Commons, the occasion seemed in comparison dull and insignificant.

'Home Rule launched. Went off quite well but no enthusiasm,'[32] scribbled Lloyd George to his wife after Asquith had introduced the Home Rule Bill on 11 April 1912; no one was 'at all excited nor interested in Home Rule', noted John Burns, one of 67 survivors of the 1893 debates in the Commons: 'a jaded House, overworked Ministry, stale subject, indifferent public'.[33]

If the Liberals lacked all conviction, the Unionists were full of passionate intensity; where ministerial contributions were tepid and boring, opposition speeches were outraged and incendiary. 'It all turns on Ulster,' confided Bonar Law and he privately admitted that he would not otherwise resist home rule only three days after the bill was introduced. 'It is a religious question . . . If Ulster, or rather any county, had the right to remain outside the Irish Parliament, for my part my objection would be met.'[34]

Privately, as we have seen from the cabinet conclusions of 6 February, the government agreed and the restive Churchill broke ranks publicly on 30 April in a remarkable Commons speech that acknowledged 'the perfectly genuine apprehensions of the majority of the people of North-East Ulster . . . It is impossible for a Liberal Government to treat cavalierly or contemptuously, for any British Government to ignore, the sincere sentiments of a numerous and well-defined community like the Protestants of the North of Ireland.' Two days later, Edward Grey followed Churchill's lead[35] and the Tories feared that the Orange card might be dashed from their hand. 'The Government may offer to exclude Ulster from the Home Rule Bill,' brooded their chief whip next day, and 'cause us grave troubles which might develop into a serious split.'[36]

They had a chance to do so when a Liberal back-bench rebel, Thomas Agar-Robartes, moved an amendment on the committee stage of the bill on 11 June 1912 proposing the exclusion of the four most north-easterly and predominantly Protestant Ulster counties (Antrim, Armagh, Down and Londonderry). Bonar Law acted publicly as he had spoken privately and a united opposition voted for the amendment, acknowledging that, if Ulster were excluded, the Tories would acquiesce in home rule for the rest of Ireland. But the government stuck to the fatal path of procrastination mapped out in their secret cabinet conclusions in February. Birrell, speaking immediately after Agar-Robartes, rejected the amendment, saying that 'it would take a very great deal of evidence from Ulster itself to lead to the belief that she desires to cut herself off from the rest of Ireland'.[37] Coming from a chief secretary persuaded that Ulster was not bluffing, this amounted to daring Ulster's Unionists to demonstrate their determination. Asquith also sidestepped exclusion and instead dished up dollops of Gladstonian platitudes.

Carson and Redmond helped Asquith stick to his policy of fudge. Carson, a Southern Unionist at heart, was not yet ready publicly to abandon the strategy of using Ulster's resistance to destroy home rule for all Ireland and accepted the amendment only as a tactic to mutilate the bill; Redmond, as Patricia Jalland has observed, in speaking against what he denounced as a wrecking amendment, 'showed his Liberal allies how they could evade the main issue and . . . provided those Liberals who followed him with a clear line of argument which had been entirely lacking in the first day's debate'.[38] Lloyd George seized the opening. Although he protested against Ulster's 'intolerable demand'[39] for a veto on giving home rule to the rest of Ireland, he said not 'a single word to justify the proposition . . . that although Nationalist Ireland has a perfect right to decide the form of government under which they shall live, Unionist Ulster shall not have the same right of self-determination extended to them'[40] and he abstained from voting on the amendment. Churchill and Grey, identified by the opposition as the cabinet rebels on Irish policy since their second-reading speeches, went further: they neither spoke nor voted and were conspicuously absent for all three days of the debate. Although five Liberals voted with the Unionists and some twenty others deliberately abstained, a government majority of 69, sustained by Lloyd George's trenchant if ambiguous speech, disguised the dissension on Ulster within the cabinet.

What seemed like a reaffirmation of the Gladstonian commitment to unitary home rule and a victory for Redmond cloaked the partitionist reality that, as early as June 1912 (at least two full years before there was the remotest prospect of the enactment of home rule) the three most senior ministers in Asquith's cabinet – the chancellor of the exchequer, the foreign secretary and the former home secretary and then First Lord of the Admiralty – refused to vote against the exclusion of Ulster.

Neither the cabinet nor the Commons considered the government's Irish policy again before Christmas 1912. Outside

Westminster, however, time did not stand so still. The next spectacular Unionist demonstration took place on English soil, at Blenheim Palace on 29 July 1912. Addressing an audience that included 120 Unionist MPs and 40 peers in one of his most notoriously inflammatory speeches, Bonar Law denounced the government as

> . . . a Revolutionary Committee which has seized upon despotic power by fraud . . . In our opposition to them we shall not be guided by the considerations or bound by the restraints which would influence us in an ordinary Constitutional struggle . . . They may, perhaps they will, carry their Home Rule Bill through the House of Commons but what then? I said the other day in the House of Commons and I repeat here that there are things stronger than Parliamentary majorities . . .
>
> I can imagine no length of resistance to which Ulster can go in which I should not be prepared to support them, and in which, in my belief, they would not be supported by the overwhelming majority of the British people.[41]

Ulster's Unionists were swift to cash Bonar Law's blank cheque and to show Birrell the 'evidence from Ulster' he had asked for in his Commons speech on the Agar-Robartes amendment. The 13,000-strong crowd at Blenheim paled in comparison with the vast numbers who signed the Ulster Covenant between 19 and 28 September: 218,206 men and 228,991 women. The covenant solemnly pledged its signatories to use 'all means which may be found necessary to defeat the present conspiracy to set up a Home Rule Parliament in Ireland' and, in the event of such a parliament being established, 'to refuse to recognise its authority'. The signatories turned out in their Sunday-best attire at meetings in villages, towns and cities throughout Ulster and beyond. 'In Dublin the Covenant was signed by two thousand men who gave proof of their birth in Ulster, in Edinburgh it was signed on the "Covenanters' Stone" in the old Greyfriars churchyard and signatures were collected in London, Glasgow, Manchester, Liverpool, Bristol, and York.' In Belfast's City Hall on 28 September, designated as Ulster Day, 'lines of desks . . . stretching for a third of a mile along the corridors, allowed 540 signatures to be taken simultaneously, and the signing went on until 11 p.m.' When the steamer bringing Edward Carson from Belfast to Liverpool cast off, 'he heard the vast crowd in the darkness begin to sing "Rule Britannia" and "Auld Lang Syne" and then "God Save the King"; and as she moved into the channel rockets burst in red, white, and blue sparks above her.'[42]

Churchill, chafing in the aftermath of Blenheim (the seat of his Marlborough ancestors and his own birthplace) and frustrated by the cabinet's timidity, urged Lloyd George again to press the case for exclusion. 'The time has come when action about Ulster must be settled. We ought to give any Irish county the option of remaining at Westminster for a period of 5 or 10 years.'[43] But Churchill's sense of urgency was not shared by his cabinet colleagues, who were infuriated by his Dundee speech on 12 September when he floated a devolution scheme to scatter ten or twelve separate legislatures throughout the United Kingdom. This was tantamount to offering Ulster separate treatment.

Armed with this new evidence of ministerial disarray, Carson again seized the initiative. At Christmas 1912 the 19 Irish Unionist MPs gave notice of an amendment to exclude all nine Ulster counties from the bill and forced the cabinet to review its Irish policy for the first time since February. The outcome was much the same, although officials in Dublin Castle were now also advising Birrell to concede the exclusion of Ulster in order improve the prospects for home rule in the rest of Ireland. The prime minister, recorded Charles Hobhouse,

> was convinced that it was merely a wrecking or embarrassing amendment. He had looked up Grey's and Churchill's speeches to see that they had said nothing which would prevent his refusal of the amendment. It was agreed that there was nothing, and the matter was very nearly settled when I said I thought it was a very important and significant step for Carson to take, and that though he and his co-signatories declared their 'fundamental and unalterable objection' to the Bill, yet they were right in saying that the responsibility would be ours if serious disturbances broke out later in Ulster which could be attributed to our refusal to exclude Ulster; moreover I was certain that we had no means of coercing Ulster, for the troops were not to be relied on, even if we wished to coerce. Then Churchill asked Birrell what really was the state of Ulster. B. said he had no very good information, but it was impossible to overestimate their real racial, religious and local abhorrence of a Dublin Parliament . . . Thereupon Ll. George and Churchill took up the running and advised no banging of the door against Ulster, Ll. George particularly strongly, and ultimately it was agreed that the P.M. should speak rejecting the actual amendment but hinting that if settlement was in the air, our attitude would be one of meeting them half-way.[44]

The cabinet's halfway-house conclusion on 31 December 1912 exposed the total disarray of government policy: the prime minister reduced to scanning the speeches of his senior ministers; the chief secretary's confession of how little he knew about the state of Ulster; the determination of Lloyd George and Churchill to secure Ulster's exclusion; the admission that sedition would infect the army; the utter indifference to Irish nationalist embitterment.

The Home Rule Bill's first dummy run dragged to its predictable close on 30 January 1913 when it was defeated in the House of Lords by 326 votes to 69. Thereafter the opposition enjoyed a major tactical advantage: the bill could not subsequently be amended without its consent (which would clearly not be forthcoming without the exclusion of Unionist Ulster) if it were to become law within the three-year cycle prescribed by the Parliament Act; and another general election would probably intervene if the government chose to initiate a second cycle. The spiral of sedition sharpened steeply next day when the formation of the Ulster Volunteer Force, a private army of a hundred thousand men who had signed the covenant, was announced.

The 1913 parliamentary session was extraordinarily short, from 10 March until 15 August, and the Home Rule Bill's second dummy run was a more pointless charade even than the first. It passed the House of Commons on 7 July and, on 15 July, the House of Lords again rejected it, by 302 votes to 64.

Another charade with intriguing implications for the future course of Irish policy had been acted out when Lloyd George and Bonar Law played two rounds of golf on the French Riviera before parliament met in March. Lloyd George's reaction to Bonar Law's elevation as leader of the opposition had been very different from Asquith's: 'The Conservatives have done a wise thing for once. They have selected the very best man – the only man. He is a very clever fellow and has a nice disposition, and I like him very much. He has a good brain.' The feeling was mutual, although Bonar Law was more cautious: 'I like Lloyd George. He is a nice man, but the most dangerous little man that ever lived.'[45] Their companionship has been identified by John Grigg as a 'striking example of personal affection and fellow-feeling transcending partisanship. The world as yet had no way of knowing that these two apparently bitter antagonists liked each other and understood each other so well.'[46] The full flowering of that fellow-feeling swiftly smothered antagonism in Lloyd George's coalition government of 1916–21 and provided the bedrock for the partition of Ireland.

4

Reaching the Realities

On 24 July 1913 the mounting threat of Ulster's Unionists taking arms against his government – now that the House of Lords had exhausted its powers to resist the Home Rule Bill – prompted King George V to summon Augustine Birrell to an audience at Buckingham Palace. The Irish chief secretary was insouciant: he nonchalantly 'discounted the seriousness of the state of things in Ulster as being due to Carson who had lost his head – not an Orangeman, a Dublin man. As for fighting, there would be no one to fight with.' Ulster's provisional government, Birrell airily predicted, 'would not last a week'. The way out of the impasse was for the opposition to table a scheme in parliament for Ulster contracting out of the bill – 'say for ten years, at the expiration of which a referendum might be taken as to whether they should come under Home Rule or not' – which the government would accept. When the king replied that Redmond would never agree, 'Birrell answered "he would have to agree!" – "But he would turn you out" – "Let him – a d—d good thing if he did!"' But, as Birrell acknowledged, '"The Opposition won't do this, because they are hoping something will turn up – that either Heaven, the King, or some other agency, will bring about a General Election and the Government will be beaten and Home Rule shelved."' He also admitted the force of the king's contention 'that apparently the Government were "drifting" and that with this "drift" his own position was becoming more and more difficult'. 'It was for the Opposition to move,' repeated Birrell, notwithstanding his admission that they would not do so. But the tension between Birrell's public bluster and his private convictions resurfaced when he wrote to Lord Stamfordham, the king's private secretary, in the first week in September, admitting that there was certainly 'great *perturbation*' among Ulster's Unionists 'and the notion that it is all bluff may be dismissed'.[1] But while the king, as he confided to his private secretary, agreed that 'there ought to be a general election before Parliament meets' and was 'perfectly prepared to tell the Prime Minister so', he thought it 'almost a certainty' that Asquith would refuse. 'Then I shall have burnt my boats and he may decide to resign and tell the country I made him do so.'[2]

An increasingly agitated king formally sought the views of the Unionist leaders and, on 31 July, Bonar Law and Lansdowne submitted a memorandum arguing that only an election would avert civil war and that, if Asquith refused to dissolve parliament in deference to the king's wishes, the king could dismiss him and send for someone who would.[3]

On 11 August George V summoned Asquith to an audience and gave him a memorandum, which he had written in his own hand on the royal yacht off Cowes, effectively arguing for the exclusion of Ulster:

The speeches not only of people like Sir Edward Carson, but of the Unionist Leaders, and of ex-Cabinet Ministers; the stated intention of setting up a Provisional Government in Ulster directly the Home Rule Bill is passed; the reports of Military preparations, Army drilling etc.; of assistance from England, Scotland and the Colonies; of the intended resignation of their Commissions by Army Officers; all point towards rebellion if not Civil War; and, if so, to certain bloodshed.[4]

Asquith, who had sedulously avoided discussing the Irish crisis with the king, looked for more time to consider his reply. He also avoided discussing the royal intervention with his ministers, although he did confide in Lloyd George[5] before the cabinet meeting on 13 August when it was agreed that there was no need to meet again until 14 October after the traditional leisurely summer holiday. Indeed the cabinet of 13 August was a fine example of the preference to talk about anything but Ireland: ministers instead discussed, *inter alia*, the desirability of putting clergymen on the Royal Commission on Venereal Disease; a proposal to establish a British-endowed university at Hangkow, the largest city in central China; an invitation to attend the Panama Exposition; and Churchill's scheme to substitute an airship patrol for British forces in Somaliland in order to 'terrify the Arabs beyond conception'.[6] Another month elapsed before the prime minister replied to the king's memorandum and began to abandon what even a sympathetic biographer describes as his 'relative inactivity on Ireland during the sessions of 1912 and 1913'.[7]

In the meantime Birrell had become much more alarmist about the Ulster situation. On 30 August he warned Asquith that police reports were predicting 'a *shindy* of large proportions' demanding 'a massive army response' and he agonised about the government's duty to declare their '*willingness* to consider the *exclusion* from the Bill of some portions of Ulster'.[8] But he still subordinated his private conviction that at least part of Ulster must be excluded to his public loyalty to the Irish Party.

On 11 September 1913, however, the Irish Party suffered 'a staggering blow' when Lord Loreburn (Lord Chancellor until June 1912, when ill health caused his replacement by Haldane, and one of the strongest opponents of exclusion while he was in the cabinet) wrote to *The Times* calling for a conference 'to consider proposals for accommodation'. Although Loreburn was suspected of acting as a stalking horse for former cabinet colleagues, his action owed more to old age, the frustrations of retirement, and jealousy of Asquith and Birrell. An apprehensive Redmond, already fearful about 'Asquith's overpowering love of compromise' and mistrustful of Churchill, 'had counted upon Loreburn and Morley as the most reliable Home Rulers in the cabinet'.[9] The Loreburn letter, Birrell reported to the cabinet, 'had an irritating and disquieting effect in Ireland, as everyone thought it originated from the cabinet: instead of being the output of an always disgruntled ex-colleague who in earlier days had said the Govt. should unhesitatingly shoot out disobedience'.[10]

Loreburn's bombshell burst just when Asquith was on the point of finally replying to the king. Asquith's memorandum echoed Birrell's and Loreburn's warnings in admitting that, if the Home Rule Bill became law,

> . . . there will undoubtedly be a serious danger of organised disorder in the four north-eastern counties of Ulster.
> . . . the genuine apprehensions of a large majority of the Protestants, the incitements of responsible leaders, and the hopes of British sympathy and support, are likely to encourage forcible resistance (wherever it can be tried); there is the certainty of tumult and riot, and more than the possibility of bloodshed.

On the other hand, if the Bill is rejected or indefinitely postponed, or some inadequate and disappointing substitute put forward in its place, the prospect is, in my opinion, much more grave. The attainment of Home Rule has for more than 30 years been the political (as distinguished from the agrarian) ideal of the Irish people. Whatever happens in other parts of the United Kingdom, at successive general elections, the Irish representation in Parliament never varies . . . It is the confident expectation of the vast bulk of the Irish people that it will become law next year.

If the ship, after so many stormy voyages, were now to be wrecked in sight of port, it is difficult to overrate the shock, or its consequences. They would extend into every department of political, social, agrarian and domestic life. It is not too much to say that Ireland would become ungovernable – unless by the application of forces and methods which would offend the conscience of Great Britain, and arouse the deepest resentment in all the self-governing Dominions of the Crown.

Asquith's analysis was chillingly prophetic – nationalist Ireland took precisely this path between 1916 and 1921 – but he still shrank from offering a solution. He saw no point in a conference, as proposed by the king and by Loreburn, unless and until the Unionists accepted the principle of home rule. Then he would be prepared to confer and 'to yield to any reasonable suggestion' about Ulster's exclusion.[11]

Asquith also wrote to Churchill, who was about to go to Balmoral as minister in attendance to the king, warning him that he would 'find the Royal mind obsessed, and the Royal tongue exceptionally fluid and voluble'. He urged him 'to emphasise the dangers of rejection, when the ship is just

reaching port. An ungovernable Ireland is a much more serious prospect than rioting in 4 counties.'[12] Although Churchill
confessed a characteristic pugnacity to Asquith – 'I wish it
were possible to do two things: (1) treat these Ulstermen fairly
and (2) give them a lesson. But I am afraid No. (1) will get
in the way of No. (2)' – he remained the cabinet's most re-
doubtable champion of Ulster's exclusion.[13]

Bonar Law was also at Balmoral and, unknown to most
cabinet ministers and to Redmond, a flurry of high-level
exchanges on Ulster followed. Bonar Law again spoke bluntly
to the king, this time about the army: 'if the Government
attempted to use troops in Belfast before they had behind
them the moral force' of a fresh electoral mandate, he was
'very doubtful whether the army would obey'.[14] He spoke
similarly to Churchill, saying that the government's 'programme was absolutely impossible without civil war' and that
the Conservatives 'would be driven in resistance to . . . ren-
dering Government in the House of Commons impossible,
with the direct result that the Army encouraged by us will not
obey their orders'.[15]

By now, as Bonar Law told Carson, the leaders of both
parties were seeking a way back from the brink of civil war;
he anticipated that Asquith would seek a private meeting with
him. Bonar Law thought 'the only way out' was 'to leave
Ulster as she is, and have some form of Home Rule for the
rest of Ireland'; other compromises involving a more general
application of devolution would be 'impossible . . . unless
there were something in the nature of a coalition', a phrase
echoing Gladstone's bipartisan proposals of 1885 and foreshadowing the coalition governments of 1915–22. But he
would do nothing that Carson opposed: 'The whole question
as to the exclusion of Ulster really turns upon this – whether

or not it would be regarded as a betrayal by the solid body of Unionists in the South and West [of Ireland].'[16]

Carson was also agonising about the 'horror of what may happen if the Bill is passed as it stands and the mischief it will do the whole empire'.[17] His personal dilemma, he admitted to Bonar Law, was inherent in his position as the Southern Unionist leader of the Ulster Unionist revolution:

> As regards the position here [in Ulster] I am of the opinion that on the whole things are shaping towards a desire to settle on the terms of leaving Ulster out. A difficulty arises as to defining Ulster. My own view is that the whole of Ulster should be excluded, but the minimum would be the six plantation counties and for that a good case could be made.
>
> The South and West would present a difficulty and it might be that I could not agree to their abandonment, though I feel certain it would be the best settlement if Home Rule is inevitable.[18]

Arthur Balfour, another influential visitor to Balmoral where he had talked to Churchill (who frankly admitted that he and 'many of his most important colleagues'[19] had always favoured Ulster's exclusion) as well as to the king, explained to Bonar Law why he preferred partition to 'the policy of letting things drift to a catastrophe'. Given that his preferred solution – a dissolution, whether advised by or forced on the government – was probably unattainable, 'the separation of Ulster from Ireland may be the least calamitous of all the calamitous courses open to us'.[20]

Privately, Carson was edging towards an exclusionist compromise. Publicly, he amplified the plans for revolution. On

24 September 1913, 500 delegates of the Ulster Unionist Council approved a plan to delegate its authority to a provisional government of 75 members (led by a Commission of Five chaired by Carson) which would seize power the moment the Home Rule Bill became law. A military council was established and the work of government departments delegated to committees on finance and business, on law, on education, and customs, excise and the post office, and so on. The meeting ended with a resolution to create an indemnity guarantee fund of £1 million to compensate the members of the Ulster Volunteer Force who might be wounded and the widows and orphans of those killed in the anticipated fighting. Carson personally pledged £10,000; a quarter of a million was guaranteed before the meeting ended, and Belfast's business community ensured that the fund had surpassed its target of £1 million by 1 January 1914. The spotlight on military preparedness intensified when a series of UVF parades throughout Ulster culminated with another massive demonstration at Balmoral in south Belfast on 27 September taking the form of a review of the Belfast division, four regiments of fourteen battalions comprising 12,000 men, led by the UVF's sixty-six-year-old commander-in-chief, General Sir George Richardson.[21]

Although the looming last lap of the third Home Rule Bill was now privately focusing government and opposition minds on seeking a formula to exclude Ulster, both sides remained publicly wedded to the confrontational theatricals of party politics. The contrast was epitomised by the antics of F. E. Smith, who was secretly seeking to revive the coalitionist spirit of the summer of 1910. Smith advised Lloyd George that he had explored the prospects of exclusion with the king and with Churchill. 'Do not attach too much importance to our speeches at the moment,' he wrote airily on 26 September.

'If people may have to go into a conference but do not know, there is a tendency to begin negotiations by putting the case high.'[22] Suiting his actions to his words, Smith next day stole the limelight at the Belfast review as General Richardson's 'galloper', the gesture that won him the nickname of Galloper Smith. Lloyd George was undeterred: 'You know how anxious I have been for years to work with you and a few others on your side. I have always realised that our differences have been very artificial and do not reach the "realities".' Lloyd George, having shown Smith's letter to Asquith and Churchill, also raised exclusion with Bonar Law, arguing that the opposition must take the initiative, but Bonar Law jibbed at giving 'the enemy the idea that we were not only ready but anxious for a settlement on those lines'.[23]

A recognition of the realities had also persuaded Asquith to edge closer towards exclusion even before the Ulster Unionist demonstration of defiance in Belfast. 'I have always thought (and said) that, in the end, we should probably have to make some sort of bargain about Ulster as the price of Home Rule,'[24] he wrote to Churchill on 19 September. But for Asquith 'the end' was not yet. Haldane, whose experience as secretary of state for war from 1905 until he became Lord Chancellor in 1912 now urged him to make proposals specifically designed to thwart an army mutiny, explained why: 'It is difficult to get the Prime Minister to make any preparations in advance of a difficulty . . . the bent of Mr Asquith's mind is towards a solution *ad hoc*; and . . . he is always inclined to optimistic views in face of a complicated situation.'[25]

Asquith came to Balmoral a week later armed not only with the Lord Chancellor's opinion but also with Birrell's advice that the king had been confused by the plethora of ministerial opinions – 'each with a stand of his own . . . Winston, Grey, Harcourt, myself – none quite the same' – and that he needed them reduced 'to a harmonious whole'.[26] But the royal needs were not met by Asquith's arrival and a bemused king noted in his diary that his prime minister admitted that the 'political situation . . . was serious, but was optimistic as usual'.[27] Indeed Lloyd George remarked on the prime minister's 'splendid form. I have never seen him better. He was not worrying about anything.'[28]

But, as the king kept up the pressure throughout Asquith's three-day visit, the shape of his prime minister's Irish strategy began to emerge. Asquith acknowledged that his government had not anticipated 'such a state of things as now exist in Ulster . . . tho' they did expect riots as in 1886'; he also 'admitted to the King that the policy at present threatened against Ulster was unEnglish and contrary to all Liberal and democratic principles'. Yet Asquith still insisted that 'Carson's attitude and speeches make it impossible to think of anything like a conference at present. Indeed such a meeting would inevitably result in either a Tea Party or a Bear Garden!' and he also dismissed the 'idea of taking any action' against Carson as 'throwing a lighted match into the powder barrel'. But the prime minister responded to the king's insistence that it was 'the duty of everyone' to avert the catastrophe threatened in Ulster by accepting that 'the ground must be broken' for a new departure and he agreed to arrange a 'quite informal and absolutely secret' meeting with Bonar Law.

Stamfordham's note of the Balmoral conversations of 6–9 October 1913[29] reveals Asquith's admission that the third Home Rule Bill could not be enacted in the form in which it had been introduced; indeed Asquith's telling the king of his assumption when the bill 'is placed on the Statute Book many months must elapse before it can be put into force' clearly foreshadows its ultimate fate.

On 8 October – when Churchill, in a controversial speech in his Dundee constituency, secretly co-ordinated with F. E. Smith and awaited with great apprehension by the leaders of the Irish Party, publicly acknowledged north-east Ulster's claim to special consideration – the prime minister succumbed; he wrote to Bonar Law inviting him to 'an informal conversation of a strictly confidential character' to explore Churchill's proposal 'as a first step towards the possible avoidance of danger to the State'.[30] When the cabinet met for the first time since the summer, on 14 October 1913, Churchill again made the running when he proposed a five-year 'exclusion of the homogeneous anti-national part of Ulster . . . *but only* "if Carson and the Tory party would accept the compromise and agree not to repeal it".'[31] He pleaded in vain. Asquith remained 'very emphatic that no concession was due to Ulster threats, and none should be given'. Birrell consoled his colleagues with the ludicrous intelligence that 'there were many rifles in Ireland but no ammunition' and 'all agreed that if the Tories wanted concessions, and would in exchange offer a permanent settlement based on an Irish Parliament and Executive, we would go to any lengths to meet them'.[32]

Two days before the crucial cabinet meeting Redmond had 'strengthened Asquith's reluctance to steer a resolute course'[33] in a vaingloriously optimistic and delusional speech to an excited crowd in Limerick when he claimed that 'the argumentative opposition to Home Rule is dead . . . All the violent language, all the extravagant action, all the bombastic threats are but indications that the battle is over.'[34] The outcome was a reaffirmation of the policy of vacillation adopted by the cabinet in February 1912. 'The Government policy on the Irish question had been settled,' confided Lloyd George. They had 'determined to let matters take their course and do nothing'.[35]

The most bizarre aspect of the cabinet discussion on the morning of 14 October was that, although the prime minister briefed his colleagues about his talks with the king, he told them nothing about his secret meeting with Bonar Law arranged for that afternoon. Bonar Law chose the meeting place: Cherkley Court, the country house near Leatherhead in Surrey of his fellow-Canadian confidant, Max Aitken, who had been instrumental in his elevation to the Tory leadership. Asquith motored down from London after luncheon to find Bonar Law playing double-dummy bridge with his host, 'the need for secrecy precluding a four'. It was the first time the two leaders had met other than on formal occasions and Bonar Law was characteristically blunt. After referring to the risk that exclusion might split his party, he admitted his reluctance to surrender the Orange card:

If the question of Ulster were removed one of the strongest points in our favour in an Election would be gone and our chance of winning it would . . . be diminished . . . At bottom, one of the strongest feelings in England and in Scotland was Protestantism, or dislike of Roman Catholicism, and . . . if Protestants of Belfast were actually killed . . . the effect in Great Britain would be not only that the Government would be beaten but that they would be snowed under.

Asquith, too, was frank about his Irish allies. He deprecated the Tory 'habit of speaking of him as absolutely dependent on the Irish . . . it was really the other way; that the

Nationalists without the support of the Liberal Party were powerless, and that if he or the Government decided on any course which commanded the support of their own party the Nationalists would have no choice but to accept it.'[36]

But the prospect of an agreement that would rid both party leaders of dependence on their Irish allies was more seductive for Asquith than for Bonar Law. The Cherkley conversations – the two leaders again met there secretly on 6 November – ended only with an understanding that Asquith would bring the matter to cabinet on 12 November.

The understanding promoted only greater misunderstanding between the two men. 'In the end I said that I would report the substance of our conversation to my colleagues in the Cabinet,' recorded Asquith, 'and if they approved of the matter going on, confidential steps might be taken by Mr Birrell to sound the Nationalist leaders.'[37] Bonar Law, however, believed that Asquith had told him 'definitely that he would propose to the Cabinet the exclusion of Ulster, either the four counties or the six – probably the six; that if they agreed he would then see the Nationalists'.[38] Whether the prime minister would *propose* or merely *report* to his colleagues was a genuine misunderstanding arising, perhaps, from Bonar Law's unfamiliarity with Asquith's style of cabinet chairmanship; it was not unreasonable to assume that a report delivered with prime ministerial authority on a conversation with the leader of the opposition was tantamount to a proposal; but that was not Asquith's way.

Another reason why Bonar Law's attitude hardened even before the cabinet met was that the Orange card glowed more seductively than ever in the light of three by-election results in the first fortnight of November. Linlithgow (7 November), Reading (8 November) and Keighley (11 November) all registered swings against the Liberals of 8.3, 11.1 and 26.5 per cent respectively.[39] The Cherkley conversations had already persuaded Bonar Law that Asquith wanted an agreement only as the 'alternative to a General Election. From a party point of view I hope the Nationalists will not agree,' he wrote to Walter Long. 'If they do, I am afraid that our best card for the Election will have been lost.'[40] The best strategy, agreed Bonar Law and General Henry Wilson (the militant Irish Unionist director of military operations and arch-intriguer, who fed the Tory leaders all the Irish secrets of the war office), 'is to make Redmond wreck the proposal'.[41] 'And then came Linlithgow and Reading,' exulted Carson. 'The Government are in a very tight place and I do not suppose that they can long remain without taking some steps toward settlement.'[42]

The pressure for a settlement had further intensified on the day of the Linlithgow by-election when Brigadier-General J. E. Gough, the recently appointed chief of staff at Aldershot and the younger brother of the ringleader of the subsequent Curragh mutiny of March 1914, came by invitation to see Lord Stamfordham for an 'absolutely confidential' conversation at Buckingham Palace. 'Unless a compromise is arranged,' warned Gough, 'there will be serious bloodshed . . . at least 60 per cent of the officers ordered to Ulster would refuse to go and 30 per cent of those not ordered there would resign their commissions.' When Stamfordham questioned whether the authorities would allow him to resign, Gough's answer was unequivocal: '"They may try me by Court Martial but they couldn't try 16 or 17 General Officers"! and such action would drive us to desperation and we should do our worst and the whole Army would be split and shattered to its foundations.'[43]

Lloyd George now added his weight to the pressure for settlement. He arranged a discreet dinner party of senior ministers at 11 Downing Street after the cabinet meeting of 12 November at which Asquith finally told his colleagues about his secret talks with Bonar Law. Lloyd George wanted to commit the cabinet to Ulster exclusion. His guests were Asquith, Crewe, Grey and Haldane, the Liberal imperialist old guard whose influence with the prime minister was profound and of long standing. Birrell was not invited: 'Ireland will require a big man at the Irish Office,' remarked Lloyd George a few days later. 'Birrell is not the man.'[44] Lloyd George proposed the 'temporary exclusion of Ulster with an automatic inclusion at the end of the term' in order to 'knock all moral props from under Carson's rebellion, and either make it impossible for Ulster to take up arms, or if they did, put us in a strong position with British public opinion when we came to suppress it'. Lloyd George's plan won the 'general approval' of his guests. Asquith 'expressed satisfaction'; Grey and Haldane were even more enthusiastic.[45]

The next day, Lloyd George sold his plan to the cabinet. It 'met with a good deal of support', reported Asquith to the king; even from John Morley (Gladstone's former chief secretary and the Irish Party's friend in cabinet), who now argued 'that to start Home Rule with a baptism of bloodshed would be fatal to its prospects'. The cabinet agreed that the prime minister should see Redmond privately to discuss Lloyd George's scheme, 'as a basis of possible compromise, but still more as the best means of avoiding armed resistance, the exclusion of Ulster (i.e. of the Protestant counties) for a definite term of five or six years, with a provision for its automatic inclusion at the expiration of that time'.[46]

The ministerial discussions of 12–13 November 1913 marked an irreversible step towards partition. Lloyd George was henceforth the real architect of Irish policy, a role he retained until his resignation as prime minister in October 1922. Birrell, no longer able to reconcile his private belief in Ulster's exclusion with his public commitment to his original bill, had no stomach to peddle Lloyd George's policy to the Irish Party and tried to resign.[47] His resignation was refused. He was too valuable for Asquith to lose: no one could better smooth the ruffled feathers of his Irish allies as he began to pick his way down the partitionist path.

Asquith met Redmond on 17 November at Queen Anne's Gate in the sumptuous house of Edwin Montagu (then a junior minister and formerly Asquith's private secretary, and who later married Venetia Stanley, the prime minister's most intimate confidante in 1913–14). He told Redmond about his talks with Bonar Law and about Lloyd George's proposal on which, he reassured Redmond, in a languid display of economy with the truth, 'neither he nor the Cabinet came to any conclusion whatever'.[48] He also asked Redmond for a memorandum of his views.

With Asquith still drifting, Lloyd George twice met John Dillon that day in an attempt to keep his hand on the tiller. Dillon argued that he and his colleagues must remain free to say that no proposal for exclusion had been made until 'the Bill was going through . . . and that then the Irish leaders might carry it in Ireland inasmuch as it was accompanied by the carrying into law of Home Rule for the rest of Ireland, thus enabling the Irish leaders to point to Home Rule as an accomplished fact, with Ulster only temporarily outside its operation'.[49] Redmond's response was in similar vein: Asquith should invite, but should not make 'offers for accommodation from the other side' which the Tories would treat as a platform for further demands. His analysis of the outlook in Ulster was ludicrously naive: 'A riot may be attempted in

Belfast and one or two other towns, but nobody in Ulster, outside a certain number of fanatics and leaders, believes in any organised rebellion, active or passive.' He was equally dismissive about the prospect of a collapse in army discipline.[50]

Redmond's memorandum told ministers what they wanted to hear and was so finely tuned to Asquith's Fabian temperament that he read it to the cabinet on 24 November, the same day he received it. Ministers seized on Redmond's 'last few words . . . *At present* negotiations were harmful and undesirable.'[51] The cabinet meetings of 24 and 25 November 1913 reaffirmed the essence of its firm but still covert commitment to some form of partition. Exclusion of Ulster there must be, but not yet. Asquith did not put it quite so brutally in his reply to Redmond, assuring him that there was 'no question at this stage of our making any "offer" or "proposal"' to Bonar Law. But the prime minister carefully loosened the bonds knotted by his Irish allies: 'We must, of course, keep our hands free, when the critical stage of the Bill is ultimately reached, to take such a course as then, in all the circumstances, seems best calculated to safeguard the fortunes of Home Rule.'[52]

In the meantime Churchill resumed the bipartisan tack with Austen Chamberlain on board his Admiralty yacht *Enchantress* – 'the sweetest of all the sweets of office', a ship of 3,800 tonnes, built in 1903, with a crew of between eighty and a hundred. The bathrooms were among its more sybaritic features: 'all assembled together side by side, and divided by partitions which did not reach the ceiling, so that one could converse agreeably with one's neighbour'. Asquith's daughter recalled an excursion in the Mediterranean 'lying lapped in hot salt water'[53] listening to Churchill's private secretaries discussing the hazards of partnering the reckless First Lord of the Admiralty at bridge. Churchill told Chamberlain that the government had never ruled out the possibility of excluding Ulster – '"*never*". Of course Redmond hated it, but they were not absolutely bound to R. and he was not indispensable to them. They would not allow Ulster to veto Home Rule, but they had never excluded the possibility of separate treatment for Ulster.' But the government must reach an understanding with the opposition if they were to break with Redmond; and Churchill 'very clearly' indicated that 'he would like to see' the Lloyd George–Balfour coalition negotiations of 1910 're-newed now'. 'Both sides had to make speeches full of party claptrap & no surrender & then insert a few sentences at the end for wise & discerning people on the other side to see & ponder.' Chamberlain realised that Churchill, Lloyd George, Grey and Asquith all 'genuinely' wanted a settlement 'but that as to the means they have no clear ideas and that the hot and cold fits succeed one another pretty quickly'; Asquith meant 'to "wait and see" and will not give his "casting vote" till the last moment.'[54]

The cabinet meeting on 25 November 1913 was a classic example of 'the hot and cold fits'. After a lengthy discussion the terms had been agreed, the prime minister reported to the king,[55] of his reply to Redmond's letter 'deprecating the making by the Government, at this stage, of any "offer" or "proposal" by way of compromise'. The key phrase was 'at this stage'. Asquith's search for compromise mirrored St Augustine's prayer for celibacy: give me chastity, but not yet. So Asquith told Redmond that the government 'were not making any "offer"' – neither were they going 'to shut the door to further conversation'. He also said that, 'before taking the responsibility of using force, we must be free to make such suggestions in regard to Ulster to the House of Commons as seem to us to be advisable'. The cabinet's sanguine conclusion that it was not the moment for compromise went hand in hand with its bellicose discussion of the need to suppress gun-running, triggered by Birrell when he 'casually remarked that he had heard from Liverpool that 1,500 rifles and 95,000 ball cartridges had been just sent to Belfast' – so much for his assertion on 13 October that 'there were many rifles in Ireland but no ammunition'. This led to the decision that a proclamation by Order in Council should be issued, saying that in the interests of *all* Ireland, arms traffic would be suspended.[56] The government had been spurred into action not by the fact that the Unionists had armed but by the fear that the nationalists might arm – or, as Asquith put it pithily to the king, 'in view of the fact that not only the Ulstermen but Nationalists and Larkinites are beginning to arm and drill'. James Larkin was the leader of the Irish Transport and General Workers' Union, some twenty thousand of whose members in Dublin were then on strike or 'locked out'.

The king had by now a shrewd idea of Asquith's strategy. 'I believe the Government intend to do nothing further for the moment with regard to a settlement by consent of the Irish question,'[57] he wrote in Sandringham on 1 December; but, when parliament met in February 1914, they intended 'to make the proposal to the Opposition that Ulster should be excluded from the Home Rule Bill for six years and then automatically to be obliged to come under the Dublin Parliament . . . I expect that Mr Redmond will probably be induced to accept the proposal.'

In the meantime the proceedings in parliament seemed increasingly irrelevant in Ireland where those nationalists, who admired the militancy of the Ulster Volunteer Force (UVF) and were frustrated by the interminable postponement of home rule, now imitated their example. 'A wonderful thing has come to pass in Ulster,' wrote Eoin MacNeill – professor of early and medieval Irish history in University College Dublin, a founder of the Gaelic League, dedicated to the revival of the Irish language, and a long-time supporter of John Redmond – in an article entitled 'The North Began' in the League's journal on 1 November 1913. The Irish Republican Brotherhood (IRB), an oath-bound secret society founded in Dublin in 1858 and dedicated to the establishment of an independent Irish republic by force of arms, which had already decided to set up a force modelled on the UVF, enlisted MacNeill's co-operation. 'I am glad that the North has "begun"', wrote Patrick Pearse, then a little-known schoolteacher, whose words have ever since resonated with physical-force republicans. 'I am glad that the Orangemen have armed, for it is a goodly thing to see arms in Irish hands . . . I should like to see any and every body of Irish citizens armed. We must accustom ourselves to the thought of arms, to the sight of arms, to the use of arms.' A steering committee to set up the Irish Volunteers first met on 11 November; on 19 November a separate Irish Citizen Army was established by James Larkin and James Connolly as a workers' defence corps in the bitter Dublin labour dispute of 1913; on 25 November Eoin MacNeill presided over the inaugural meeting of the Irish Volunteers and some 3,500 men enrolled. 'Ireland armed', Pearse told the cheering crowd, would 'make a better bargain with the Empire than Ireland unarmed.' Drilling began within a week.[58]

Ministers might persuade themselves that their decision to proscribe arms traffic was 'in the interests of *all* Ireland' but the contrast between their reaction to the reality of Unionist sedition and the prospect of nationalist sedition was stark indeed. The Ulster Volunteers had been drilling and arming for over a year but the royal proclamation of 4 December prohibiting importation into Ireland of arms and ammunition was issued only days after the first Irish Volunteers were enrolled. Irish nationalists, outraged at such blatant discrimination, would have been still more incensed had they known, as Redmond knew, that the government took its decision on the very day that the Irish Volunteers were inaugurated. To Redmond and his party the new development 'was a nightmare' and the government's decision the first of 'many irretrievable blunders'[59] that shook 'the constitutional [nationalist] movement to its foundations' and which, by 1918, had destroyed the Irish Parliamentary Party at Westminster.

The year 1914 began much as 1913 had ended: with the prime minister secretly negotiating with opposition leaders behind the backs of most ministers and of his Irish allies. His third Cherkley meeting with Bonar Law had taken place on 10 December, but since Asquith was not yet prepared to go 'further than Redmond would allow him to go, their conversation was inevitably abortive'.[60] Bonar Law felt Asquith 'was in a funk about the resistance of Ulster . . . I am convinced he will not face that when it comes to the point . . . he is quite at sea and does not in the least know what he can do.'[61]

The search for a bipartisan solution now persuaded Asquith to approach Carson. They met secretly, again in Edwin Montagu's house at Queen Anne's Gate, on 16 December, when their conversation, though fruitless, was sustained by the camaraderie of the bar. 'They are old professional friends,' the prime minister told the king, 'and he feels that he can speak with greater ease and freedom to Carson than to Mr B. Law whom he does not know at all intimately.'[62] So Asquith persevered and sent Carson 'a few rough suggestions' in his own hand which he did not show the cabinet and which were 'entirely unknown to the Nationalist leaders'; indeed the deluded Redmond was not told of his meeting Carson until nearly two months later.

The core of Asquith's suggestions was a variant of home rule within home rule: 'a "statutory Ulster" with undefined geographical boundaries would have powers of veto in an Irish Legislature'. Carson discussed the proposal with Bonar Law, as Asquith had assumed he would, and on 27 December dismissed it as 'useless' because its 'basis is the inclusion of Ulster in the Irish Parlmt.' On 8 January 1914, after another abortive meeting with Carson on the 2nd, Asquith tried again and contrasted his own preference for 'veiled exclusion' with Carson's preference for 'naked exclusion'; in Carson's words, 'that Ulster should remain as at present under the Imp. Parlmt. & that a Dublin Parlmt. should have no legislative powers within the excluded area. Ulster wd. therefore send no members to the Dublin Parlmt., but would continue as at present to send members to the Imp. Parlmt.'[63] Asquith, about to depart for a week in Antibes, let matters rest. But the exchanges marked the moment when the prime minister, *pace* his assurances to Redmond, *had* made the first offer of Ulster's exclusion and it had been refused.

After Asquith's return from Antibes, a crisis over Winston Churchill's insistence on increased naval expenditure in the estimates for 1914–15 absorbed the cabinet and ensured that Irish policy still stuttered through 'hot and cold fits' throughout January. The ministers 'doing their utmost "to down Winston"'[64] – McKenna, Runciman, Samuel, Simon, Hobhouse and Pease – cared little whether they forced him out of the cabinet over his naval estimates or over Ulster but they formed a nucleus of resistance to an early offer to Ulster's Unionists that reinforced Asquith's and Redmond's preference to postpone concessions on exclusion until the last moment.

The complexity of Lloyd George's position in the navy crisis further paralysed Irish policy. Loyalty and liking tied him to Churchill, but his role as chancellor of the exchequer as well as his identification with the radical, Little England wing of the party cast them as opponents on the naval estimates; he brooded that 'there comes a time when one cannot allow oneself to be influenced by personal considerations'. Hence his attack on Churchill in an interview in the *Daily Chronicle* appealing to the 'conscience' and 'noblest traditions' of liberalism and calling for a reduction in armaments expenditure.[65]

The interview prompted a procession of irate ministers to Asquith – Grey, Seely and Samuel – and won some sympathy for Churchill, then hunting wild boar in Les Landes with the Duke of Westminster.[66] When Asquith saw Churchill and Lloyd George together (on 20 January, after his return from Antibes), Lloyd George said to Churchill's face what he had been saying behind his back:

> There was a strong impression among important people, and those not merely Churchill's opponents on the question of naval armaments, that if he did not resign on that he would resign on the Irish question and that therefore it was useless to make concessions to him, and Lloyd George challenged him to say if this were so or not. Churchill greatly confused and taken aback. Had no such intention, but could not commit himself in advance etc. Asquith expressed his full confidence in him and so the matter ended.[67]

On 22 January Asquith finally came clean with the cabinet about his secret conclaves with Bonar Law and Carson. Lloyd George yet again urged 'an early announcement' of the government's exclusionist offer 'which he thought the Irish would accept'[68] and the cabinet decided on its tactics for the coming session: that Asquith should announce his terms to Carson as soon as parliament reassembled to make it 'impossible for Opposition to abet rebellion in face of them. Cabinet united in determination to meet force by force. Churchill had now finally agreed to stand in with the rest.'[69]

On 2 February Asquith met John Redmond for the first time since he had effectively surrendered the principle of Ulster's exclusion to Bonar Law and Carson. The prime minister unveiled a nightmarish scenario, according to Redmond's account of their meeting, founded on the king's conviction 'of the reality of the Civil War threat'; the king therefore wanted a general election because 'he must be assured that he had his people behind him' before assenting to the Home Rule Bill. Otherwise Asquith thought it 'quite conceivable' that the king would dismiss his ministers and ask Bonar Law to form a government in order to force a dissolution. In that event, even if the Liberals were returned to power, 'the sequence of the Parliament Bill would have been broken, the last two years would have been wasted, and the work would have to be begun all over again. This the government was determined to avert by every means in their power.' Asquith had therefore decided that 'for the safety of Home Rule' he must make an offer to the Ulster Unionists of such a kind that, if they rejected it, 'it would deprive them of all moral force and avert any action by the King'.[70]

'I had Birrell with me at the Leviathan interview,' Asquith confided to Venetia Stanley – his nickname for Redmond illustrating his sense of encumbrance at his Irish alliance. 'I developed the situation with such art as I could master, until the psychological moment arrived for discharging my bomb.

My visitor shivered visibly & and was a good deal perturbed, but I think the general effect was salutary.'[71] Redmond, Asquith told the cabinet next day, 'was prepared to concede anything the effect of which was temporary, but the permanent exclusion of Ulster he would not however consider for a moment'.[72] Therein lay the dilemma that Asquith's government could never escape: for Redmond, partition could be only temporary; for Carson, it must be permanent. After consulting his colleagues, Redmond responded that the government should make no proposals on exclusion that would be rejected by the opposition but should instead reiterate its readiness 'to consider favourably all proposals consistent with an Irish Parliament, an Irish executive, and the integrity of Ireland'.[73] On the same day, Birrell, who had said nothing at the meeting on 2 February, had what Asquith, preoccupied with cooking up a compromise, described as 'a rather gloomy second interview with our Leviathan. The "breadcrumb" stage has not yet been reached – if it ever will be. I must brace myself to fresh culinary efforts.'[74]

The amendment of the Home Rule Bill, envisaged by the government since February 1912, was now a matter of urgency. Ulster exclusion, the menu on which government and opposition had privately agreed in principle, must now be force-fed to Redmond and his party.

On 5 February the cabinet, still wrangling over the naval estimates, postponed consideration of Irish policy; but the cabinet of 9 February, the day the parliamentary session opened, was wholly devoted to Ireland. 'Cabinet just arisen,' wrote Birrell to Redmond:

> Great difference of opinion disclosed . . . But *eventually* it *seemed* to be the view of the majority that it was better he

[Asquith] should say nothing . . . What he will say I don't know – only what he *won't* . . . I feel sure the Cabinet won't be willing to wait *very long* before making up their minds as to what *ought* to be offered publicly to Ulster. When the Bill comes on, if not before, they will *insist* on a plain statement, whatever the consequences – not with much hope of *acceptance*, but to make good their intentions and clear their consciences.[75]

Say nothing: 'wait and see' was still the order of the day. In the debate on the King's Speech, although Asquith 'admitted the gravity of the situation, and for the first time admitted also that the obligation for taking the initiative rested with the Government',[76] he otherwise said nothing. Yet again it was Lloyd George who mapped the government's path to partition in a memorandum copied to Redmond. There was nothing new about Lloyd George's plan. He had simply dusted down the proposal he and Churchill had first urged on the cabinet two years before: 'that every county should be given the option of "contracting out" – really to apply to Ulster, but nominally for every part'. What was new, after two wasted years, was the imminence of an election given that 'this House of Commons cannot last beyond December 1915'. The cabinet had never formally rejected Lloyd George's original proposal in February 1912; it had merely shelved it. Now, on 25 February 1914, the cabinet endorsed his self-appointed role as their Irish negotiator and deputed him and Birrell

. . . to state to Redmond and Dillon the attitude of the Govt. which was this: it was necessary to make concessions to legitimate fears in England and Ireland, which were thought quite groundless but recognised as sincere; that permanent exclusion of any part of Ireland was undesirable and undesired by any part in England or Ireland; that temporary exclusion of the four north-eastern Counties either singly or *en bloc* would be considered by the Govt. if it would be accepted by the Opposition, *an acceptance which for political reasons they would probably not concur in* [author's italics].[77]

The italicised phrase is a testament to the tenacity with which Asquith's government clung to its cabinet conclusion of two years before: that the Home Rule Bill should apply to the whole of Ireland but that the government was free to amend it as it thought expedient. By February 1914 ministers deemed it expedient to urge on Redmond what Lloyd George had urged on them in February 1912. They did so not because they believed their proposal could resolve the impasse but because they hoped it might finesse the Orange card in the forthcoming election.

Asquith was absent from the critical meeting on 27 February when Lloyd George and Birrell received Redmond, Dillon and Joe Devlin (the nationalist MP for West Belfast) at the Treasury. 'The P.M.'s trouble is that he hates anything unpleasant or in the nature of a row,' observed Lloyd George. 'He hates an unpleasant interview. He said to me, "I think you had better have a preliminary conversation with the Irish." He thought it would be an unpleasant and troublesome task!'[78] And so it was. An unhappy Redmond sought an assurance that 'whatever scheme was put forward by the Government would be their last word' and that the Irish Party would not later be asked for further concessions. Lloyd George disingenuously agreed. That unpleasantness disposed of, Asquith participated in a second interview in 10 Downing Street on 2 March and reaffirmed the assurance. In a memorandum submitted later that day, Redmond stressed the 'enormous risks' of alienating his supporters, especially in Ulster. He then summed up the limits of his party's concessions: 'We are ready to give our acquiescence to the solution of the standing out for three years by option of the counties of Ulster as the price of peace.' But acquiescence, he emphasised, would not stretch to his party's voting for the concessions if the opposition forced a division; and the right to opt out was 'limited to three years, covering the period when a General Election must take place'.[79]

Asquith's reply in his own hand on 4 March elegantly demonstrated the harsh reality of Redmond's impotence of which Asquith had spoken to Bonar Law at Cherkley: the nationalists had now no choice but to accept whatever the government decided.

> I am obliged to you for your memorandum which I communicated to the Cabinet today. Without tying our hands (should the proposals referred to be accepted by the Opposition) in regard to matters of detail which might reasonably form the subject of further negotiations and accommodation, we agree that the conditions for which you stipulate are in the circumstances reasonable and proper.[80]

The prime minister had harpooned his Leviathan. The formula gave him the freedom to do what Redmond most feared: use the concession of temporary exclusion as an instrument for demanding its prolongation. Indeed the next demand was presented even before the proposals were formally communicated to the opposition; it was accelerated by an embarrassing press leak to the *Daily News* – which published the cabinet decision of 4 March next day – and by the king, whose immediate response to the decision was to urge a longer period of exclusion on his prime minister.[81]

On the morning of 6 March Birrell called on Redmond and told him that the price had been doubled, from three years to six. Leviathan thrashed helplessly on the harpoon: 'Mr Birrell, however, put it to us in such a way that we feel we cannot refuse to consent to an extension of five, if you still think that absolutely essential,'[82] he wrote to Asquith, who insisted on six because five might span the life of only one Westminster parliament; and six it was in the white paper published on 9 March 1914. 'This is a real triumph for your diplomacy,'[83] exulted Churchill in a congratulatory note to the real architect of the policy of partition, David Lloyd George.

When what F. E. Smith had described as the 'realities' were finally reached in March 1914, John Redmond did indeed have to agree to the government's change of course, just as Birrell had predicted in his audience with the king in July 1913. The reality was that if the Home Rule Bill were to be enacted, Ulster would be excluded. What was now alone at issue was how much of Ulster and for how long.

5
1914: Britain's Irish Crisis

Asquith spelled out the government's plan to exclude Ulster when he moved the second reading of the Home Rule Bill for the third and last time on 9 March 1914. The Unionists were unmoved. If this was the government's 'last word', responded Bonar Law, the position was 'a very grave one'; and he left it to Carson to speak for Ulster. Carson's dismissal of the six years wrung by Asquith from the reluctant Redmond was as memorable as it was contemptuous: 'We do not want a sentence of death with a stay of execution for six years.' Indeed the phrase has echoed so resoundingly down the years that it has deafened historians to the larger significance of Carson's welcome for the irrevocable partitionist shift in Irish policy marked 'by the acknowledgement of the principle of exclusion . . . The moment you admit the principle of exclusion the details of the principle may be a matter that may be worked out by negotiation.'[1]

Carson and Bonar Law accepted that the principle of partition had now been established. Two problems remained: first, whether the exclusion of Ulster would be temporary or permanent; second, what part of Ulster would be excluded.

But ministers were not yet ready to negotiate. As Winston Churchill listened in the House of Commons to Carson's withering rejection of the policy he and Lloyd George had put in place, he passed an emotional note to F. E. Smith, his bipartisan ally in 1910 and 1913: 'My dear, . . . if that is the answer to all that we have offered, there is nothing for it but a trial of strength in which believe me I shall enter with the deepest sorrow, but without doubt or fear. Alas, alas — W.'[2]

Such sentiments were not confined to Churchill. Carson's ringing rejection of their olive branch made ministers more militant when the cabinet met on 11 March to review a memorandum from Birrell on the growing threat posed by the Ulster Volunteer Force, which by then was reckoned to be at least 80,000 strong and to have at least 17,000 rifles, as against about 23,000 regular troops in Ireland of whom about 9,000 were quartered in Ulster. Police reports indicated plans 'to seize, by coups de main, police and military barracks, and depots of arms and ammunition', reported Asquith to the king; the cabinet had appointed a committee, consisting of Crewe, Birrell, Churchill, Jack Seely (the new secretary of state for war) and John Simon (the attorney general), 'to look into the matter in all its aspects'.[3]

But it was Lloyd George, although not a member, who again made the next move. 'Settled with the Irish and carried my plan through the Cabinet today,'[4] he wrote cryptically on 11 March to his brother, and he persuaded Churchill to deliver 'a speech that will ring down the corridors of history'. As a minister known to have favoured conciliation for Ulster, Churchill could now say that, 'having secured a compromise, the Ulstermen will either have to accept it or take the consequences'. Although Asquith was 'rather alarmed' – 'My game is more the olive branch,'[5] he remarked to Lloyd George – he did not dissent and Churchill's speech, at Bradford on 14 March, threw down the gauntlet. 'We are not going to have the realm of Great Britain sink to the condition of the

Republic of Mexico,' he declaimed. 'If all the loose, wanton and reckless chatter we have been forced to listen to these months is in the end to disclose a sinister revolutionary purpose, then I can only say to you, "Let us go forward and put these grave matters to the proof."'[6]

Churchill's speech had just the impact Lloyd George wanted. 'The fat is in the fire,' he exulted to his brother; the speech 'has enraged the Opposition but it has bucked up our supporters tremendously . . . I am glad that I was largely responsible for it.' Now, he hoped, Asquith would relinquish his olive branch: 'The P.M. is ready for anything.'[7] Churchill, who had designed his Bradford speech to restore his popularity with the Liberals after his fall from grace over the naval estimates, was duly received with rapturous cheers from the Liberal benches when he returned to the House of Commons.[8] The cabinet discussed 'the new situation' at an emergency meeting called by Asquith on 17 March. 'There was great harmony,' he told Venetia Stanley, 'and Winston preened himself and was stroked by all the others.'[9] Ministerial militancy sharpened because Crewe, the sub-committee's chairman and Asquith's watchdog, had fallen ill, leaving Churchill and Seely, ministers for the armed forces, who had served together in the South African war, to make the running.

Like Churchill, Seely was first elected as a Tory MP in 1900 but switched to the Liberals in 1904. Popular on both sides of the House, not least for the stories he told against himself, the new secretary of state for war was not renowned for his intelligence. He once recalled telling Balfour about a mountaineering accident that had left him concussed for months: 'Balfour, turning to me with his benevolent smile, said slowly, "My dear Jack, that explains it all!" Perhaps it does!'[10] Seely's and Churchill's swashbuckling temperaments, compounded by an engrained militarism and, perhaps, an insecurity about their common past as Tory renegades, encouraged them to behave more belligerently towards the Ulster Unionists than cabinet colleagues with less suspect Liberal credentials. But, temporarily at least, their belligerence struck a chord with cabinet colleagues, including the prime minister.

It was a nice irony that the crucial cabinet meeting authorising military plans to contain the threat of Unionist rebellion in Ulster took place on St Patrick's Day. The prime minister's cabinet letter to the king spelled out the wider dimensions of the sub-committee's conclusions. Any additional troops needed would be supplied by moving forces from Britain. Churchill had arranged that the forthcoming manoeuvres of the 1st Battle Squadron would take place at Lamlash, on the Isle of Arran in the Firth of Clyde, in close proximity to Belfast, and a cruiser would be stationed 'at or near Carrickfergus'. The Royal Irish Constabulary in Ulster, 'who are scattered in very small detachments over the countryside, should be placed under the authority of a single Commanding Officer at Belfast'.[11] The cabinet's plans were communicated to Sir Arthur Paget, the general officer commanding in Ireland, at a war office conference which began next day at noon.

The plans bear an uncanny and scarcely coincidental resemblance to proposals that Haldane had urged on the prime minister and the cabinet in September 1913: 'sending at once' for Paget and 'discussing with him the necessary measures' and appointing the director of military planning at the war office, General Nevil Macready (who had 'exhibited useful qualities of judgement and tact' in his handling of the Welsh miners' strike of 1912) as 'a special Staff Officer'[12] in Belfast. Seely had first sent Macready to Belfast and Dublin in November 1913 to report on police inadequacies and on 'the military administration of the command' but he was told on his return to London, on 24 November, that, for the moment at least, 'the Government intended to do nothing'. In March 1914 Asquith again sent Macready to Ulster 'on a not very clearly defined mission', although, working directly to the war office rather than under Paget, he was 'empowered to take command of the troops in Ulster in certain eventualities'.[13]

There were two reasons why the government's military plans swiftly collapsed in disarray: first, the political intrigues of the war office's director of military operations and diehard Irish Unionist, Major-General Henry Wilson; and, second, the Curragh mutiny, triggered by the ineptitude of General Paget in communicating his orders to his officers in Ireland.

Wilson had spelled out his views on the possible use of troops against Ulster Unionists to the chief of the Imperial General Staff, Field-Marshal Sir John French, in November 1913. 'I told him that I could not fire on the North at the dictates of Redmond & this is what the whole thing means. England qua England is opposed to Home Rule, & England must agree to it before it is carried out.'[14] French had told Wilson the substance of that morning's discussion with Paget on the afternoon of 18 March and Wilson immediately leaked the plans to Carson at dinner that night.[15] This was just the beginning of Wilson's extraordinary machinations with the opposition leaders: between 21 and 31 March he saw Bonar Law ten times in ten days – six times at Bonar Law's home, three times at his own home and once at a lunch when Carson was also present.[16]

The next day, Thursday, 19 March, saw high drama in the House of Commons, at the war office, at the admiralty and among the now forewarned Ulster Unionists; Wilson's warning had been reinforced that morning by Lady Londonderry,

who was received by Carson in bed when she called with a letter from a friend in Dublin advising her that 'the Government
are going to try and frighten Ulster this week'.[17] Carson
decided that his Commons appearance that afternoon would
be his last until after the Ulster question was settled. His place,
he told a tense and expectant House, was in Belfast, and,
having taunted ministers with what he knew of their plans,[18]
rushed from the Palace of Westminster to catch the 6 o'clock
boat train.

Paget also took a boat train that night, to Holyhead, and
arrived in Dublin at 7.30 a.m. the next morning, Friday, 20
March. He might have been tired when he addressed his
senior officers, six generals and one colonel, in his small office
at Parkgate adjoining the Phoenix Park, the headquarters of
the Irish command. He was certainly emotional. He began by
stating that 'what he had to say might appear theatrical. But
the situation was very serious . . . The whole place would be
in a blaze, he thought, to-morrow . . . "Active operations were
about to commence against Ulster."' But Paget's histrionics
were insignificant in comparison with a concession he claimed
to have extracted from Seely:

First: Officers actually domiciled in Ulster would be
exempted from taking part in any operation that might
take place. They would be permitted to 'disappear' (that
being the exact phrase used by the War Office), and when
all was over would be allowed to resume their places
without their career or position being affected.

Secondly: Officers who stated that they would be
unwilling to serve might tender their resignations, but
these could not be accepted. And officers doing so would
be forthwith dismissed from the Service.

He concluded by telling General Hubert Gough, the officer commanding the 3rd Cavalry Brigade at the Curragh, that a squadron of cavalry was to be ready 'to march northwards next morning if required'. Gough responded by saying that 'he could not claim exemption as a resident of Ulster, but that, on account of birth and upbringing, and many friendships, he did not see how he could bear arms against the Ulster loyalists'.[19] Gough returned to the Curragh, spoke to his officers, and reported back to Paget that afternoon that 60 of the 70 officers on duty in his brigade 'prefer to be dismissed' rather than carry out a duty that 'involves the *initiation* of active military operations against Ulster' and that a further five officers 'are domiciled in Ulster and claim protection as such'.[20]

The significance of the events at the Curragh on Friday, 20 March 1914, has been obscured by the pedantic preference for the term 'Curragh incident' to describe what contemporaries called the 'Curragh mutiny', a preference originating in the understandable reluctance of both government and opposition to acknowledge the enormity of the crisis.

Ministers had an obvious incentive to minimise the challenge to their governmental authority both during and after the crisis. The outbreak of war in Europe so soon afterwards was another retrospective, but even more powerful, motivation to shy away from any suggestion of mutiny. The opposition's reaction was more complex. In the short term, they had a vested interest in playing up the crisis in order to maximise the embarrassment to the government. But, once their objective of preventing the government using the army to sustain its Ulster policy had been accomplished, it was not in the Unionist interest to highlight how their intrigues with Henry Wilson and other elements in the military establishment and at court had endangered the proper relationship between government and army. Within a matter of months, moreover, the Great War demanded that government, opposition and military establishment close ranks and make light of the Curragh crisis.

Yet neither historiographical understanding nor the bizarre element of choice in the orders issued by Paget can blur the political significance of the episode: an elite corps of British army officers had revolted against the Irish policy of the democratically elected government. The prevailing orthodoxy among historians, epitomised by Ian Beckett, is that 'no direct orders of any kind were disobeyed by any officer or man'; indeed 'all the precautionary movements . . . were fully complied with'; and that 'Paget's error in appearing to offer a choice to his subordinates as to whether to obey orders or not on the morning of 20 March is all the more culpable.'[21] Keith Jeffery, Wilson's latest and best biographer, has put it more succinctly. Although 'no orders had been disobeyed, the declaration wrung from Seely and the others in practice limited the government's legitimate freedom of action. It was a kind of pre-emptive mutiny.'[22] At 7 o' clock on the night of Friday, 20 March, two hours after the House of Commons had adjourned for the weekend, the first official intimation of the Curragh mutiny reached the war office in the shape of a curt telegram from Paget.

It was symptomatic of the spirit of sedition that the news was first conveyed not to the government but to the opposition. Henry Wilson, called home from the war office to be briefed by General Johnnie Gough, who had a telegram from his brother, Hubert,[23] at the Curragh;[24] Bonar Law, independently informed by an anonymous telegram from the Curragh camp delivered to him in the House of Commons at 5.46 p.m., which he showed to his dinner companions[25] (who included Milner, Lady Londonderry, and F. E. Smith); Carson and Craig (to whom the news was rushed at the UVF head-quarters at Craigavon 'from the Curragh by motor-cyclists'[26]) – all knew what had happened at the Curragh before the prime minister or his cabinet colleagues. While Unionist dining rooms were buzzing with excitement, the prime minister had been out dining unawares; not until midnight was he called back to Downing Street where he found Churchill, Seely and French waiting with what even the ever phlegmatic Asquith described as 'some pretty alarming news'.[27]

The next morning, Saturday, 21 March, *The Times* broke the Curragh story in its later editions and the king, outraged that he had been told nothing of the crisis, carpeted Seely at the palace.[28] Asquith's unwonted militancy collapsed. He told Churchill that, 'in view of the prevalent excitement in this country . . . the movement of the ships should be delayed'. Churchill complied and at 5.30 p.m. on Saturday the battle squadron, then abreast of the Scilly Isles en route to Lamlash, was diverted to Southampton. On Sunday afternoon the prime minister soothed the king, saying that his government had no larger intention 'beyond the movement of troops into Ulster for the protection of ammunition, stores, and outlying barracks' and promised him 'that no movements, naval or military, should take place without his being informed'.[29]

Asquith, despite retaining his customary sang-froid – indeed his letters to Venetia Stanley suggest that he was unsurprised by the army revolt – had no illusions about the gravity of the crisis. There was 'no doubt' that if the government 'were to order a march upon Ulster . . . about half the officers in the Army – the Navy is more uncertain – would strike. The immediate difficulty in the Curragh can, I think, be arranged but that is the permanent situation, & it is not a pleasant one.'[30] Attention was deflected from this 'permanent situation' by the government's ham-fisted handling of 'the immediate difficulty' created by Gough's extracting from Seely a written assurance that, 'in the event of the present Home Rule Bill becoming law', the army would not 'be called upon to enforce it upon Ulster under the expression maintaining law and order'.[31] The consequences proved chaotic for ministers, 'hurriedly summoned' to what a Liberal backbencher later derided as 'an extraordinary jumble'[32] of a cabinet. Yet again Edward Grey was standard-bearer for the Liberal imperialists, arguing that 'we cannot and ought not to use force to bring the Home Rule Bill into operation till the opinion of the country has been taken on the situation'.[33] Churchill, backed by Lloyd George, who was still 'all for fighting', remained the most resolute: as First Lord of the Admiralty, he bragged belligerently that 'whatever might be the indiscipline in the Army, the Navy was prepared for anything'.[34]

Seely's 'peccant paragraphs', as they were later christened by Balfour, made nonsense of the cabinet's alleged determination to resist making 'terms with mutinous officers'. They stated that, although the government retained the right to use the crown forces in Ireland 'to maintain law and order and to support the civil power in the ordinary execution of its duty . . . they have no intention whatever of taking advantage of this right to crush political opposition to the policy or principles of the Home Rule Bill'. At first sight, this humiliating collapse of the government's efforts to resolve what Asquith had described as 'the immediate difficulty' seemed to have compounded its embarrassment. That was certainly the sense conveyed in the House of Commons and in the Tory press in the weeks that followed.

In the longer term, Seely's bungling disguised the graver reality of the 'permanent situation': that senior army officers had effectively declared that they would not obey orders to implement the government's Irish legislation. Instead, the spotlight switched to what divided one arm of government, the war office, from the cabinet as a whole. Seely's playing the bungling cavalier provided the government with a ready-made scapegoat, although Asquith initially declined his offer of resignation at cabinet on 25 March. But French and Ewart (the adjutant general) were determined to resign, on the point of honour that 'their initials to Seely's document were a pledge to the soldiers at the Curragh that they would not be asked to initiate proceedings in Ulster'.[35] 'This is splendid,' Henry Wilson, who had assiduously inflamed French's sense of honour, exulted in his diary. 'Rang up B.L. [Bonar Law] & told him & added that it was now his business to drive the wedge deep into the Cabinet by causing the downfall of Seely, Morley & Haldane. A good day's work.'[36] Seely duly followed suit as Asquith, who had already combined the office of secretary of state for war with his premiership, had anticipated.

Once Asquith received confirmation of the resignations he broached his scheme to an approving king. His Commons announcement that he would assume Seely's ministerial responsibilities drew enthusiastic cheers from the Liberals and taunts of 'Cromwell' from the Unionists. Asquith's move dampened outrage among the government's supporters much as his magisterial calm at the war office steadied the army. But the parliamentary genius of the stratagem was that it enabled him immediately to vacate his seat in the Commons under the law that, until 1918, required MPs to seek re-election on accepting cabinet office. Asquith, piously pleading the advice of his attorney general, John Simon, 'cleared out at once'[37] and thereby denied the opposition the opportunity again to question either prime minister or secretary of state for war for the next two tense weeks. When Asquith's unopposed re-election as the member for East Fife enabled him to resume his seat on 14 April, the parliamentary storm had abated and the Unionists had vented much of their spleen and, on 29 April, he told the Commons that he would answer no more questions on the Curragh episode.

Meanwhile the Ulster Unionists had rubbed salt in the wounds of a government bereft of the authority to use its own armed forces to implement its legislative will. Fred Crawford, acting for the Ulster Unionist Council, had bought some 25,000 rifles and 3 million rounds of ammunition in Germany and shipped them in the vessels *Fanny* and *Clydevalley*. On the night of 24–25 April 1914 they were landed at Larne, Donaghdee and Bangor and distributed throughout northeast Ulster. The logistics were sophisticated – the UVF threw a cordon of checkpoints around Larne, granting access only to those on UVF business, and huge convoys of cars queued to unload the arms and ammunition – but the wider implication of such a spectacular coup was political: the Larne gun-running made it almost impossible for the Unionist leaders to agree to any settlement short of the permanent exclusion of at least the six north-eastern counties of Ulster.

Now the government's Irish policy was in tatters. It was bad enough that what Asquith had described as his 'immediate difficulty' had ended in humiliation. Much worse, however, was the reality of his 'permanent situation': that a Liberal prime minister could not rely on the armed forces to implement any Irish legislation that the Ulster Unionists opposed. There was no point, in effect, in the government's proceeding even with the diluted and partitionist Home Rule Bill already forced down the throat of a reluctant John Redmond. Nationalist Ireland, waiting for the Liberals to deliver home rule ever since Gladstone's conversion in 1885, would have to wait again.

'No single officer or man in Ireland, or elsewhere, disobeyed a single order,' wrote Seely about the events of March 1914. 'Harm had been done. But disaster had been averted.'[38] But at what political cost was the fig-leaf of military discipline held in place? That the government abandon its Irish policy and issue no orders which the army, and the king, deemed *politically* unacceptable. 'Asquith executed the heroic gesture of becoming war minister himself,' wrote R. C. K. Ensor in his volume of the *Oxford History of England* published more than fifty years ago. 'His followers supposed that this betokened a drastic policy, such as only a prime minister could put through; in fact, it heralded a policy of surrender, such as only a prime minister could put over.'[39] The surrender was unconditional: when the prime minister took over at the war office and discovered Henry Wilson's role in plotting with the Unionists, he did nothing.

Ensor's assessment is borne out by the contemporary response of Charles Hobhouse, an increasingly isolated radical voice in the cabinet, who tried to induce his colleagues

> . . . to consider what actual steps should be taken if the Ulster Provisional Govt. was actually set up. But no one felt inclined to move until the trouble actually arrived. History if it concerns itself with us at all will write us down as either the most patient, wise, foreseeing Govt. this or any country ever had, or else as the [?most] inept, blind, and cowardly crew that ever disgraced Downing Street. No middle judgment will be possible.[40]

Although historians, with the innate caution of their breed, customarily cling to middle judgements, many have followed Hobhouse and Milner's biographer, A. M. Gollin, in identifying 'the problem of Ireland . . . as one of the major failures of British statesmanship. The Irish crisis of 1912–14 was more terrible than any other in recent English history, for, during those years, the system of parliamentary democracy, so long accepted as the traditional method of politics in England, was shaken to its foundations.'[41]

Asquith's problem, Patricia Jalland has argued, was that his 'well-ordered legal mind . . . did not instinctively relate to the play of passion in others' and 'had difficulty in taking Irish Nationalism and Ulster Unionism entirely seriously, since they involved such a large element of emotional commitment. His temperament and legal training convinced him that the Irish Problem could be solved by the usual constitutional procedures of British parliamentary politics.'[42] Roy Jenkins has elaborated on how Asquith's unswerving Liberal commitment to those constitutional procedures was what inhibited him from ordering the arrest of the openly seditious Unionist leaders:

> To lock up the leaders of the opposition would have been a bold stroke for any government. For Asquith it would have been a fatal one. It would have undermined the whole position he was trying to maintain. The House of Commons was the one battleground on which the Liberals always won. It was therefore in their interests to pretend that it was the only one which counted . . . Asquith's stand was on the inviolability of the parliamentary system. To maintain this stand he had to pretend that the system was working normally, even if it was

not – and this meant that, whatever they did, he could not lock up his principal opponents.[43]

The leaders of the Irish Parliamentary Party were of like mind and offered 'no alternative but "to proceed calmly with the Bill" . . . The fatal weakness of Redmond's position was that the Liberals had everything to lose if they provoked violent resistance';[44] hence their pusillanimous reaction to the Larne gun-running when the cabinet was informed that 'the Irish party were very strongly against "prosecutions"'.[45]

The Curragh conspiracy exploded Asquith's and Redmond's pretence of normality. Deprived of the veto of the House of Lords to resist home rule, the king and the army empowered the Unionists with an alternative, albeit unconstitutional, veto over the government's Irish policy.

The most compelling acknowledgement of the failure of British parliamentary democracy in Ireland is what Robert Blake, the doyen of historians of the Conservative Party, wrote in his biography of Bonar Law:

The truth is that Parliamentary democracy depends on certain conditions, which, because they have usually prevailed in England over the last two hundred and fifty years, tend to be taken by Englishmen for granted. In the last resort it depends upon a minority accepting majority decisions, and this acceptance in its turn depends upon the majority not taking decisions which the minority regards as genuinely intolerable. In England, the remarkable homogeneity of the population, the absence of violent disputes, the general agreement over the fundamentals of society, have made such conditions prevail. Minorities accept majority decisions, because they know

that these decisions will not be insufferable and because
they know that the majority of today will become the
minority of tomorrow. As a result we have the swing
of the electoral pendulum, the political neutrality of the
Army and the Civil Service, the whole tradition of peaceful change which is England's greatest contribution to the
science of government.

But in Ireland these conditions did not apply. Ireland
was – and is – a land of bitter, irreconcilable, racial and
religious conflicts. The Protestant minority could never
hope by any swing of pendulum to become the majority.
The two nations in Ireland were separated by the whole
of their past history. They were divided by rivers of blood
and bitterness. It was absurd to expect the conventions
which prevailed in placid England would be accepted by
the Ulster Protestants with all this fear, suspicion and
hatred in their hearts. For of all political disputes, nationalist disputes are the most bitter and recalcitrant. They
are very seldom settled by peaceful means within the
framework of a liberal constitution. On the contrary,
they are usually resolved, as Bismarck observed, not by
Parliamentary majorities but by blood and iron.[46]

If one substitutes 'Catholic minority' for 'Protestant minority', Blake's argument offers a prescient analysis of why the
polity of Northern Ireland collapsed some fifteen years after
he wrote. Some may be tempted to dismiss the passage as
stereotypical of that Anglo-Saxon attitude so well captured
in Perry Curtis's classic analysis of anti-Irish prejudice in
Victorian Britain[47] which finds comfort in contrasting English
tolerance and placidity with Irish bitterness and bloodshed.
But that would miss the point for it was English identification

with just such Ulster Protestant fears that provided the ideological dynamic for partition.

'We must all now endeavour to get the new order of things arranged in a way that will be fair to the Protestants in Ireland,' urged Lord Roberts, the feisty commander-in-chief in the South African war, in a letter to Balfour that described how his grandfather – 'a Protestant clergyman – helped to keep peace in the County of Waterford during the rebellion of 1798 and [his] father served as a subaltern in the Waterford Militia at the same time'.[48] 'I have always wished the Catholics in Ireland to govern themselves,' wrote Lord Esher to Margot Asquith in the aftermath of the Curragh mutiny. 'We have shown ourselves unfit to govern a community of Catholics; this, over centuries. But we are not half as unfit to govern Catholics as they are to govern the Protestant community. That is the whole ethical and political aspect of the situation.'[49] Although such flagrantly anti-Catholic sentiments were rarely committed to paper, they coloured the mentality of government and opposition. Esher, as the king's liaison with ministers, moreover, would scarcely have written in such terms to the prime minister's wife were he not satisfied that she was of like mind. The home-rule crisis of 1912–14, as Daniel Jackson has observed, 'was the last time that religion and politics seriously intersected in British politics. Furthermore, Home Rule provided an issue which cut across the sectarian divisions *within* Protestantism.'[50]

Robert Blake's Bismarckian dictum that nationalist disputes are more usually resolved by blood and iron than by parliamentary majorities was not lost on those Irish nationalists who were fast losing their faith in parliamentary democracy as a result of the Curragh conspiracy and the Larne gun-running. The numbers of Irish Volunteers increased dramatically: from under 2,000 at the end of 1913 to 160,000 by July 1914. This so alarmed John Redmond that he issued a public statement on 9 June 'explaining that he must control the Volunteers or take steps which would, in effect, either split the movement in two or break it up altogether';[51] although a split was temporarily averted when the Volunteer leaders grudgingly yielded before Redmond's national prestige, a militant minority was already set on a revolutionary course.

Meanwhile the cabinet fiddled while Ireland armed. The Curragh crisis having derailed his government's quest for a resolute Irish policy, Asquith reopened lines of communication to Bonar Law and Carson, whom he met secretly on 5 May, when 'a good part of the morning was furtively spent in the silken tents'[52] – once more pitched in Edwin Montagu's opulent house at Queen Anne's Gate. Again there was no agreement about the terms of Ulster's exclusion, but it was agreed that some such terms would be incorporated in a separate amending bill that would be immediately introduced so that it could receive the royal assent at the same time as the Home Rule Bill. Bonar Law noted with satisfaction that Asquith had 'stated more than once in a most emphatic way that he would be no party to the coercion of Ulster'.[53]

Asquith's amending bill, which feebly repeated the earlier offer of exclusion for six years by county option so scathingly rejected by Carson, was attacked not only by the king but by senior cabinet colleagues. The king denounced it as 'useless' since its terms had already been 'repudiated by Ulster'.[54] Edward Grey objected '"very dourly" . . . in favour of excluding Ulster (to be defined by Commission) "until such time as Parliament may hereafter determine"'. Lloyd George agreed and told the king that the Lords should 'put into' the amending bill 'complete exclusion of Ulster and a redefining of area . . . "limited exclusion is already gone; all the fight would be over area"'.[55] Augustine Birrell drew up an even more damning indictment following one of his rare visits to Ulster: 'However useful the proposals of our Amending Bill may be (1) as a means of keeping the door open, and (2) as an answer to the cry that we are "coercing" Ulster, they present no solution to the difficulties of the situation.'[56]

Despite the foreign secretary and the Irish chief secretary, as well as Churchill and Lloyd George, all despairing of the futility of his policy, Asquith plodded on. Crewe's speech, when he introduced the amending bill in the House of Lords on 23 June, appalled the Irish Party. But when Dillon denounced his 'inviting root and branch amendments and his abject thanks to Carson for keeping order as monstrous', he got cold comfort from John Morley, who 'actually said "Carson has won and the sooner the public knew it the better"'.[57] The Lords' response to the amending bill showed that Carson indeed held the whip hand: they deleted the six-year time limit and the county-option provision in favour of a wrecking amendment (proposed by Lord Lansdowne in the interests of the Southern Unionists) providing for the permanent exclusion of all Ulster.

'For the first time Asquith was brought up against a complete *impasse*',[58] and even his self-admitted 'ingrained and much-tried optimism'[59] began to crumble. The parliamentary deadlock forced him back into the secrecy of Queen Anne's Gate where he saw Carson on 7 July. Again, the meeting came to nothing, although Asquith presciently observed that Carson thought that his 'more extreme followers' would prefer the exclusion of six counties rather than the whole of Ulster. 'They are apparently afraid that a big entire Ulster would gravitate towards a United Ireland.'[60]

Persuaded of the inevitability of partition, Asquith now sought consensus on the area of an excluded Ulster. His intermediary, Lord Murray of Elibank, the former Liberal chief whip, first saw Redmond on 30 June. By 2 July, after acting as go-between with Carson and Bonar Law, Elibank was 'convinced that the only point which at present could be truthfully regarded as an absolute deadlock was the question of the inclusion or exclusion of Tyrone'.[61] Asquith agreed and on 15 July asked Elibank

> . . . to find out whether C. [Carson] & his friends would *definitely* treat, if I made them an offer to exclude Antrim, Derry, Down (except the Catholic parts of the South), Armagh (except South), North Fermanagh, with the possibility of a split Tyrone: provision to be made on both sides for the migration at State expense of Protestants & Catholics into & out of the excluded area . . . Of course I said I could not *guarantee* that Redmond wd. assent, but if C. falls in, I shall have to put on the screw to R.[62]

That Asquith went so far as to cost the expense of migration in and out of the excluded area – his estimate was £11 million – was a measure of the attention he was now giving to the details of a partitionist settlement. But he had said nothing of his secret designs to Redmond when he met him on 13 July. Indeed the deluded Redmond recorded that Asquith 'approached all these questions with an open mind . . . and gave the most specific assurances that no large concessions would be agreed to without the fullest discussion with us'.[63]

Four days later Asquith again went behind Redmond's back to see Bonar Law, saying that 'it would be a crime if civil war resulted from so small a difference' over Tyrone, and even offering to 'give up the time limit clause altogether'.[64] So blatant a betrayal of Redmond was a measure of Asquith's desperation, for, by 15 July, when his amendment bill as castrated by the Lords received its first reading in the Commons, the paralysis of the parliamentary system was complete. The government could not proceed with an unamended home-rule bill when it had publicly conceded the principle of excluding at least part of Ulster, albeit only temporarily. Yet neither could it proceed with an ultra-Unionist amendment bill that permanently excluded all of Ulster.

Although Asquith had been irritated by the king's continual and 'very one-sided' importunities about Ulster and had stalled in response to royal overtures throughout May and June for an all-party conference on Ireland,[65] he no longer had room for manoeuvre at what he melodramatically and uncharacteristically described as 'this most critical time of my life'.[66] He finally conceded when he saw the king, on 17 July, and agreed that the 'silken tent' should next be pitched in Buckingham Palace. Asquith gave way because he calculated that 'the pressure to settle is bound to become more & more severe' if he failed to get any amending bill through parliament; the king might then refuse his assent to the Home Rule Bill unless 'an immediate dissolution follows'; if his ministers refused to agree, 'he will politely dismiss us & send for Ministers who will agree'. Indeed the king had broadly hinted as much to Lord Crewe on 6 June when he had expostulated against his ministers expecting him 'to put his name to a Bill which they themselves believed would result in civil war'.[67] A general election under such circumstances was what the Tories had always wanted and what Asquith had always avoided for, as he told Venetia Stanley, it 'would be one of the worst things that c[oul]d happen to the country, or (I suspect) to the Liberal party'[68] – or, what he did not say but what he assuredly knew, to Asquith himself.

The conference held at Buckingham Palace between 21 and 24 July 1914 was 'designed to serve a time-honoured purpose of conferences and committees – that of delaying the day of decision', concluded Nicholas Mansergh. 'So much it achieved – and no more.'[69] Although Asquith admitted that the conference would be 'unable at the moment to attain a definitive settlement', he argued that 'it will certainly postpone and may avert dangerous and possibly irreparable action'.[70] Asquith and Lloyd George represented the government; Bonar Law and Lansdowne the opposition; the Irish nationalists and Unionists, more predictably, were represented by John Redmond and John Dillon, and by Edward Carson and James Craig. The inclusion of Lloyd George rather than Birrell publicly confirmed that he was now the minister who shaped Irish policy. The composition of the Tory delegation was also significant; the king had sought Balfour's inclusion, but Asquith successfully objected on the grounds that Balfour was 'in this matter a real wrecker'[71] – seven years later Lloyd George similarly ensured Balfour's exclusion from the British delegation that negotiated the Anglo-Irish Treaty of December 1921 for much the same reason.

The prime minister's opening statement identified 'the two serious outstanding points': first, the area of Ulster to be excluded from the terms of operation of the Home Rule Bill; second, the time limit for exclusion, which had already been the subject of such exhaustive and futile negotiation since the beginning of 1914. Despite Unionist objections, it was agreed to discuss area first; and, when it proved impossible to reach agreement on area, the conference broke up without even discussing the question of the time limit.

The collapse of the conference drove even the phlegmatic Asquith to the brink of despair after a sterile day discussing

> that most damnable creation of the perverted ingenuity of man – the County of Tyrone . . . The extraordinary feature of the discussion was the complete agreement (in principle) of Redmond & Carson. Each said, 'I must have the whole of Tyrone, or die; but I quite understand why you say the same.' The Speaker [of the House of Commons who chaired the conference] who incarnates bluff unimaginative English sense, of course cut in: 'When each of two people say they must have the whole, why not cut it in half?' They wd. neither of them look at such a suggestion . . . Nothing could have been more amicable in tone, or more desperately fruitless in result . . . I have rarely felt more hopeless in any practical affair: an impasse, with unspeakable consequences, upon a matter which to English eyes seems inconceivably small, & to Irish eyes immeasurably big. Isn't it a real tragedy?[72]

Yet, although the conference was utterly unproductive, it was a landmark on the path to the partition of Ireland. It marked the moment when the leaders of the two major parties in Britain and in Ireland collectively acknowledged that partition, in whatever shape or for whatever time, was unavoidable. Thus even John Redmond recorded, at the end of the first day's deliberations, that 'it was generally understood that there was no possibility, with any advantage, of discussing any settlement except on the lines of exclusion of some sort'.[73]

Two things obscured a clear view of this partitionist landmark. First, the secrecy surrounding the conference proceedings, which was so strict that there was no official record of

the proceedings; second, the prior agreement that no statement should be published in the event of a breakdown without the approval of all parties. Redmond, conscious of the
concessions on exclusion that Asquith had already wrung
from him and vulnerable to nationalist criticism on that
account, had insisted on both preconditions when the conference began.

Two days after the conference collapsed, the graphic contrast between the British government's response to Unionists
and nationalists running guns into Ireland further undermined
Redmond's position as the leader of Irish constitutional
nationalism. Darrell Figgis and Erskine Childers had bought
1,500 rifles and ammunition for the Irish Volunteers in Ham-
burg in May 1914. In a publicity counter-coup to the Larne
gun-running, Childers landed the bulk of the cargo in broad
daylight on 26 July in Howth, a small fishing port some
twelve miles north of Dublin, and a thousand rifle-bearing
Irish Volunteers marched into the city centre. The quantity
was minuscule when compared with what the UVF had
landed and distributed throughout north-east Ulster without
hindrance in April, but what happened in Dublin on 26 July
was very different.

Troops of the King's Own Scottish Borderers, returning to
barracks having failed to disarm a column of Irish Volunteers
en route, opened fire on a jeering crowd in Bachelor's Walk:
they killed four and wounded 30. The headlines in the next
day's *Daily Chronicle* on the bloodshed in Bachelor's Walk
included TERRIBLE SCENES IN THE STREETS, BAYONET
CHARGE AND BULLETS, WOMEN AND CHILDREN VICTIMS.
To outraged Irish nationalists the upshot has been pithily
described by Michael Laffan: 'The army, apparently so
reluctant to move against organised Ulster gun-runners, was

prepared to kill hostile but unarmed Dublin civilians.'[74] Patrick Pearse seized the political opportunity: 'The army is an object of odium and derision and the Volunteers are the heroes of the hour. The whole movement, the whole country, has been re-baptised by blood shed for Ireland.'[75]

Asquith's despair deepened: 'The malignity of fortune could hardly have devised a more inopportune coup . . . the whole thing in any case must react most unfavourably on the chances of peace & settlement . . . Irish history is a long chapter of untoward and impish accidents.'[76] But fortune had by then in store that ghastlier malignity triggered by the assassination at Sarajevo, which was about to sweep the Irish crisis into an oblivion that endured for five years.

6

'Cutting off One's Head to Get Rid of a Headache'

By August 1914 the Irish crisis had brought Britain to the brink of civil war. 'The British Constitution and the conventions upon which it depends', in Robert Blake's words, 'were strained to the uttermost limit; and, paradoxically, it was the outbreak of the First World War which, although it imperilled Britain's very existence, probably alone saved Britain's institutions from disaster.'[1] That paradox explains the otherwise inexplicable sense of elation that suffused the government at the coming of war. Although 'it is almost certain that Asquith never became Venetia [Stanley's] lover in a physical sense',[2] his love for and dependence on her was then at its most intense and his letters to her most revealing of his state of mind. 'The most dangerous situation of the last 40 years', he mused on 26 July, 'may have incidentally the good effect of throwing into the background the lurid pictures of "civil war" in Ulster.'[3] And, on 28 July: 'What you say à propos of the War cutting off one's head to get rid of a headache is very good. Winston on the other hand is all for this way of escape from Irish troubles, and when things looked rather better last night, he exclaimed moodily that it looked after all as if we were in for a "bloody peace"!'[4]

Eight months later, on St Patrick's Day 1915, he wrote of 'an early call from John Redmond who brought me some bunches of shamrocks . . . I spoke to him of Birrell's possible retirement . . . Redmond is aghast at the thought, and says that B. ought to be kept on at any cost – even if he never goes near the [Irish] Office, wh. is being admirably run by [Sir Matthew] Nathan.' But Asquith insisted on discussing alternatives to Birrell 'if only to indicate which in [Redmond's] opinion was the worst . . . He has a considerable respect, tho' not much liking for [Herbert] Samuel [president of the Local Government Board], but shudders at the gibes which [Tim] Healy & others would pour forth at the spectacle of Dublin Castle ruled by a brace of Jews.' Samuel and Nathan, the under-secretary at the Irish office, were both Jewish. He also recounted how Redmond had 'received a present of a record Irish Wolfhound, no less than 9½ hands high, for the new Irish corps . . . almost too big to give to a battalion or regiment but one never heard of a whole Division having a Mascot. I advised him to hand the beast over to the General & leave him to parcel it out at his discretion.'[5] It was a far cry from wrestling with maps of Tyrone and Fermanagh but the prime ministerial musings were still shot through with relief at his escape from the Irish imbroglio on the first anniversary of 'that dismal Curragh business . . . now it is all dead and securely buried as Queen Anne'; a week earlier he had described his career as 'almost a classical example of *Luck* . . .': 'above all (at a most critical and fateful moment . . .) in the sudden outburst of the Great War'.[6]

Such musings against the backdrop of the slaughter on the western front might seem callous, even obscene, but Asquith could not foresee the horrors of a prolonged war in which his own son and the sons of many cabinet colleagues would feature in the monstrous casualty lists. In August 1914, his twin perspectives, as prime minister and as leader of the Liberal Party, were quite different. As prime minister, he had averted the real danger of civil war and, as the editors of his letters have observed, 'contemporaries regarded it as his greatest achievement that he led a united country into the war'.[7] As Liberal leader, he had held his party together throughout all the Irish vicissitudes of 1910–14, something Gladstone had so signally failed to do in 1886. Asquith had succeeded, moreover, not only in retaining the office of prime minister for himself but in keeping his party in power. He had thwarted the Conservative Party's demands for a general election on the Irish issue, a general election that by-election results, the best guide to the popular mood at a time when opinion polling was unknown, suggested the Liberals would lose.

Ireland had been the touchstone of British party politics, the most important single issue distinguishing Liberals from Conservatives, ever since Gladstone had embraced home rule, and this was never more true than in 1914. War changed all that: henceforth the parties, united in pursuit of the supreme national interest of victory over Germany, shunned what divided them and embraced what united them. Bipartisanship was no longer a matter of choice but of necessity. This powerful impetus towards consensus made imperative the immediate resolution of party-political differences on Ireland, which had previously seemed intractable. Asquith's earlier attempts in 1914 to lead Bonar Law and Carson down the bipartisan path, first charted by Lloyd George and Churchill in 1910, had failed because, with an election in prospect, the Tories found confrontation more seductive than compromise; they discarded the Orange card only when war was inevitable and an election unthinkable.

Compromise came quickly. On 30 July, Asquith was drafting his speech on the amending bill incorporating his government's terms for the exclusion of Ulster,

. . . in the Cabinet room with a map of Ulster, & a lot of statistics about populations & religions . . . when a telephone message came (from of all people in the world) Bonar Law, to ask me to come and see him & Carson at his Kensington abode. He had sent his motor which I boarded . . .

I found the two gentlemen there, & B Law proceeded to propose in the interest of the international situation, that we should postpone for the time being the 2nd reading of the Amending Bill. He thought that to advertise our domestic dissensions at this moment wd. weaken our influence in the world for peace &c. Carson said that at first he had thought it impossible to agree, as it wd. strain still further the well-known & much-tried 'tension' of his Ulstermen, but that now he had come to see it was a patriotic duty &c.

Asquith seized the opening; he saw Lloyd George and Grey as soon as he got back to Downing Street and they clinched the deal. He then saw Redmond who, jumping at the 'excellent chance of putting off the Amending Bill', made what Asquith described as 'a really useful suggestion: namely, that if we wd. put off the Amending Bill till next session, he would agree that the operation of the Home Rule Bill (to be put of course on the Statute book now) should be suspended until the Amending Bill becomes law'.[8]

This, then, was the compromise that put Ireland on ice for the duration of the Great War. Redmond agreed to the suspension of home rule; Asquith agreed to the suspension of partition. Neither realised how long the war would last or how all would have changed utterly before these issues were again addressed at Westminster. Redmond's fateful proposal was yet another reiteration of his party's refusal to come to grips with the Ulster Unionists' right to self-determination. The core of the crisis of 1912–14 had nothing to do with a home-rule settlement for nationalist Ireland about which unanimous, if sometimes grudging, agreement had evolved and everything to do with settling terms for the exclusion of Ulster from that settlement. Redmond's compromise obscured that political reality and instead restored the political fiction that had endured, albeit for different reasons, from 1886 until 1912: that Ireland could be treated as a unitary entity. In so doing, he nourished the nationalist delusion that the partition of Ireland was avoidable.

'I feel as if a great weight were off my chest,' wrote Asquith, on 18 September 1914 as the third Home Rule Bill, accompanied by the Suspensory Bill, went through all stages in the Commons 'on oiled castors in about 7 minutes'.[9] The Suspensory Act provided that the Home Rule Act would not come into effect until an indefinite date 'not being later than the end of the present war'. It was also accompanied by an explicitly partitionist assurance from Asquith to the Unionists that 'the employment of force, any kind of force, for . . . the coercion of Ulster, is an absolutely unthinkable thing . . . a thing which we would never countenance or consent to'. Asquith's declaration, as Nicholas Mansergh has observed, 'carried, despite the wartime qualification, an unmistakable ring of finality. There would be no coercion of Ulster, with the Ulster Unionists left in effect to decide what was coercion. To that the government was now pledged.'[10]

The immediate announcement of the royal assent, on 18 September, to what was now the Government of Ireland Act 1914, was greeted with wild enthusiasm in the Commons by Liberals and nationalists and by the embittered absence of the Unionists, who had walked out of the House en bloc. Embitterment was as misplaced as enthusiasm, for the ultimate achievement of home rule was more apparent than real. For the Ulster Unionists, if not for the Southern Unionists outside whatever parts of Ulster might ultimately be excluded, the Suspensory Act disguised what was in reality a victory. By the summer of 1914 ministers had gone too far down the path of partition to reverse their tracks. Lloyd George and Churchill had been committed to the exclusion of Ulster since February 1912, Grey since the summer of 1912; Asquith and the Liberal government were publicly and irrevocably committed to partition once Asquith offered the exclusion of the six north-eastern counties of Ulster in the House of Commons on 9 March 1914. The Suspensory Act disguised but it did not reverse this commitment to the principle of partition.

The Nationalist Party, on the other hand, lost more than it gained from a formula that deprived it of its *raison d'être*. Forty years after its foundation as a separate party, its members appeared to have achieved their goal and yet they had nothing to show for it: no parliament to set up in Dublin, no offices to fill, no patronage to dispense, no trappings of power to cover their impotence in the vortex of a war that sucked up all political energy for four long years. Redmond, again in Mansergh's words, was 'blindly dismissive of what alone could save him, namely getting his hands on the levers of power'; incredibly, in the brief debate on the Suspensory Bill, he spoke 'in terms of astonishing negation, saying that, with an army being created, "the idea is absurd that under these circumstances a new Government and a new Parliament could be erected in Ireland"'.[11]

The war also posed Redmond a new and dangerous question about Ireland's role in the war and the compatibility of that role with nationalist aspirations. His own attitude was unambiguous: on 20 September 1914 he urged his followers to join the British army, most controversially in an open-air speech from what is now a fairway of Woodenbridge golf course in County Wicklow within yards of the hotel where Éamon de Valera, who was to succeed him as the leader of Irish nationalists, had honeymooned in 1910. He called on the Volunteers to serve 'not only in Ireland itself, but wherever the firing line extends'. The initial enthusiasm for the war, in nationalist Ireland as throughout the other nations of Europe, and his own popularity in the immediate aftermath of home rule's enactment prompted a large majority – some 150,000 'National Volunteers' to follow Redmond. These were opposed by fewer than 10,000 anti-war 'Irish Volunteers' (secretly manipulated by the revolutionary Irish Republican Brotherhood). But the longer the war dragged on, the more Volunteers were slaughtered on the western front and the more unpopular Redmond and his party became.

The erosion of Redmond's power at Westminster and, consequently, in Ireland, became quickly apparent. The wartime spirit of co-operation between Liberals and Conservatives destroyed the leverage exerted in the House of Commons by Redmond over Asquith's government since the 1910 elections. 'Redmond's hold of the balance of power has now disappeared', observed Tim Healy, the anti-Parnellite MP who became the first governor general when the Irish Free State was established in December 1922, 'and he will be I fear treated accordingly.'[12] The consequences became explicit on 25 May 1915 when bipartisan politics found full expression in the formation of the first coalition government.

Although Asquith retained the premiership, all Redmond's leading Unionist adversaries during the bitter battles over

home rule now joined the government: Bonar Law, Lansdowne, Balfour, Chamberlain, Long – men who had spent
much of their political lives, dating, in some cases, back to
the 1880s, fighting against home rule – obtained cabinet
appointments. So too, and this was the most sickening blow
of all for the Nationalist Party, did Edward Carson, whose
endorsement of sedition in the shape of Ulster's provisional
government was now no barrier to his appointment as attorney
general. For the moment Ireland was not an issue, but the
power and influence these men could wield in cabinet if and
when it again became an issue was enormous. Redmond, on
the other hand, rejected Asquith's thrice-repeated invitation
to join the cabinet as 'impossible' because of his party's
'principles and history'.[13] In the light of Redmond's absence,
Carson's appointment, as Alvin Jackson has argued, 'apparently affirmed Ulster militancy while simultaneously slighting
Irish constitutionalism'.[14]

From now until the Irish settlements of 1921–2 the key to
understanding Britain's Irish policy was that it was the policy
of a coalition government. Between 1910 and 1914 Unionists had emphasised, indeed exacerbated, their differences
with the Liberal government on Ireland. Within a period of
five years, between 1906 and 1910, the Conservative Party
had lost three general elections, an experience then unique in
its history, and the Orange card, which had turned up trumps
so often in the past, seemed to be all it had left in its hand.
Once the Tories were back in government, the Orange card
became irrelevant. The Liberals were now their allies, not
their enemies; it was in neither party's interest to rake over
the embers of Irish controversy.

This had two consequences. First, both Liberals and Conservatives wanted to avoid the Irish issue if at all possible, to

minimise straining the coalition. Second, and again in the interests of the coalition's cohesion, *if* the Irish nettle had to be grasped, there was a powerful incentive towards compromise, an incentive of a kind lacking in the normal workings of the British party system as it had developed around the turn of the century. The impetus, in short, was towards agreement on Ireland where previously it had been towards disagreement, and agreement, in the context of coalition, meant partition.

These considerations lead us directly to a profound difficulty confronting historians (especially Irish historians) of British–Irish relations: the problem of reconciling an appreciation of the significance of the momentous events that occurred between 1916 and 1919 for the future course of Irish history with an equal recognition of the British government's almost utter indifference to what was happening in Ireland. Because of the Great War and because of the institutionalisation of bipartisanship embodied in the coalition governments of 1915–22, Ireland is never again as important to Britain as it had been in 1910–14 because it is never again so deeply embedded in the warp and weft of British party politics.

The high drama of Irish history after 1916 – the Easter rebellion, the execution of the rebel leaders, the growing strength of Sinn Féin and the revolutionary nationalists culminating in the enormous electoral defeat they inflicted on the Nationalist Party in the 1918 election, the consequent unilateral establishment of an independent Irish parliament (the first Dáil) in Dublin in January 1919, the Irish war of independence of 1919–21 and all that followed in its wake – tends to obscure this fundamental fact. To Irish nationalists it seemed (and seems) almost incomprehensible that the British refused to attribute a significance to the events of 1916–21 at least comparable to the significance they attached to the events of 1910–14.

Yet a frank recognition of that refusal is essential to an understanding of the British government's Irish policy after 1914. The Great War absorbed all the energies of ministers. For as long as it continued, they had neither time nor inclination to turn to Ireland and, if they did discuss Ireland, it was only because the exigencies of war strategy demanded it. Their Irish policy or, more accurately, their lack of any coherent Irish policy, was founded not on any concern for the harmony of British–Irish relations but on their determination that Ireland must not hinder the imperial war effort.

It was precisely because of that understandably obsessive concern with the war effort, moreover, that the Great War conferred as many advantages on the forces of Irish revolutionary nationalism as it did disadvantages on the Nationalist Party. 'England's difficulty is Ireland's opportunity' is so well worn a slogan of Irish separatists that it is too easily forgotten how long it had been since international difficulty had created such opportunity. Not since the battle of Waterloo had Britain been drawn into a major war involving all the great powers. The 120 years of the Act of Union were, for the most part, a period of unparalleled tranquillity in the history of Britain's relations with the European continent. It is no coincidence that, just as one great European war played a decisive part in making the Act of Union, the next great European war played a decisive part in breaking it.

The prime minister spent the Easter weekend of 1916 at his country home, resting from the responsibilities of running the war and preparing for a crucial Commons debate on conscription. He drove back to Downing Street late on Easter Monday (24 April) with Maurice Hankey, the secretary to the war committee, and arrived just after midnight. Only then did he learn of the rebellion* that had erupted in Dublin earlier that day. Asquith, recorded Hankey, 'merely said "well, that's something" and went off to bed'.[15] Thus did the Irish question emerge from the oblivion to which it had been consigned in September 1914.

The languor of Asquith's reaction epitomises the impact of the war on Irish policy. Ireland, which from 1912 to 1914 had held the centre of the political stage, had, by Easter 1916, been driven into the wings, if not out of the theatre.

Although the rebels were members of the Irish Volunteers and of the Citizen Army, led respectively by Patrick Pearse and James Connolly, the rebellion was masterminded by the secret and revolutionary Irish Republican Brotherhood. The seven signatories of the proclamation, *The Provisional Government of the Irish Republic to the People of Ireland*, posted when the rebels seized the General Post Office and several other major buildings in Dublin on 24 April, were all members of the IRB's military council. Martial law was proclaimed in Dublin city and county on 25 April and, on 26 April, British artillery and the gunboat *Helga* shelled buildings occupied by the rebels. Birrell and General Sir John Maxwell, the newly appointed commander-in-chief, arrived in Ireland the next day. On 29 April – after 450 persons had been killed (more than a hundred of whom were British soldiers) and nearly 3,000 wounded – the unconditional surrender of Pearse and Connolly on behalf of the provisional government ended the rebellion. On 1 May the first 400 of some 2,000 captured insurgents were sent to Britain for internment.

* The conventional Irish usage is 'Easter Rising' but, to the British, it was a rebellion (generally misnamed the 'Sinn Féin rebellion') and, since this is a history of Britain's Irish policy, that term is here preferred. The authorities in Dublin Castle had described the minority, anti-war Irish Volunteers as 'Sinn Féin' Volunteers[16] since the split of September 1914.

Until that point Asquith's government had reason for relief, even, perhaps, for self-congratulation: the rebellion had been swiftly suppressed and, more important, appeared to have been repudiated by Irish public opinion. It was not, reported Birrell in his last letter from Ireland to Asquith, 'an *Irish* Rebellion – it would be a pity if *ex post facto* it became one, and was added to the long and melancholy list of Irish Rebellions'.[17]

But all was 'changed utterly' by the sentences of death handed down by the courts martial. Death transformed the leaders into martyrs and gave birth to the 'terrible beauty' immortalised in William Butler Yeats's 'Easter 1916'. Fifteen executions were carried out between 3 and 12 May: all seven signatories of the proclamation and all the Volunteer commandants except one were shot. Éamon de Valera escaped death because of his American birth.

Asquith had played Pontius Pilate when he and his cabinet colleagues washed their hands of responsibility on 27 April, deciding that martial law should be proclaimed over Ireland and that General Maxwell should be given plenary powers to administer it. The decision signalled what Charles Townshend has well described as 'the eclipse of civil government and "politics" generally'. The best generals were obviously serving on the western front or in the Middle East, and Maxwell, who was not the government's first choice, was a general 'in enforced semi-retirement after a period in Egypt . . . it seems that his main qualification for the job was his complete lack of any previous contact with Ireland – "no past record", as Asquith characteristically put it'.[18] On 6 May, as Asquith told the king, Maxwell had been given discretion in individual cases, 'subject to a general instruction that death should not be inflicted except upon ringleaders and proven murderers, and that it is desirable to bring the executions to a close as quickly as possible'. Behind these decisions loomed 'the awful corroding presence of the Great War itself . . . Where death had become a commonplace, if a hateful one, of what account were the deaths of a few rebels? And of rebels, moreover, who had struck at a nation and empire when they were already reeling from repeated defeats?'[19] – and of rebels, furthermore, whose proclamation had invoked the Germans as 'gallant allies in Europe'.

The cabinet's attention was more sharply focused by the resignation of Augustine Birrell as chief secretary on 1 May. Birrell had tried to resign before, but this time, heavily criticised for his failure to act on well-founded intelligence reports warning of rebellion, he insisted. Even Liberal ministers thought, as Christopher Addison confided to his diary, that 'dear old Birrell will have to go'.[20] Unionist ministers were more vitriolic. 'No one takes the thing as other than the usual Irish tragic comic opera,' wrote the Earl of Selborne, the president of the Board of Agriculture, but 'everyone thinks that Birrell is a scandal.' Since the coalition had been formed eleven months before, 'Birrell has never once mentioned the subject of Ireland and we have had no knowledge whatever of the state of affairs there. As everything seemed calm we assumed that it was calm. Now it appears that Birrell and [Sir Matthew] Nathan [under-secretary for Ireland since October 1914] have had any number of warnings which they neglected on principle.'[21] Birrell had now to pay the price for what Charles Townshend has called Dublin Castle's 'quietist consensus'.[22] Asquith accepted his resignation with 'infinite regret' and bade farewell on 2 May to one of the few survivors from his first cabinet: 'I don't remember what he *said*,' Birrell wrote, 'but I do know he *wept* and stood staring out of the window jingling some half-crowns in his pocket.'[23] Nathan resigned the next day.

The Unionists immediately tried to seize the vacancy. Bonar Law wanted Walter Long (the last chief secretary, in 1905, in a Conservative government and Carson's predecessor until 1910 as leader of the Irish Unionist MPs) or Robert Cecil; but Asquith, after consulting Redmond, refused.[24] None of the leading Liberals, in symptomatic contrast, had any appetite for the occupancy of Dublin Castle. Ireland, so often regarded as a sentence of exile, seemed an even more remote back-water against the backdrop of war. Although Redmond urged the appointment of an experienced Liberal minister – Samuel, Runciman or McKenna – his own first choice was Edwin Montagu, who in July 1915 had married Asquith's beloved Venetia Stanley. It was, perhaps, a measure of Asquith's instinct of how disruptive the appointment might prove for his already shaky coalition government that he first offered the post neither to an ardent home-ruler nor to a committed Unionist, but to a liberal-minded Jew; a disconcerted Montagu declined on the grounds of 'his own Jewish race, his lack of physical courage and interest in the Irish race'.[25]

So Asquith, as Roy Jenkins observed, 'in despair for a Chief Secretary' to send to Dublin, 'sent himself';[26] his assumption of temporary responsibility for the Irish portfolio after Birrell's resignation mirrored his taking over the war office when Seely resigned after the Curragh mutiny. When Asquith arrived in Dublin at two o'clock on the morning of 12 May, Maxwell immediately assured him that there would be no more executions, but the damage had already been done, as Maxwell's own prescient assessment a month later made plain:

There is a growing feeling that out of Rebellion more has been got than by constitutional methods, hence Mr Redmond's power is on the wane, therefore this desire to curry favour with the people on the part of the M.P.s by agitating for the release of Sinn Féiners.

It is becoming increasingly difficult to differentiate between a Nationalist and a Sinn Féiner.

Mourning badges, Sinn Féin flags, demonstrations at Requiem Masses, the resolutions of public bodies are all signs of the growth of Sinn Féin.

Recruiting [for the war effort] in Ireland has practically ceased . . .

If there was a General Election very few, if any, of existing Nationalist M.P.s would be re-elected so there is a danger that Mr Redmond's party would be replaced by others perhaps less amenable to reason.[27]

Asquith affected less interest in political prognosis than in weeding out the 'Sinn Féin (or so-called) prisoners – very good-looking fellows with such lovely eyes',[28] he observed after a visit to Richmond barracks where they were awaiting transfer to England and Wales. As prime minister in charge of the war effort, moreover, he soon despaired of 'this most perplexing and damnable country'.[29]

Asquith instead turned to Lloyd George, urging him 'to take up Ireland; at any rate for a short time. It is a *unique* opportunity and there is no one else who could do so much to bring about a permanent solution.'[30] Margot Asquith was even more flattering: 'You will settle it and the whole Empire will be grateful for ever . . . if you want to please Henry and me and do a *big thing* settle Ireland. Anyone with wit and a sense of humour must enjoy Ireland, trying as the Irish are.'[31]

Ambition, rather than wit or a sense of humour, led Lloyd George to accept. He was scathing about Asquith's having 'brought back absolutely nothing. He had no plan and he funked the task of endeavouring to make a settlement.' The real attraction of the appointment, which Asquith told the Commons was at the unanimous request of his cabinet colleagues, was that it effectively gave Lloyd George 'the reversion of the Premiership'; suspicious that there might be 'other motives' for the appointment, he was determined that it should not block – even if it did not ease – his passage into 10 Downing Street.[32]

In practice, that meant Lloyd George could not offend the Unionist powerbrokers in the coalition – Bonar Law and Carson, in particular – who would shortly determine the identity of Asquith's successor. Indeed one newly appointed Unionist minister, the Earl of Crawford, was surprised at how speedily Lloyd George gave way to Bonar Law when a draft home-rule bill excluding the six Ulster counties 'only for the period of the war and twelve months later' was brought before cabinet on 19 July and he agreed that the bill 'must be . . . redrafted to make exclusion of Ulster definitive and final'.[33] So tight by then was the Unionist grip on Irish policy that only one Liberal minister, Herbert Samuel, challenged it.

The story of Lloyd George's unsuccessful 1916 negotiations with Redmond and Carson is well known. Lloyd George, mindful of the futility of the Buckingham Palace conference of 1914, spoke separately to the two Irish leaders in the first instance, using what one of his secretaries described as his favourite negotiation technique: 'He would take one party into one room and tell them one thing, and the other into another room and tell them another, and thus influence their minds and bring them together.'[34] But the strategy collapsed when Carson and Redmond formed contradictory impressions of his basic proposal. Carson believed that the Government of Ireland Act of 1914 would be given immediate effect but that the six north-eastern Ulster counties would be permanently excluded. Redmond understood that this exclusion would be only temporary; Lloyd George's apparent duplicity was a product of his negotiating technique of trying to reconcile the irreconcilable by telling one set of politicians one thing, and their opponents something rather different, in the hope that, before these misunderstandings had been cleared up, a mood of good will would have been generated in which differences would seem insignificant and a compromise emerge.[35]

The negotiations also fell foul of the conflict of interest between Ulster Unionists and Southern Unionists. Ulster Unionist leaders preferred to 'have six counties excluded than the whole Province, because the proportion of Unionists in six counties is so much greater' and, as the secretary of the Ulster Unionist Council, R. Dawson Bates, explained, 'They had consciously left any reference to the Southern Unionists out of the terms of their resolutions accepting the exclusion proposals, and expressed great surprise that Lord Lansdowne or Mr Walter Long should be prepared to take any very strong step in supporting opposition by the Southern Unionists.'[36]

But where the Ulster Unionists saw an opportunity to advance their exclusion, Southern Unionists saw an opportunity to insist that home rule should not be implemented in any shape or form, the Government of Ireland Act of 1914 notwithstanding. Their sense of siege and isolation had been intensified by the war's fragmentation of their minority status in nationalist Ireland: 'Trinity College Dublin and the Belfast University are depleted. Protestant Theological Colleges are closed' was the typical reaction of one Southern Unionist. 'In this neighbourhood [Colbinstown, County Wicklow] there is hardly one Unionist who is left – all have joined the Army.'[37] Southern Unionists countered claims that the Easter rebellion necessitated the immediate introduction of home rule with the argument that the rebellion confirmed that home rule was a cloak for ultimately separatist aspirations and ought never to have been conceded. They had powerful allies in the cabinet, notably Walter Long, Lansdowne and Selborne, and a stream of correspondence deluged Bonar Law with protests and abuse.[38] It was Lansdowne who delivered the *coup de grâce* when he attacked the compromise in a House of Lords speech on 11 July. Once the ambiguities inherent in Lloyd George's negotiating technique became public knowledge, his initiative was doomed to fail. The ensuing welter of recriminations did little damage to Lloyd George or to Carson but further corroded the authority of Redmond in nationalist Ireland because it made his acceptance of partition public knowledge.

Lloyd George's 1916 negotiations were as significant as they were short-lived. This was the first illustration of the stranglehold Unionist ministers exerted on the Irish policy of the coalition governments of 1915–22, a stranglehold tantamount to a power of veto. For Irish Unionists and their English fellow-travellers, unlike the other groupings attached to the coalition, Irish policy ranked in importance with the conduct of the war. If their wishes on Irish policy were disregarded, they were ready to threaten to bring down the government, whatever the state of the war. Such blackmail was a most potent weapon, which greatly deterred the coalition leaders – and Lloyd George in particular – from undertaking Irish initiatives in the future. Lloyd George himself saw the 1916 negotiations as the last chance of a settlement before the war ended. 'Heaven knows what will happen then,' he told John Dillon.

I shudder at what may happen meanwhile in Ireland. The country must be governed and if it cannot be ruled through and with the assent of the Irish people, there is no doubt it will have to be governed by force. In the middle of a great war you could not tolerate a rebellious or a seditious Ireland. But nobody knows better than you what coercion would mean under these conditions. People are getting accustomed to scenes of blood. Their own sons are falling by the hundred thousand, and the nation is harder and more ruthless than it has ever been.[39]

Lloyd George's prediction was as accurate as it was ominous. Never again during the war did he grapple with the Irish problem. One reason why he attempted in the summer of 1916 what he was not to attempt again until the end of 1919 was that he had not yet become prime minister. If he failed where so many had failed before him, it would scarcely tarnish his reputation. If he succeeded, it would be a feather in his cap. 'If I pull it off, it will be a big thing,'[40] he told Lord Riddell. Asked if he thought he would 'bring it off' after his appointment to 'solve the Irish problem' had been greeted by a great ovation in the House of Commons, Lloyd George replied. 'You know I am that kind of beggar. I always *do* think beforehand that I am going to bring things off.'[41]

The 1916 negotiations are also significant as a middle ground between the negotiations of 1914 and the negotiations of 1920–21. In 1916, as in 1914, Redmond and Carson were the protagonists. Never again were representatives of the British government, of the Unionist majority in Ulster and of the nationalist majority in the rest of Ireland to come together to try to solve the Irish problem within a common framework of reference, a framework founded on the fact that all three

led parties in the Westminster parliament. Yet even here, perhaps, Lloyd George's preference for negotiating separately
with Carson and Redmond is symptomatic of the coalition's
preference for treating Ireland and Ulster as separate problems needing separate treatment.

Whatever his motivation, there can be no doubt that Lloyd
George blazed the trail towards partition during the 1916
negotiations. On 12 June, for example, Carson persuaded the
Ulster Unionist Council to accept his proposal for the immediate implementation of home rule subject to the exclusion
of the six north-eastern counties; on 23 June, Redmond persuaded the Ulster Nationalist Conference in Belfast to vote
for exclusion. In early July partition achieved the status of a
white paper with the publication of *Headings of a Settlement
as to the Government of Ireland*.[42]

Although the collapse of the negotiations meant that the
issue of whether exclusion would be temporary or permanent
remained unresolved, that the Unionist and nationalist leaders
had otherwise endorsed partition was now a matter of public
record. 'The only gainers', observed W. Alison Phillips in
The Revolution in Ireland, published in 1923, 'were the Sinn
Féiners, who from this moment never allowed the Irish people
to forget that Redmond and his party had consented to the
"partition of Ireland."'[43] The 'real point' was 'the future of
the excluded area', argued Asquith in a personal and strictly
confidential letter to Redmond on 28 July after the breakdown of the negotiations: Carson wanted to preclude the
possibility of 'automatic inclusion'; Redmond wanted to keep
'effectively open, the possibility of revision and review at an
early date'.[44] The 'real point', *pace* Asquith, was that Lloyd
George had endorsed Carson's position from the beginning
of the negotiations. 'We must make it clear that at the end of

the provisional period Ulster does not, *whether she wills it or not* [author's italics], merge in the rest of Ireland,'[45] he wrote on 29 May in a letter accompanying the draft Heads of Settlement which he asked Carson to show to Craig.

The Unionists secured the chief secretaryship and further tightened their grip on the coalition's Irish policy even before Lloyd George succeeded Asquith. 'For Chief Secretary we must have a Unionist,' Asquith told Redmond when the negotiations collapsed, and he thought Henry Duke (the MP for Exeter and a distinguished sixty-one-year-old barrister without previous ministerial experience) 'by far the best man. He is "almost persuaded" to be a Home Ruler.'[46] Asquith, as so often in his dealings with Redmond, was disingenuous. Duke's Unionist credentials were impeccable: speaking in Exeter in 1912 of Ulster's right to resist home rule, he had insisted that the 'killing of men who so resist is not an act of oppression – it is an act of murder'.[47]

Duke's appointment on 31 July was swiftly followed by a sop to the nationalists in the unseemly shape of the Liberal Lord Wimborne, known as 'the Rebounder' in Dublin society because of his survival as viceroy following his exoneration by the Hardinge commission of inquiry into the rebellion; the nickname also reflected his reputation as the best judge of good wine and of bad women in Ireland. 'Some of the ladies who had visited the [Viceregal] Lodge said he was so fearful a bounder that they would die rather than return,'[48] Asquith's daughter-in-law confided to her diary during a 1916 visit to Dublin. 'I shudder to think of the scenes enacted in the sitting-room. He really ought to restrain himself with the natives.'[49] Other sops followed in 'a form of "Rome rule"', seeking to placate nationalist Ireland by putting Catholics in control of the state apparatus[50] centred on Dublin Castle. The key post of under-secretary (the head of the Irish civil service) went to Sir William Byrne, a fifty-seven-year-old English Catholic and an assistant under-secretary at the home office. General Joseph Byrne, an Irishman and 'a devout Roman Catholic' who had been on General Maxwell's staff, was made inspector general of the Royal Irish Constabulary, and, in November, Maxwell himself was replaced as Irish GOC by another Irish Catholic, General Sir Bryan Mahon. Yet another Irish Catholic, former nationalist MP and then solicitor general in Ireland, James O'Connor, subsequently became the Irish attorney general.

But such Irish policy as existed during the Great War was shaped in Downing Street, not in Dublin Castle, and the formation of Lloyd George's first coalition tightened the Unionist stranglehold. This was most notable in the Unionist dominance of the small war cabinet of five to seven members he established as the supreme policy-making body of British government between December 1916 and January 1919. Apart from Lloyd George himself and the Labour leader, Arthur Henderson (replaced by George Barnes in 1917), the other three members of the first war cabinet were all Unionists: Bonar Law, Lord Curzon and Lord Milner. Milner had been appointed 'as a surrogate for Carson',[51] who was himself a member from July 1917 until January 1918, when he resigned over Irish policy. When Milner also resigned, in April 1918, he was replaced by yet another Unionist, Austen Chamberlain, who sought specific assurances on Irish policy before accepting the appointment.[52] Only briefly – between June and July 1917 and, after Carson's resignation, between January and April 1918 – were the Unionists denied an overall majority in the war cabinet.

The war cabinet minutes, moreover, reveal its almost utter indifference to Ireland. Between 18 January 1917 and 6

March 1918 there was only one substantive discussion of Irish policy and this notwithstanding the fact that the war cabinet, under Lloyd George's chairmanship, met on every weekday. Yet this thirteen-month period witnessed a string of four by-election victories for Sinn Féin at the expense of the nationalists; the anti-partition declaration of 8 May signed by sixteen Catholic and three Protestant bishops; the release on 16 June of the remaining prisoners convicted of participating in the rebellion; the Irish Convention which met between July 1917 and April 1918; the election of Éamon de Valera as president of Sinn Féin on 25 October 1917 and as president of the Irish Volunteers two days later; the enfranchisement of all men over twenty-one and of most women over thirty; and the death of John Redmond (on 6 March 1918) and his succession by John Dillon as leader of the Irish Parliamentary Party.

Lloyd George had signalled his determination to ensure that Ireland helped rather than hindered winning the war in the course of his statement of government policy to the House of Commons on his appointment as prime minister. 'The real solution of the Irish problem' was to produce a 'better atmosphere . . . to help us, not to solve a political question, but to help us to do something that will be a real contribution to the winning of the War.'[53] He was as good as his word. From now until the conclusion of the peace treaties Lloyd George sought only to achieve that objective. The new prime minister, encouraged by Henry Duke,[54] who had been retained as chief secretary, first tried to improve the atmosphere by a Christmas gesture of good will: the release of untried Irish political prisoners, imprisoned in Frongoch and Reading gaols since the Easter rebellion. The gesture was designed for international rather than for Irish consumption: Lloyd George wanted to persuade the Americans, and President Woodrow Wilson in particular, that he was redressing Irish nationalist grievances.[55]

7

'Blood in their Eyes': The American Dimension

The early years of the Great War demonstrated that Britain alone could no longer tilt the deadlocked balance of power in Europe and enlisting the United States as an ally became the primary objective of British foreign policy. This consolidation of Anglo-American relations, the nurturing of the so-called 'special relationship', has impinged on Britain's Irish policy until today.[1]

The sinking of the *Lusitania*, torpedoed without warning by a German U-boat 14 miles off the Old Head of Kinsale on the south-west coast of Ireland on 7 May 1915 was the catalyst for the gradual erosion of the American policy of neutrality declared by President Woodrow Wilson on the outbreak of war; 128 of the nearly 1,900 people who lost their lives were American and Wilson's appeals that the Germans abandon their policy of unrestricted submarine warfare went unheeded. But the Easter rebellion of 1916 threatened the British policy of eliminating causes of friction with the United States. In June 1916 Lord Aberdeen, the Liberal viceroy in Ireland from 1906 until 1915, who was then in New York, advised that the executions of the rebel leaders had 'occasioned a severe shock to a large body (1) of Irishmen in the U.S. who previously had little or no sympathy with the Sinn Féiners and (2) to a number of Americans, whose attitude towards England has hitherto been entirely friendly, especially in relation to the War'. The Irish vote would be influential in the forthcoming presidential election and it was imperative to secure 'an arrangement that will deter the mass of opinion . . . from moving in the pro-German direction'.[2]

Cecil Spring-Rice, the British ambassador in Washington, likewise advised on how American, and Irish-American attitudes in particular, had been 'changed for the worse . . . They have blood in their eyes when they look our way.'[3] Spring-Rice's advice fell on deaf ears in the foreign office where his views were suspect because of his Irish, albeit Protestant, birth and because, after two terms in Washington, formerly as an embassy secretary and, since 1913, as ambassador, he was thought to have gone native. Many senior foreign office officials, moreover, were fervent Unionists; none more so than the permanent under-secretary until June 1916, Arthur Nicolson, who 'believed that the Liberal Government had cynically resurrected Home Rule for party gain and had thereby provoked righteous resistance'. Only months before Britain declared war on Germany, Nicolson had gloated to the British ambassador in Berlin about the UVF's Larne gun-running: 'I hope you were amused by this "coup" . . . so wonderfully organised and so beautifully carried out.'[4]

Unionists resented and resisted the encroachment of the American dimension because they recognised its potential for shifting the Irish balance of power in the nationalist interest. Lord Salisbury had attacked Lloyd George's 1916 home-rule proposal on the grounds that 'it is in America that the real motive for this policy is to be found',[5] while Walter Long threatened to resign rather than impose Lloyd George's scheme on Ulster 'as an Imperial necessity and in order to avoid American complications'.[6] Both Salisbury and Long circulated their views to Unionist, but not to Liberal, colleagues in the cabinet.

No amount of Unionist bluster, however, could disguise the government's determination to sanitise Irish policy for American consumption, as its campaign of character assassination against the homosexual Roger Casement in July 1916 so grotesquely demonstrated. Casement had been captured shortly after disembarking from a German submarine on a mission for the Irish Volunteers on the eve of the Easter rebellion; unlike the other rebels, he was tried in London – the attorney general, F. E. Smith, leading for the prosecution – and, on 29 June, was convicted of high treason and sentenced to death by hanging. American pleas for leniency had begun even before the trial but the predominant official view, in the phrase of the British ambassador to France, was 'hang him and chance public opinion in the States'.

When the cabinet discussed the matter on 5 July several ministers, including Grey and Lansdowne, counselled that Casement be 'kept in confinement as a criminal lunatic' rather than 'executed without any smirch on his character, and then canonised as a martyr in Ireland and America'. When that view did not prevail, ministers and home office and foreign office officials set about vindicating Casement's execution by circulating photographed extracts of graphic descriptions of homosexual acts from his diary, through the British Embassy in Washington (which targeted members of the Roman Catholic hierarchy as well as congressional leaders), to the American ambassador in London and to carefully selected American journalists.[7] Asquith himself delivered the *coup de grâce* at a luncheon on 1 August with the American ambassador, Walter H. Page. The prime minister, noted the ambassador in a memorandum for President

Woodrow Wilson, 'showed a very eager interest in the [American] Presidential campaign, and he confessed that he felt some anxiety about the anti-British feeling in the United States . . . *He spoke of the unmentionable Casement diary, which shows a degree of perversion and depravity without parallel in modern times.* "In all good conscience to my country and to my responsibilities I cannot interfere."'[8] The italicised sentence was silently deleted when the ambassador's biography was published in London in 1930. When Casement was hanged at Pentonville gaol on 3 August 1916 most American critics had been effectively silenced, although to make assurance doubly sure the British naval attaché in Washington, Captain Guy Gaunt, continued disseminating copies of the choicer pages from Casement's diaries for three weeks after his death.[9]

Woodrow Wilson's re-election as US president had done nothing to exorcise the American spectre when Lloyd George became prime minister. Indeed the need for 'a settlement of the Irish question' in order to release troops tied down in Ireland and for the 'maintenance of good relations with the United States'[10] was emphasised in a memorandum produced by Maurice Hankey, secretary to the newly constituted war cabinet, at its inaugural meeting. An exchange between Arthur Balfour, who had succeeded Edward Grey as foreign secretary, and Walter Page in March 1917, on the eve of Balfour's departure on a diplomatic mission to Washington, went to the heart of the matter. Why, asked Balfour, were the British so unpopular in the United States? 'It is the organised Irish,' replied the American ambassador. 'Then it's the effect of the very fact that the Irish question is not settled. You've had that problem at your very door for 300 years. What's the matter that you don't solve it?'[11]

Lloyd George delegated the problem to his new personal secretariat or brains trust, the 'Garden Suburb', so called because of its makeshift offices in the garden of 10 Downing Street; from then until the end of the war the Garden Suburb played an important role in shaping Irish policy. The head of the secretariat was W. G. S. Adams, Gladstone Professor of Political Theory and Institutions at Oxford, '*the* man to create the subject of political science in Oxford'[12] and a home-ruler 'who had spent formative years in Ireland' working for Horace Plunkett in the Department of Agriculture and Technical Instruction. Another who made an even larger contribution to Irish policy was Philip Kerr, later Lord Lothian, who was born into the Scottish Catholic aristocracy but became a Christian Scientist. Kerr was one of Lord Milner's protégés, an ardent imperialist and the first editor of *The Round Table* (where he had written in September 1916 that Ireland's separation from the Empire was 'not only suicidal but impossible'); he had also been associated with the movement to make federal devolution the Unionist Party's alternative to home rule. Kerr's rejection of the Catholic Church, and his consequent attitude to the religion of the majority of Irishmen, was such that Plunkett, a tolerant observer, feared that he was incapable of dispassionate judgement in Irish matters.[13]

Adams made the running when, on 1 March 1917, he urged Lloyd George to 'state plainly that the settlement of the Irish question depends on the Irish themselves, and that what Irishmen will agree on England and the Empire will accept'.[14] He suggested an Irish convention to draw up such a settlement. Lloyd George gave Adams's paper to Bonar Law and Carson the next day[15] – he invariably went immediately to the Unionist leaders whenever Ireland surfaced during his premiership – but Carson jibbed, arguing that the proposal would produce no 'useful result, as the moment the convention was started it would be found that the persons nominated were not really able to bind their followers in any way'.[16]

The American dimension assumed an even larger significance when the United States, having severed diplomatic relations with Germany on 3 February 1917, formally declared war on 6 April. Within a month six American destroyers were moored at Queenstown, the major British naval base in Cork Harbour, and the influx of some 7,000 American naval personnel in 1917–18 prompted a sermon at the Catholic cathedral warning parents 'to look out for their young daughters especially since there had lately arrived on our shores hundreds of vultures, yea I might say thousands of them, who were preying upon the purity of our daughters of Queenstown'.[17]

On 10 April President Wilson personally typed a confidential message to his secretary of state, Robert Lansing, instructing the American ambassador in London to tell the prime minister unofficially and most confidentially that 'the failure so far to find a satisfactory method of self-government for Ireland' alone stood in the way of 'absolutely cordial' Anglo-American co-operation.[18] Lloyd George welcomed the intervention, as well he might given that he himself had inspired it: he had communicated secretly with Wilson through Walter Page 'asking him to send a message urging that the Irish question should be settled. He thinks if he can get this it will be a very great help, & will influence Carson.'[19] But a 'most secret' annexe to a telegram from Washington from Arthur Balfour, that most Irish-Americans would acquiesce in partition, although they would not welcome it publicly, strengthened Carson's hand.[20] 'Carson was his difficulty,' Lloyd George explained over breakfast to the editor of the *Manchester Guardian*; 'Bonar Law said that if Carson went out he must go out and that meant the complete breakup of the Government.'²¹

Carson's continued insistence on permanent exclusion was the rock on which the recommendations prepared by a Unionist-dominated sub-committee (Duke, Curzon and Addison) – providing for a poll of the six excluded counties 'to be taken within a specified period after the war with a view to the incorporation in the Home Rule area of any county where a majority of the voters shall support inclusion, and to be repeated after a period of not less than seven or more than ten years if there shall still be at that time an excluded area'²² – foundered at a war cabinet meeting on 16 May. But a chink of light had appeared the night before in the unlikely setting of a banquet in the House of Lords where Redmond, seated beside Lord Crewe, was astonished to learn that Lloyd George was sending him yet another formal offer of the immediate establishment of a home-rule parliament excluding the six counties. This was Redmond's last chance to try to salvage his party's fortunes with the power, patronage and popularity that might accrue if a home-rule parliament in Dublin was set up without further delay, albeit only for twenty-six counties, but he instead declared that he and his party were 'irreconcilably opposed' to such a scheme.

Mounting disillusion with the horrors of war – Redmond's own brother, William, was killed in action on the western front on 7 June – meant that the tide of Irish by-election results was already flowing against the Irish Parliamentary Party. The Sinn Féin candidate, Count Plunkett (the father of Joseph Mary Plunkett who had been executed after the 1916 rebellion), had won a seat in North Roscommon on 5 February; on 9 May, only a week before Lloyd George's offer, Sinn Féin's Joseph McGuinness, imprisoned in Lewes gaol, defeated the nationalist candidate in South Longford. Yet, unaccountably, 'time, Redmond still believed, was on the side of the Nationalists as against Lloyd George'.[23] Pressed for an alternative by Crewe, Redmond said that 'he saw no hope now except by the summoning of an Irish Conference, representative of all interests, to draft a national constitution'.[24] Crewe hurried with the news to 10 Downing Street in the early hours of the morning. Lloyd George seized the opening, which coincided with Professor Adams resurrecting his own hobby horse of an Irish convention; two paragraphs incorporating the offer of a convention were appended to Philip Kerr's draft of Lloyd George's offer to Redmond. On 17 May Redmond replied, expressing his party's irreconcilable opposition to the home rule/exclusion proposal but supporting a fully representative convention 'summoned without delay'.[25]

On 21 May the prime minister duly announced in the House of Commons 'a convention of Irishmen of all parties for the purpose of producing a scheme of Irish self-government'. Lloyd George, noted his mistress, was 'very bucked' that 'the Irish question has suddenly taken a turn for the better'; he is 'hopeful that peace may reign for a few months at least in that quarter, though I do not know whether he has any hopes of the Convention ultimately solving the Irish puzzle'.[26] Frances Stevenson's scepticism was as well founded as Lloyd George's elation. The convention did nothing to solve the Irish puzzle, but it did give the prime minister a breathing space of eight months.

The Irish Convention, which first met in Dublin on 25 July 1917 and ended on 5 April 1918, exemplified Lloyd George's determination to mollify nationalist, and thereby American, opinion without deflecting ministerial energy from the war effort. From a British perspective, the merit of the convention's format was that its representation was exclusively Irish. The point was spelt out by F. E. Smith during an American speaking tour in an interview with the *Boston Post* in January 1918: 'Let them keep on talking. If they don't agree it's the fault of Irishmen and not of the English, for there is not an Englishman on the Convention. It's an Irish problem and not an English problem.'[27]

The convention, its historian has remarked, 'could be considered a declaration of faith in the principles of nineteenth-century liberalism . . . that if men of goodwill got down together and discussed rationally their political differences, by conversion and compromise they could reach agreement.'[28] But Lloyd George's coalition was not the nineteenth-century Liberal Party and the convention was no more than a token genuflection by the Liberals within its ranks to battered Gladstonian deities. Asquith might, perhaps, have retained a vestige of belief in such deities; Lloyd George did not. For Lloyd George, in the words of Tom Jones, was 'never, as Gladstone was, a crusader for Home Rule';[29] for him, Ireland was never 'a cause, but a problem that had to be solved'.[30] The convention was 'nothing more to Lloyd George than a most respectable and plausible way of marking time for months on end',[31] not so much an attempt to solve the Irish problem as yet another attempt to shelve it – what F. S. L. Lyons has called 'a gigantic irrelevancy'.[32] This was best illustrated by the response of what were now the two most dynamic political groupings in Ireland: the Ulster Unionists and Sinn Féin, the 'two classes of Irish opinion' which, as Lloyd George admitted to the House of Commons in 1920, had nothing to do with the convention reports and which after the 1918 election 'were the two sections which between them represented the whole of Ireland'.[33] The 'one positive result' of the convention, as Nicholas Mansergh has observed, 'was that the Cabinet *appeared* to have a policy on Ireland, which was important in the English [and the American] political context, but which, in its Irish, may well have been worse than having none'.[34]

The Ulster Unionists, although they reluctantly agreed to participate in the convention, did so merely as an exercise in imperial public relations; they attended, according to Mansergh, 'only in order to convey their "inexorable opposition" . . . to Home Rule or any variant of it'.[35] They made it plain, moreover, just as Carson had anticipated, that they would be in no way bound by whatever decisions the convention might make. They would merely submit such decisions for the consideration of their own governing body, the Ulster Unionist Council, which appointed a committee to choose and then to ride herd on their representatives to the convention. Their delegation, argued one member of that committee, should include 'two or three men of first-rate ability with a wide as well as a practical knowledge of industry and commerce who will be able to flatten out clever, plausible [nationalist] gasbags . . . The rest of our men should, I think, be chosen for character.'[36] For 'character', one may fairly read obduracy and a refusal to compromise, particularly on the issue of Ulster's permanent exclusion, on which Carson had stood firm since 1914.

Sinn Féin was even more obdurate and uncompromising. Bolstered, first, by the release on 16 June of Éamon de Valera and all other convicted prisoners remaining in British gaols after the Easter rebellion as a gesture of good will towards the convention; and, second, by de Valera's crushing defeat of the nationalist candidate in the East Clare by-election on 10 July, they were dissatisfied by the number of delegates they were offered and refused to play any part whatsoever in the convention. De Valera explained why during his by-election campaign: 'The Unionists of the north were consistent in their desire to remain part of the British Empire; the only other position was the Sinn Féin position, completely independent and separate from England. How then could they have conciliation?'[37] Sinn Féin, in short, unlike the Irish Parliamentary Party under the leadership of John Redmond as it had evolved since 1914, would play no role in trying to shape the geographical dimensions of a partitionist settlement but would simply denounce it as an evil never to be countenanced.

Yet on the rare occasions when Ireland surfaced in their deliberations, the war cabinet was complacent about Sinn Féin's advance. On 4 July 1917, for example, when 'Lord Midleton, the Lord Lieutenant [Wimborne], General Mahon, and the head of the Irish Constabulary and Dublin Police gave evidence regarding the disturbed state of Ireland and disaffection among Sinn Féiners', the war cabinet concluded that 'the general trend of evidence, though serious, did not cause great anxiety'. But it was taken aback by 'a terrific outburst by Henry Duke, the Irish Secretary, who . . . spoke like a man overworked and overwrought and on the verge of a breakdown'.[38] Eunan O'Halpin has described Duke as 'a kind, fussy lawyer, ill equipped for the pressures of government'; he was an 'excitable, confused and ineffective' chief secretary 'incapable of resolving questions on his own initiative. For the Cabinet Ireland was a nuisance to be got rid of, yet Duke bothered them repeatedly over the smallest issues.'[39]

All this was abundantly illustrated on 23 October when the war cabinet had its most substantive discussion of Irish policy in 1917. There was a full attendance: Lloyd George, Bonar Law, Carson, Milner, Curzon, Barnes and the South African leader, General Smuts. Duke and four other ministers from outside the war cabinet – three more hardline Unionists (Balfour, Long and Derby) and one Liberal (Fisher) – were also present. The meeting considered the terms of Duke's proposed Commons speech that afternoon reporting on 'a continuous propaganda of extreme Republican doctrines, incitements to rebellion, and the enrolment, for seditious purposes, of young men who, owing to the non-application of compulsory military service, were available in Ireland in large numbers' and cited extracts from de Valera's seditious speeches. Duke argued that the logical consequence of the cabinet's approving his speech was the immediate arrest of de Valera and the prosecution of between fifty and a hundred others under the Defence of the Realm Act.

The war cabinet, impatient with Duke's agonising, was dismissive: 'the Irish question was so small a matter in relation to the vast problems with which the Government was confronted, when the situation was viewed as a whole, that it might be undesirable to pay too much attention to it, particularly if it would involve this country in serious difficulties', the worst of which was 'the effect of a drastic policy in the United States of America'. Such apprehensions about American perceptions coloured the decision to approve Duke's speech and his proposal to arrest de Valera and prosecute whomever else he deemed necessary, subject to the Department of Information immediately telegraphing the substance of his speech, and, in particular, the seditious extracts from de Valera's speeches, to the United States.[40] But Duke shrank from grasping the nettle and, after consulting his principal advisers in Dublin Castle, he advised Lloyd George that 'the known facts and the suspected intentions of the revolutionists would not warrant a whole scale scheme of arrests'.[41]

The war cabinet discussions of October 1917 illustrate how, even on those rare occasions when Irish policy was reviewed, it was subsumed in the larger issues of the war. They similarly reveal that fateful blend of indifference and vacillation tempered with anxiety about the American dimension that characterised Irish policy during the war years. A more dramatic illustration was yet to come. The war cabinet's most prolonged and detailed Irish discussions took place in the spring of 1918 when the only crisis in Irish policy between the aftermath of the Easter rebellion and the war's end prompted consideration of Irish policy at five separate meetings.

Two factors precipitated the Irish crisis in the spring of 1918: first, the imminent collapse of the Irish Convention and, second, the acute manpower shortage on the western front, which strengthened the perennial Unionist demand for the extension of compulsory military service to Ireland.

When Lloyd George had questioned Duke about 'the practicability and advisability of Conscription for Ireland' in January 1917, he was told that 'with a national settlement in Ireland conscription could be applied without grave risks', but that it could be applied only 'without such a settlement . . . at the cost of much disturbance and some bloodshed now and intensified animosities henceforward'.[42] Little had changed in December 1917 when, at a breakfast meeting with the Unionist members of his government in Lord Derby's house, the prime minister mused aloud about manpower over the cigars. 'Ireland ought to be conscripted' but that 'would immediately smash up the Convention' and make 'the normal conduct of [parliamentary] business . . . impossible', quite apart from the distressing effect on 'allied opinion abroad . . . were England to be convulsed'[43] in an Irish crisis. In the meantime, Carson was getting 'sicker and sicker' because the war cabinet refused 'to face the music over conscription for Ireland. He makes his views perfectly plain, and when they ask his views and opinion on plans for raising more men in Great Britain, he refuses point-blank and takes no part in the discussion.'[44]

Both nationalists and Ulster Unionists believed 'that the Government is not really serious about the Irish Convention, in the sense that it regards it chiefly as a useful method of keeping Ireland quiet during the war', Philip Kerr warned Lloyd George; unless that impression were dispelled, 'the Ulstermen will refuse to make any real concessions and the nationalists will simply manoeuvre for position when the inevitable breakdown occurs'.[45] Ulster Unionist obduracy was indeed the rock on which the Irish Convention seemed about to founder; and, on 11 January 1918, Professor Adams urged Lloyd George 'to contemplate the departure of Carson from the Cabinet'.[46] The next day Lloyd George wrote a personal and confidential letter to Bonar Law, saying that he took

... a very serious view of the Irish situation. If the Southern Unionists and Nationalists agree, as they are likely to, the position of any Government that refuses to carry out that compact will be an impossible one. I simply could not face it. For if the Government refused to act under these circumstances, everyone in GREAT BRITAIN and through-out the world – notably in AMERICA – would say we were sacrificing the interests of the War to that of a small political section. In fact they would say we were doing it merely because Carson was in the Government ...

The Irish in AMERICA would be more rampageous than ever, and Wilson's position, embarrassing enough as it is now with Germans and Irishmen on his flank, would become untenable. The Irish are now paralysing the War activities of AMERICA . . . This is the opportunity for ULSTER to show that it places the Empire above everything, and if the little Protestant Communities of the South, isolated in a turbulent sea of Sinn Féinism and Popery, can trust their lives and property to Midleton's scheme, surely the powerful Communities of the North might take that risk for the sake of the Empire in danger. If AMERICA goes wrong we are lost. I wish Ulster would fully realise what that means. I am afraid they don't.

Beg Barrie [an Ulster Unionist delegate to the Convention] . . . to lift his Province to the high level of this opportunity. If ULSTER declines then if the Government do not deal with the situation, the only alternative is for Carson to take the responsibility for running the War; form his own Cabinet; run IRELAND on ULSTER principles, and take the risks with AMERICA. I certainly cannot accept the responsibilities in the present critical situation of directing the War with a great row in IRELAND over the refusal of the British Government to accept a scheme proposed by the Protestant Unionists of three Irish Provinces.[47]

Lloyd George rarely did important business by letter and such a portentous letter to Bonar Law was in marked contrast with his ordinarily informal style of dealing with the leader of the Unionist Party. Its real purpose may have been to put on record the arguments why Bonar Law must not follow suit if or, as seemed increasingly likely, when Carson defected. Bonar Law and Milner, wrote Lady Carson in her diary on 15 January, 'have hinted to Edward that they may not be able to stay in the Cabinet if Ulster is coerced to come into Home Rule; but I hope they will prove as brave when the time comes'.[48] On 14 January Lloyd George and Adams met Law to discuss his intervention with H. T. Barrie; but next day the Midleton plan unravelled at the convention when the Catholic bishops, backed by Joe Devlin, the charismatic Belfast nationalist leader, 'ran amok'[49] and withdrew their support. Although the prospect of any broad-based agreement, even excluding the Ulster Unionists, emerging from the convention was thereafter doomed, Carson claimed that 'it was impossible for him to remain . . . while they are trying to settle Ireland';[50] he duly resigned from the war cabinet on 21 January so as to be 'entirely unfettered'[51] in responding to the deepening Irish crisis.

Lloyd George immediately launched an exercise in damage limitation at another Derby House breakfast with all the Unionist ministers next morning when the newspapers were full of Carson's resignation. Having stressed his fears about President Wilson's nervousness and other American repercussions in the event of the convention's now inevitable collapse, 'Lloyd George paid a heartfelt tribute to Carson's loyalty and single-minded spirit', saying he had resigned 'to devote himself to conciliation, to work for a settlement among the Ulstermen'. The prime minister reserved his bitterness for the 'wreckers' and, in particular, for Ireland's Catholic bishops – 'to be defeated by Maynooth is indeed an added humiliation'.[52] He again denounced 'the priesthood' and praised Carson even more extravagantly at another breakfast with Liberal ministers the next morning.[53]

But Carson returned from Ulster in trenchant mood, insisting that it would be an 'act of treachery' to bring the 1914 act into effect before the end of the war and floating a speculative 'system of federation for the whole United Kingdom . . . let the south and west of Ireland have their act with any necessary safeguards and let Ulster stand out until such time as England and Scotland can be brought in'.[54] Bonar Law meanwhile was 'inclined to favour separation of Ulster and colonial government for the rest of Ireland',[55] whereas Balfour told Carson that he wanted 'to keep Ulster as she is, and to disinterest ourselves completely from the South and West of Ireland, except in so far as it may be necessary to prevent its coastline being used by Enemy Powers'.[56] The triumvirate of Unionist leaders was agreed only on its commitment to some form of partition. Its triad of conflicting Ulster utopias shows how difficult it was for Lloyd George to frame an Irish policy that would command Unionist support even in the war cabinet, let alone in parliament or in Ireland; it also explains the incoherent response when the last great German offensive on the western front catapulted Ireland to the top of the war cabinet's agenda at the end of March.

The pressure to introduce conscription in Ireland then intensified with Henry Wilson, now the chief of the Imperial General Staff, leading the charge when the scale of British casualties became apparent. On 25 March, an 'anxious' war cabinet decided to have a bill drafted extending the age limits for military service to run from seventeen to fifty-one years of age and, for the first time, to include Ireland in the legislation.[57] Irish conscription was discussed again, briefly, on 27 March and more fully the next day, when Lloyd George reopened the question of whether Ireland should be included in the new bill; he also asked if the summoning of parliament should be postponed pending the Irish Convention's final report, which might ease the difficulty of applying conscription in Ireland.[58] 'It might be possible, by introducing Home

Rule, to soften the effect of compulsion in Ireland', wrote Hankey in his diary, 'but every day's delay is dangerous, as the recruits whether from England or Ireland are urgently needed.' But there was 'no decision'.[59] Henry Wilson was more brutally honest: 'Convention is, of course, dead, but these men can't or won't see it.'[60]

The war cabinet wobbled again on 1 April when it considered a telegram from Lord Reading, the British ambassador in Washington (saying 'that the effect in America would be very bad if Compulsory Military Service were applied to Ireland'), and acknowledged that the prime minister's personal preference for 'the compromise of dealing simultaneously with the Home Rule and Compulsory Military Service questions might result in merely stirring up trouble in the North as well as in the South of Ireland'.[61]

The war cabinet's dilemma was pitilessly exposed at another meeting on 3 April when, with Bonar Law in the chair in Lloyd George's absence, the discussion was even more rambling and indecisive.

If the Nationalists were promised Home Rule, to be followed by conscription, they would not accept. If their opponents were asked to accept conscription which was to be followed by Home Rule, they would equally object: while if both Home Rule and conscription were to be brought in together, opposition would be general. In the minds of the Unionists the great point of conscription was that it would imply the maintenance of a United Kingdom.

Government policy, in short, was founded on the maxim that if they had to offend any of the Irish, it would be as well to offend all the Irish or, as Lord Milner, ever the pro-consul, told his war-cabinet colleagues, 'A settlement in Ireland would never be attained unless it was imposed: it should be imposed, therefore, on both sides.'[62]

When Bonar Law and Carson dined with Lloyd George on 5 April they agreed that the convention, which met for the last time that day, was 'finished and nothing agreed' and that Lloyd George should 'try his hand at settling things'.[63] The next morning, after yet another meeting of the war cabinet, Lloyd George spelled out to a larger meeting of all government ministers his 'Irish policy – i.e. girding the conscription bill with the Home Rule Bill'.[64] On 9 April he introduced the bill in the Commons. 'We must press these proposals through the House with all the support at our command', he told Bonar Law the next day, 'on the ground that the military need is overwhelming.'[65] Lloyd George stuck to his twin-track policy despite objections from Dublin Castle and from his war cabinet secretariat; Hankey tried in vain to persuade him 'to take a more conciliatory line with Ireland . . . but the P. M. was quite implacable'. But even Lloyd George, supported by Carson, shrank from making priests liable for conscription under the terms of the bill, saying that 'the priest meant more in Ireland than he did here. If they were taken the women would lose their heads.'[66]

Prime-ministerial implacability was rooted in determination to avoid a breach with Unionist allies. If this entailed seeming more Unionist than the Unionists, then so be it. It was a strategy Lloyd George was to adopt again and again at moments of cabinet crisis on Ireland, especially in 1920–21, in the interests of preserving his parliamentary majority. In April 1918, he pursued it to such effect 'at Lord Derby's breakfast table' that at least one Unionist minister, W. C.

Bridgeman, concluded 'that he is rapidly making up his mind to throw in his lot with the Conservative Party'.[67]

Hence Lloyd George's turning to Walter Long, whose Irish Unionist credentials were impeccable, when the war cabinet asked him to appoint a committee to draft a home-rule bill. Long, who thought linking home rule with conscription 'absurd', was patently surprised at the prime minister's telephone call asking him to preside over a committee 'to draw [up] Home Rule Bill!!! I can't refuse.'[68] There were five Unionists on Lloyd George's nine-man committee: Long, Duke, Curzon, Austen Chamberlain (who had joined the war cabinet and agreed to sit on the committee only on condition that any home-rule bill would be compatible with a federal system for the United Kingdom[69]), and George Cave, the home secretary. The rest of the committee was made up of the Labour and Empire representatives in the war cabinet (Barnes and General Smuts) and three Liberals (Addison, Fisher and the solicitor general, Gordon Hewart).

Tom Jones, Lloyd George's Welsh compatriot who had become deputy secretary to the cabinet in 1916 and was to play a key role in shaping Irish policy from now until 1925, acted as secretary when the committee first met on 15 April. Walter Long set the pace, disingenuously suggesting that the committee's task was 'to produce a bill which would pass the House of Commons'; that meant a bill with 'a federal complexion. With this the Ulster Unionists would accept one parliament in Ireland.'[70] He had been more honest a few days earlier in a memorandum to Lloyd George arguing that any legislation must safeguard Carson's position to the extent of making it 'thoroughly satisfactory' and warning of strikes in the Belfast shipyards and their effect on the war effort.[71]

By 16 April, however, when the Military Service Bill received its third reading in the Commons, apprehensions about its impact on Irish nationalist opinion had intensified. General Mahon, the Irish GOC, reported that he was 'satisfied, from reliable information received and from various incidents which have occurred already, that on conscription becoming law, armed insurrection is intended'.[72] The Catholic Church's opposition would erode the loyalty of the police; and he would need 12,000 more men plus aeroplanes and artillery. The chief secretary, Henry Duke, was also 'very serious on Irish situation . . . Revolution imminent, priests receiving confession – the whole country united against conscription.'[73] The bill, if passed as it stood, Duke told Lloyd George, would 'produce a disaster'; the Nationalist Party would abandon Westminster and join Sinn Féin and 'in view of the conditions existing in Ireland conscription could not be immediately enforced'.[74] Duke also urged that a measure of home rule be passed simultaneously and asked to be allowed to resign as chief secretary if his advice was not followed.

A ludicrously gung-ho report from Lord French – proposing *inter alia* 'the proper use and employment of aircraft . . . to put the fear of God into these playful young Sinn Féiners' – was more attuned to the war cabinet's hawkish mood than the nervous pessimism of Mahon and Duke. French's reappearance on the Irish political scene for the first time since his resignation over the Curragh mutiny and his disastrous tenure in 1914–15 as commander-in-chief of the British expeditionary force in France followed his creation as the Earl of Ypres and appointment as commander-in-chief of home forces in 1916. His report was a result of a fact-finding visit to Ireland in that capacity.

But Duke's forebodings were vindicated on 16 April when, at the close of the debate on the Military Service Bill, John Dillon led the Irish Parliamentary Party out of the House of Commons back to Ireland to join in the synchronised campaign of all Irish nationalists against conscription – a disillusioned John Redmond had died of heart failure in London on 6 March after an operation for gallstones. Never again were the elected representatives of nationalist Ireland to sit at Westminster. On 18 April, when the bill (providing for the imposition of conscription on Ireland by Order in Council) was enacted, a conference assembled in Dublin's Mansion House to co-ordinate opposition. Dillon and Devlin represented the Irish Parliamentary Party; Éamon de Valera and Arthur Griffith, Sinn Féin; other nationalist interests and the Irish Labour Party were also represented. De Valera's key role rested on his election as president of Sinn Féin on 25 October 1917 and, two days later, as president of the Irish Volunteers (more commonly known as the Irish Republican Army from 1919). That he drafted both the declaration and pledge agreed by the conference revealed how rapidly power was changing hands in nationalist Ireland.

That evening, moreover, Sinn Féin scaled new heights of respectability when the Catholic bishops conferred on it 'the moral sanction of a legitimate political party and removed it from the realm of theological and moral suspicion' when de Valera was one of the conference delegates they received at Maynooth. Until then, as David Miller has argued,[75] the bishops had probably possessed the power, 'if not to crush Sinn Féin, as least to forestall the overwhelming mandate which it received eight months later'. They instead effectively endorsed Sinn Féin by immediately issuing a manifesto sanctioning resistance to conscription 'by every means that are consonant with the law of God' and instructed that arrangements for taking the anti-conscription pledge be announced from the pulpit of every Catholic church in Ireland on the following Sunday. The next day, 19 April, the Sinn Féin candidate in the Tullamore by-election was elected unopposed after the withdrawal of the nationalist candidate. On 23 April a one-day general strike in protest against conscription paralysed all Ireland, outside Belfast: shops and factories closed; trains and trams came to a standstill; even the pubs were shut, although not even the strike stopped racing at Punchestown.

Although conscription was never introduced, its imminence brought nationalist Ireland to the brink of revolution. The crisis devastated what remained of the Nationalist Party's credibility, partly because Sinn Féin had blazed the anti-conscription trail, and partly because abandoning Westminster, as Henry Duke had predicted, was also seen as jumping on the Sinn Féin bandwagon. Giving Sinn Féin a free run in the Tullamore by-election, moreover, notwithstanding having beaten off its challenge in the three previous by-elections in 1918, seemed to signify nationalist acquiescence in Sinn Féin's ascendancy, although two of the results – Waterford (John Redmond's seat) and East Tyrone (occasioned by the resignation of Redmond's son, Captain William Archer Redmond, who instead contested and won Waterford) – were scarcely indicative of a national trend.

It was unsurprising that John Dillon should have concluded that Lloyd George's letting 'loose *Hell* in Ireland' was

a Machiavellian plot to escape from the necessity of granting Home Rule and to do so at such a time and in such a way as will embroil us with the American Government and the American people, and make it safe for

England to have a regular quarrel and stand-up fight with Ireland . . . Considering L.G.'s action in bringing forward his measure applying conscription to Ireland hot-foot on our three successive victories over S.F. at the last three elections . . . it is hard to escape from the conviction that he deliberately adopted the policy of destroying the constitutional party in Ireland and throwing the country into the hands of the revolutionary party.[76]

Although Irish distractions from the war effort at so critical a moment deepened Lloyd George's disenchantment with Ireland and the Irish – 'Lloyd George was full of abuse of Ireland', noted Henry Wilson, 'and said he wished my d—d country was put at the bottom of the sea'[77] – there is no evidence to sustain Dillon's theory that Lloyd George was secretly conspiring to destroy the constitutional party; but neither is there evidence that he was other than entirely indifferent to its destruction. For Lloyd George the destruction of the constitutional party in nationalist Ireland counted for nothing when cast into the scales against the crisis on the western front and his determination to preserve the cohesion of the coalition.

Lloyd George and Bonar Law, complaining that 'Duke had given no steady counsel',[78] began the search for a new chief secretary. When Fisher, a Liberal already in the cabinet as president of the Board of Education, declined because he had no appetite for enforcing conscription, they opted for another Liberal, Edward Shortt.

Lord French had meanwhile warmed to his theme of blood and thunder, advising Lloyd George that 'Ireland should be at once put under complete Martial Law, and that a purely Military Government should rule it, under the guidance of the War Cabinet, for at least the next two months'.[79] This was music to Lloyd George's ears, as C. P. Scott, the editor of the *Manchester Guardian*, was horrified to discover when he spent an hour with the prime minister and Philip Kerr, the most hawkish of his Irish advisers, on 21 April. Lloyd George

started right away by saying he was determined to put Conscription through in Ireland. He knew there would be trouble – rioting, bloodshed, but it was better to face all that and get it over . . . If men were to be shot they were to be put up against a wall and shot on the spot, as happened in the Paris Commune. Kerr concurred. The executions after the Dublin rising, spread out day after day, a fresh batch every morning for breakfast, had been intolerable . . .

The question . . . was really one of principle. The control of the armed forces of the Crown by Parliament had been conceded in every proposal for Home Rule and was now being disputed. The right to levy troops was part of the same right and must be asserted at all costs. To deny it was virtually to claim independence. The demand for Dominion status was really a demand for the right of secession, since the Dominions were virtually independent States and could secede at any time they chose. It was better to face the matter at once and go through with it. [Abraham] Lincoln had had the same difficulty to meet and had met it by force and he should not shrink from the same course.

Seemingly seduced by French's bizarre argument that 'with armoured-cars and aeroplanes you don't need a great many troops' to enforce conscription, Lloyd George told Scott 'he was putting French in command'.[80]

But although Lloyd George remained determined, in Kerr's phrase, to 'make the two measures strictly coordinate and force them both through', the Unionists were wavering. By 27 April, Walter Long, sensitive to the supreme irony of his role as principal architect of a home-rule bill – 'What an occupation for me!'[81] he had written in his diary on 19 April – had broken ranks. The Irish situation had 'entirely altered' since the cabinet established his committee to draft a home-rule bill, he told Bonar Law. 'How can we proceed to set up a Government in Ireland when the hierarchy of the R.C. Church have declared war against the King's Government?'[82] Carson, writing on the same day to Bonar Law, was even more apocalyptic: Roman Catholic prelates were 'claiming the right to lay down when the people are entitled to resist the Imperial Parliament' and it was 'evident that slightest provocation will lead to a religious war in the North'.[83] Bonar Law tried to hold the line, denying Carson's bitter accusation that he had broken his solemn pledge about imposing home rule on Ulster: 'Our policy as to the connection between Home Rule and conscription is as stated by the Prime Minister. We have agreed to nothing else.'[84]

But when Lloyd George, 'furious against the priests, thinks English public opinion would applaud violent enforcement of conscription . . . wants the aeroplanes to disperse crowds', clung to his hard line at another divided meeting of ministers in Downing Street[85] on 29 April, Bonar Law disagreed, saying that 'personally he was against introducing conscription, but the Tories would have withdrawn support if he hadn't'.

By now the dual policy of home rule girded by conscription was in total disarray. The Conservative and Unionist

Party was threatening to split apart. The prime minister was at loggerheads with Liberal ministers, with his war cabinet secretariat and with his 'Garden Suburb' (except for Philip Kerr). The war cabinet had lost faith in Dublin Castle and Dublin Castle derided the war cabinet's Irish policy. Ireland was in a worse state of unrest than at any time since the Easter rebellion. Lloyd George, needing an excuse for another shift of Irish policy and in particular an excuse to drop the home-rule bill in deference to Unionist pressure, found it in the so-called 'German plot'.

The German plot had its origins in the arrest of a Corporal Joseph Dowling of the Connaught Rangers (who as a prisoner of war in Germany had joined Roger Casement's brigade) after he landed by canvas canoe from a German submarine on a deserted island off County Clare on 13 April and the subsequent arrest, on 16 April, of two 'Sinn Féiners' in a sailing boat in Dublin Bay where they were allegedly trying to communicate with a German submarine.[86] Ministers made little of this when they were informed on 16 April and, as Bonar Law admitted ten days later, 'as regards evidence about Sinn Féiners' relations with Germany we have nothing I am told that would be proof in a court of law . . . Duke tells me they have nothing except what comes from [Admiral] Hall [the director of Naval Intelligence] and which I am told is not proof.'[87]

It was Austen Chamberlain who recognised the larger political possibilities of the episode in a late-night letter in his own hand to a grateful Lloyd George who 'came back full of fight over Ireland' from a visit to the western front on 4 May to discover that all his 'colleagues except Austen had funked'.[88] 'If Hall has moral proofs of cooperation between Sinn Féin & Germany,' wrote Chamberlain, then although it may be insufficient for a jury it will be sufficient for America & I think for the people & I should publish it simultaneously with French's arrival in Ireland or with his first definite action against de Valera & other Sinn Féin leaders. Such a publication if amounting to moral proof would be our justification & might not improbably break up the alliance between the Hierarchy & Nationalists on the one hand & the Sinn Féiners on the other . . . I think we have a good case & a winning case if we act *wisely* & *firmly*.[89]

Walter Long endorsed Chamberlain's point two days later, fulminating against the German menace and declaring it the 'first duty of the Government to deal with this sedition and treason with an unsparing hand'.[90]

French was duly sworn in as Lord Lieutenant of Ireland on 5 May 1919 on the understanding 'that it is proposed to set up a quasi-military government in Ireland with a soldier as Lord-Lieutenant'. The clerk to the Privy Council, Almeric Fitzroy, who administered the oath to French, observed that 'so far as he defined his own position, he is going to Ireland prepared to carry out the instructions of the Cabinet as a soldier obeying orders, even if the attempt to enforce conscription was to deluge the country with blood'.[91] Henry Duke was replaced as chief secretary by Edward Shortt, a colourless and uncontroversial fifty-six-year-old Liberal barrister without any previous ministerial experience. On the same day that French was sworn in, General Mahon (GOC Irish Command) retracted his assessment of 23 March that conscription could be introduced in Ireland, albeit with difficulty, on the grounds that he had not anticipated the vehemence of the Catholic Church's opposition: 'It is not only conscription now that has to be considered but also a miniature religious war; the after effects and bitterness of which will remain in Ireland for generations.'[92]

The draconian policy won the day and the strategy of sugaring conscription with home rule finally collapsed at a meeting of the cabinet's Irish committee on 9 May when Long argued that it was 'idle, criminal, to apply conscription to Ireland today' with the Irish administration in Dublin Castle 'against you'. Edward Shortt, who had taken the precaution of ensuring that Long supported his appointment as chief secretary,[93] agreed, subject 'to no steps being taken to enforce conscription'.[94] This Long–Shortt alliance proved as incongruous as it sounded. For the next two years Irish policy was more frequently shaped by the bond between Long and French, whose power base was bolstered by a seat in the cabinet. Hence the committee's unanimous decision, recorded in Tom Jones's minute for the war cabinet,

> *that as a preliminary to proceeding with Government policy either in respect of conscription or of the grant of self-government to Ireland, it was first necessary that the new Irish Administration should restore respect for government, enforce the law and, above all, put down with a stern hand the Irish–German conspiracy which appears to be widespread in Ireland . . .* Until this has been done neither branch of the Government's policy had any chance of success . . .
>
> The early introduction of the Home Rule Bill is an impossibility and the Committee were of one mind in deprecating any statement in Parliament, which would seem to imply that the Bill could be taken at an early date.[95]

Home Rule, first postponed at the outbreak of war, postponed again after the collapse of Lloyd George's 1916 negotiations, was to be postponed for a third time with a predictably disastrous impact on the popularity of Ireland's beleaguered constitutional nationalists.

The war cabinet rubber-stamped the committee's recommendation the next day, incorporating the italicised passage in their own conclusions. Although the rest of the meeting, devoted to discussing the wording of the draconian proclamation French and Shortt would bring with them when they crossed to Dublin that night, was inconclusive, it showed that ministers were fully aware of the flimsy evidence on which they intended to base the arrest of the alleged 'leaders of rebellion in Ireland'. General Smuts, for example, warned that the government would be discredited 'if they made a great deal of pro-German activities in Ireland, and then found out that the evidence of such activities was not very considerable or convincing'. But Bonar Law cynically swept aside such niceties: 'even if the evidence were complete, there would be no public trial [necessary under the Defence of the Realm Act], and the public would not know what evidence was in the possession of the Government'. Lloyd George yet again was less concerned with British opinion than with what, in Austen Chamberlain's phrase, would 'be sufficient for America'. He wanted a reference in the proclamation 'not only to the Empire, but also to the Allies, as the Proclamation would be published in the States . . . the Sinn Féiners were entering into treasonable relations not only with the enemies of England, but with the enemies of the United States, France and Belgium'.[96]

Such considerations again loomed large on the evening of 22 May when, most unusually, a meeting of the war cabinet was exclusively devoted to Irish policy – specifically, to discussing with Long and Shortt the terms of the announcement justifying the arrest and deportation without trial to British gaols of 73 Sinn Féin leaders, including Éamon de Valera, Arthur Griffith and W. T. Cosgrave. Smuts was the first to cast doubt on 'the adequacy of the evidence' presented by Shortt. Curzon followed, noting 'that the last evidence of communications between the German Government and the Sinn Féiners was more than a year old', and asking 'whether the Government were not exposing themselves to the charge that they had had this information for more than a year and had not prosecuted'. The arrests were carried out under a regulation (14B) of the Defence of the Realm Act providing for the detention of 'persons who are under suspicion of acting in a manner prejudicial to public safety', but there was no question of preferring 'definite charges against the individual persons who have been interned'.[97]

Although the war cabinet was unwilling to recommend any prosecutions, not even in the case of de Valera, which was specifically discussed, for Lloyd George and Long the issue was not whether but how the arrests could best be justified. But when the prime minister called in the director of Naval Intelligence, Admiral Hall, Curzon remained unconvinced, pointing out that Hall's statement 'provided ample evidence of German designs but not of Sinn Féin complicity'. The meeting ended with ministers struggling to reassure themselves with a conclusion as pompous as it was disingenuous: that, if they had not acted, 'an impeachment might well have been made out against them'. This was accompanied by an acknowledgement that 'the case required most careful presentation to the public'.[98]

An exchange of telegrams between Walter Long and Lord Reading, the British ambassador in Washington, confirms that the American dimension dictated British policy throughout the conscription crisis. Long wanted Reading to leave no stone unturned in his efforts to persuade President Woodrow Wilson that evidence of the German plot should first be published not in Britain but in the United States and the arrests were postponed for a day while a telegraphic reply from Washington was awaited. Although Reading's efforts were in vain, it is the attempt rather than its failure that is significant.[99]

The way was now clear for a draconian policy in Ireland. French in Dublin, supported in London by Long, who was used by Lloyd George as the war cabinet's go-between with Dublin Castle, pursued a policy that appealed to the majority at Westminster and in Britain. That policy was confirmed when its Irish committee finally interred the dual policy in a report on 14 June, which concluded that,

> . . . in view of the new information which has come into the possession of the Government as to the disturbed state of Ireland and as to the effects of priestly denunciations upon the police, that the immediate enforcement of conscription is impossible . . . The same circumstances destroy for the time being the chance of any agreed settlement of the Irish Government. The lawlessness which prevents conscription is itself the strongest argument against the establishment of a Government dependent on the support of a population so utterly out of hand . . .
>
> In view of the fact that no Bill can be introduced at present it seems highly undesirable without further instructions to continue the meetings of the Committee which lead the public to believe that a Bill will shortly be introduced.[100]

And so it was that Walter Long initialled the death sentence on yet another alleged and abortive attempt to introduce home rule. The war cabinet duly executed that sentence on 19 June but publicly pretended they had not done so by instructing their spokesman, Curzon, to base his speech 'on the assumption that the dual policy had not been abandoned, although the Government must be judge of the time and method of its application'.[101]

The conscription crisis epitomises the impact of the Great War on Britain's Irish policy. It provides the classic example of how that policy wobbled and wavered with the ebb and flow of war, of how it was utterly indifferent to how it benefited Sinn Féin and disadvantaged Ireland's constitutional nationalists, of how it was shaped by the need to nurture Anglo-American relations rather than by any intrinsic concern for harmony in Anglo-Irish relations, by the pursuit of victory on the western front rather than by any ambition to resolve the Irish question.

It was the war that put home rule on ice; it was the war that restored the Unionists to office; it was the war that demanded the executions after the Easter rebellion and that then, and again in 1918, dictated internment without trial, thus empowering Sinn Féin and the Irish Volunteers while destroying the Irish Parliamentary Party; it was the war that conceived, brought forth and nourished the 'terrible beauty' of Yeats's 'Easter 1916'.

'I have no belief in my power of getting any man's ear. Who listens to men of my trade?' wrote Yeats to Lord Haldane in the dying days of the Great War. Yet it is that same letter of Yeats that best captures the intangible but incalculable consequences of the conscription crisis for the course of Anglo-Irish relations.

If conscription is imposed upon Ireland it will be neither imposed nor met in cold blood. I have just been speaking to a man who said to an officer this morning, 'Why do you want conscription with the war nearly at an end?' And the officer had replied, 'We want the charm of teaching these people a lesson.' He went on to explain that a barber at Kingstown had refused to shave him, and the refusal of that barber may yet cause some man's death. There will be incidents that become anecdotes and legends according to whether they are told by the educated or by the poor, and the legends of the poor never die. Each side will have its wrongs to tell of and these will keep England and Ireland apart during your lifetime and mine. England will forget the anecdotes in a few years but the legends will never be forgotten.[102]

8

1919: French Leave

The Great War precipitated the progressive, although subterranean, erosion of Britain's commitment to the Union with Ireland; this was linked to the collapse of the old world order and the emergence of the United States as a global power. Henceforth the British perspective on Ireland had to take account of the Anglo-American alliance, and to reconcile the American ideological commitment to self-determination, embodied in Woodrow Wilson's '14 Points', with its Irish policy. While the Government of Ireland Act placed on the statute book in 1914 embodied self-determination for Irish nationalists, it had signally failed to do so for Ulster's Unionists, notwithstanding the assurance embodied in the Suspensory Act that their position be reconsidered after the war. The phenomenon of coalition government, as we have seen, accelerated the momentum towards partition and the likelihood of self-determination for Unionist Ulster. One measure of how the erosion of Unionism even within the Conservative and Unionist Party was the response to a questionnaire circulated by Conservative Central Office to its district agents throughout Britain at the time of the abortive home-rule initiative in April 1918. There were three questions:

1 Whether Unionist feeling was hostile to any home-rule proposal?

2 Whether it was felt that, provided Ulster was properly safeguarded, such proposals should be entertained?

3 Whether a home-rule measure would be more acceptable if it were consistent 'with the application of the federal principle to all parts of the United Kingdom'?

The answers showed that 'the one thing on which all are united is that in any home-rule proposal the safeguarding of Ulster is essential'; they also showed that many British Unionists viewed the introduction of home rule with equanimity and had no interest in the federal principle. The opinion of a Mr Box, the agent for north-east Yorkshire, was not untypical: 'Settlement of the question would be welcomed – people sick of the Irish question. Safeguards for Ulster insisted upon. Present time considered inopportune. Federal question not considered.'[1]

This shift in Tory attitudes to the Union with Ireland eased Bonar Law's role in helping Lloyd George cobble together the published letter constituting the coalition's election manifesto in November 1918. The letter, devised by Lloyd George to stitch the Unionists into the coalition, and ostensibly from Lloyd George to Bonar Law, was in fact drafted by Bonar Law.[2] It minimised the risk of disagreement between the coalition parties on Irish policy:

There will be no political peace either in the United Kingdom or the Empire so long as the present state of affairs continues. The situation in regard to Ireland is governed by two fundamental facts. The first, that the Home Rule Act of 1914 is upon the statute book; the second, that in accordance with the pledge that has been given by me in the past, and, indeed, by all party leaders, I can support no settlement which would involve the forcible coercion of Ulster.[3]

Lloyd George put it more bluntly at a luncheon with Edwin Montagu and Churchill: 'he was a Home Ruler, that Home Rule must be given to Nationalist Ireland, Ulster must not be coerced, that this had been Asquith's policy, that it was his policy'. In fact, as Churchill 'reminded him', it was the policy that Lloyd George and Churchill had together 'forced upon Asquith'.[4]

The election results, declared on 28 December, revealed an overwhelming victory for the coalition government, which won 478 seats out of 707. But a more important statistic for the future of Irish policy was the dramatic shift in the parliamentary balance of power between the coalition Conservatives (335 seats) and the coalition Liberals (133 seats). The 23 non-coalition Conservatives and 25 Irish Unionists ensured that Irish legislation henceforth coming before the House of Commons had to surmount the obstacle of what was, in effect, an overall Conservative and Unionist majority. The shift in the balance of Irish seats was even greater: Sinn Féin won 73 seats (25 of them unopposed) while the constitutional nationalists retained only 6; the Unionists' representation, 26 seats, remained much the same. Sinn Féin's refusal to take its seats at Westminster, in accordance with its election manifesto, gave an even more cataclysmic dimension to this shift by ensuring that the Ulster Unionists henceforth enjoyed a ratio of the order of four to one in respect of the Irish representation in the House of Commons.

Lloyd George was now, in the words of his friend Lord Beaverbrook, 'a Prime Minister without a party'.[5] The Tory stranglehold on Irish policy tightened immeasurably: Lloyd George could proceed only as far and as fast as his predominantly Conservative cabinet would permit, unless he wanted to hasten the fate that finally overtook him in October 1922 when the Tories ditched him for one of their own. In the immediate aftermath of electoral victory, this mattered little. But any threat to the coalition's cohesion would pose a threat to his tenure of 10 Downing Street, and Ireland, as always since the formation of the first coalition in 1915, seemed the likeliest source of such a threat. The parliamentary arithmetic hardened Lloyd George's instinct for the bipartisan resolution of the Irish question which had first surfaced in his coalition proposals in 1910 and explains why in future ministerial discussions of Irish policy he so often adopted a stance more unionist than the Unionists.

For the moment, however, any such threat to the coalition's grip on office had been averted by the formula in the election manifesto and Ireland could yet again be put on the back burner. Walter Long, who continued to act as what Lord French described as Dublin Castle's 'liaison officer with the Cabinet',[6] summed up the government's 'absolutely sound' position: 'they are pledged to try and find a Home Rule solution, but they decline to move in this direction at present owing to the condition of the country'.[7]

Once the election was out of the way the priority was peace in Europe rather than 'political peace' in the United Kingdom of Great Britain and Ireland. For much of 1919 the Paris peace conference absorbed governmental energy much as the war had done since 1914. It especially preoccupied the prime minister: in the first half of 1919 Lloyd George was in Paris from the opening of the conference on 12 January until mid-February and from 5 March until 29 June.

Lloyd George had wanted to suspend the normal procedures of cabinet government during the peace conference –

the other members of the British delegation were Bonar Law, Balfour, George Barnes (the former Labour member of the war cabinet who had resigned from the Labour Party when it withdrew from the coalition in 1918 in order to join the delegation) and a representative prime minister of a dominion – but Bonar Law's compromise of leaving the war cabinet in place until the end of the conference was instead adopted. Bonar Law's membership of the delegation was nominal 'since his responsibilities as functional head of the Government required him to spend most of his time in London' and Lloyd George 'practically disappeared from domestic politics'. But, in effect, Lloyd George got his way, because as Bonar Law's latest biographer has observed,

Its absentees left the War Cabinet no more than a rump, and Bonar Law soon fell into a routine of consulting with Lloyd George in Paris, then hurrying back to London to communicate their conclusions to various ministers . . . Bonar Law (usually helmeted and swathed in a fur-lined leather flying suit) made many of these journeys by aeroplane, which earned him the unsought distinction of being the first British statesman regularly to employ air transport.[8]

Although the war cabinet continued to meet in London, policy-making on Ireland, as on everything else, was paralysed in Lloyd George's absence. 'Everything gets hung up while you are away,' complained the king to his prime minister when he was about to return to Paris. 'No one seems capable of taking any decision.'[9] The cabinet secretary, Maurice Hankey, writing on Christmas Day 1918, brooded that Lloyd George was trying to 'absorb too much into his hands. He seems to have a sort of lust for power: ignores his colleagues or tolerates them in an almost disdainful way'.[10] Edward Shortt, when moving from the Irish office to the home office in January 1919, correctly predicted 'that while the Peace Conference is sitting, it will be impossible to get Lloyd George to appreciate the situation and what should and can so easily be done'.[11] 'Lloyd George means to take a bold line on the Irish question the moment he is able to give the matter his personal attention, and appear before the world as the man who succeeded where Gladstone failed.' But, as Horace Plunkett remarked, 'the trouble is that while he is waiting for his opportunity England and Ireland are losing theirs'.[12]

Sinn Féin had meanwhile seized the opportunity to capitalise on its stunning victory in the general election. On 21 January 1919, the 37 of the 73 Sinn Féin MPs who were not in prison assembled in Dublin's Mansion House and unanimously adopted a provisional constitution of their unilaterally established Irish parliament (Dáil Éireann), which proclaimed the establishment of an independent Irish republic. On that same day the first shots were fired in the guerrilla war of independence when the Irish Volunteers (shortly to be renamed the Irish Republican Army) killed two RIC constables escorting a cart of gelignite at Soloheadbeg in County Tipperary. On 3 February, Michael Collins, the effective leader of the IRA, engineered Éamon de Valera's escape from Lincoln gaol; the remaining Sinn Féin internees were released between 6 and 10 March. On 1 April de Valera was elected president of Dáil Éireann but the Sinn Féin delegation sent by the Dáil to Paris to seek recognition of the Irish Republic and to lobby for admission to the peace conference failed to achieve either objective. On 4 April, Collins, now also the Dáil's minister of finance, launched the first national loan to bankroll a revolutionary war, and on 1 June, de Valera left Ireland for the United States where he spent the next eighteen months garnering financial and political support.

The IRA's initial focus in what is known either as the 'War of Independence' or the 'Anglo-Irish War' of 1919–21 was the ostracisation of the police. This soon became a campaign of attacking and burning RIC and coastguard stations, especially in remote rural areas, and then of killing soldiers as well as policemen. 'Favourite targets of the IRA,' in Tom Bartlett's words, 'apart from soldiers and policemen, were informers or "touts", a catch-all category that appears to have included the likes of tinkers, tramps, ex-servicemen and Protestants.'[13] Although the scale of sectarian murders is the subject of enduring historiographical controversy, there can be no doubt that at local level, most notably in Cork, the IRA targeted some Protestants simply because they were Protestants.

This upheaval in the Irish political landscape did nothing to ruffle the serenity of a cabinet savouring its own sweeping election victory. Lloyd George's voluminous collection of papers, for example, reveals no interest in, let alone distress at, the rout of the Irish Parliamentary Party or at the revolutionary nationalists' rapid and unilateral implementation of the Sinn Féin agenda. Yet Lloyd George himself, ever the realist, had anticipated Sinn Féin's victory two months before the election when, breakfasting with Liberal ministers in 10 Downing Street, he told them that 'we shall have to negotiate some day with the men who *do* represent Ireland'.[14] But Paris beckoned and that day was to be long deferred.

Paris was a happy time for Lloyd George and Frances Stevenson. Lloyd George's wife came to Paris for the first three weeks of the conference but, once she had returned to London, Frances Stevenson enjoyed greater social status and easier intimate access to the prime minister in her role as his confidential secretary. 'The sleeping arrangements were complicated and revealing,' according to John Campbell, the chronicler of their relationship. 'While most of the British Empire delegation – including Frances – were housed in the Hotel Majestic', Lloyd George had a flat of his own in the rue Nitot with Arthur Balfour ensconced in the flat upstairs:

> They both – particularly Frances – looked back on 1919 as the most exciting period of their long relationship . . . While the statesmen were settling the future of the world during the day, Paris was one big party in the evenings . . . For the British, the Majestic was the centre of this social whirl . . . The Saturday-night dances at the Majestic became particularly famous – or notorious.

One such dance, wrote Frances Stevenson in her diary, 'was a most amazing affair – a most cosmopolitan crowd – the last touch was put on it when Lord Wimborne [Lord French's predecessor in Ireland's Viceregal Lodge denounced as such a "fearful bounder" by Asquith's daughter-in-law] arrived with a crowd of wonderful ladies'. Marshal Foch, the French commander of the allied armies in 1918 and an intrigued spectator at the Majestic, once asked, 'Why do the British have such sad faces and cheerful bottoms?'[15]

The unshakeably sanguine Lord French dismissed the first meeting of the Dáil as 'a ludicrous farce' and predicted that 'these seventy-three devils will soon go bag and baggage over to Westminster'. Walter Long, who always kept his finger on the Irish pulse, even when his ministerial colleagues were preoccupied elsewhere, no less misguidedly agreed 'that the Sinn Féin MPs would troop off to Westminster as soon as they discovered they could not draw their salaries'.[16] French fell ill early in February, however, and for the next two months Ian Macpherson (who had become chief secretary on 10 January when Edward Shortt was elevated to the home office) took the helm in Dublin. Although Macpherson was a Liberal, his inveterate hostility to Sinn Féin was reflected in Walter Long's having first proposed his appointment in March 1918 when Long himself was offered but declined the post. What Long had instead sought from Lloyd George was a watching brief 'at the head of all the Departments concerned to represent the Cabinet . . . I would go to Ireland occasionally and thereby obviate the need for the futile expedient of bringing the Irish Govt. over here.'[17] And, after Long became First Lord of the Admiralty in the cabinet reshuffle of January 1919, so it came to pass.

The Admiralty yacht *Enchantress*, reported the *Weekly Irish Times* on 24 May 1919, had moored at Kingstown [now Dun Laoghaire], eight miles south of Dublin, on the morning of 20 May: 'Mr Long's visit is understood to be unofficial and he is said to be travelling for the benefit of his health.' Long did not disembark but that night entertained Lord French to dinner. 'The Lord Lieutenant motored from the Viceregal Lodge, attended by Mr Saunderson, his private secretary, and arrived at Kingstown at 7.40 p.m. He was conveyed to the Admiralty yacht in a launch from the *Enchantress* . . . At 8.20 p.m. the Chief Secretary and Mrs Macpherson also arrived from Dublin . . . and went off to the *Enchantress*.'

Where Winston Churchill had used 'the sweetest of all the sweets of office' to entertain his cabinet colleagues on cruises around the Mediterranean, Walter Long used it as his mobile headquarters for the governance of Ireland. But few *Irish Times* readers would have guessed that these four men –

Long, French, Saunderson and Macpherson – were master-minding the campaign for the defeat of Sinn Féin and the IRA. Long, whose protégé John Taylor, the assistant under-secretary in Dublin Castle, had become the 'dominant force' in the Irish administration since January 1919, had also per-suaded French to appoint Saunderson as his private secretary. Saunderson was the son of Long's predecessor as leader of the Irish Unionist MPs, Colonel Edward Saunderson, and, as Eunan O'Halpin has observed, 'distrusted all Catholics on principle. As private secretary he was able to steer French away from political conciliation, and he brought him into close contact with leading Ulster unionists. Saunderson also kept Long privately informed of the affairs of the administra-tion.'[18] The commonest cause of friction between Lord Lieu-tenant and chief secretary, moreover, was absent because both French and Macpherson had seats in Lloyd George's 1919 cabinet. Indeed Macpherson soon admitted to Lloyd George that his regime was being compared to those of Balfour and Forster – the sobriquets of Bloody Balfour and Buckshot Forster had been bywords for coercion in the 1880s – and apologised if his own policies were embarrassing the prime minister at the Paris peace conference.[19] The diaries of Lord Riddell suggest Macpherson need not have worried. Riddell, the chairman of the *News of the World* and the liaison officer between the British delegation and the press at Paris and other conferences, was one of Lloyd George's closest confidants, a regular golfing partner and companion at Sunday luncheons. Yet his diaries disclose no references whatever to the deterio-rating condition of Ireland in the first half of 1919, just a soli-tary Irish reference to Lloyd George's amusing Balfour during a Sunday stroll about the grounds of Fontainebleau with the revelation that Balfour's 'insolent' method of treating the Irish

Parliamentary Party when Lloyd George first entered the House of Commons in 1890 'interested me immensely'.[20]

But the arrival in Paris on 11 April of a three-man American Commission on Irish Independence did cause embarrassment. The commission had been appointed by an Irish-American umbrella group (the Irish Race Convention) after a stormy meeting with President Woodrow Wilson, who refused to press Ireland's right to self-determination, saying that the Irish question was a domestic British problem in which he could not interfere. But Wilson suppressed his initial instincts 'to tell the Irish-Americans "to go to hell"'[21] and, 'in order to help the President' with the Irish vote in America, Lloyd George agreed to the 'three accursed Americans' travelling to Ireland 'to study the situation on the spot'.[22]

The commission's mission in Ireland, from 3 to 12 May, infuriated French and Macpherson, who complained to Lloyd George that it 'has revived the prestige of Sinn Féin, has bewildered the loyalists and has given your enemies good ground upon which to attack your administration'.[23] Outrage at republican bravado during the commission's visit, such as the meeting of Dáil Éireann on 9 May, the last occasion when the deputies of the first Dáil had the temerity to meet in public session, prompted Macpherson, backed by Austen Chamberlain, to advise the war cabinet to proclaim Sinn Féin an illegal organisation. Liberal ministers, headed by Fisher, demurred. Bonar Law, in the chair in Lloyd George's absence in Paris, postponed a decision; he acknowledged that Macpherson had been appointed on the basis 'that the Cabinet gave him a free hand' but feared the repercussions of 'suppressing an organisation which represented a great part of the South of Ireland'.[24] Bonar Law took up the matter twice with Macpherson in the next forty-eight hours, writing to him in his own hand saying that Carson shared his reservations and seeking to talk to him before he 'definitely recommend[ed] the proclamation of Sinn Féin to the Cabinet'.[25] But Macpherson and French persisted and urged that Sinn Féin and all related bodies – the Sinn Féin organisation, the Sinn Féin clubs, the Irish Volunteers, Cumann na mBán (established in 1914 as the Irish republican women's auxiliary corps to the Irish Volunteers) and the Gaelic League – in effect the core of political life in nationalist Ireland, be proclaimed illegal.[26]

It was a pivotal moment in the evolution of the hardline policy and Bonar Law clearly recognised it as such. He advised the absent Lloyd George that

> we are coming up against another division about Ireland
> . . . I do not wish the question to be raised in the Cabinet
> till you have had an opportunity of considering it for you
> know that every Cabinet is too inclined to jump at what
> they call 'the strong line'. I spoke to Carson about it and
> . . . he was inclined to take my own view which is that
> to proclaim Sinn Féin means in effect putting an end to
> the whole political life of Southern Ireland and that we
> should find that it could not be effectively done.[27]

Walter Long pressed 'the strong line'[28] on Lloyd George from the *Enchantress* and, although lavish in his praise of the French–Macpherson regime, also urged root-and-branch reform of the RIC. Long's influence on French was immense: French and Long, Richard Holmes, French's biographer has written, 'were birds of a feather: their robust friendship was cemented by a mutual interest in horseflesh and it survived even the trials of Ireland'.[29] 'I like Walter Long's idea to employ some discharged soldiers in the RIC,'[30] wrote French to Macpherson, a proposal foreshadowing the transformation of the RIC (already ostracised by Sinn Féin's supporters) into the notorious Black and Tans.

Liberal ministers, apprehensive about the draconian drift in Irish policy, also sought the prime minister's ear. Shortt, Fisher and Addison, reported Tom Jones, were 'very concerned about the state of Ireland and disturbed at the suggestion that Sinn Féin be "proclaimed". They recognise that no constructive policy can be developed in the P.M.'s absence but they don't want the pitch queered in the meantime.'[31] But the hardliners had the edge because Lloyd George, unlike Bonar Law and Carson, gave carte blanche to Dublin Castle. When Bonar Law went to Paris for the signing of the Versailles Treaty, the decision sent by telegram after he talked to Lloyd George was that they declined 'to oppose the view of the Irish Government in this matter as long as the latter think it is the only possible way of dealing with the question'.[32] Even Erskine Childers, a member of the Sinn Féin mission vainly seeking access to the peace conference, recognised the diehard mood of the British delegation: 'Partition and devolution seem to be their only ideas,' he concluded after meeting Philip Kerr and Lionel Curtis who had 'the official view of Ireland as a stab-in-the-dark rebellious province which didn't help us in the war'.[33]

'D. hates returning home,'[34] wrote Frances Stevenson, on 29 June, the day the prime minister came back from Paris to be wreathed with laurels, literally by the public and metaphorically by the House of Commons. He was in no mood to abandon his strategy of giving French and the hardliners in Dublin Castle a free hand, despite warnings about the implications for Anglo-American relations. 'It is impossible to exaggerate the harm which is being done by the Irish situation,'[35] reported William Wiseman, the British consul general in New York to the British delegation in Paris, after de Valera arrived in the United States to campaign for the recognition of the Irish Republic. French pressed on undaunted and the Order proclaiming as illegal Sinn Féin, the Irish Volunteers and kindred republican organisations was duly issued on 4 July. Next day a fatigued but indifferent Lloyd George left London for a fortnight's holiday in Criccieth, north Wales.

But the delights of France in 1919 were not yet exhausted and from 20 August until mid-September Lloyd George took a house near Deauville, found for him by Lord Riddell. The party comprised ministers and initially included both the prime minister's wife and his confidential secretary.

The hardline policy emanating from Dublin Castle was not only politically bankrupt, it was militarily ineffective. On 30 July 1919 the 'Squad', a hand-picked team of IRA assassins working directly to Michael Collins, killed a detective working for the 'G' Division of the Dublin Metropolitan Police, the first shots in their attack on the heart of the British intelligence system in Dublin. In August there were eleven attacks on police and the RIC's inspector general recognised a 'deliberate campaign to break the morale of the force',[36] which had already necessitated vacating outlying barracks and fortifying the remainder for defence. Public antagonism was not only directed at the police, as a plaintive entry in French's diary for 10 September revealed: 'I gave a garden party at the VRL [Viceregal Lodge]. About 1,000 people came. Nearly 2,000 were invited.'[37] But policy-making by proclamation continued apace and, on 12 September, Dáil Éireann was proclaimed illegal throughout Ireland. 'For the present,' wrote Bonar Law two days later in response to an inquiry from the king, 'the policy of His Majesty's Government must be what it has been throughout . . . supporting the Irish Government in taking whatever measures they think necessary to secure orderly Government in Ireland.'[38]

In September 1919, with the Home Rule Act of 1914 due to come into force once the last of the peace treaties had been ratified, the Irish horizon of His Majesty's ministers could no longer be confined to orderly government. 'Find out . . . the exact terms of the Home Rule Act,' instructed the cabinet secretary, Maurice Hankey, from France. 'The point I want to get at is how soon after the ratification of Peace it comes into force if no action is taken.'[39] The 1914 act could not be allowed come into force because it made no provision for the exclusion of Ulster and breached the commitment in the 1918 election manifesto not to coerce Ulster. The first serious review of constitutional policy since the outbreak of the Great War now began only because it could no longer be postponed.

Whereas the main principle of the bills introduced in 1886, 1893 and 1912 had been to provide home rule for Ireland, the main principle of the new bill was to provide separate treatment for Ulster. Ambiguities were at an end and the momentum down the partitionist path was now irresistible. On 23 September 1919, at lunch with Lord French in Downing Street, Lloyd George led the way, arguing that Ireland's 'three southern provinces should be together under one parliament'; he arranged for French and Macpherson to see him alone immediately before the cabinet 'on Irish matters' scheduled for 25 September. It was richly appropriate that when, on leaving Downing Street, French called on his old friend Henry Wilson, the *éminence grise* of the Curragh mutiny, and told him that the prime minister had agreed to accept the freedom of Belfast, 'Henry . . . was delighted.'[40]

1 Herbert Henry Asquith, prime minister 1908–16, in 1915 when the Great War had enabled him to do what he always wanted to do about Ireland: nothing.

2 Augustine Birrell, chief secretary for Ireland 1907–16: 'I crossed that odious Irish Channel . . . because the Prime Minister of the day asked me to do so. I expect most, if not all my predecessors, would have given the same answer.'

3 Asquith and Birrell (seated on either side of Mrs Asquith) in Ireland, 1912.

4 Andrew Bonar Law and Edward Carson at the Balmoral demonstration that launched the Ulster Unionist campaign against the third Home Rule Bill, 9 April 1912.

5 The Ulster Volunteer Force parade at Balmoral, Belfast, 27 September 1913, after the Ulster Unionist Council had established a provisional government.

6 John Redmond at a meeting of Irish National Volunteers, 1914.

7 Dublin in ruins after British artillery had shelled republican positions during the 1916 rebellion. Nelson Pillar, which was unscathed but was destroyed by the IRA in 1966, is in the background.

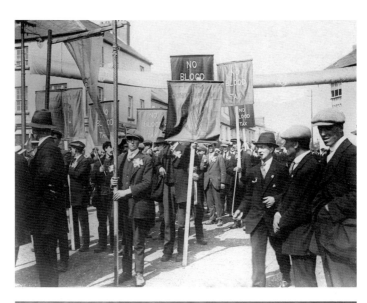

8 An anti-conscription meeting at Ballaghaderreen, County Roscommon, May 1918.

9 Coercion: Ian Macpherson, chief secretary 1919–20, and Lord French, Lord Lieutenant 1918–21, who directed Dublin Castle's repressive regime of 1919–20.

In Sacred Memory of

THE

BRITISH

OFFICERS

WHO WERE BRUTALLY MURDERED IN IRELAND.

on Sunday November 21st. 1920.

They died for their Country.

PROGRAMME of the

Funeral Procession

on Friday November 26th. 1920.

10 Conciliation: the team of British officials seconded to Dublin Castle in 1920 who paved the way for opening negotiations with Sinn Féin; seated, from left to right, are Geoffrey Whiskard, Andy Cope, John Anderson and Mark Sturgis.

11 Funeral programme for the intelligence officers killed on the orders of Michael Collins on 'Bloody Sunday', 21 November 1920.

12 King George V, accompanied by Queen Mary, at the first meeting of the Northern Ireland Parliament in Belfast City Hall, 22 June 1921.

13 Frances Stevenson, Lloyd George's secretary and mistress, and Philip Sassoon, at Sassoon's luxurious house in Lympne where Lloyd George secretly briefed Bonar Law in August 1921 on his negotiations with Sinn Féin.

14 Prayer vigil of Sinn Féin supporters in July 1921 at Downing Street where Éamon de Valera was meeting David Lloyd George.

15 Winston Churchill and Nevil Macready, general officer commanding the British forces in Ireland, arriving at Inverness Town Hall for an emergency cabinet meeting on Ireland, 21 September 1921.

16 British troops with their horses at Dublin's North Wall during the 1922 evacuation of what became the Irish Free State.

17 David Lloyd George, prime minister 1916–22. His successful negotiation of settlements in 1920–21, first with the Ulster Unionists and then with Sinn Féin, solved the Irish question that had bedevilled British politics since 1886. Portrait by Sir John Lavery, 1922.

The next day French met Walter Long to co-ordinate strategy. Long was the only minister (other than Carson) to display a continuous interest in Irish policy, even during the war years; his influence was never negligible and frequently decisive because he filled the vacuum that so often passed for Irish policy. This was especially true in 1919 when he was so close to French and Macpherson. It now fell to this triumvirate to co-ordinate the terms in which Lloyd George asked the cabinet to review Irish policy. The process had in fact begun on 16 September during one of Long's regular visits to Ireland on board the *Enchantress* when he dined with French in Kingstown harbour, and French again met Long in London on 22 September, the day before his lunch with Lloyd George. Having received Long's blessing for a memorandum on the state of Ireland when he called on him at the Admiralty on 24 September, French met Macpherson to make plans for the vital cabinet meeting on the following day.[41]

Long also fired off a formidable memorandum to Lloyd George on 24 September. His principal recommendations were two:

1   That the Government of Ireland [Dublin Castle] shall be given in public the assurance of the entire confidence and support of His Majesty's Government, who are determined that treason, crime, and outrage, shall not be allowed to continue.
2   That on the adoption of the Federal scheme for the United Kingdom, Ireland shall receive such Parliaments as may be thought necessary. Obviously there must be two – one for Ulster and another for the three southern provinces.

Long acknowledged that his prescription would not satisfy Sinn Féin. 'But nothing short of the setting up of a Republic would satisfy Sinn Féin. Therefore why not recognise the fact and say so frankly?'[42] Long's memorandum and a supportive joint memorandum from French and Macpherson provided the framework for the cabinet's discussion on 25 September. But a railway strike, which began that day and lasted until 5 October, again deflected attention from Ireland and it was not until 7 October that the cabinet appointed a twelve-strong Irish committee, under Long's chairmanship and with French and Macpherson serving ex officio.

Long's chairmanship of the committee fireproofed Lloyd George's premiership against the flames of a Tory revolt on Ireland. His appointment, in Richard Murphy's words,

> . . . guaranteed the acquiescence of back-bench Conservative M.P.s, amongst whom Long was extremely popular; it re-assured the Ulster Unionists, for short of asking Sir Edward Carson to draft a bill – an absurd prospect – there was no one else who would receive as much trust from Ulstermen; and it indicated that the southern loyalists would not be given short shrift in the attempt to find a quick solution.[43]

The committee's anodyne terms of reference, to 'examine and report on the probable effect on Ireland and on the United Kingdom and on opinion abroad of each of the possible Irish policies', gave Long a blank cheque to propose partition along the lines of his own memorandum proposing two parliaments and of Lloyd George's injunction to French about putting the three southern provinces 'under one parliament'.

The other key appointment on the committee was that of Philip Kerr as secretary. Kerr's influence with Lloyd George had grown dramatically ever since he first had steered Irish policy in 1917–18 and he had become what Kenneth Morgan has described as 'the Prime Minister's most intimate private confidant . . . a man who represented the Prime Minister's views to foreign heads of government or the domestic newspaper press, with the merest nod of acknowledgement to the Foreign Office'.[44] Kerr's appointment helped Long to work in tandem with Lloyd George and this was reflected in the committee's decision when it first met at the Admiralty on 14 October:

> . . . that in the first instance they would confine themselves to discussing main principles of action and that when these principles had been agreed upon, the Prime Minister should be consulted. In the event of the Prime Minister agreeing to the main principles of action suggested by the Committee, a Bill could then be worked out.

The two other decisions taken at the same meeting – that the committee would not simply recommend the repeal of the 1914 Act but 'must suggest some alternative policy'[45] and that they would meet for two hours on Tuesday, Wednesday and Thursday of every week – showed Long's determination to seize his chance to direct Irish policy. Although Long's committee took only one decision at their next meeting, on 15 October, it was fundamental to all that followed: they would proceed on the basis

> . . . that there should be two [parliamentary] Chambers, one for the north and another for the south of Ireland with a Common Council with certain powers for the whole of Ireland. Such a scheme not to be inconsistent

with a Federal System of Government for the United Kingdom.[46]

On 4 November 1919, Long's committee presented the cabinet with its First Report on the Irish Question,[47] the document that signalled the most decisive shift in Britain's Irish policy since Gladstone drafted his first home-rule bill in 1886.

The committee's point of departure was

> . . . that in view of the situation in Ireland itself, of public opinion in Great Britain and still more of public opinion in the Dominions and in the United States of America, they cannot recommend the policy either of repealing or of postponing the Home Rule Act of 1914. In their judgement it is essential, now that the war is over, and that the Peace Conference has dealt with so many analogous questions in Europe, that the Government should make a sincere attempt to deal with the Irish question once and for all.

The committee took the view that there were only two practical limitations on its freedom of action: first, the government's commitment 'against any solution which would break up the unity of the Empire'; second, the commitment that 'Ulster must not be forced under the rule of an Irish Parliament against its will'. The first commitment excluded any proposal 'for allowing Ireland or any part of Ireland to establish an independent republic'; the second precluded them 'from again attempting what has so often failed in the past', namely the establishment 'of a single parliament for all Ireland'.

Long's committee also specifically rejected the policy of establishing 'a home rule parliament for all Ireland, and providing for the exclusion of some part of Ulster either by the clean cut, or by allowing the people of Ulster to vote themselves out by county option or some system of plebiscite'. They likewise rejected the notion of a single parliament for Ireland within which Ulster would be given special securities 'against forced Dublin control' either by 'artificial over-representation' or by the constitution of an Ulster committee with power of veto within such a parliament. Their preference was for the kind of partition favoured both by Long and by Lloyd George even before the committee had been appointed, namely:

> . . . to establish one parliament for the three southern provinces and a second parliament for Ulster, together with a Council of Ireland composed of members of the two Irish Parliaments, to discharge certain immediate functions, but mainly to promote as rapidly as possible, and without further reference to the Imperial Parliament, the union of the whole of Ireland under a single legislature.

The rationale for the Council of Ireland was spelled out in an explanatory memorandum[48] 'as a means for enabling Ireland to work out her own salvation'.

Partition, in other words, would be imposed by the British, but the ending of partition would be a matter for the Irish. If, however, 'either Northern Ireland or Southern Ireland chooses to be impractical' the two parliaments would 'be left with full legislative and administrative powers over local affairs'; the memorandum piously hoped that the 'inconvenience' of such a course would 'lead to a more reasonable attitude'. The beauty of the device, from a British perspective, however, was that 'there is no coercion; there is no subordination of one part to another or to the whole'. If the agreement necessary 'for bringing the two parts of Ireland into harmony' was not forthcoming, then the two parliaments if they so chose 'may remain isolated, with each master within its own house . . . The central body may remain a kind of county council or become a sovereign parliament.' The argument was worthy of Pontius Pilate: the determination of Ulster Unionists to remain masters in their own house was scarcely in doubt.

But why did Long's committee abandon the traditional Unionist stance of assuming that an excluded Ulster would remain a fully integrated part of the United Kingdom? They argued that exclusion, whether of the entire province of Ulster or of the six north-eastern counties, 'would leave large nationalist majorities under British rule, which would clearly infringe the principle of self-determination'; it would be impossible

> . . . to convince Irishmen themselves or Dominion or American opinion that Great Britain was sincere in its policy of home rule unless it withdraws its control from the domestic affairs of Ireland altogether. British rule in the domestic affairs of Ireland has been the root of the Home Rule movement from start to finish. If it is retained anywhere in Ireland the opponents of Great Britain will be able to say either that Great Britain is ruling nationalist majorities against their will, or that it is giving its active support to Ulster in its refusal to unite with the rest of Ireland.

Again and again the report reiterated the attractions of 'the complete withdrawal of British rule from all Ireland in all matters not especially reserved' and the need to destroy 'the tap root of the Irish difficulty by providing for the complete withdrawal of British rule from the whole of Ireland in the sphere of its domestic government'.

The committee also insisted that its report was

> . . . entirely consistent with the Government pledges to Ulster. The Committee's proposal that Ulster should be called upon to govern itself cannot in any sense be called coercion . . . The proposal will certainly deeply affect Ulster. But if the withdrawal of British rule and the establishment of a local legislature in Ulster is necessary in order to heal the feud which has estranged Ireland and Great Britain for so many decades, and which is now seriously imperilling the relations of Great Britain both with the rest of the Empire and with the United States of America, the sacrifice which Ulster will be called upon to make in assuming control of its own local affairs is one which the Imperial Government and Parliament is clearly entitled to ask its people to make.

The report concluded by stressing that the proposal followed 'the Peace Conference by respecting the principle both of responsible government and of self-determination' and that it followed 'all American and Imperial precedents'. Withdrawing British rule from Irish local affairs 'takes away the reproach of coercion which is the principal ingredient in Irish hostility to Great Britain, and in American and Dominion suspicion of British policy'. Philip Kerr's influence is evident in these repeated references to American and Dominion opinion.

Some of the omissions from the committee's report were as revealing as its contents. Not once, in the course of some three and a half thousand words, does the word 'Unionist' appear, notwithstanding the presence of such Unionist stalwarts as

F. E. Smith (now ennobled as Lord Birkenhead), Worthington-Evans and Long himself on the committee. Although Birkenhead and Worthington-Evans endorsed the report, they submitted a separate memorandum arguing that the bill of which it was the embryo should not be passed until it became clear that 'responsible people with the necessary following both in the South and North of Ireland will accept the offer and form the Governments necessary to maintain law and order'; they also anticipated that 'the Sinn Féiners will reject the offer with contempt and that the Ulstermen will not welcome it'.[49]

The report was never intended to satisfy Sinn Féin; indeed Long had said as much in his memorandum of 24 September to Lloyd George. But it was Lord Birkenhead who gave the game away in a personal appendix to the report that stands as one of the starker monuments to cynicism in British cabinet records:

I assent to this proposed Bill as affording an ingenious
strengthening of our tactical position before the world.
I am absolutely satisfied that the Sinn Féiners will refuse
it. Otherwise in the present state of Ireland I could not
even be a party to making the offer, for I believe that
if the Sinn Féiners did accept their Parliament, they
would only use it for the purpose of forwarding
separation.[50]

Birkenhead, who had 'inherited Lancashire Protestant prejudices from his lay preacher grandfather'[51] and who had visited Dublin in mid-October when French noted that 'his views accord very well with Macpherson and me',[52] makes a persuasive preliminary witness for the case that what became the Government of Ireland Act of 1920 was not so much an attempt to settle the Irish question as an attempt to settle the Ulster question.

Although the first criticism that surfaced when the cabinet considered the committee's report on 11 November was that 'Ulster has hitherto always taken the standpoint that its citizens were entitled to be in all respects on the same footing as citizens of Great Britain and under this scheme they would be subject to a different *régime*', the cabinet swung behind Long and Lloyd George, largely because 'from the point of view of our relations with the Dominions and the United States of America a mere repeal or postponement [of the 1914 act] would be very undesirable'.[53] Two jeremiads, from Edward (now Viscount) Grey, to whom Lloyd George had given specific pledges about proceeding with Irish legislation when he persuaded him to go temporarily to Washington as ambassador in August 1919, were circulated to the cabinet with the committee's report. 'In Anglo-American relations one comes on Irish difficulty everywhere. It poisons atmosphere,' Grey had telegraphed on 4 October. 'A statement of Irish policy on self-government lines is now very desirable.'[54]

The cabinet duly approved the report in principle and asked Long's committee to draft 'resolutions intended to be introduced in Parliament'.[55]

The next step was to seek the blessing of the Ulster Unionists for the committee's report. Herbert Fisher saw James Craig, soon to become Northern Ireland's first prime minister, that afternoon and reported back to Long's committee on 13 November that Craig wanted only six counties, rather than the entire province of Ulster, to come under the jurisdiction of the northern parliament.[56] Craig's reasoning was simple: the six north-eastern counties (Antrim, Armagh, Down, Fermanagh, Londonderry and Tyrone) was the largest area with a decisive Protestant majority in which Unionist power could be guaranteed in perpetuity. Indeed the argument in the committee's first report – that the nine-county proposal 'will enormously minimise the partition issue . . . it minimises the division of Ireland on purely religious lines. The two religions would be not unevenly balanced in the Parliament of Northern Ireland' – were precisely the reasons why the Ulster Unionist leaders preferred six counties. The last thing they wanted was to minimise the partition issue.

The cabinet debate on the area of Northern Ireland was not finally resolved until the spring of 1920 and in the meantime Ulster's right to remain a fully integrated part of the United Kingdom was taken up by Arthur Balfour in a blistering five-page critique.

> Six counties of Ulster should be out of the Bill, and only Home Rule areas should be compelled to endure Home Rule . . . such unity as Ireland possesses is mainly the work of England . . . she has never, in all the centuries, been a single, organised, independent State; and . . . if she were not surrounded by water, no human being would ever think of forcing the loyal and Protestant North into the same political mould as the disloyal and Roman Catholic South.[57]

Balfour's traditional Unionist clarion call rang with the echoes of an antediluvian past and attracted minimal support from Conservative ministers when the cabinet returned to the subject on 3 December, but, unusually, it provoked what its minutes identify as an 'interchange of views as to the ultimate aim of the Government's policy'.[58] The discussion, 'based on the hypothesis that the policy of the Union on old lines was no longer sufficient and that some development in the direction of self-government was necessary', centred on three proposals:

1 Balfour's proposal of a parliament for the south and west 'but that the Six Counties should be allowed to vote in favour of remaining part of the United Kingdom for all purposes'.

2 Long's committee's parliament for the south and west of Ireland and another parliament 'for the whole of Ulster'.

3 Craig's alternative of a parliament for the south and west of Ireland and 'a parliament for the Six Counties'.

The cabinet first ruled Balfour's proposal out of court – a decision to which he insisted, at cabinet on 10 December, on being recorded as opposed;[59] thereafter, as he confided in Lord Midleton (the Southern Unionist leader at the Irish Convention who had formerly served in his cabinet) Balfour disagreed 'with almost everything the Government [did] about Ireland'.[60]

> While some views were expressed in favour of keeping Ulster, or at any rate the six counties, permanently separate from the remainder of Ireland, the general feeling was that the ultimate aim of the Government's policy in Ireland was a united Ireland with a separate Parliament of its own, bound by the closest ties to Great Britain, but that this must be achieved with the largest possible support, and without offending the Protestants in Ulster: in fact, as Sir Edward Carson had put it, Ulster must be won by kindness; and this ultimate aim could only be achieved by something like general consent in Ireland.

Again, 'Ulstercentricity' was paramount. Sinn Féin's aspirations figured not at all and Nationalist aspirations only in some distant utopia. The cabinet was still wobbling on the issue of six counties versus nine. Although it initially agreed that Long's committee should work out a bill 'for a Parliament for Ulster as well as for the three Southern Provinces', it also agreed that 'if, after the introduction of the measure in Parliament, it was found that the limitation of the Parliamentary area to the six counties was more acceptable, the question might be reconsidered'. Strip away the circumlocution and the real decision is clear enough: the Government of Ireland Bill would initially provide for a nine-county Northern Ireland, but if Ulster's Unionists and their parliamentary allies found six counties 'more acceptable', then six counties they could have. The Conservative Party, in particular, in George Boyce's words, 'could hardly fly in the face of Ulster Unionist opinion . . . Ulster had to be bought off, and the price of peace was the six counties.'[61]

On 15 December the cabinet was duly informed

> . . . that further conversations with the Ulster leaders had confirmed that they were doubtful whether the Northern Parliament of Ireland would be able effectively to govern the three Ulster counties where there was a Nationalist majority, and greatly preferred that the scheme should be applied only to the six Protestant Counties.

They were also told that Craig, in a private conversation with Worthington-Evans, 'had suggested the establishment of a Boundary Commission to examine the distribution of population along the borders of the whole of the six Counties, and to take a vote in those districts on either side of and immediately adjoining that boundary in which there was a doubt as to whether they would prefer to be included in the Northern or the Southern Parliamentary Area'. This procedure was consonant with the practice at the peace conference, 'where, whenever possible, the boundary had been adjusted on ethnological grounds',[62] and it was referred to Long's committee. On 19 December Lloyd George told the cabinet that he had seen Craig who had reaffirmed his preference for six counties.[63]

In the meantime the IRA had intensified its campaign and on 19 December it upped the ante by attacking Lord French, as he recorded in his diary, 'with bombs and revolvers'[64] outside Dublin's Phoenix Park. Lloyd George reacted with what an overwrought Macpherson regarded as callous indifference: 'There was no expression of regret for my friend . . . nor was their expression of sympathy for us both . . . in our difficult task. He simply said, "They are bad shots."'[65]

But the failed assassination attempt on French was an inauspicious backdrop for Lloyd George's statement in the House of Commons on 22 December 1919 introducing the resolutions of Long's committee on what became the bill for the partition of Ireland. He was deeply depressed by 'the difficulty of his task and by the whole situation. I never saw him so gloomy,' observed C. P. Scott, the editor of the *Manchester Guardian*. 'He had to propose something, but obviously he had little faith in his own plan.'[66] Yet pessimism prompted a fine flight of rhetoric in Lloyd George's first major Commons speech on Ireland since the war:

There never has been, and there never will be, a perfectly acceptable time [for an Irish initiative]. There is a path of fatality which pursues the relations between the two countries and makes them eternally at cross purposes. Sometimes Ireland demands too much; sometimes when

Ireland is reasonable England offers too little; sometimes when Ireland is unfriendly England is sulky; sometimes when England has been friendly, Ireland has been angry; and sometimes when both Britain and Ireland seem to be approaching towards friendship, some untoward incident sweeps them apart and the quarrel begins again. So the fitting time has never been and never will be. But it is always the right time to do the right thing; and Britain can afford now more than ever, and better than ever, to take the initiative.[67]

In Lloyd George's case, as his biographer John Grigg has recognised, 'rhetoric was nearly always accessory to action, not, as with many politicians, a substitute for it'.[68] Although in this instance action was intermittent, the speech marks the inauguration of the initiative that finally brought the Act of Union to an end.

Lloyd George's rhetoric reduced all but one member of the House, Edward Carson, to silence. The Ulster parliament, he conceded, had attractions: 'Once it is granted . . . [it] cannot be interfered with. You cannot knock Parliaments up and down as you do a ball, and once you have planted them there, you cannot get rid of them.' But Carson saw in the Commons what Balfour had seen in cabinet – the destruction of the Union – and bitterly accused Lloyd George that where the Unionists 'wanted to stay with you, and where you had no cause of complaint against them, you still want to kick them out as if they were of no use, to please somebody else'.[69] The harsh truth for Unionists was that they no longer were of use but had become an embarrassment because the Irish garrison protective of British strategic interests in earlier centuries had become redundant.

9

1920: Ulster – the 'Fundamental Issue'

Disagreement about the territory of Northern Ireland rumbled on into 1920 when the resumption of the peace conference again detained Lloyd George in Paris; on 5 February Tom Jones noted that 'Long's Committee reserved for Cabinet decision question of inclusion of Six Counties or whole of Ulster in Northern Parliament.'[1] Lloyd George wanted the issue resolved before the cabinet met and he asked Bonar Law to convene another meeting of the Irish committee. Long's committee stuck to the terms of its first report and Bonar Law reported to the cabinet that the meeting, which he chaired, on 17 February in 11 Downing Street, recommended 'that the whole province of Ulster should be included in the Northern Parliament'.[2] But Long himself was wavering. 'People in the inner [Ulster Unionist] circles', he reported after a visit to Ulster, 'hold the view that the new province should consist of the six counties, the idea being that the inclusion of Donegal, Cavan and Monaghan would provide such an access of strength to the Roman Catholic Party that the supremacy of the Unionists would be seriously threatened.'[3]

Arthur Balfour also threw his weight against a nine-county Northern Ireland. In a powerful letter, which Lloyd George circulated to the cabinet before their decisive meeting on 24 February, Balfour argued that 'if the Peace Conference had drawn the boundary it would '*not* have included in the Protestant area so large and homogeneous a Roman Catholic area as that (say) of the greater part of Donegal'. Balfour then laid bare the reasoning behind the Ulster Unionists' preference for six counties:

> If you have a *Hibernia Irredenta* within the province of Ulster, you will greatly add to the difficulties of the Ulster Parliament; you will reproduce on a small scale all the troubles which we have had at Westminster during the forty years between the advent of Parnell on the political stage in 1878, and the blessed refusal of the Sinn Féiners to take the oath of allegiance in 1918; and you will throw upon the Executive at Belfast the same embarrassments from which the Executive in Dublin is now suffering.
>
> If this, or anything like this, happens, there will be no Irish settlement. Whereas, if you carry out logically the principle of self-determination, you need fear no effective agitation either outside Great Britain or in Ireland for re-uniting the two fragments of the Island which your Home Rule Bill divides. Any movement on behalf of the south and west to force the north-east into an unnatural unification will be without excuse, and will appear to be, what it really is, a mere struggle for domination.[4]

On 24 February 1920, the cabinet, with Lloyd George back in the chair, finally capitulated before the onslaught of Long, Balfour and the Ulster Unionists; it reversed its committee's recommendation and gave the Ulster Unionists what they wanted: a Northern Ireland of six counties.[5] The bill received its first reading in the House of Commons the next day.

A fortnight later, on 10 March 1920, a conference of the Ulster Unionist Council endorsed the bill. Carson, who chaired but took no part in the debate, believed, on the one hand, that there was 'no alternative to the Union but separation' and, on the other, that the bill's enactment should not be opposed. Tom Moles, a Belfast MP, defended the desertion of their fellow Unionists in Donegal, Cavan and Monaghan on the grounds that, 'in a sinking ship, with lifeboats sufficient for only two-thirds of the ship's company, were all to condemn themselves to death because all could not be saved?'[6]

Walter Long remained resentful about accusations that his committee 'were governed by any Ulster views or prejudices'. They 'had no communications with Carson',[7] he insisted to Philip Kerr; the mode of address ('My dear Philip') underlined his intimacy with Lloyd George's closest adviser. Kerr spelled out the political realities for C. P. Scott. The bill, despite its defects, 'was the best that could be got from the existing Government. It would at least accomplish two essential things: it would take Ulster out of the Irish question which it had blocked for a generation and it would take Ireland out of English party controversies'. Lloyd George was more blunt: the bill must be passed 'at all costs . . . Nothing could be done to amend it to which Carson objected'. But the starkest illustration of the bill's enduring 'Ulstercentricity' was that even Herbert Fisher, the leading Liberal on Long's committee who, with Kerr, had done much of the drafting of the bill, admitted that 'he had no expectation that it would be accepted by Sinn Féin as a settlement'.[8] But that did not matter as Bonar Law's response revealed when he was asked during his speech on the second reading whether Ulster's parliament would be put into operation if the bill was rejected by the 'rest of Ireland': 'Most certainly,' he replied.[9]

The Ulster Unionists were satisfied. Although James Craig felt inhibited about speaking on the second reading because of his position in the government as a parliamentary secretary (he was translated from pensions to the Admiralty under Long on 2 April 1920), his brother, Charles, had no such qualms:

> The Bill practically gives us everything that we fought for, everything we armed ourselves for, and to attain which we raised our Volunteers in 1913 and 1914 . . .
>
> We would much prefer to remain part and parcel of the United Kingdom . . . but we have many enemies in this country, and we feel that an Ulster without a Parliament of its own would not be in nearly as strong a position as one in which a Parliament had been set up, where the Executive had been appointed and where, above all, the paraphernalia of Government was already in existence . . . We should fear no one and . . . would then be in a position of absolute security.[10]

'The greatest danger to the success of our Irish policy', Walter Long had written to the prime minister on 26 December 1919, 'lies in the attempts, now being widely made, to spread the view that "the Government are not in real earnest, that the [Government of Ireland] Bill is only intended for window-dressing"', and he urged Lloyd George publicly to support whatever French and Macpherson deemed necessary to crush the 'campaign of crime and outrage'[11] in Ireland. Long's letter puts the government's dilemma throughout 1920 in a nutshell. Its legislative policy was in place once the Government of Ireland Bill was introduced, but its security policy was in a shambles. It was one thing for British politicians to reach a consensus on legislating 'for the complete withdrawal of

British rule from the whole of Ireland in the sphere of its domestic government', but it was quite another thing for them to acquiesce in the effective destruction of British government over large parts of Ireland in advance of that withdrawal. Hence what Long described to Lloyd George as the 'double-barrelled' policy of firm repression of crime and constitutional reform.[12]

But the two barrels were not easily synchronised. The Government of Ireland Bill dragged its slow length along throughout 1920 and was not enacted until 23 December. Meanwhile British forces struggled to retrieve the ground they had lost to the IRA in 1919 and to restore a semblance of stability sufficient to enable them to set up the two parliaments provided for in the bill. Their inability to achieve the second explains their lethargy in proceeding with the first.

The attempt to assassinate French in December 1919 triggered the gradual intensification of violence and by 20 February 1920, when he imposed a curfew in Dublin, French admitted that 'we are up against a powerful conspiracy – something more than the "scallywags" we thought'.[13] But curfews did nothing to counter the IRA's new campaign of daylight assassinations, which included Assistant Commissioner William Redmond of the Dublin Metropolitan Police (DMP) on 21 January; Alan Bell (a resident magistrate who was making significant progress in seeking out secret bank accounts where Michael Collins had hidden the proceeds of his national loan), who was taken off a tram and shot at Ballsbridge on 20 March, and Frank Brooke (a member of the Irish privy council, friend of Lord French and a railway director), who was shot in his office in Westland Row station on 20 July. What had become the first of Britain's twentieth-century urban guerrilla wars was, like all such wars, a vicious and

squalid business. French's language about 'a powerful conspiracy' reflected his dawning realisation that British forces
were in fact fighting a war, albeit a war in which they never
accorded their guerrilla adversaries the status of belligerents
but continued treating them as criminals. General Shaw
reached a similar conclusion in his valedictory letter[14] after he
had learned that he was to be replaced as commander-in-chief
in Ireland.

Shaw's replacement was General Sir Nevil Macready,
whose Irish experience went back to the Curragh crisis, when
he was designated as officer commanding in Belfast, and he
had served as adjutant general in 1916–18. Lloyd George
liked him and had even invited him to the private dinner in
Frances Stevenson's Paris apartment celebrating the third anniversary of his appointment as prime minister.[15] Macready's
role commanding the troops in aid of the civil power during
the Tonypandy riots in 1910 and his appointment as commissioner of the London Metropolitan Police in 1918–20,
when he had to handle the police strike of 1919, emboldened
the prime minister to commend him to the House of Commons as combining 'both military and police experience and
remarkable powers of organisation with exceptional judgement and tact'. Bonar Law agreed: 'The Viceroy and the
Government thought it was essential they should have somebody at the head of the forces in Ireland who understood the
police system, and who could in some way co-ordinate the
military and police.'[16]

Macready detested Ireland and the Irish: 'I cannot say I
envy you,' he had written to Macpherson on his appointment
as chief secretary, 'for I loathe the country you are going to
and its people with a depth deeper than the sea, and more
violent than that which I feel against the Boche.'[17] Only his

admiration for Lord French, 'his old chief', persuaded him to return to 'the island [he] hoped never to set foot in again'[18] when he was summoned from lunch at the Garrick to 10 Downing Street on 23 March 1920 and found Lloyd George, Bonar Law, Walter Long and French in conclave. But Macready's anti-Irish sentiments were impartial, for he also loathed Ulster's Unionists. Ulster, he admitted to Frances Stevenson shortly after he assumed command in Dublin on 14 April, 'is the one point on which I am prejudiced, because ever since my days in Ulster in 1913–14, I have always looked upon the leaders of that movement as rebels'.[19] Macready was appalled by his first impressions of Dublin Castle. 'Before I had been here three hours, I was honestly flabbergasted at the administrative chaos that seems to reign here,' he wrote to Long, who copied his letter to Lloyd George, 'especially as regards the RIC we are sitting on a volcano.'[20] The upshot was an investigation into the workings of Dublin Castle led by Warren Fisher, the new permanent secretary to the Treasury and head of the civil service.

On the Saturday before he took up his appointment in Ireland, Macready revealed in his memoirs, he 'had the honour of lunching at Windsor with Their Majesties the King and Queen'.[21] What he does not reveal is that the king then asked him to 'write personally' on the state of Ireland, establishing a channel of communication so secret that not even the prime minister seems to have been aware of its existence. Macready's first report,[22] on 27 April 1920, complained that 'the official machine' at Dublin Castle was largely 'in the hands of one man', the arch-Unionist, John Taylor. Taylor had been Walter Long's protégé since he had served as his private secretary during his tenure as chief secretary for Ireland in 1905 and had become assistant under-secretary at the Castle in 1918.

Macready disingenuously exculpated his 'old chief', Lord French, from responsibility for Taylor's machinations in short-circuiting James MacMahon, the Catholic permanent under-secretary, saying that he understood they were 'at the sole instigation . . . of the late Chief Secretary'. Macpherson was a soft target since on 12 April Lloyd George had replaced him with Hamar Greenwood, well described by Charles Town-shend as 'a Canadian Liberal with an Imperial style of oratory and Conservative political tendencies, whose bluff courage and sanguine outlook seemed well suited to this discouraging task'.[23] Greenwood had only a year's experience as a junior minister and 'Lloyd George thus kept to the coalition's habit of handing the Irish portfolio to a cabinet newcomer – prob-ably because more established figures would not touch it . . . Greenwood, though brave, was not bright, and he was not to contribute much to Irish policy in his two years as Chief Secretary.'[24]

Macready, while 'looking forward' to Greenwood's arrival 'to ascertain his policy', warned the king that 'no permanent solution' would be found without restoring 'in some degree the moral courage of those who do not agree with extreme measures'. Until then trial by jury would remain 'a mere farce'; he also foresaw that, 'unless the Civil Law can be depended upon, it would seem we are drifting towards Mar-tial Law'. Macready's professed diffidence 'in saying anything in regard to the political aspect' was also disingenuous. His political influence in shaping British policy until his final departure from Ireland on 17 December 1922 was immense and his thinking is apparent in embryo in this first report to the king: 'Nothing but the widest possible interpretation of Self-Government will bring any degree of satisfaction to the country.'

But Macready was ahead of his time and Lloyd George reaffirmed Long's 'double-barrelled' policy at a conference on the Irish situation in 10 Downing Street on 30 April attended by Bonar Law, Long, French, Greenwood and Denis Henry (the Irish attorney general) and three of Lloyd George's officials, Kerr, Hankey and Tom Jones.

> Disorder must be put down at whatever cost. If there were a truce it would be an admission that we were beaten and it might lead to our having to give up Ireland . . . the Cabinet would support any demand to maintain order. Home Rule would be an utter failure unless and until order were restored. On the one hand they had to restore order and ensure the sympathy of moderate people and on the other they ought in Parliament to be proceeding simultaneously with the provision of remedial measures.[25]

But Macready was becoming increasingly sceptical about French's hardline strategy now embraced by Greenwood; so, too, was William Wylie, the law adviser to the Irish government, whom Lloyd George and Bonar Law met because Macready described him as 'the one who knows the country and the feelings of the people best . . . of the many people I have seen since I came over here'.[26] Marked out for retribution by Michael Collins because of his role as crown prosecutor at the courts martial after the 1916 rebellion, Wylie had also been commended to Philip Kerr as having 'the best political brain of any lawyer in Ireland . . . Ulster Protestant stock, Dublin bred', a 'Protestant Home Ruler who is not regarded with aversion by the average Ulsterman (probably because he is a great horse coper)'.[27] Wylie told Greenwood that 'the root reason why the present administration of Ireland is so difficult is that there is no body of people (or call it public opinion) behind the administration' and he denounced 'semi-martial measures' and the confusion of 'crime with politics'.[28]

'I am unhappy about Ireland,'[29] Lloyd George admitted to Bonar Law after he had listened to Wylie's views on the futility of coercion. Bonar Law reacted similarly. Indeed Wylie so 'impressed and depressed' the Conservative Party leader that he wanted 'to postpone the Irish Bill'; but, after talking to the Unionist chief whip, Lord Edmund Talbot, Law conceded that further postponement of the bill would be equated at Westminster 'and still more in Ireland'[30] with its abandonment.

In Lloyd George's absence through illness Bonar Law chaired a critical ministerial conference on Ireland on 11 May: it decided that 'all the requirements of the Irish Executive should be promptly met'. The war office would hold eight of the thirty-seven available battalions in readiness to proceed to Ireland; deficiencies in respect of mechanical transport, signal personnel, intelligence and the secret service would be remedied and 'a Special Emergency Gendarmerie' would be raised as a branch of the RIC.[31] This became the force whose wanton indiscipline, whether in the guise of 'Black and Tans' or Auxiliaries, incurred widespread domestic and international criticism. The proposal 'that a special body of Ex-Service men here in England should be enlisted on special terms as gendarmerie to be used in Ireland', Bonar Law reminded Lloyd George, was one they had 'discussed before'; although it 'would cause a great row politically . . . at first sight I am inclined to be in favour of it. It is, however, so important that I will keep back any decision until you return.'[32]

On 12 May, Warren Fisher presented his report[33] to his political master, the chancellor of the exchequer, Austen

Chamberlain. It was a devastating indictment of Dublin Castle whose requirements he and his ministerial colleagues had endorsed only the day before.

> The Castle Administration does not administer. On the mechanical side it can never have been good and is now quite obsolete; in the infinitely more important sphere (a) of informing and advising the Irish Government in relation to policy and (b) of practical capacity in the application of policy it simply has no existence . . . The prevailing conception of the post of Under Secretary – who *should* be the principal permanent adviser of the Irish Government in civil affairs appears to be that he is a routine clerk . . . The Chief Secretary, for his part, appears to be under the illusion that a Civil Servant – even though he has the position and emoluments of permanent head of the Irish administration – is entirely unconcerned with the exploration or settlement of the problems which the Irish administration exists to solve.

Fisher proposed the appointment of joint under-secretaries. James MacMahon, a Catholic with nationalist sympathies, had been under-secretary since 1918 but, after Shortt's departure as chief secretary, had been sidelined by the hard-liners under the French–Macpherson–Taylor regime. Fisher described MacMahon as 'not devoid of brains' but lacking 'initiative, force and driving power' and without any 'experience of running a big show or shaping policy'. But Fisher urged his retention partly because of Macready's argument that he enjoyed the confidence of the Catholic hierarchy and partly because his views were 'more in keeping with twentieth-century sentiment than those expressed by the ascendancy party and the supporters of indiscriminate coercion . . . his advice would be on the side of judicious moderation'. For the key appointment of the joint under-secretary who 'would rapidly acquire the real control' Fisher nominated the exceptionally able Sir John Anderson, already chairman of the Board of Inland Revenue at the age of forty and whose meteoric career eventually was to lead him into Churchill's cabinet in World War II. Fisher also proposed the retirement of Walter Long's protégé, the assistant under-secretary John Taylor, then on a month's leave, and his replacement by one of Fisher's subordinates in composing his report on Dublin Castle, Alfred Cope, formerly a detective in the Customs Service and then second secretary at the ministry of pensions. Another member of Anderson's team was Mark Sturgis, a former private secretary to Asquith when he was prime minister, who kept a fascinating diary of his days in Dublin Castle. When asked how Anderson, Cope and he had come together to such high positions, the insouciant and socially assured Sturgis, who taught Anderson to ride when they were in Dublin, 'replied that Anderson came in through the front door, Cope via the back door and himself through the drawing-room window'.[34]

On 15 May Fisher sent an even more savage supplementary report[35] to Chamberlain, Lloyd George and Bonar Law:

> With the notable exception of General Macready . . . the Government of Ireland strikes one as almost woodenly stupid and quite devoid of imagination. It listens solely to the ascendancy party and (previous to General Macready's arrival) it never seemed to think of the utility of keeping in close touch with opinions of all kinds. The phrase 'Sinn Féin' is a shibboleth with which everyone not a 'loyalist' is denounced, and from listening to the people

with influence you would certainly gather that Sinn Féin and outrage were synonyms. If you ask whether it is not the case that two-thirds of the Irish people and over 70 of their MPs are Sinn Féin and that the murder etc. gang are a few hundreds, they admit this is so; they admit also that the bulk of the population has no desire to murder or be murdered and that its passive attitude is due to impaired morale.

Nor did his admission that the Government of Ireland Bill was 'quite outside' his province deter Fisher from concluding with a critique of its fundamental flaw: 'It seems to have no friends in Ireland. The ascendancy party would no doubt prefer the status quo, plus universal coercion; the nationalists and moderate Sinn Féiners would apparently be content with something on the lines of Dominion Home Rule.'

Fisher's more drastic proposals to conciliate nationalist opinion fell on deaf ears in Downing Street. Lloyd George could not abandon his strategy of sounding as hawkish as his hardline Tory ministers. However privately disconcerted Lloyd George and Bonar Law might have been by critics of coercion, it was politically impossible for them to be 'moved by Fisher's case for a conciliatory policy', but 'they were sufficiently impressed by his arguments for *administrative* reform to give him sanction to bring to Ireland a team of talented officials from British departments'.[36] The immediate appointment of the officials hand-picked by Fisher to head the Irish administration explains why his intervention was such a major landmark in the history of British policy. 'Away with the cant of "Measures not men"!' an earlier prime minister, George Canning, had once exclaimed. 'If the comparison must be made, if the distinction must be taken, men are everything, measures comparatively nothing.' The time was not yet ripe for Fisher's measures, but Fisher's men now ran Dublin Castle and they went on running Dublin Castle until December 1922 when the British withdrew from what then became the Irish Free State.

Although not even the most senior officials in Dublin Castle could dismiss policies pursued by their political masters in such scathing tones as the head of the civil service, Fisher's men were essentially supportive of Fisher's measures. Their arrival in Dublin further undermined French's authority (already threatened by the presence of Greenwood and Macready) during his last twelve months in the Viceregal Lodge, and created a climate in which the seeds of concilia-tion were more likely to germinate. The corollary was the col-lapse of the Unionist-oriented apparatus of repression so long predominant in Dublin Castle at the very moment that the cabinet had reaffirmed its commitment to a repressive policy. The hawks, as we shall see, remained a formidable force: most notably in the 'Special Gendarmerie' under General Hugh Tudor, the de facto chief of police in Ireland and a personal friend of Churchill, and in the reorganised intelligence machinery under the direction of Ormonde Winter who was appointed deputy chief of police and director of intelligence for Ireland in May 1920; but Fisher had ensured that hence-forth the doves also enjoyed access to the levers of power in Downing Street.

'I am glad to see you all back alive'[37] was the prime minis-ter's greeting when, on 31 May 1920, Anderson, Greenwood and Macready attended their first conference with ministers. The discussion was rambling and discursive with Greenwood and Macready expressing scepticism about French's commit-ment to coercion. Churchill ('It is monstrous that we have some 200 murders and no one hung') and Lloyd George ('I feel certain you must hang') were the most bellicose ministers. The Irish attorney general's response ('Substantially, no') when Lloyd George asked, 'Can you get convictions from Catholics [Catholic jurors]?' prompted an inconclusive discussion of the benefits of martial law.

The cabinet had another meeting with its Irish advisers on 23 July, the day after Macready, Anderson and Mark Sturgis had met Warren Fisher at the Treasury and agreed that 'the Government must come out for Dominion Home Rule'.[38] The unanimity of Macready, Anderson, Cope and Wylie the next day that 'no amount of coercion could settle the Irish question' made a profound impression, not least on the prime minister who remarked that if 'the view of the experts . . . [were] known to the public, it would be impossible to go on with the Government [of Ireland] Bill'. Their advice, complained Birkenhead, amounted to abandoning the Government of Ireland Bill and replacing it with some form of Dominion Home Rule. Churchill, who proposed raising a force of 30,000 men in Ulster for deployment throughout Ireland, opposed concessions which 'would be claimed as a victory by the Sinn Féiners'; so did Balfour, who favoured 'fighting the prevailing disorder' and going on with the bill. The foreign secretary, Curzon, went to the heart of the matter: 'This programme of mingled coercion, plus the Government Bill, meant there would be no real attempt to settle the Irish Question for six months.' Twelve months would have been a better estimate. He favoured granting the experts' request that they should 'explore the grounds on which a pact could be concluded'. But it was Hamar Greenwood, notwithstanding his demonisation by Irish nationalists as the chief secretary responsible for the outrages of the Black and Tans, who made the most prescient contribution:

Sooner or later the Government of Ireland must be brought into accord with the views of the Irish people. If by some pronouncement or Conference, or in any other way, you could encourage the decent Sinn Féiners, the hierarchy and the Southern Unionists and get them agreed, it would be a great help. In the meantime there was nothing to do but to increase the powers of the Executive. As a result of such a policy many will be shot and many will be worn out, but even after that was done it would still be necessary to get into accord with the Irish people.

This was 'the first real discussion in his time in the Cabinet of the Irish Question',[39] observed Herbert Fisher, the Liberal minister who had been in the cabinet since December 1916, but the Ulster hurdle remained. The new men in Dublin Castle were understandably unaware of the extent to which the bill had been primarily conceived to resolve the problem of Ulster, not the problem of Ireland. For, as Curzon pointed out, the real 'difficulties turned around Ulster' because 'the price to be paid for Dominion Home Rule was that Ulster was to be left as part of England . . . and . . . the Ulster people were now wedded to the institutions about to be given to them under the Government Bill'. Lloyd George's horror of any recrudescence of Ulster Unionist opposition made him cling instead to the 'double-barrelled' policy and to the alleged virtues of the bill, claiming that 'if the powers therein were offered to Wales the Welsh people would say they were being offered too much'. He wound up the meeting by asking for 'the definite and final proposals of the Irish Government for the enforcement of the law'. Tom Jones's private proposal[40] to the prime minister next day that he should seek a middle way between the Scylla of coercion and the Charybdis of talking to Sinn Féin by announcing an offer of dominion home rule as a final settlement likewise fell on deaf ears.

Ulster again loomed large when Philip Kerr briefed President Woodrow Wilson's special emissary, Colonel Edward House, at Claridge's Hotel on 29 July.[41] Kerr wanted House to act as a mediator and, although the proposal fell through because Sinn Féin decided 'there could be no negotiations except between accredited representatives of the "Irish Nation" and official representatives of the British Government',[42] the briefing was highly significant because Kerr spelled out the two conditions governing the British perspective on any future negotiations with Sinn Féin. The first was Britain's vital strategic interest in Ireland: 'Under no circumstances could any British government agree to any arrangement which paralysed or interfered with its effective control of Ireland for purposes of defence.' The second condition was that the government could never be 'party to the coercion of Ulster in any shape or form'. It must therefore 'be dealt with as a separate entity' and 'must either be excluded altogether from any arrangement with Sinn Féin or it must be brought into the negotiations as an equal party only being bound by its own consent'.

The aftermath of the Downing Street conference of 23 July 1920 removed the last obstacles to the creation of the polity of Northern Ireland. Craig seized the initiative after a summer of sectarian rioting and murder in Ulster. Disturbances in Derry in June resulted in 18 deaths and on 25 June the Ulster Unionist Council's standing committee had revived the Ulster Volunteer Force (under the command of Wilfred Spender. Expulsion of Catholics from shipyards and engineering works in Belfast was accompanied by rioting and over a dozen deaths in July; more rioting, arson and looting in late August resulted in some 30 deaths and the imposition of a curfew on 31 August. 'Dublin Castle appears to be entirely out of touch with feelings in the North,' complained Craig to Bonar Law next day; it was favouring rebels at the expense of loyalists. With Sinn Féin 'already the predominant factor over a considerable portion of the province', loyalist leaders might have to endorse '*organised* reprisals against the rebels'. The situation had become 'so critical that unless urgent action is taken, civil war on a very large scale is inevitable'.[43]

'The Irish, like the poor, are always with us,'[44] bemoaned Maurice Hankey, then accompanying Lloyd George at the Lucerne conference; and, in the prime minister's absence, Bonar Law chaired a ministerial conference summoned to hear Craig's assessment on 2 September. Only three ministers were present and they were all hardline Conservatives – the others were Balfour and Robert Horne, the president of the Board of Trade.

Craig gave a very alarmist view of the situation in Belfast and sought approval for an eleven-point shopping list amounting to a blueprint for the administrative partition of Ireland, even before the Government of Ireland Bill had been enacted. His demands included the immediate appointment of an under-secretary in Belfast, as opposed to Dublin Castle, as the civil authority responsible for law and order in the six counties; that the commander-in-chief Ireland (Macready) should likewise devolve his powers in the six counties to Belfast, and that the UVF should be used as the nucleus of an armed Special Constabulary and Special Constabulary Reserve for duty in the six counties. What Craig wanted, in sum, went well beyond the established Ulster Unionist demand that the six counties should never come within the jurisdiction of a Dublin parliament; he now demanded that the six counties no longer be governed from Dublin Castle but from Belfast. Balfour agreed that the bill justified 'separating Ulster administratively from the rest of Ireland', as did Horne, who supported the immediate enrolment of special constables, but Bonar Law came to the defence of the Dublin Castle officials and pointed out that, 'if we armed Ulster, public opinion in this country would say the Government was taking sides and ceasing to govern impartially'. In the absence of the chief secretary, the discussion was adjourned.[45]

Macready and Anderson immediately threw their weight against government recognition of the UVF, the 'same force', thundered Macready in a secret memorandum to Bonar Law, 'who, for their own opinions, armed against the Government of the day in the early part of 1914'.[46] Disciplining regular troops was difficult enough but a remobilised and rearmed UVF 'would undoubtedly consist entirely of Protestants, and no amount of so-called loyalty is likely to restrain them if the religious question becomes acute . . . the arming of the Protestant population of Ulster will mean the outbreak of civil war in this country, as distinct from the attempted suppression of rebellion with which we are engaged at present'.

Macready's threat to resign if the UVF was recognised was of long standing and Mark Sturgis, effective assistant undersecretary and a sparkingly indiscreet diarist on the workings of Dublin Castle in 1920–21, noted its revival the day after Craig's démarche.[47] Macready's threat worked, at least in so far as there was no recognition of the UVF when the adjourned conference of ministers reassembled on 8 September with Lloyd George back in the chair and with Greenwood present. But, given Lloyd George's 'tacit approval'[48] for the UVF, it was hardly surprising that Craig got the guts of what he wanted. First, that Greenwood 'should take the necessary steps through the Divisional Commissioner of Police to organise a force of Special Constables in ~~Ulster~~ Ireland [*sic*]'[49] and, second, that he 'should appoint an Assistant Under Secretary for the six counties of the Northern part of Ireland'.

A relieved Bonar Law reassured Carson, 'I feel sure that the move about Ulster is right and I was very glad to get it agreed.'[50] The rewording of the cabinet minute betrayed the gulf between the government's ostensible policy and their 'actual motivations'; to write 'Ireland' in pen over ~~Ulster~~ in typescript was disingenuous nonsense when only in Ulster were there sufficient 'well-disposed persons' to establish a Special Constabulary. The circumlocution 'six counties of the Northern part of Ireland' for Northern Ireland likewise reveals a reluctance to admit that the measures amounted to 'what was practically a secession of the six counties from Dublin Castle's control'. The denials of the new assistant under-secretary notwithstanding, his appointment *was* 'a preliminary step towards partition'.

The appointment as 'midwife to the new province of Ulster',[51] the phrase coined by a future prime minister of Northern Ireland, Basil Brooke, fell to Ernest Clark, a protégé of Anderson; Clark had first to say that he 'was not by any chance a Roman Catholic', and was put 'on show' by Greenwood before Craig and the other Ulster Unionist leaders prior to his appointment. He passed the vetting process with flying colours and 'from the start worked consistently and uncompromisingly for the interests of the future Northern Ireland government'. His first task was to organise the Special Constabulary and he relied so heavily on the advice of Craig, Spender and Basil Brooke that, as he admitted to Anderson, the Ulster Unionists 'got the force "practically on their own conditions"'.[52] With the creation of Clark's post in September

1920, as John McColgan has argued, 'The policy of solving the Ulster question as a prerequisite to an overall settlement had taken a tangible form even before the Government of Ireland Act was passed.'[53]

Lloyd George meanwhile 'remained firm', despite Scotland Yard's anxieties about threats to his life, as tensions rose during the prolonged hunger strike in Brixton prison of Terence MacSwiney, Sinn Féin's Lord Mayor of Cork and commandant of the IRA's 1st Cork Brigade. The prime minister's 'present policy',[54] noted Hankey from Lucerne on 7 September, 'is to pass the Irish Bill, establish a parliament in Ulster and, if southern Ireland refuses to establish a parliament, withdraw from the interior, occupying the ports only and collecting there the customs and excise duties'. Although Lloyd George urged his family 'not to be anxious' on his behalf, he was not unaffected by the tension among his police guardians. 'Ireland is a hell's broth. Potas y Diafol [Devil's broth],'[55] he wrote in a letter home.

On 29 September 1920, before parliament reassembled to complete its consideration of the Government of Ireland Bill, Walter Long made another intervention on behalf of the Ulster Unionists in a memorandum for the cabinet committee on Ireland. Having first rejected the mounting demand for dominion home rule, Long urged abolishing the provisions in the bill reserving certain services 'until North and South are united' and instead proposed 'definitely' giving 'to each Parliament control of all Irish administration, excluding finance'. Although he admitted that his recommendation 'might tend to perpetuate the division between North and South', Long argued that 'many years must elapse before such a complete change takes place in Southern Ireland as would alone justify the North in uniting with them and forming a single Parliament. If and when this time comes, the Irish will be able to pass their own "Act of Union".'[56]

But Bonar Law hesitated. He had not yet discussed how the bill should be handled in the coming session with Lloyd George or anyone else, although he accepted that its terms must be cut and dried before parliament met. Ulster, however, remained paramount. He felt the best strategy was to get the bill through 'as it stands with as little alteration as possible without a row with Ulster'. It was impossible for the moment 'to have any sort of understanding with the Sinn Féiners'; but, since such an understanding might be possible later, the fewer concessions – whether financial or otherwise – the better, 'for whatever we give at present would not be looked upon as final but would be regarded as a jumping off ground for further concessions'.[57] Lloyd George agreed, as he invariably did with Bonar Law on Ireland, that it would be a mistake to make concessions when 'the prospects of getting anything in return were so small. Nothing would be left with which to negotiate if the Irish adopted a conciliatory attitude'. What was important was that 'Ulster meant to work this Bill.' The South 'would use it . . . to extort something further.'[58] A ministerial conference on 13 October accordingly decided that no changes of principle should be made in the bill's financial clauses.

Although Long had failed to secure the deletion of the provisions enabling partition to be reversed, his intervention had momentous implications: the principal architect of the Government of Ireland Bill had abandoned even the pretence that it could provide for the eventual reunification of the Ireland it was now partitioning. It also provoked a clear admission from Lloyd George that, just as Birkenhead had asserted in his addendum to the cabinet minutes a year before, he never expected that the bill would come into force in the South.

Meanwhile the 'hell's broth' grew hotter by the day. 'Tudor made it very clear that the police and the Black and Tans and the 100 Intell[igence] officers are all carrying out reprisal murders,' recorded Henry Wilson in his diary on 23 September. 'At Balbriggan, Thurles and Galway yesterday the local police marked down certain SFs [Sinn Féiners] as in their opinion the actual murderers or instigators and then coolly went and shot them without question or trial. Winston saw very little harm in this but it horrifies me.'[59] On 17 October Macready advised the government that, 'if the present state of affairs' continued, steps must be taken 'to regularise reprisals for outrages committed upon troops'.[60] His alternative was the introduction of martial law. Lloyd George was willing to authorise reprisals but, as he told Henry Wilson, he 'wanted to wait till the American [presidential] elections are over'.[61] Tension increased following Terence MacSwiney's death on 25 October 1920 on the seventy-fourth day of his hunger strike and the execution of Kevin Barry in Mountjoy gaol on 1 November (the first such execution since May 1916). Enrolment of recruits for Ulster's Special Constabulary Force began on the same day. On 10 November Churchill, admitting that regular troops in Ireland were getting out of hand, sought authorisation for official reprisals 'within certain strictly defined limits . . . regulated by officers of not less than divisional rank', but a nervous cabinet, shaken by mounting press and public criticism, decided that 'the moment was not opportune' and instead instructed Greenwood to 'do all in his power to prevent houses and creameries being burned by the RIC and the troops as reprisals'.[62]

The RIC's sacking of Balbriggan, a town in north County Dublin, after the assassination of the local head constable, opened the floodgates of public condemnation of reprisals and drew indignant headlines in the Conservative as well as the Liberal press. *The Times*, the *Daily Express*, the *Scotsman*, and, more predictably, the *Manchester Guardian*, the *Daily Chronicle*, and the *Daily News* were but some of the newspapers to join in the chorus of criticism. Members of parliament (including some Tories as well as Liberals and Labour) and representatives of the churches and trade unions likewise expressed outrage at the disingenuous defence of reprisals Greenwood periodically offered to a disbelieving House of Commons. 'The sheer weight of the press interest in Ireland, not just from Britain but from the rest of the empire, the USA and Europe, created a stream of bad publicity that none of Greenwood's evasions and denunciations [of journalists] could counter.'[63]

But for the moment the government kept its nerve. The 'hawks' still held the upper hand in the autumn of 1920, largely because of the perception that they were beating the IRA. Regulations issued by Order in Council under the Restoration of Order in Ireland Act of 3 August had given the Military Authority sweeping additional powers.[64] By mid-September even the perennially pessimistic Macready claimed that, although there had been no 'marked change in the general military situation . . . things are beginning to improve'.[65] On 25 September, Greenwood told Bonar Law, 'The tide has turned . . . the hostiles are getting frightened and . . . the mass of Irishmen are losing faith in Sinn Féin as a winning side.'[66] Macready concurred and advised the cabinet next day of an improvement in army and police morale and an increase in IRA casualties, but he also shrewdly predicted that this would make the 'extremists' feel that 'desperate measures are necessary. We may therefore expect to see a temporary increase of murder and outrage.'[67] The general military situation continued 'to improve', until mid-November according to the weekly reports to the cabinet's Irish situation committee.[68] There was 'some talk of [the IRA's] "fighting to the end", but I think they're beat', exulted Mark Sturgis on 11 November. 'We're on top and I'm sure they know it.'[69] 'We have murder by the throat!' declaimed the prime minister to a glittering audience at the Lord Mayor's banquet in London on 9 November.

Such hubris did not survive the twin British military disasters in late November. First came 'Bloody Sunday', 21 November 1920, when Macready's prediction was fulfilled as Michael Collins's 'Squad' (the Active Service Unit of the IRA's Dublin Brigade) shot dead fourteen suspected British intelligence officers in their Dublin homes. 'Eight were certainly intelligence officers',[70] either part of Dublin District Special Branch (informally established in the summer of 1919 and under army control since March 1920) or of Ormonde Winter's intelligence department in Dublin Castle. British reprisals were immediate: the commandant and vice-commandant of the IRA's Dublin Brigade (Peadar Clancy and Dick McKee) were shot out of hand by Auxiliaries and the Black and Tans opened fire at a Gaelic football match in Croke Park that afternoon, killing twelve. The mood in London swung instantly from 'extreme apathy to almost panicky activity'.[71] Great barricades went up in Downing Street and King Charles Street; the closure of all the galleries in the House of Commons was frustrated only by the Speaker's insistence that the House must first so resolve, and 200 ex-officers were re-enlisted 'to roam armed and in plain clothes about the Houses of Parliament and the Government offices'.

Worse was to come: on 28 November 1920, the IRA's 3rd Cork Brigade killed every man of an eighteen-strong Auxiliary patrol in an ambush at Kilmichael. The Kilmichael ambush,

Lloyd George pointed out to the cabinet, was 'of a different character' from previous IRA operations. The others were 'assassinations'; Kilmichael 'was a military operation and there was a good deal to be said for declaring a state of siege or promulgating martial law in that corner of Ireland'.[72] The cabinet agreed and martial law was duly proclaimed by Lord French in Cork, Kerry, Limerick and Tipperary on 10 December; there followed the sack of Cork city by the Black and Tans and Auxiliaries on 11–12 December and on 30 December the martial-law area was extended to include Counties Clare, Kilkenny, Waterford and Wexford.

Bloody Sunday and Kilmichael marked pivotal points in the guerrilla war against the IRA because they made nonsense of assumptions that the end was in sight. There was no more talk of having murder by the throat. If Lloyd George had learned nothing else from the Great War, he had learned to distrust the optimism of generals. He had, moreover, long anticipated the necessity of talking to Sinn Féin. 'We shall have to negotiate some day with the men who *do* represent Ireland,'[73] he had told Liberal ministers in mid-October 1918, two months before Sinn Féin had even acquired its democratic mandate in the general election. Lloyd George was 'quite ready for a chat with Sinn Féin when the time comes',[74] Philip Kerr again assured one of those ministers, Herbert Fisher, in June 1920.

Fisher was the conduit for Lloyd George's first secret soundings with Sinn Féin in October 1920 when Arthur Griffith, then the acting president of Sinn Féin in the absence of Éamon de Valera in the United States, had asked Patrick Moylett, a successful businessman from the west of Ireland with good contacts in Britain who had been involved in the Irish Volunteers since 1914, to go to London to meet John Steele, the London correspondent of the *Chicago Tribune*, whom he had first introduced to Moylett at lunch in Dublin's Shelbourne Hotel. Steele gave Moylett an introduction to Philip Kerr, who happened to be away, and Moylett instead met C. J. Phillips, an official attached to the foreign office's political intelligence department and then Fisher's secretary.[75] Griffith responded positively to Moylett's report of his three-hour interview with Fisher and, on 18 October, charged him to return to London to try to persuade the British government to recognise Dáil Éireann. Before returning to Phillips, Moylett sought out a number of those he described as Lloyd George's 'immediate political friends'. These included Wickham Steed, the editor of *The Times*; H. W. Massingham, editor of *The Nation*; J. A. Spender, editor of the *Westminster Gazette*; Arthur Henderson, the chairman of the Labour Party; and H. G. Wells, who had just returned from a fact-finding mission to Moscow for Lloyd George. Wells perspicaciously told Moylett 'to tell Griffith to stick it, that Lloyd George might not be ready for peace just then, but that he would be ready in six months' time'. There followed further meetings with Fisher and Phillips and, on 29 October, Phillips told Moylett that 'the Prime Minister was interested in what I had to say and he asked me would the "Dáil" [the first time the word "Dáil" was used by the British] agree to nominate men to meet three or four from England to discuss the basis of a formal conference'. Phillips put his proposal in writing and when Griffith read it 'he actually broke down with emotion'. Michael Collins was also 'delighted'. On 12 November Phillips asked Moylett whether, as a prelude to a conference, the Dáil would 'stop the police and soldiers being murdered in return for the British "ceasing reprisals"'. Griffith's response persuaded Lloyd George of Moylett's credibility.[76] Then came Bloody Sunday.

Privately, the pragmatic Lloyd George cared little about the fate of the intelligence officers killed on Bloody Sunday; '"I suppose this ends all further hope,"' said Moylett when he was ushered into the prime minister's presence on the very next day. 'To which Lloyd George replied, "Not at all. They got what they deserved, beaten by counterjumpers."'[77] 'Ask Griffith for God's sake to keep his head, and not to break off the slender link that had been established' was Lloyd George's message passed by Philip Kerr to John Steele. 'Tragic as the events in Dublin were, they were of no importance. These men were soldiers and took a soldier's risk.'[78] Hamar Greenwood was also unsympathetic and told the king's private secretary that 'he was astonished at the carelessness of those who lost their lives yesterday morning – not one of them had a revolver, whereas he never goes to bed without a revolver by his side and always carries one on his person'.[79]

Moylett and Phillips met every day in Downing Street in the week after Bloody Sunday discussing 'the question of a settlement in detail from every angle' against the backdrop of a message from Lloyd George that 'if the conference was not held while the coalition government existed a settlement would never be effected, as one of the English parties would not allow the other party to make a settlement'. During one such meeting Phillips took a phone call from an irate prime minister asking who had ordered the arrest, on 26 November, of Arthur Griffith.[80] The Moylett–Phillips negotiations ran into the sand after Griffith's arrest for, although Lloyd George later denounced it as 'a piece of impertinence on the part of the military', his policy remained 'a double one: to crush murder and [make] peace with the moderates'.[81]

But the result of Bloody Sunday and the Kilmichael ambush was that, while the first barrel of the double-barrelled policy (pushing through the Government of Ireland Bill and establishing a parliament in Belfast) remained firmly in place, the second barrel (defeating Sinn Féin) was modified. Henceforth coercion was diluted with the prospect of negotiation; the doves in Dublin Castle, notably Andy Cope, sought not to crush Sinn Féin but to talk to them. Anderson best described Lloyd George's modified policy: 'Cracking the whip with one hand and holding out the carrot in the other – he intends to show clearly that war on the gunmen is *à l'outrance* and at the same time to encourage the peacemakers.' The divide between the warriors and the peacemakers in Dublin Castle was stark and the tensions acute and, sometimes, incongruous as when, as Mark Sturgis confided to his diary, 'Our Judge Wylie was hiked off a tram the other day to be searched at the point of a revolver "Come down yer bloody Irish barsterd" – Tudor's Tactful Tough!'[82]

But Ulster, as always, took priority. While Lloyd George was privately convinced of the need to talk to Sinn Féin, the Northern Ireland settlement had first to be put in place. Hence the cabinet discussion on Christmas Eve 1920 (the day after the enactment of the Government of Ireland Bill) on postponing 'any future approach to Sinn Féin until the Government of Ireland Act was brought into operation'.[83] The Act 'might come into operation any time in February, and the North was anxious to get it working at once', Lloyd George told a conference with his military advisers on 29 December, but this would be 'awkward' if intimidation by Sinn Féin prevented it from coming 'into operation in the South as well'.[84] On 30 December the cabinet instructed the chief secretary to start the machinery for setting up the Northern Ireland parliament. Such was the anxiety immediately to give the Ulster Unionists what they wanted that it was even agreed to explore the possibility of holding the Northern Irish election before the election to the Southern parliament.[85] 'The policy is to get the Parliament set up in Ulster, to undertake an intensive propaganda as to what the Act gives in Southern Ireland which, it is hoped, will then be led to follow Ulster's example,'[86] noted the cabinet secretary in his diary the next day.

Peacemaking was a casualty of these Ulster-oriented policy priorities and it was no coincidence that the attempts of Dr Clune, the Australian Catholic Archbishop of Perth, to mediate between Lloyd George and Sinn Féin also collapsed in the last week of December 1920. Although the cabinet's insistence that there could be no truce unless the IRA surrendered its arms was the main reason why Clune's efforts failed,[87] the Ulster factor was also significant; Philip Kerr's response to Clune's criticism of the act's embodiment of partition was that 'the Government thought that the kindest way out was to settle the fundamental issue beyond question now'.[88] At the end of 1920 when the Government of Ireland Bill had been enacted, as at the end of 1919 when it was introduced, Ulster remained 'the fundamental issue'.

Yet although the time was not ripe for Lloyd George to drop the whip, neither did he discard the carrot. Hence the instructions, issued on 2 January 1921,[89] not to arrest Éamon de Valera, who had returned from his prolonged mission to the United States on the very day that the Government of Ireland Bill received the royal assent, 23 December 1920. The coincidence was appropriate. 'So far as British legislation can effect it, the partition of Ireland has been virtually accomplished,'[90] recorded Belfast's *Irish News*. Lloyd George had long anticipated negotiating with de Valera, 'the one man who can deliver the goods',[91] in Hamar Greenwood's phrase. But the status of Northern Ireland would form no part of such a negotiation.

10

From Partition to Peace

The government's campaign of 'counter-terror',[1] spearheaded by the Black and Tans and Auxiliaries, including government-authorised reprisals in the martial-law area, continued unabated in the early months of 1921. Not even the viceroy proved immune to the random depredations of the crown forces. Lord French had sent six dozen bottles of a champagne he disliked to be sold on his account in Neary's, a pub off Dublin's Grafton Street popular to this day. Three dozen had been sold when, on 10 February 1921, 'Neary's place was raided by "Black & Tans" or "officers" [Auxiliaries] – not at the moment clear which – who stole a lot of whisky and cigars and two cases of His Ex's champagne! H E in a black rage what with his loss and the fear that the story will get out – Hard to keep so excellent a story to ourselves,'[2] Mark Sturgis wrote gleefully in his diary.

On 30 January, Lloyd George told Bonar Law of suggestions that de Valera wanted to see him secretly. Bonar Law 'tried to put the subject off'. Lloyd George persisted, saying that Auckland Geddes, the British ambassador in Washington, took so 'gloomy' a view that 'in the interests of peace with America I think we ought to see de Valera and try to get a settlement'. Bonar Law was unyielding and immune to Tom Jones confiding in him the next day how 'intensely' he felt about 'the ghastly things that were being done' in Ireland. Bonar Law responded that 'coercion was the only policy: that in the past it had been followed by periods of quiet for about 10 years: that this was the most we could hope for from the present repression, and that he had come to the conclusion "that the Irish were an inferior race"'.[3] Bonar Law, Tom Jones unsurprisingly advised John Anderson a fortnight later, was 'one of the most persistent opponents of conciliation and had greatly influenced the P.M. throughout'. Anderson demurred; he felt Lloyd George 'was the person really responsible for the policy of reprisals', citing the behaviour of General Tudor who, whenever he came to London to see the prime minister, returned to Dublin 'very much strengthened in his policy'. He contrasted this with the attitude of General Macready who 'had given such drastic orders against indiscipline to the military that they were now, as Anderson put it, "living in the odour of sanctity"'.[4]

On 17 March, St Patrick's Day, Bonar Law gave Lloyd George freedom of manoeuvre to prepare the ground for talking to Sinn Féin when he sensationally announced that he was resigning all his offices on medical advice. But he did not resign his parliamentary seat, leaving the way open for his return to politics at a time of his own choosing. It is difficult to dispute Paul Canning's conclusion that Bonar Law's illness was 'at least partly psychosomatic'[5] for, as Lloyd George later learnt circuitously through his doctor, 'Bonar's plea of illness and his sudden departure . . . were due to one thing only – cold feet about Ireland.'[6]

Law's was the third crucial resignation within six weeks. Edward Carson, having refused a formal invitation to become the first prime minister of Northern Ireland on 25 January, announced his resignation as leader of the Ulster Unionists on

4 February; he went back to 'hold the fort at Westminster',[7] where he accepted a lordship of appeal. Walter Long, intermittently bedridden with spinal arthritis since the end of October 1920 – his stream of correspondence hectoring Lloyd George about Ireland dries up after June – had finally resigned from the cabinet on 13 February.[8] In March, too, Lord French, deprived of Long's staunch protection and 'still a symbol of coercion' – the phrase is Charles Townshend's – 'was retired from the Lord Lieutenancy much against his will'.[9] He was succeeded by Lord Edmund Talbot, Viscount Fitzalan. Fitzalan, the brother of the Duke of Norfolk and a Unionist of long standing, had been the Conservative Party's chief whip since 1913, but he was also a leading Catholic layman and an opponent of the 'counter-terror'. The appointment on 22 April 1921 of the first Catholic viceroy since the reign of James II was a clear signal of conciliation, despite an occasional hitch in the transition. Macready later regaled Lloyd George, Frances Stevenson and Tom Jones at a luncheon in 10 Downing Street with an account of the restoration of the chapel at Dublin Castle for Catholic services. It was decided to 'secure a suitable picture of the Madonna, Joseph, and the infant Jesus to hang above the altar. When the Viceroy and his Lady arrived to inspect the Chapel they found a picture of Charles the Second, Lady Castlemaine and their baby!'[10] Also noteworthy was the departure later in 1921 of another hardliner, Philip Kerr, who had shaped so much of Lloyd George's Irish policy since 1918 and who left Downing Street to become editor of the *Daily Chronicle*; the vacuum left by his departure was filled by the more liberal and conciliatory Tom Jones.

Carson, Long and Bonar Law, the Ulster Unionists' three leading advocates in the corridors of power, stood down only when the Northern Ireland parliament had been secured.

Despite the consequent relaxation of the diehard stranglehold on Irish policy, Lloyd George hastened slowly, his antennae always attuned to his inability to move further or faster than the Conservative ministers who were the backbone of his government. At a personal level he had little in common with the new leader of the Conservative Party, Austen Chamberlain, and Frances Stevenson wrote of how he missed Bonar Law, 'an ideal companion with whom he could laugh & joke and enjoy himself. He cannot do that with Chamberlain, who is pompous to the last degree, & has become increasingly so since he took Bonar's place.'[11] But Chamberlain's personality, Liberal Unionist origins, 'intrinsic loyalty' and 'convinced Coalitionist' attitudes[12] made him a much more malleable instrument in Lloyd George's hand when he finally decided the time was ripe to seek an accommodation with Sinn Féin.

In the immediate aftermath of Bonar Law's resignation, the obstacles to elections, South and North, preoccupied Dublin Castle. Holding elections in the South was 'little less than folly'[13] unless a truce could be first arranged with Sinn Féin, wrote Macready on 19 March to Frances Stevenson. She had a soft spot for Macready, whose private secretary enjoyed a sexual relationship with the general as she did with the prime minister, and he invariably wrote to her rather than directly to Lloyd George, whose aversion to reading correspondence was notorious. This ploy guaranteed that Macready's views were brought to Lloyd George's attention. The alternative to truce, argued Macready, was the countrywide imposition of martial law. Lloyd George demurred; Ulster, as ever, came first and Mark Sturgis, who lunched with the prime minister and chief secretary on 21 March, noted that Lloyd George preferred 'to make no changes until the North has its Parliament and then see what changes ought to be made in the South'.[14]

By March 1921 Liberal Party workers were warning Lloyd George that anger at reprisals in Ireland was threatening his own constituency seat and by mid-April Liberal ministers were complaining about the crown forces' indiscipline and the need for a truce.[15] On 6 April the Bishop of Chelmsford and nineteen other English Protestant prelates and ministers attacked 'the whole reprisals policy' in a letter to *The Times* and called for a negotiated truce.

Lloyd George's reply, designed for 'propaganda purposes both in Ireland and the United States'[16] as well as in Britain, rested on the rights of Ulster. Once the 1918 election had at last secured an all-party mandate from the electorate to give home rule to Ireland, 'the only unsettled question was the treatment of Ulster, and as to that, both the Liberal Party had recognised in 1914, and the Irish Nationalists in 1916, that if there was to be a peaceful settlement Ulster must have separate treatment'. After reciting a litany of Sinn Féin's alleged atrocities and declaring that the fundamental issue was the same as in the American civil war, 'an issue between secession and union', an analogy clearly designed for American consumption to which he would repeatedly return in the months ahead, he reaffirmed the primacy of Ulster:

It has never been our policy to refuse compromise about anything but the Union itself and the non-coercion of Ulster. Throughout the whole of last year when the Home Rule Bill was before Parliament, I invited negotiations with the elected representatives of Ireland, stating that the only points I could not discuss were the secession of Ireland and the forcing of Ulster into an Irish Parliament against its will.[17]

The cabinet was preoccupied by a miners' strike throughout the first half of April and discussion of whether or not the elections to the Southern parliament should be postponed was deferred until 21 April.

'The decision is to let the elections go on,' Bonar Law was told by Tom Jones, who kept him informed of Irish policy throughout his stay in France.

> In Ulster there will be bloodshed, and in the south the Sinn Féiners will be returned without contest. They will refuse to take the oath and the Government will have to decide whether to try some sort of truce or Constituent Assembly or Crown Colony. Meanwhile no General will name a date when murder will cease, and the Chief Secretary has dropped his optimism of six months ago and now talks of pacification in years rather than months.[18]

The cabinet set its face against accommodation when it met again for a rambling discussion of Irish policy on 27 April, a few days after the publication of Lloyd George's letter to the bishops. Opinion remained divided about the merits of seeking a truce,[19] but there was a clear consensus against postponing the elections in the South, partly on the grounds that 'if you postpone the operation of the Act and repeal the writ to have an election, at the same time as Ulster is conducting one, you will lay yourself open to the criticism that this is only an Ulster measure',[20] which, of course, is precisely what it was.

On the same day, Carson launched a missive at Lloyd George from the sidelines, arguing that procrastination would convince Sinn Féin that its 'murder campaign' could kill the act completely and arguing that its coming into operation in the North would be no hindrance to a future settlement in the South.[21] Lloyd George would never antagonise Carson, even after his elevation to the House of Lords, on anything touching Ulster Unionist interests; 'the door to Lloyd George is Carson', noted Mark Sturgis, and 'the door to getting almost anything . . . from the Government is agreement with Carson'.[22]

Meanwhile Andy Cope arranged a 'theatrically clandestine' but essentially pointless meeting on 5 May between de Valera and James Craig, who was in Dublin visiting the viceroy. It was unsurprising that nothing came of it given that both men thought the meeting had been requested by the other. De Valera did all the talking and Craig listened to his 'harping on the grievances of . . . the last 700 years', although de Valera did divulge that 'we can get more out of England by refusing to work the [Government of Ireland] Act than by working it', a disclosure that winged its way instantly to Lloyd George.[23] But the meeting was a watershed because it signalled that Craig had no objection to negotiating with Sinn Féin 'provided it did not hurt Ulster's Unionist interests' and, as Paul Bew has pointed out, 'If "Orange" Craig, a former British minister, could talk directly with de Valera, it became absurd to deny'[24] that Lloyd George might also talk to him.

Basing a truce on the meeting between Craig and de Valera was 'preposterous', Lloyd George told the cabinet on 12 May, the day before election nominations closed. Although the cabinet was split after a long debate, a majority agreed that it 'would be a mistake for the Government to take the initiative in any suspension of military activities in Ireland, and that the present policy should be pursued'.[25] The essence of the cabinet's decision, reported Beaverbrook to Bonar Law the next day, was 'to reject all overtures for a truce during the elections – except on condition of surrender of arms. The division of

opinion was sharp.' All the Liberal ministers bar one, Alfred
Mond, were for truce. All the Conservatives, bar Curzon,
sided with the prime minister. Lloyd George, who feared 'for
the permanency' of Chamberlain's leadership of the Conservative Party, was accordingly 'meeting the whole of the Tory
party in relays' at Lord Derby's Thursday breakfasts, where
he spoke of '"the long tradition and unbroken loyalty of Tory
party" as the instruments with which he would crush out
insurrection in Ireland' and where he extolled the virtues of
'Bloody' Balfour's repressive regime at the Irish office in the
1880s 'in terms of unbounded admiration'.[26]

It was Balfour, rather than Chamberlain, his erstwhile and
still overawed subordinate on the Tory front bench from
1902 to 1911, who made all the running at the cabinet meeting on 12 May, arguing vehemently against any advance on
the 1920 Act.

> Behind Irish politics, behind the moderates, there is the
> real force making for change and that force always makes
> for independence, which this Cabinet won't give . . . I
> want no further concessions made, for if made they'll only
> strengthen the Republicans. The main thing we hope for
> from the Home Rule Act is – not that Ireland is going to
> be better governed but that we've made our Irish policy on
> all fours with our European policy of self-determination,
> and which no American can say is unfair.

Lloyd George concurred. Stick, not carrot, remained the order
of the day: the 'reasons which influence me', he told his colleagues, 'are Balfour's'.[27] Hamar Greenwood, noted Mark
Sturgis, was 'used as the "Stick Shaker" to the last', so much
so that when he put 'a lot of pacific stuff' into one speech,

Lloyd George 'made him cut it out, keeping the "offer" stuff for himself'.[28]

Voting in the election to the Northern Ireland parliament took place on 24 May 1921 and the Ulster Unionists' majority, 40 seats out of 52 (Sinn Féin and Joe Devlin's Nationalists won 6 apiece), exceeded their expectations. 'It would take a very brave man', exulted Carson to Bonar Law, 'to take away Ulster's parliament.'[29] The Sinn Féin candidates in what the 1920 act termed 'Southern Ireland' – who won 124 out of 128 seats – treated the election as an election to the second Dáil, but its first session did not take place until 16 August, nearly two months after the Northern Ireland parliament came into existence.

On 25 May, the same day that the IRA destroyed Dublin's Custom House (and much of Ireland's national archives) in an action in which they suffered about a hundred arrests, the cabinet considered a clutch of memoranda[30] on the general military situation in Ireland from Laming Worthington-Evans, the secretary for war, from Henry Wilson, then chief of the Imperial General Staff, and from Macready. 'The present state of affairs in Ireland, so far as regards the troops serving there, must be brought to a conclusion by October,' declared Macready; otherwise practically all the troops and 'the great majority of their commanders and staffs' would have to be relieved. The 'general view', according to Fitzalan, was that 'now it must be peace or real war and no fooling'.[31]

The cabinet prepared for 'real war' on 2 June when they decided 'that Martial Law should be proclaimed throughout the 26 Counties if the Southern Parliament does not function', which was already a foregone conclusion, but they left the door to peace ajar when they also decided that 'no announcement of this policy should be made at present'.[32] Anderson elucidated the policy on his return to Dublin Castle: after 12 July, '14 days after the summoning of the Southern Parliament, such days being an essential period for members to take the oath – if there is no intervening settlement Martial Law and War will fall on the 26 counties like a sword of Damocles'.[33]

But Anderson and Cope were preparing for peace, not war. On 28 May the American consul, Frederick Dumont, acting at Anderson's request, sent for Patrick Moylett, Sinn Féin's interlocutor with Lloyd George in 1920, and told him that the British wanted to meet de Valera. Moylett relayed the information through W. T. Cosgrave, Dáil Éireann's minister for home affairs, and a sceptical de Valera agreed to Moylett's venturing into the lion's den of Dublin Castle. Macready must also have known of the peace overture as Colonel Brind, his senior general staff officer, was the intermediary to whom Moylett was introduced by Dumont on 29 May in the lavatory of the Shelbourne Hotel; Brind, Moylett recalled, 'had a face as red and as round as a well-shaped tomato'. Moylett met Cope for the first time the next morning. '"We are willing to acknowledge that we are defeated," said Cope. "There is nothing else for us to do but to draft . . . four hundred thousand men and exterminate the whole population of the country, and we are not willing to do that . . . We are willing to withdraw our whole establishment, from the lowest policeman to the highest judge."' His only qualification to a complete British withdrawal was that 'they would want the use of the ports in war time'. Cope also stressed that 'he had superseded both the Lord Lieutenant and the Chief Secretary . . . although he was only an ordinary civil servant he was here to make peace'.[34]

But the copper-fastening of partition still took precedence over peace. A preliminary meeting of the House of Commons of the Northern Ireland parliament took place on 7 June when the cabinet, with James Craig as prime minister, was appointed. It was also decided that, on 22 June 1921, the king would go to Belfast and formally open the first session of the new parliament.

King George V, who was a severe critic of reprisals and 'felt he had not been sufficiently advised and consulted' about his government's Irish policy, was encouraged to turn his Belfast speech into an olive branch for Sinn Féin by General Smuts, the South African prime minister, who was in London for the Imperial Conference. Smuts's 'strong sense of there being a real opportunity of touching Irish sentiment' also impressed Edward Grigg, Philip Kerr's successor as Lloyd George's private secretary, who argued that 'in Green Ireland, the King's speech presents an opportunity which will not come again of putting us British right with the English-speaking world . . . even if the Goidels [sic] were untouched by the King's words, the rest of the world would be'.[35]

Smuts outlined his ideas in a note to the indisposed prime minister, then resting in Wales on medical advice.[36] The situation in Ireland was 'an unmeasured calamity', which poisoned 'both our Empire relations and our foreign relations'; reprisals were 'frightfully expensive in a financial no less than a moral sense; and what is worse, they have failed'. The 'establishment of the Northern Parliament definitely eliminates the coercion of Ulster' and cleared the road 'to deal on the most statesmanlike lines with the rest of Ireland'. Smuts, who enclosed a draft declaration for insertion in the King's Speech, suggested that it

. . . should foreshadow the grant of Dominion status to Ireland, and point out that the removal of all possibility of coercing Ulster now renders such a solution possible. The promise of Dominion status *by the King* would create a new and definite situation which would crystallise opinion favourably in Ireland and elsewhere. Informal negotiations should then be set going with responsible Irish leaders.[37]

The king meanwhile was 'greatly distressed' about the speech Craig had drafted for him to deliver in Belfast: 'He feels he is being made the mouthpiece of Ulster in the speech rather than that of the Empire.' Grigg agreed and dismissed the 'doctrine' that Craig, rather than Lloyd George, was 'ultimately responsible' for the King's Speech as equivalent to endorsing 'the claim of Ulster to dictate the King's utterances. It makes the King a provincial partisan.'[38]

While Smuts and Grigg were urging peace, the cabinet's Irish Situation committee, chaired by Chamberlain, was contemplating war. Macready, reported Tom Jones on 15 June to the ailing prime minister,

set forth in the baldest and, as Balfour said, 'most ensanguined hue', what was involved in the extension of Martial Law and 'Crown Colony Government' to the South. His object . . . was to make it perfectly plain to the cabinet that if coercion is to succeed at all it can only succeed by being applied with the utmost thoroughness and that only by so doing can the spirit of the soldiers and police be sustained. He made no concealment of his own personal belief (shared by John Anderson) that the policy of coercion will not succeed, but will instead 'land this country deeper in the mire'. But he insisted that half-hearted coercion made the position of the troops and

police farcical. 'It must be all out or another policy' . . .
Throughout the discussion Macready reiterated his
main point: Does the Cabinet realise what is involved?
Will they go through with it? Will they begin to howl
when they hear of our shooting a hundred men in
one week?[39]

On 20 June Macready resorted to his favourite back channel
of a 'Very Secret' letter to 'My dear Miss Stevenson' to brief
Lloyd George. 'The policy of coercion [was] a mistake', but if
the cabinet decided 'coercion was the only policy' he would
do his best 'to carry it out for them'. But 'the more people
that are killed, the more difficult will be the final solution,
unless while the killing is going on a body of opinion is growing up imbued with a strong sense that the Government have
made a generous and definite offer to Ireland'.[40]

Macready's politically repellent depiction of the extension
of martial law was designed to sway the cabinet towards
conciliation and it worked. Chamberlain's nervousness about
parliamentary reaction and Bonar Law's making himself
scarce in France from where he signalled his willingness to
'give the South anything or almost anything' provided
nothing was forced on Ulster, together with the royal aversion to reprisals, gave Lloyd George the space he needed to
change course. When Lord Stamfordham, the king's private
secretary, called at Downing Street on 17 June to reiterate the
king's complaints about being 'kept in the dark . . . and the
intense anxiety throughout the whole of the Dominions for
some solution other than that of the government's present
policy regarding Ireland', Lloyd George at once agreed that a
completely new speech should be drafted. The task was given
to Edward Grigg and the king approved the revised version

given him by Lloyd George personally at Windsor the next day.[41] The king's Belfast speech was essentially an appeal 'to forgive and forget'. Although there was no foreshadowing of dominion status beyond the wish that 'every man of Irish birth, whatever be his creed, and wherever be his home, should work in co-operation with the free communities on which the British Empire is based', what it said was less significant than what was left unsaid. It contained not a word in condemnation of the IRA which might sound a discordant note in the atmosphere of conciliation it sought to create.

Lloyd George seized on the new mood on 24 June at a hastily summoned ministerial conference about Ireland, immediately followed by a cabinet meeting. He proposed that the king's appeal be followed up by a letter inviting Craig and de Valera to London to discuss an accommodation. The letter, which Cope would take to Dublin that night, would, like the king's appeal, offer no terms. There was no dissent and the letter, from which all references to the cessation of hostilities as a precondition to the conference were deleted, was released by Lloyd George once Cope reached Dublin.[42]

Ulster's position was yet again punctiliously shielded. Although the initiative was designed for Dublin, that the invitation to de Valera, 'as the chosen leader of the great majority in Southern Ireland', was coupled with an invitation to Craig, as 'Premier of Northern Ireland', amounted to a de facto recognition of partition. Craig's 'confidential' preliminary reply of 26 June was complacent but unyielding. Lloyd George could count on his ultimate acceptance, but it would be delayed so that he could carry all his supporters. 'I too have difficulties. Moreover, I feel that by not "jumping in" at once I may be helping de Valera to come along.'[43]

De Valera's initial reply on 28 June objected on the grounds that the invitation denied 'Ireland's essential unity' and he invited Craig as well as Southern Unionist representatives to a conference in Dublin's Mansion House before replying in full. Craig inevitably rejected de Valera's invitation and Midleton, who did attend on behalf of the Southern Unionists, explained to Lloyd George that de Valera refused to attend a conference at which Craig was also present because he denied Ulster's right to have 'an equal voice with the Irish people of whom he [de Valera] was the only accredited representative'.[44]

On 5 July Smuts went to Dublin to meet de Valera, as an 'unofficial' intermediary, and his report to the cabinet the next day posed two separate questions: first, whether Lloyd George would agree to meet de Valera without Craig and, second, whether de Valera's demand for a truce as a precondition to a conference was acceptable. Once the principle of a truce had been accepted, Balfour, 'the most irreconcilable Minister' in all recent cabinet meetings on Ireland, seized the chance to highlight the partitionist divide: he 'was all for meeting de Valera apart from Ulster and doing everything to mark the division between them'. It was duly agreed 'to meet the Southerners apart from the Northerners' subject only to the perennial Ulster Unionist right of veto, that the prime minister would 'find out whether Craig had any objection'.[45] Smuts immediately warned de Valera about the dangers of offending Lloyd George's Ulster Unionist sensitivities:

In replying to Lloyd George and proposing a conference of two instead of three (against which in itself I see no objection) you should avoid any form of language which will reflect on or belittle the position of Ulster. I see no objection to your stating that the dispute is now between the Irish Majority and the British Government, and the conference for a settlement should be between the two. But the less said about Ulster the better.

De Valera bore Smuts's 'counsel in mind' when he simply telegraphed to Lloyd George on 8 July that he was ready to meet him to discuss 'on what basis such a conference as that proposed can reasonably hope to achieve the object desired'.[46]

The terms of the truce were duly agreed on 9 July at a meeting in Dublin's Mansion House with Macready and Cope; it came into effect at noon on 11 July 1921 and paved the way for the negotiations that led to the Anglo-Irish Treaty of 6 December 1921. On that day H. A. L. Fisher, one of the senior Liberal ministers in the coalition government, 'inquired how many British lives had been lost in the Irish troubles. The answer came, 506. So at the end of it all, and despite our excruciating agonies, the Irish troubles had cost fewer losses than were incurred on the quietest day on the Western front.'[47]

The truce cleared the way for the British government to enter into face-to-face talks with Sinn Féin and the first meeting between Lloyd George and de Valera took place in 10 Downing Street on 14 July. Emotions ran high as crowds outside sang and said the rosary, and even Lloyd George, veteran of so many international conferences, was not immune. Frances Stevenson had never seen him

. . . so excited as he was before de Valera arrived, at 4.30. He kept walking in and out of my room & I could see he was working out the best way of dealing with Dev. . . . He had a big map of the British Empire hung up on the wall in the Cabinet room, with its great blotches of red all over it. This was . . . to impress upon Dev. the greatness

of the B.E. & the King. . . . D. said he was very difficult
to keep to the point – he kept on going off at a tangent,
& talking in formulas and refusing to face facts.[48]

At first Lloyd George kept the cabinet in the dark and
confided only in the key Tories, Chamberlain and Balfour,
with whom he had conferred at Chequers the day before he
met de Valera – Chamberlain as leader of the Conservative
Party and Balfour, whose intellect and negotiating skills he
had admired since 1910 and as the most intransigent Unionist in the cabinet who he feared might wreck the chances of a
settlement. He was already brooding about the group chemistry of negotiating with Sinn Féin, and Hankey, the cabinet
secretary, sensed that he wanted Tom Jones, his fellow Welshman, in charge of secretarial arrangements because he 'did
not want an Anglo-Saxon to run the show!' He later got both
Balfour and Hankey out of the way for the final phase of the
negotiations by sending them to Washington for the naval
conference of November 1921–February 1922.[49]

When Lloyd George did consult the cabinet, on 20 July, he
kept carefully within the boundaries of the terms drawn up at
the cabinet meeting of 25 May. The text of the offer to de
Valera, drafted by Edward Grigg and 'worked over by
Chamberlain, Balfour and Smuts', was endorsed with verbal
changes; although 'Balfour squirmed . . . at terms . . . so contrary to all the views [he] had ever held on Ireland . . . he gave
in gracefully' and cabinet unanimity was preserved.[50]

Ulster, as always, 'was the real difficulty'. James Craig had
made no bones about his intentions when, on 11 July 1921,
the day the truce came into force, he chanced to meet Mark
Sturgis in the Carlton Club. Sturgis asked him if he had any
message for his colleague in Dublin Castle, the prime minister's

intermediary, Andy Cope. Craig's reply revealed the essence of Ulster Unionist strategy in the months ahead: 'Tell Cope I'm going to sit on Ulster like a rock, we are content with what we have got – let the Prime Minister and Sinn Féin settle this and if possible leave us out.'[51]

What de Valera 'chiefly seemed to want', reported Tom Jones to Bonar Law, allegedly recuperating in France,

> was *Irish unity* – that we should not *impose* partition, that there should be an All-Ireland Parliament with real financial and other powers, while leaving to Ulster the autonomy she now enjoys so long as she wishes to retain it . . . The crux of the problem as usual is the relation of Ulster to this question of unity.

Jones then summarised Lloyd George's offer formally handed to de Valera on 20 July. 'Briefly it is "Dominion status" with all sorts of important powers, but no Navy, no hostile tariffs, and no coercion of Ulster. There is a Territorial Force for Ulster, and for the South. It is *hoped* they will contribute to the [war] Debt, etc.'[52]

What Bonar Law described as Jones's 'long and interesting letter' was intended to deflect him from plunging back into the political fray as the standard-bearer of Ulster Unionism. Tory backbenchers, unhappy with Chamberlain, were already pressing him to return.[53] 'The real difficulty of the Irish business', he replied from the Golf-Hôtel du Touquet in Étaples,

> . . . will prove now as always in the past, to be Ulster. I greatly fear that de Valera will find it impossible to treat Ulster as entirely outside his sphere and on the other hand I am sure that no settlement can be carried in England

which imposes anything on the new Ulster Parliament which they do not freely accept. If anyone can carry it is the P.M. and success would be almost as big as winning the war. The longing for peace on both sides of the Channel is a strong lever but I am afraid of the partition difficulty. *Personally, now that the Unionists in the South are all for agreement with Sinn Féin, I would give the South anything or almost anything, but I would not attempt to force anything on Ulster . . .*

The P.M. is very wise and can estimate the forces on all sides better than anyone probably, but I earnestly hope he will not make what I am sure would be the mistake of trying to put pressure on Ulster to accept any arrangement which brought them in any way under the control of a Dublin Parliament, however shadowy that control might be.[54] [author's italics]

Bonar Law's message to Lloyd George was brutally plain: give what you must to Dublin, but hands off Belfast.

De Valera rejected Lloyd George's proposals at what the prime minister described to the king as 'a pretty hopeless' meeting on 21 July when he

. . . demanded that Ireland should have Dominion status *sans phrase*, any condition such as that regarding the Royal Navy, which we consider vital to the safety of these islands to be left for arrangement at a subsequent date between the British and Irish Governments. He also demanded that Ulster should become a part of the Irish Dominion. Failing this, he demanded, as his only alternative, complete independence for Southern Ireland.[55]

Lloyd George replied that if that represented de Valera's last word there was nothing left to discuss except when the truce should end, but it was agreed that the truce should continue while de Valera returned to Dublin to prepare counter-proposals.

The British now tried to persuade Sinn Féin of their inability to sway Northern Ireland's government. On 25 July, Tom Jones told Art O'Brien, Sinn Féin's official spokesman in London, of the impossibility of Lloyd George's tackling 'the North-East Ulster difficulty' without losing Tory support. O'Brien replied that 'England had made this difficulty, and . . . should deal with it'.[56] But the concerted efforts of Lloyd George, Austen Chamberlain, Smuts and Andy Cope to budge Craig were all in vain:

> Craig's 'safe' line is that all Ulster wants is to remain part
> of Great Britain. That they didn't want 'HR [home rule]'
> but having got it mean to keep it. He admitted he had
> gone back on his promise to co-operate with de Valera
> to get anything short of a Republic which would give
> Ireland peace – he now simply says that his people will
> not have one Parliament mostly and ostensibly for fear of
> RC [Roman Catholic] plots to do down the Protestants.[57]

Craig also set about sealing the Conservative Party's support at a series of meetings with 'most of the Unionist leaders', including Austen Chamberlain, Lord Birkenhead and Lord Salisbury, who 'promised to stand by Ulster'.[58]

British twitchiness at the prospect of the talks collapsing intensified when the prime minister went to Paris on 7 August, before de Valera had formally replied to the offer of 20 July. Such was the character of the post-war coalition government, as A. J. P. Taylor has written, that 'Lloyd George, on the hunt for success, had to handle every problem himself: peace abroad, reconstruction at home, Ireland, the Empire'.[59] None of his cabinet colleagues had his single-mindedness or negotiating flair and the 'Big Beast'[60] (Beaverbrook's nickname, which well illustrated Lloyd George's predominance over his cabinet colleagues) kept the strings of Irish policy firmly in his own hands.

With Lloyd George in Paris, it fell to Austen Chamberlain to take delivery of de Valera's formal reply to the British offer of 20 July. There were, Tom Jones delicately informed Lloyd George, 'slight indications of apprehension of Mr Chamberlain's handling of the situation in your absence. His own nervous manner conveyed a feeling of mild panic to his colleagues' when they heard Chamberlain's 'palpitating account'[61] of de Valera's reply. The upshot was that Worthington-Evans sought instructions about troop movements and Hamar Greenwood about the police as if 'Michael Collins was about to break the truce in ten minutes or at most a quarter of an hour'. Yet, despite Chamberlain's bungling, the crisis was real, and de Valera's letter 'practically refusing' the British terms[62] prompted Lloyd George's immediate return from Paris on the night of 12 August. Although the prime minister described the de Valera document as 'a silly answer', he was in high good humour when Jones briefed him as they motored from Victoria Station to Downing Street that evening. Nor was he unduly disturbed by the news from another of his secretaries 'that the Whips were very disgruntled with Chamberlain's handling of the House'. When Jones 'added that Chamberlain was much too nervous to be left to handle Ireland', Lloyd George merely 'jerked out with a wave of his hand, "He's a bloody fool"',[63] before going off to dress for a working dinner in 11 Downing Street, Chamberlain's residence. Also present were Churchill, Birkenhead, Greenwood, Fitzalan and Edward Grigg, who drafted a reply to de Valera which Lloyd George presented to the cabinet the next morning.

The cabinet's deliberations hinged on whether the de Valera document constituted a rejection of the British proposals and, in particular, of dominion status, or whether it was rather a 'clumsy attempt' to keep negotiations going. Cope's telegram from Dublin Castle, arguing for the open-door interpretation, swayed the meeting, but it had been a close-run thing for, as Fitzalan explained to his subordinates in Dublin Castle, the cabinet, and Chamberlain in particular, had come 'within an ace'[64] of taking de Valera's letter as a refusal to negotiate.

On 17 August a cabinet committee was established to review the military options in the event of Dáil Éireann's rejecting the British terms. Six of the seven members of the British delegation in the subsequent Anglo-Irish negotiations of October–December 1921 (Lloyd George, Chamberlain, Birkenhead, Churchill, Greenwood and Worthington-Evans) were members of this high-powered committee, which effectively hammered out in advance the boundaries of the British negotiating position. The other members were Shortt, Fisher and Lord Lee of Fareham (who had made a gift to the nation in 1917 of the Chequers estate as a residence to be used by prime ministers) and its composition epitomised Lloyd George's strategy of talking only on terms that were acceptable to the Conservative leadership, a strategy to which he clung limpet-like throughout the exchanges with de Valera in the weeks ahead. He also took care to brief Bonar Law, whom he persuaded briefly to return from France to join him at Lympne,[65] Philip Sassoon's luxurious house in Kent – such was Sassoon's wealth that, speaking as the local Unionist MP in the immediate aftermath of the

Curragh mutiny to a meeting of the Folkestone battalion of the National Reserve, he had offered, 'in the event of hostilities breaking out in Ulster, to provide at his own expense a vessel to take the battalion over to Ireland'.[66] Lloyd George then left London for a holiday in Flowerdale House, Gairloch, an isolated village on the west coast of Scotland.

The prime minister's strange Scottish holiday, on which he was accompanied by both his wife and his mistress, was marred by incessant rain with most of the party falling prey to colds and chills and Lloyd George himself having to have a tooth extracted by a local dentist. 'The confusion here is indescribable,' reported one of the cabinet-office secretaries to Tom Jones. 'There is one room as an office into which everyone crowds – *no* telephone and a PO [post office] with a single line, one mile away. Thirty miles from the nearest railway station . . . and only one car!'[67] Communication problems about responding to de Valera's next message caused Lloyd George peremptorily to summon a cabinet meeting in Inverness Town Hall, fifty miles away, on 7 September. The group of seven ministers who 'scowled and growled' on the night-sleeper from Euston included an outraged Chamberlain, who had refused to go up earlier for an informal meeting of ministers in Brahan Castle – 'I simply splutter with rage,'[68] he told his sister – and the home secretary, Edward Shortt, who sought solace in a bottle of whisky.[69] In the meantime most of Lloyd George's Irish advisers were already in, or en route to, Scotland, including Fitzalan, Anderson, Cope, Macready (who arrived in a destroyer[70]) and Tudor. The discussion in Inverness Town Hall hinged on the choice between inviting de Valera 'to a conditional conference on the basis of no separation, no republic' or of inviting him to an 'unconditional' conference.

Lloyd George, surprised that 'the "no condition" party . . . were clearly in the ascendant', could not ignore a formidable Conservative 'conditional' phalanx reinforced by the crypto-Conservative Churchill, 'breathing fire and slaughter', and the Irish chief secretary. Two senior and staunchly Unionist ministers, Balfour and Curzon, both of whom had argued against the truce in the key cabinet division of 12 May, moreover, were absent. So Lloyd George stuck to his strategy of siding with the hardliners by

> . . . making really one main point: if the Conference started without securing in advance Irish allegiance to the Crown and membership of the Empire, the discussion would become entangled in the Ulster problem; that de Valera would raise the question of Fermanagh and Tyrone, where we had a very weak case, the Conference might break on that point, a very bad one. He would rather break – if there was to be a break – now, on allegiance and Empire. All this he delivered very gravely, and it obviously shook some of his wobbling colleagues.[71]

The core of the ultimate British response, which went through nine drafts, stated that the correspondence had 'lasted long enough' and sought a 'definite reply' as to whether de Valera was 'prepared to enter a Conference to ascertain how the association of Ireland with the community of nations known as the British Empire can best be reconciled with Irish national aspirations',[72] the formula that ultimately opened the door for the conference.

When the Dáil cabinet met on 9 September, they agreed on a reply that simply reiterated Lloyd George's formula. They also appointed their negotiating team.[73] When the president,

Éamon de Valera, declined to 'take part in the conference as a representative', it was agreed that the delegation would be chaired by Arthur Griffith, minister of foreign affairs; the other delegates were Michael Collins, minister of finance and the effective leader of the IRA's guerrilla campaign; Robert Barton, minister of economic affairs; Éamonn Duggan, Dáil deputy for Louth and Meath and a negotiator of the truce arrangements; and George Gavan Duffy, a lawyer and the Dáil's envoy at Rome. These decisions were ratified when Dáil Éireann met in private session on 14 September and the names of the Irish negotiators, who were given plenipotentiary powers, were announced to the press immediately afterwards. But de Valera's reply went beyond simply accepting Lloyd George's invitation: it included an assertion that the Irish 'nation has formally declared its independence and recognises itself as a sovereign State' and were entering into negotiations 'only as the representatives of that State'.[74] This precipitated a renewed flurry of telegrams, culminating in 'a fresh invitation' to a conference in London on 11 October despatched to de Valera on 29 September and accepted by him the next day.

Contemporaries and successive generations of historians alike have consequently focused so bright and unwavering a spotlight on the negotiations, which began on 11 October and concluded with the signing of the Articles of Agreement for a Treaty between Great Britain and Ireland in the early hours of 6 December 1921, as to cast into deep shadow the importance of what had gone before. But the critical debate on the British government's Irish policy took place *before*, not *during*, the Treaty negotiations. Michael Collins later observed that it was not the Treaty but the acceptance of the invitation to negotiate that formed the compromise. Similarly, from a

British perspective, the crucial compromise was the cabinet decision to issue the invitation to negotiate. The decisive shift in British policy took place between May and July and the essence of that compromise, which the British never diluted, was embodied in the proposals Lloyd George handed to de Valera on 20 July – summarised by Tom Jones as '"Dominion status" with all sorts of important powers, but no Navy, no hostile tariffs, and no coercion of Ulster'.

The length and intensity of the cabinet's debate on Irish policy between May and September 1921 was a great source of strength to the British delegation and, above all, to Lloyd George, throughout the treaty negotiations. Maurice Cowling has described how between April and the end of June he had been vulnerable to critics in cabinet plotting to displace him from the premiership 'on the ground, among others, that he had no Irish policy'.[75] Churchill and Birkenhead had been the principal plotters but Lloyd George had disarmed them by engaging them at every step of the way, a process culminating in their inclusion in the prime minister's proposed six-strong negotiation team endorsed by the cabinet on 6 October – the other three were Chamberlain, Worthington-Evans, and Greenwood (Gordon Hewart, the attorney general who was not in the cabinet, was also to attend for constitutional questions). Three Conservatives and three Liberals, but, more to the point, all except Chamberlain had argued for entering into the conference without preconditions other than no separation and no republic. Little wonder, then, that, having endured such exhaustive discussions on its negotiating position, the cabinet also agreed that there was no need to give its delegation any specific instructions.[76] By including Churchill and Birkenhead, because, as Beaverbrook observed, 'they were too dangerous to leave out',[77] Lloyd George cemented the cohesion of the British delegation behind the Irish policy laboriously pieced together during the previous months and inextricably linked the success of the conference with the survival of his coalition government.

The tortuous evolution of policy and the constant toing and froing between Dublin Castle and Downing Street afforded another advantage to Lloyd George: he was well briefed on the idiosyncrasies of his Irish adversaries long before the conference began. 'On the whole I think it is a good thing that Michael Collins is one of them,' Lord Fitzalan had advised a month earlier. 'Remember they are plenipotentiaries and must not take advantage of de Valera's absence to delay and refer back to him.'[78] Four days later, Fitzalan offered an equally prescient description of Arthur Griffith's attitude towards Ulster: 'He has stated that he would work to get in the whole of Ireland; failing this, he would work for the 28 counties, but that he was not going to fight if he could only retain the 26.'[79]

The gross disparity in negotiating experience between the British and Irish delegations was also evident before the conference began. Churchill, Birkenhead and, above all, Lloyd George had honed their negotiating skills at national and international level over decades. Revolutionaries on the run, such as Collins, or imprisoned, as was Griffith in 1916–17, in 1918 and again between December 1920 and July 1921, had no remotely comparable experience. This handicap was reinforced, moreover, by the failure of the Dáil cabinet to undertake an exercise approximating to the British cabinet's painstaking evolution of a coherent negotiating policy with clearly defined boundaries. Indeed the Sinn Féin strategy, even the very name 'Sinn Féin' ('Ourselves') with its emphasis on the virtues of self-reliance, revealed a mentality scornful of negotiation. The first act of Dáil Éireann, declared its *ceann comhairle* (speaker) at its inaugural meeting on 21 January 1919, was to break with Britain. Until the truce ended the Anglo-Irish war, Sinn Féin's solution to the age-old problem of the constitutional relationship between Britain and Ireland had been as simplistic as it was psychologically satisfying: the declaration of an independent, sovereign republic and the denial that there was any legitimate connection between the two islands. The truce marked the point when such simplicities were discarded. As de Valera admitted to the Dáil, 'Negotiations were necessary because we held one view and the British another.'[80] But the revolutionary distrust of talking to the enemy was not so easily shed. 'The greatest strength of the British people lies in their inveterate belief that, whatever else happens, they and their leaders will blunder horribly,' mused Lionel Curtis, one of the British officials involved in the negotiations, in August 1921. 'The greatest weakness of the Sinn Féin government . . . is that it is almost void of any admission to the world or themselves that they can either think what is wrong or do what is wrong. That is exactly what the Greek writers meant by "hubris"; the frame of mind which, on their theory, the gods instil into people whom they have marked for destruction.'[81]

There were other reasons why Sinn Féin's experience in 1919–21 inhibited the development of negotiating skills. The Dáil had met on only twenty-one days before the truce and only four of those meetings, and none later than May 1919, were held in public. Meetings were short and poorly attended due to the imprisonment of many deputies and fears of further arrests by British forces. The Dáil, moreover, was a one-party assembly where there was no opposition to be persuaded or convinced. 'Incredibly', as Kevin Matthews has pointed out, 'the Irish delegates were sent to London without a detailed alternative to Lloyd George's 20 July proposals'[82] of '"Dominion status" with all sorts of important powers, but no Navy, no hostile tariffs, and no coercion of Ulster'. The incredible becomes explicable when set in this context of the primitive and one-dimensional politics of Dáil Éireann, an assembly that was little more than a forum where the representatives of Sinn Féin could talk to themselves.

The Irish delegation was crippled, moreover, by Éamon de Valera's refusal to head the Irish plenipotentiaries, a decision that baffled and incensed his colleagues at the time and has ever since been criticised as a gross evasion of the responsibilities of leadership. His own retrospective explanations have been well summarised by Patrick Murray: they included 'that he remained at home to avoid compromising the Republic, as a reserve against the tricks of Lloyd George, to be in a better position to rally a united nation . . . to oblige the delegates to refer home before taking decisions . . . [by creating] through himself, a final court of appeal to avert whatever Britain might attempt to put over'.[83] De Valera knew from his own talks with Lloyd George in July of the extreme difficulty of the negotiations that lay ahead. He knew, too, that any Irish negotiating team would be callow and inexperienced compared with their British counterparts, who would also enjoy the advantage of playing at home. In theory, his strategy of denying finality to what might happen in Downing Street by insisting that the final decision be taken in Dublin seemed shrewd. In practice, it was fatally flawed because of the inherent contradiction between the plenipotentiary status of the delegates and their agreement to sign nothing in London that had not first been endorsed by the Dáil cabinet in Dublin. First, because de Valera failed adequately to explain his reasoning to the plenipotentiaries before the talks began; the corollary was that it never occurred to de Valera that the ultimate decision about an agreement might be made in London and not in Dublin. Second, because the bonding that took place between the plenipotentiaries on their wearying journeys by sea and rail and during their long hours in London silently corroded de Valera's authority with consequences that proved disastrous.

11

The Treaty Negotiations: 'We are after a settlement'

The appearance of the Irish delegation at 10 Downing Street at 11 o'clock on the morning of 11 October 1921 marked the most historic shift in the British government's Irish policy since the creation of the United Kingdom of Great Britain and Ireland in 1801. 'Great crowds of people assembled at the entrance to Downing Street to watch the arrival of the conference delegates,' reported the *Irish Times* the next day.

> One feature of the demonstration . . . was that while the crowd on one side of the street shouted the names of prominent Irishmen, the crowd on the opposite side of the street cheered each name vigorously. They varied this by cries of: 'Shall we have a Republic?' which received the hearty response of 'Yes'. Others came out with the popular Irish battle cry of 'Up the Rebels'. Many Sinn Féin flags were waved, while the enthusiasts sang 'God Save Ireland' to the tune of 'The Old Land' song.
>
> The crowd was not all one way of thinking, and occasionally there was a retort to the Irish demonstration by the calling for cheers for prominent English statesmen, the names of Mr Gladstone and Mr Lloyd George figuring prominently. The exchange was entirely good-natured, however, and subsequently the waiting crowds

settled down to the singing of hymns. The watchers blended with their demonstration occasional resorts to prayer, most of them kneeling as they recited the Rosary.

There were neither prayers nor hymns around the cabinet table where the Irish delegation took their seats, according to the *Irish Times* 'on the side nearer the Horse Guards Parade with the British delegates on the side nearer to Downing Street', but no one was more keenly aware of the historic nature of that morning than David Lloyd George. Never before had British ministers met Irish revolutionary nationalists, 'the first time we have [had] the physical force party round a table in direct discussion',[1] as he said a month later at the first cabinet meeting on Ireland since the negotiations began. He also reported that the Irish delegates 'are simple; they have none of the skill of the old nationalists; these men are not accustomed to finessing'. There could be no turning back. Failure would trigger the end of his premiership and the collapse of his coalition government on which all the British delegates were also dependent for their political survival.

'We are after a settlement – that was our objective,'[2] Lloyd George curtly reminded his colleagues halfway through the negotiations. This determination to achieve agreement was the key to the British negotiating strategy: it hinged on identifying and massaging the offence out of any elements that would prevent the Irish plenipotentiaries from signing a draft treaty. Short of that and subject to the constraints in the British proposals Lloyd George had given to de Valera on 20 July, the British delegates, and Lloyd George in particular, were largely indifferent to the small print of any agreement. What mattered was the fact of a settlement, not its details.

The Irish delegation's naivety and inexperience, starkly apparent in its failure to present an alternative position paper when the talks began, gave the British an advantage from the first moment when Tom Jones circulated fresh copies of the proposals of 20 July. 'However much amended, the basic paper at any conference is apt to determine the parameters of subsequent discussion,' Nicholas Mansergh has observed. 'This was to prove no exception.'[3] The opening sessions of the conference were essentially preparatory and focused on redrafting the five restrictive reservations in the British proposals: naval access to Irish ports, air facilities, the constitutional position of dominions in relation to war and defence, and a free-trade area between Britain and Ireland. There remained the two issues likeliest to obstruct agreement: Ulster and the relationship with the crown, and when Lloyd George invited Arthur Griffith to address the Ulster problem at the fourth plenary session, on 14 October, the negotiations moved into a more substantive phase.

Yet again the Irish delegation was caught off guard because de Valera was still revising the so-called 'Ulster clause' in Dublin. So Griffith took refuge in a classic Irish nationalist critique: 'an elaborate, not to say prolix, exposition of the unnaturalness of Partition'[4] that elicited a remarkable response[5] pitting Lloyd George's pragmatism against Griffith's idealism.

THE P.M.: Perhaps I may now state our point of view.
  Attempts have been made to settle the Irish problem since
  1886 on the basis of autonomy. Gladstone, who was the
  outstanding figure of his time with 40 years of political
  experience, tried to do it but he came up against Ulster . . .
  We tried from 1911 to 1913. Ulster defeated Gladstone,
  Ulster would have defeated us. Mr Churchill and I were

for the [third Home Rule] Bill. Mr Chamberlain and the Lord Chancellor were opposed. They with the instinct of trained politicians saw that Ulster was the stumbling block. They got the whole force of the opposition concentrated on Ulster. Ulster was arming and would fight. We were powerless. It is no good ignoring facts however unpleasant they may be. The politician who thinks he can deal out abstract justice without reference to forces around him cannot govern. You had to ask the British to use force to put Ulster out of one combination in which she had been for generations into another combination which she professed to abhor and did abhor, whether for political or religious reasons. We could not do it. If we tried, the instrument would have broken in our hands. Their case was 'Let us remain with you.' Our case was 'Out you go or we fight you.' We could not have done it. Mr Churchill and I warned our colleagues. Mr Gladstone and Asquith discovered it. I cannot say I discovered it because I was always of that opinion. You have got to accept facts. The first axiom was whatever happened we could not coerce Ulster. There was the same strain in the argument of de Valera as I have [heard] here this morning, that Ulster would come in if we let her alone . . . It is a mistake to assume that the population of Ulster for the time being is opposed to partition. It is not. I am glad that de Valera has come to the conclusion which we favoured that force is not a weapon you can use. It would break in your hands. We should have a terrible civil war and you would draw men from all parts into the vortex of the whirlpool. Mr Collins shakes his head. He knows Ireland. I know Great Britain and the Empire. It would resolve itself into a religious war. You do not want to begin your new life with a civil war which would leave you with desolation in its train. Therefore I am glad that we are agreed that force is impossible. What is your alternative?

MR GRIFFITH: You should withdraw your support [for Ulster].

THE P.M.: We proposed to come out. We begin with (1) no force and are left with the only alternative, (2) persuasion without any pressure from us.

The Irish delegates might have discounted Lloyd George's impassioned defence of his Ulster policy over the previous decade as mere rhetoric, an example of his wizardry with words. If they did, they were wrong. Although political expediency dovetailed with intellectual conviction, Lloyd George meant every word he said. Expediency demanded that the composition of the British delegation, like the composition of Lloyd George's coalition government since 1916, must reflect both sides in the battle over the third Home Rule Bill: Lloyd George and Churchill *had* supported the bill; Austen Chamberlain and F. E. Smith, now Lord Birkenhead, the Lord Chancellor, sitting directly across the table from Michael Collins, *had* opposed it. The Tory opposition *had* centred on Ulster and Ulster *had* armed in revolt. When the government sought to contain illegal force with legal force, the instrument of the army *had* broken in their hands at the Curragh. On the other hand, Lloyd George and Churchill *had* been intellectually convinced since 1911 that Ulster must be excluded from the terms of the bill and they *had* so warned their cabinet colleagues. Lloyd George *was* 'always of that opinion'. Given that the commitment not to coerce Ulster had been written in stone since Lloyd George and Bonar Law had stitched together their 1918 election manifesto, persuasion without pressure was indeed 'the only alternative'.

At no time during the seven weeks of negotiations that followed did Lloyd George retreat from the position he here staked out. Given Craig's already expressed determination to sit on Ulster like a rock, that meant doing nothing to disrupt the Ulster settlement he had already put in place. Although the absence of Bonar Law, convalescing in France, and Balfour, shunted away to Washington, together with the retirement of Carson and Long, had expanded Lloyd George's freedom of manoeuvre, his outburst reflected his awareness that the problem of Ulster retained the potential to wreck yet another attempt to solve the problem of Ireland. James Craig and Bonar Law might not have been the elephants in the room, but they were the elephants outside the door, who, if provoked, could still wreak havoc. Lloyd George devoted as much energy to soothing the Ulster Unionists as to negotiating with Sinn Féin's plenipotentiaries.

De Valera's draft of the 'Ulster clause' was to hand on 17 October. Its provisions were tortuous and, instead of tabling the draft,[6] Griffith returned to his theme of 14 October, urging that 'the Six Counties should be allowed to choose freely whether they would be in North or South'.[7] Lloyd George admitted that 'the logical unit would have been [the province of] Ulster', as Walter Long's committee had initially proposed in November 1919. The six-county boundary embodied in the 1920 Government of Ireland Act, he insisted, was 'a compromise, not our proposal, but a compromise' to escape the Ulster impasse that had wrecked every previous bill, and no compromise was 'logically defensible'. But he was a worried man. 'This is going to wreck settlement,'[8] he scribbled in a note slipped to Tom Jones.

The sixth and seventh plenary sessions, on 21 and 24 October, dealt with three other matters on which the British regarded the Irish delegation's attitude as 'vital': allegiance to the king; 'whether Ireland is prepared to come freely into the fraternity of nations known as the British Empire', and whether Ireland would accept in principle the British claims for defence facilities in Irish ports.[9] But Ulster again loomed large when, at the end of the seventh and final plenary session, it was agreed that Lloyd George and Chamberlain would meet privately with Griffith and Collins. The British, Griffith wrote hurriedly to de Valera later that night,

> ... talked freely – Chamberlain frankly. The burden of their story was that on the Crown they must fight. It was the only link of Empire they possessed.
>
> They pressed me to say that I would accept the Crown provided we came to other agreements. It was evident that they wanted something to reassure themselves against the Die-Hards. I told them I had no authority. If we came to an agreement on all other points I could recommend some form of association with the Crown ...
>
> [I] told them the only possibility of Ireland considering association of any kind with Crown was in exchange for essential unity – a concession to Ulster ...
>
> We agreed to proceed on basis of settling all other points, leaving Crown to last.[10]

That 'the only way to reconcile Ireland to the Crown was to secure Irish unity' was how Lloyd George and Chamberlain summarised the Irish position at a meeting of the British delegation later that night; 'this did not mean a denial of autonomy to Ulster, but Ulster and Ireland could not be equal'.[11]

The next day, 25 October, Griffith and Collins discussed Ulster with Chamberlain and Gordon Hewart, the attorney general. The British line remained 'we are committed to the six-county area – what can we do?' but they raised the possibility of 'the six-county area remaining as at present, but coming into the All-Ireland Parliament'.[12] When Chamberlain reported Griffith's continued insistence that the Irish representatives 'could not recommend allegiance to the King unless they got the unity of Ireland' they saw no room to manoeuvre. 'We can't give way on Six Counties; we are not free agents,' declared Churchill; Birkenhead agreed, although he admitted that the British stance on the six counties 'is an impossible one if these men want to settle, as they do'. Lloyd George, knowing that a breach with Churchill and Birkenhead would spell the end of his premiership, swiftly charted a new negotiating strategy:

> I would not now resume discussion on Ulster with Sinn Féin. I would review whole situation either by stating our position asking them to give answers on vital things and then say: 'We understand your position on Ulster is so and so.' On Ulster we would have to say something about area, e.g. Six [counties] or Nine [counties], willing to discuss that. Willing also (this put vaguely) to consider any machinery by which unity of Ireland should be reorganised or strengthened. If they accept all subject to unity we are in a position to go to Craig; if they don't the break is not on Ulster. My proposal is put Ulster on one side and ask S. F. for their views in writing.[13]

So it was agreed and the meeting ended with Birkenhead, ever the realist, demurring at Chamberlain's suggestion that Lloyd George should see Craig and urging that he instead see Carson. Carson, unsurprisingly, was 'quite obdurate' and said 'he cannot possibly give in on Ulster'.[14]

Lloyd George's greater worry was 'the attitude of Bonar Law' who had 'come back quite recovered' from his illness and who was again

> . . . taking an active interest in politics . . . He was very reasonable and moderate up to a point. Then suddenly you touched him and he blazed up. At heart he was an Orangeman and a fanatic and the Orange fanaticism was there. He had brought it with him from Canada. He might at any time, in defence of what he regarded as an attack on Ulster, lead a Tory revolt.[15]

But Lloyd George saw opportunity as well as danger in Bonar Law's return and impressed on Churchill and Birkenhead that Bonar Law would replace him if he resigned on Ulster, calculating they would not want to put Bonar Law in 10 Downing Street.[16]

Lloyd George's determination to protect his Unionist flank shaped the official British note given to the Irish delegation on 27 October. It urged the need to 'get unequivocal answers on the main issues. "If this is not done it makes it very difficult for my Unionist colleagues who, we must remember, have been fighting this business for the last thirty years."' The upshot was 'categorical questions on allegiance, Empire and defence' but, again at Lloyd George's suggestion, the document as a whole was 'governed by a preamble "subject to agreement being reached on the question of Irish unity"'.[17] The British document, Tom Jones privately assured Erskine Childers, the hardline republican secretary to the Irish delegation, should not be taken at face value; it was designed to placate Lloyd George's Unionist adversaries who 'were threatening to resign from the Cabinet, their tactics being

[to] force a break on the Crown, Navy etc. and so safeguard Ulster'.[18]

The point was underlined when Lloyd George and Birkenhead sought another meeting on 27 October with Griffith and Collins before they replied in writing to the British note. The 'gist' of the hour-and-a-half-long conversation, reported Griffith to de Valera, 'was that if we would accept the Crown they would send for Craig i.e. – force "Ulster" in, as I understood'.[19] That Griffith should equate sending for Craig with forcing Ulster in, given that 'coercing Ulster' was always anathema to Lloyd George, showed more misunderstanding than understanding. But that was unsurprising: the Irish delegation, conditioned by Sinn Féin's revolutionary experience, despised politics as the art of the possible. That scorn for political realities was apparent in Michael Collins's response when C. P. Scott pointed out to him that 'Lloyd George was fighting their battle hard under great difficulties and had done wonders in bringing over the Tories'. No previous prime minister 'who had taken the Irish question in hand was in a position to "deliver the goods". He surely had a right to expect some help from those he was helping.' Collins's reply reeked of revolutionary disdain: 'I know nothing about your politics. I have only to think of Ireland.' Collins wanted peace, he told Scott, 'but one could not sell the honour of one's country any more than one could sell the honour of a woman. Ireland *was* a nation. Every Irishman felt it in himself. It was not a theory. "It was there."'[20]

But Lloyd George's fear that the Tories would desert him on Ulster was also there and it was reinforced by the Irish reply on 29 October. Hamar Greenwood, mindful of Canadian analogies and 'very much more instinctively sympathetic'[21] to Irish demands than his cabinet colleagues, reacted positively.

'We have secured allegiance, membership of the Empire, naval control, acknowledgement of debt and neutrality is gone.' The outstanding 'decisive factor' was 'how a parliament for all Ireland can be set up while at the same time an Ulster parliament can carry on'.[22] But Austen Chamberlain's reaction, as the Tories' titular leader, disturbed Lloyd George: Chamberlain 'did not know what the document meant' and told Tom Jones to 'tell the Irish we were being fooled'.[23] Jones met Éamonn Duggan on Saturday night and asked him if Griffith would send Lloyd George 'a private letter' stating 'that the official Reply did in fact mean acknowledgement of allegiance, common citizenship and Imperial Defence' with the aim 'of putting the P.M. in a position on Monday to face the House with the confidence born of the knowledge that the Sinn Féiners would give him the three essentials'.[24] Although Duggan baulked, the Irish delegation agreed to yet another private meeting before Lloyd George spoke in the Commons.

The meeting took place on Sunday night in Churchill's house where Lloyd George and Birkenhead were dining. Lloyd George regarded Birkenhead's support as 'essential'; most Unionists would follow him rather than Chamberlain whom 'they regarded as a Liberal Unionist'. When Tom Jones telephoned the prime minister and advised him, in Welsh, that Griffith and Collins distrusted Churchill and Birkenhead, Lloyd George met Griffith alone.[25] Their meeting, reported Griffith to de Valera, lasted about three-quarters of an hour and revolved around Lloyd George's complaint that the Irish reply

. . . was so worded that he did not know where he stood. He had to meet the Die-Hards next day and he would easily beat them so far as a Parliamentary majority was concerned, but the Crown, free partnership with the

British Empire and facilities for the British navy on the Irish coast – these were vital matters. The bias of his speech had to be towards peace or war with Ireland. If [Griffith] would give him personal assurances on this matter he would go out to smite the Die-Hards and would fight on the Ulster matter to secure essential unity.[26]

Lloyd George said that 'he could carry a six-county Parliament subordinate to a national Parliament'. Alternatively, 'he would *try* to carry a plan for a new boundary or a vote on the inclusion or exclusion of the whole of Ulster as a unit, but he was not hopeful of doing so'.[27]

Although Lloyd George duly routed the diehards on 31 October by 439 votes to 43, he did so by acquiescing in the Ulster Unionists' demand for the transfer of executive power to the Northern Ireland government. The transfer took effect under two orders in council made by the king on 9 November under section 69 of the Government of Ireland Act of 1920. 'Partition was now legally complete'[28] and Lloyd George's room for manoeuvre in his dealings with the Northern Ireland government correspondingly diminished.

Ireland remained the focus of the diehards' attack on Lloyd George because, as Maurice Cowling has argued, they 'identified resistance to Sinn Féin with the defence of civilisation, believed in the Irish Union as the fundamental principle of the Conservative Party and thought Lloyd George likely either to concede what de Valera wanted or to force an anti-Ulster election in England in order to get power to make Ulster give it'.[29] The next diehard offensive was deferred until 17 November when the Conservative Party conference took place in Liverpool, 'a citadel of Tory Democracy since Disraelian times, founded on working-class sentiment directed against the Irish

Catholic immigrants'.[30] Meanwhile the British delegates, flushed with their parliamentary triumph of 31 October, resumed negotiations with Griffith and Collins next morning. Their immediate objective was unchanged: to get a letter from Griffith to Lloyd George 'embodying' Griffith's replies to Lloyd George in their private conversation 'to produce against Craig'.[31] Griffith's letter of assurance went through three drafts before Griffith and Collins handed it to Birkenhead at the House of Lords at noon on 2 November and Griffith agreed to meet Lloyd George for further discussions later that day.

In the meantime Lloyd George received another Unionist shot across his bows in the shape of a letter from Arthur Balfour, then en route from London to Washington where he was to lead the British delegation at the naval conference: 'We are all agreed that we cannot and ought not to coerce Ulster. We are all agreed that if Southern Ireland fully and frankly accepts the three conditions it will be very difficult, not to say impracticable, to coerce her.' After a typically Balfourian blast against the Irish claim to 'political unity as based on bad history and bad logic', he bleakly concluded that, if neither North nor South could be coerced, Ireland could not be governed. 'If we cannot govern Ireland, I think we should resign; leaving it to others to solve a problem which we have honestly done our best to deal with, but where, through no fault of our own, we have failed.' Balfour's request that his letter be shown to Chamberlain and Birkenhead added venom to his parting shot.[32] But the beleaguered prime minister stuck to his guns when he and Birkenhead met Griffith and Collins at a quarter to seven that evening at 10 Downing Street – Chamberlain joined them later – and hammered out the final draft as signed by Griffith later that night.

The letter reiterated Griffith's verbal assurances on the British delegation's three 'vital' points: the Commonwealth, the crown and naval defence. He agreed to recommend 'a free partnership of Ireland with the other States associated within the British Commonwealth'; that 'Ireland should consent to a recognition of the Crown as head of the proposed association of free states'; and that 'the British navy should be afforded such coastal facilities as may be agreed to be necessary pending a [defence] agreement'. Griffith also stated that his 'attitude . . . was conditional on the recognition of the essential unity of Ireland'.[33] That proviso meant that the negotiations remained focused on Ulster because there could be no settlement without a formula for 'essential unity'.

When Birkenhead met Griffith and Collins at the House of Lords the next day he assured them that 'if Ulster proved unreasonable', Lloyd George's government 'would resign rather than use force against Ireland'.[34] 'In such an event no English Government is capable of formation on a war-policy,' exulted Griffith to de Valera; they were 'up against Ulster and we, for the moment, are standing aside. *If* [author's italics] they secure "Ulster's" consent we shall have gained essential unity and the difficulty we shall be up against will be the formula of association and recognition.'[35] But it is unlikely that Lloyd George ever intended to resign over Ulster unless he lost his parliamentary majority. A more plausible interpretation is that he dangled the threat of resignation over the heads of Chamberlain, Churchill and Birkenhead to ensure their continued loyalty and Griffith's misplaced elation rested on the frail foundation of that italicised *If*.

Lloyd George's first meeting with Craig took place on Saturday, 5 November, and Frances Stevenson described his state of mind the next day, after a week in which he had hardly taken his mind off the Irish negotiations 'for one minute'. Although she felt that he had 'successfully wangled Churchill & Birkenhead' to the point where they were 'all out' for settlement, Bonar Law, 'influenced by Carson, & also by the hope that this may be his chance of becoming Prime Minister', was still 'proving difficult'. Craig had at first been 'quite obdurate & would concede nothing' and Lloyd George was 'rather hopeless about it'; but by evening he felt 'he had extorted from him considerable concessions, the most important being an all-Irish Parliament'. The concessions were unconfirmed, however, and Lloyd George still worried that Bonar Law 'will come in expressly to coerce the South'[36] if and when Lloyd George refused do so.

Craig's attitude stiffened the next day, moreover, after he and Wilfred Spender, the secretary to the Northern Irish cabinet who had re-established and commanded the Ulster Volunteer Force in 1920, went to the war office and extracted crucial concessions from Worthington-Evans, the secretary of state for war, and Henry Wilson, the Ulster Unionists' staunchest ally during the Curragh mutiny and now chief of the Imperial General Staff. It was agreed that the Northern Ireland government could use its new executive powers to employ Spender's 'special constabulary' and the RIC to maintain order. Craig, with his security flank now secured, confided in Worthington-Evans that he found it 'impossible to agree to an all-Ireland parliament'.[37]

Fresh from his triumph at the war office, Craig went straight to Downing Street and effectively rejected Lloyd George's terms. A despairing Lloyd George, more depressed than at any time since the conference had begun, finally accepted that Craig would 'not budge an inch'; he told Tom Jones to prepare Griffith and Collins for the break-up of the conference and again talked of resignation rather than 'coercing the South'. But his ingenuity was not yet exhausted:

> He then said – 'There is just one other possible way out.
> I want to find out from Griffith and Collins if they will
> support me on it; namely that the 26 Counties should
> take their own Dominion Parliament and have a Boundary Commission, that Ulster should have her present
> powers plus representation in the Imperial Parliament
> plus the burdens of taxation which we bear. I might
> be able to put that through if Sinn Féin will take it.
> Find out.'[38]

The next day, 8 November, Lloyd George told a meeting of 'the British Seven' that Craig's 'attitude had changed from willingness to discuss all-Ireland parlt to absolute *non possumus*'. If Ulster refused he would tell the king that, while his ministers were pledged not to coerce Ulster, they could not advise the coercion of south-west Ireland because of opposition from the dominions and the likelihood that the United States would break up the Washington naval conference. He would accordingly resign and advise the king 'to send for somebody else',[39] almost certainly Bonar Law.

Although Chamberlain and Birkenhead undertook not to serve under Bonar Law, Lloyd George told Tom Jones of his suspicion that Worthington-Evans, Curzon and Baldwin, lured by 'the nose bags of office', would 'all go over to Bonar if the opportunity comes'. Tom Jones's job was to shut off that opportunity and he immediately went to see Griffith and Collins in the Grosvenor Hotel, used by the Irish delegation as one of their London bases. He pointed out that a Bonar Law government would have a large Tory majority in the

House; it was 'all important' to keep Lloyd George 'at the helm'. He then dangled Lloyd George's bait of 'the Southern Parliament plus Boundary Commission' as his own suggestion. Collins did not like it 'at all because it sacrificed unity entirely'. Jones 'agreed, but what was the alternative? Chaos, Crown Colony Government, Civil War?'[40] Griffith, however, 'was not alarmed' and Jones departed, promising to sound out the prime minister on what was in fact the prime minister's own proposal!

Griffith's report of the meeting of 8 November to de Valera is striking evidence of the success of Lloyd George's stratagem: Craig was 'standing pat' and refusing either 'to come under any all-Ireland Parliament' or 'to change Six-County area'. If the Northern Irish government refused the proposal Lloyd George intended to put to them, 'that they should accept the 6-County area under an Irish Parliament', he would give his resignation to the House of Commons and 'Birkenhead and Chamberlain will probably resign along with him'. Bonar Law would then 'probably form a Militarist Govt. against Ireland'. Griffith then outlined the alternative: that Lloyd George would 'offer to set up a Govt. for the 26 Counties with all the promised powers, and appoint a boundary commission to de-limit "Ulster", confining this Ulster to its Partition Act powers. This would give us most of Tyrone, Fermanagh, and part of Armagh, Down, etc.' Griffith concluded that the scheme was 'partly bluff, but not wholly' because 'the Conference may end this week. If so, all policy dictates it should end on the note of "Ulster" being impossibilist, in order to throw the Dominions against her'.[41]

Griffith's response threw a lifeline to Lloyd George. The next afternoon, 9 November, Tom Jones returned to Room 125 at the Grosvenor Hotel and nudged Arthur Griffith, this time accompanied by Duggan and not Collins, further along Lloyd George's path. Not for nothing did the biblical text in silk threads over the prime ministerial bed in 10 Downing Street read: 'There is a path which no fowl knoweth and which the eye of the vulture hath not seen.'[42] He said that Lloyd George was prepared to play the boundary commission as an absolutely last card if he could feel sure that Sinn Féin would take it, if Ulster accepted. 'We are not going to queer his pitch,' replied Griffith. 'We would prefer a plebiscite, but in essentials a Boundary Commission is very much the same.'

Griffith's acceptance of the boundary-commission proposal was 'enough' for Jones and his report allowed a 'perfectly satisfied' Lloyd George[43] to wriggle off the horns of his Ulster dilemma. He was further reassured by a letter from Churchill putting 'on record' the government's 'duty' to press forward with its policy until it was defeated in the Commons. 'Such a policy might well include the creation and recognition of an All-Ireland Parliament, subject only to the condition that no physical force would be used against Ulster from any quarter.'[44] Buoyed up by success, the prime minister told Jones to summon a meeting of the British Seven the next morning before the whole cabinet assembled that afternoon for its first meeting since the start of the Irish negotiations.

The British Seven reviewed Lloyd George's letter to Craig, which he wanted recast to bring the Ulster Unionists up against the financial disadvantages of staying out of an all-Ireland parliament by making them subject to the same tax regime as in the rest of the United Kingdom, as opposed to the more favourable financial settlement embodied in the 1920 Government of Ireland Act. Lloyd George explained his thinking to Frances Stevenson: that an all-Ireland parliament be set up for a year with Northern Ireland having the option to withdraw after six or twelve months; but they could with-draw 'only by coming back as part of the U.K. & paying the same taxes as the U.K. . . . . They have their hands on their hearts all the time, but if it comes to touching their pockets they quickly slap their hands in them. "I know. . . . My wife is a Presbyterian!"'[45]

Lloyd George's financial leverage scheme 'came as a great and sudden revelation', which upset the Unionists on the British delegation, especially Worthington-Evans, who main-tained 'that Ulster was to get all her powers under the 1920 Act and therefore there could be no change in the matter of finance . . . The atmosphere was at once electric.' The Union-ists also jibbed at the florid language of the draft and, after Chamberlain tartly reminded Lloyd George that 'we were now not writing to Celts but to Anglo-Saxons', it was agreed 'to "de-floridise" the first half of the document and to "con-certina" the second half'.[46]

Lloyd George presented the revised draft, hastily prepared by Lionel Curtis over a solitary lunch of sandwiches and port,[47] that afternoon, 10 November. So far there had been no need to consult the cabinet, the prime minister told his col-leagues, because 'we knew our instructions'. But Craig now sought written British proposals to which he had promised a written reply. The Tories once more rumbled to the defence of the Northern Irish government, Curzon complaining that Craig 'spoke of being betrayed, surprised, dismayed, turned out of the British system'.[48] But Lloyd George's key allies, Chamberlain, Birkenhead and Churchill, held firm. The cabi-net duly approved the achievements of the negotiations to date, although 'emphasis was laid upon the importance of exercising the greatest patience in the conduct of negotiations with the Cabinet of Northern Ireland'.[49]

Lloyd George dispatched his letter immediately after the cabinet meeting and Craig's reply duly reiterated his rejection of an all-Ireland parliament; Craig also proposed that Northern Ireland should become a dominion 'based on "equality of status" with the South', a proposal that came 'as a shock to those accustomed to receive their passionate assurances of union'.[50] Lloyd George showed Griffith the exchange of correspondence at lunch in Philip Sassoon's house in Park Lane on 12 November and told him that he and his colleagues were 'sending a further reply to the Ulstermen – refusing their Dominion proposal, but offering to create an All-Ireland Parliament, Ulster to have the right to vote itself out within 12 months, but if it does a Boundary Commission to be set up to delimit the area, and the part that remains after the Commission has acted to be subject to equal financial burdens with England'. Lloyd George also extracted from Griffith an assurance not to embarrass him during the Liverpool conference by repudiating the proposal, an assurance that Griffith described to de Valera as a 'guarantee that while he was fighting the "Ulster" crowd, we [the Irish delegation] would not help them by repudiating him'.[51] Tom Jones immediately embodied Griffith's undertaking in a short memorandum that Lloyd George was later to use to devastating effect in the dying hours of the negotiations.

Meanwhile the conference had effectively ground to a halt. 'No progress has been made since last weekend,'[52] wrote Michael Collins to de Valera on 12 November. Nor would there be progress, Andy Cope advised the Irish delegation, until 'the pro- and anti-Ulster parties test their strength'[53] at the Conservative Party conference at Liverpool. The outcome at Liverpool and, indeed, the fate of Lloyd George's negotiating strategy now depended on Bonar Law. Thanks to J. P.

Croal, the editor of the *Scotsman*, who on 12 November asked Bonar Law to dictate his views to one of his journalists, we have a remarkably comprehensive account[54] of the alternative strategy he had urged on Lloyd George at dinner on 10 November. The key to Bonar Law's position was that 'Ulster will not go into an all-Ireland Parliament at present and that the immediate effect of trying to force her in would be trouble in Ulster not very different from civil war'. His alternative, he told Lloyd George, was

> Don't confine your bullying to Ulster. Try it on the Sinn Féiners too. Say to them, 'I have tried to put through this settlement. Ulster in spite of all the pressure I have put on it is immoveable, and the [Conservative] party on which I rely will be hopelessly broken up. However much I wish it, it can't be done. I therefore make this proposal to you – For your own part of Ireland frame your own constitution, and if it is within the Empire we will accept almost anything you propose. Not only so, but if it is possible we will carry an Act of Parliament that the moment Ulster is willing to join with you she can do so automatically.

If Sinn Féin refused such a proposal, Bonar Law suggested a second option which he himself could not 'advocate' but which he 'would not oppose':

> I would say to them, 'Very well go to the devil in your own way – govern your own part of Ireland as you please. If you form a constitution within the Empire and behave decently to Protestants there and make no attempt against Ulster, we will not interfere with you. We will allow trade to go on as at present. On the other hand if

you don't behave decently we will spend no more British blood in Ireland. We will fight you by an economic blockade. We will allow no intercourse of any kind between Ireland and the United Kingdom.'

Bonar Law's exposition is significant on two counts. First, predictably, because it demonstrated the strength of his determination to protect Northern Ireland from coercion in any guise. Second, less predictably, because of what it reveals of his indifference to whatever settlement might be concluded in respect of nationalist Ireland, an indifference that became important when he ultimately succeeded Lloyd George as prime minister in October 1922. But in the short term the first count was what mattered. Although Bonar Law told Croal that if Lloyd George 'goes on with his present proposals' he would oppose him and 'try to get the Conservative Party to follow', he also insisted that there had been no breach in his 'personal friendship' with Lloyd George with whom he was again dining the next night; his own preference, moreover, was not 'to have anything to do with politics until next session'.

Bonar Law was sufficiently reassured by talking to Lloyd George to abandon all thoughts of leading a revolt at Liverpool; indeed he did not even attend the conference and the threat to the government's survival evaporated. But Austen Chamberlain remained suspicious of Bonar Law, 'an Ulsterman by descent and spirit, a very ambitious man . . . itching to be back in politics where he is disposed to think the first place might & ought to be his'.[55] In his absence the mood at Liverpool was ambivalent. While 'there was a universal sympathy for the Irish Loyalists North and South' and a 'determination to defend Ulster', reported Salisbury, there was also 'a very strong desire to avoid civil war and a general wish not to break up the Irish Conference until everything had been tried to secure peace with honour'.[56] Austen Chamberlain further conciliated Bonar Law at a lunch on 23 October. A misunderstanding had arisen, explained Chamberlain, because

> Bonar had somehow got it into his head that we Unionists contemplated, not indeed the physical coercion of Ulster, but a legislative procedure which would make Ulstermen rebels against the law of the land. He appears to have thought that we had at one time contemplated, and might now [be] contemplating the passage into law of an Act for the creation of an All-Ireland Parliament to which Ulster would be legally subject without her own consent being obtained and under which Ulstermen who refused obedience would be technically rebels even though we did not use force to compel their obedience. I told him that we did not contemplate and never had contemplated the possibility of such a procedure. Relieved of this fear he appeared to have no difference with us. He would not object to anything that we were proposing to give to the rest of Ireland.[57]

Safe from the danger of a diehard revolt, Lloyd George now hastened the preparation of a draft British treaty.[58] On 16 November Tom Jones presented the British draft to Griffith. Griffith described it to de Valera as 'not the draft of a Treaty but tentative suggestions'[59] to which the Irish should reply 'with a similar document'. But, again, it was the British draft that determined the course of the continuing negotiation. Its essence was a reiteration of the restrictive reservations in their proposals of 20 July coupled with a formulation of what Lloyd George had agreed with Griffith about Northern

Ireland. The Irish response, delivered on 22 November, was drafted mainly by Childers and took the form of a typed two-paged memorandum prefaced by a note stating that the proposals were contingent on the essential unity of Ireland being maintained. It effectively ignored the British reservations and made no mention of Northern Ireland until the final clause which baldly provided that 'in the event of the existing legislature of the North East of Ireland accepting its position under the National Parliament, Ireland will confirm the legislature in its existing powers and will undertake to provide the safeguards designed to secure any special interests of the area over which it functions'.[60]

'This is no use,' was the immediate reaction of Lloyd George. 'They are back on their independent state again . . . There is nothing here about safeguards for Ulster . . . [He] was thinking really not of the specific safeguards . . . but of Ulster's right to contract out of an All-Ireland Parliament.'[61] Lloyd George's outrage was genuine. 'The Irish negotiations have a taken a turn for the worse – seriously,' he wrote to his wife. 'This time it is the Sinn Féiners. Last week it was the Ulsterites. They are both the sons of Belial!'[62]

Lloyd George now played Bonar Law's card of 'bullying the Sinn Féiners'. He first ordered Tom Jones to tell them that 'unless they withdrew their document he would have to break off the negotiations' but when Jones left 10 Downing Street to arrange an appointment with Arthur Griffith, he was called back and instructed, this time in the presence of Chamberlain and Birkenhead, instead

> . . . to tell the Sinn Féiners that the document filled him with despair, Ministers were busy men, they had spent weeks and weeks on this matter and apparently made no

progress whatever. 'Are they in the Empire or are they out? Are we to control Naval defence or are we not? . . . Where are the safeguards for Ulster? Do they accept or do they not safeguards enumerated on Friday and of which Griffith made a note? All my colleagues would share my view of this document. If they are not coming into the Empire, then we will make them.' All these remarks, said with great vehemence, to which I listened in complete silence, were followed by F. E. [Birkenhead] and Chamberlain with accompanying remarks of approval.

Tom Jones prevented the collapse of the conference when he soft-pedalled his instructions at his meeting with Griffith and Collins in 22 Hans Place that afternoon. He 'did not tell them they could "pack up and go home" but made . . . them understand that, unless the letter was withdrawn or explained away, the P.M. . . . would have no option but to send them a letter that day breaking off negotiations'. But he also suggested that 'there were explanations' that might 'modify [British] objections'. When he returned to Downing Street he 'found the P.M. resting on a couch in the drawing room . . . I sat down by his side and, beginning in Welsh and passing into English, spoke as quietly and soothingly as I could about the interview . . . telling him that they had gone off to consider his message with their colleagues.' The sense that the talks were on the brink of collapse pervaded a cabinet meeting that afternoon when first Birkenhead, then Chamberlain and finally Lloyd George himself all passed notes to Tom Jones seeking information about what had happened. '"Were they very truculent?", asked Lloyd George, referring to Griffith and Collins. I scribbled back, "Nervous, rather firm, not at all truculent."'[63]

Lloyd George, however, was also nervous because, as Edwin Montagu remarked, he 'could not afford to let the negotiations fail'.[64] Both sides pulled back from the brink when Lloyd George, Chamberlain and Birkenhead met Griffith, Collins and Barton in Downing Street to discuss the Irish memorandum the next morning. After Lloyd George spoke of 'the grave view he and his colleagues took of the reply . . . there was a long and not unfriendly discussion' that cleared the air. Afterwards Lloyd George was 'in a much milder mood. He hardly referred to the question of a rupture but asked rhetorically, "Why did they bring that pip-squeak of a man Barton with them? I would not make him a private secretary to an Under-Secretary."'[65]

A further conference took place the next morning, 24 November, in the House of Lords with Birkenhead and the attorney general, Gordon Hewart, representing the British, and two constitutional lawyers, Gavan Duffy and John Chartres, accompanying Griffith and Collins. The discussion never got beyond the first two clauses of the Irish memorandum, dealing with issues of authority, the Commonwealth and the crown, and the only outcome was 'a promise by Sinn Féin to provide a formula embodying their conception of the Crown and allegiance. For the first time this issue was made absolutely clear to both sides.' The British were pessimistic – Lloyd George again thought 'it looked like a break', but he sat tight and awaited the outcome of the Irish delegation's deliberations with their colleagues in Dublin where they returned on the night of the 24th.

On Monday, 28 November, an impatient Lloyd George rang Tom Jones from Beaconsfield, where he had been playing golf, and asked him to bring Griffith and Collins to Chequers so that they could give him the Irish reply in person.

But the Irish shrank from accepting prime ministerial hospitality and Tom Jones delivered their reply. The formula read: 'Ireland will agree to be associated with the British Commonwealth for all purposes of common concern, including defence, peace and war, and political treaties, and to recognise the British Crown as Head of the Association.'[66] Lloyd George 'read the Sinn Féin letter aloud' to Tom Jones and Frances Stevenson 'and remarked "This means war."' But when Birkenhead and Robert Horne arrived at Chequers they were more sanguine. 'They did not think this was the Irishmen's last word. Anyway it was a bad ground for a break. At 10.10 Arthur Griffith and [Éamonn] Duggan arrived. They left at 11.45 and ten minutes later L.G. went off to bed with the remark in Welsh "Gwell" [better].'[67]

The British stance at Chequers was that, while 'no British Government could attempt to propose to the British people the abrogation of the Crown', they would put any phrase the Irish wanted into the treaty 'to ensure that the function of the Crown in Ireland should be no more in practice than it is in Canada or any Dominion'. The next afternoon, 29 November, Lloyd George pushed the conference into its final phase at a series of three meetings in Downing Street. A meeting of the British Seven to consider the oath of allegiance at three o'clock was followed at four by another meeting of Lloyd George, Chamberlain and Birkenhead with Griffith, Collins and Duggan when the British confirmed the Chequers conversation 'and specifically offered to put a phrase in the Treaty ensuring that the Crown should have no more authority in Ireland than in Canada'.[68] The 'essentials' of the final British proposals were hammered out at another meeting at 5.30 p.m. between the British triumvirate and their parliamentary draftsmen and constitutional lawyers. Lloyd George's formula that Ireland 'have the same national status as the Dominion of Canada and be known as the Irish Free State'[69] emerged from his exchanges with Chamberlain and Birkenhead.

The draft treaty was delivered to Arthur Griffith on the evening of 30 November, although the Irish delegates won some further amendments, principally on the financial articles, before travelling to Ireland on the evening of 2 December for a meeting of the Dáil cabinet on Saturday, 3 December. Their voyage was prolonged by a collision between the mail-boat and a schooner and they were exhausted when they arrived at Dublin's Mansion House for a fractious and inconclusive meeting constrained by the deadline of their having again to set off for London that evening.

The five delegates were split. Griffith was 'in favour of the Treaty'. He refused to break on the crown 'and thereby hand to Ulster the position from which she had been driven'. Duggan agreed with Griffith and believed the 'Treaty to be England's last word'. Collins was 'in substantial agreement' with Griffith and Duggan; 'the non-acceptance of a Treaty would be a gamble as England could arrange war in Ireland in a week'. Barton and Gavan Duffy opposed acceptance. Barton thought 'England's last word had not been reached and that she could not declare war on question of allegiance'. Gavan Duffy wanted the treaty to be rejected by the Dáil and 'sent back amended'. While there was unanimity that the oath of allegiance could not be accepted 'if not amended', the level of support for de Valera's suggested amendment – 'I ____ do solemnly swear true faith and allegiance to the constitution of the Irish Free State, to the Treaty of Association and to recognise the King of Great Britain as Head of the Associated States' – was unclear and de Valera again refused to 'join the delegation in London at this stage of the Negotiations'. But

Griffith, despite reiterating his refusal to 'take the responsibility of breaking on the Crown', agreed that 'he would go before the Dáil' and that he would tell Lloyd George that 'the document could not be signed . . . that it is now a matter for the Dáil, and to try and put the blame on Ulster'.[70]

In the last analysis, the details of the discussions in Dublin had little bearing on the signing of the treaty. What mattered was what happened in London. It was a measure of the sense of make or break in both delegations that the next meeting took place on a Sunday, when Griffith, Barton and Gavan Duffy met Lloyd George, Chamberlain, Birkenhead and Horne in Downing Street at five o'clock on 4 December. Michael Collins was so '"fed up" with the muddle'[71] that he stayed away. After Griffith had read out de Valera's 'counter proposals', the British retired for a ten-minute private conclave. When they returned, Lloyd George declared that, 'although they might have considered some change in the form of the oath, this was a refusal . . . to enter the Empire and accept the common bond of the Crown'. Griffith's attempts 'to work back on Ulster' came to nothing and the discussion broke down with an agreement that the Irish delegation would formally submit its proposals the next day and that the British would respond with 'a formal rejection'; they would also inform Craig that 'the negotiations were broken down'.[72]

Tom Jones again dragged the conference back from the brink of collapse when he went to see Griffith at midnight in 22 Hans Place and spent an hour with him alone. Griffith, he reported to Lloyd George, in a three-page memorandum hastily scribbled at 1.30 on the morning of 5 December, 'was labouring under a deep sense of the crisis and spoke throughout with the greatest earnestness and unusual emotion', so much emotion that Tom Jones sanitised the version of the memorandum[73] in his privately printed and subsequently published diary. Griffith said that 'he and Collins had been completely won over to belief in [Lloyd George's] desire for peace' but their 'Dublin colleagues' had not;

> ... they are told they have surrendered much ('the King' and 'Association with the Empire') and got nothing to offer the Dáil in return ... Cannot you [Lloyd George], he pleaded, and this was the burden of our talk, get from Craig a conditional recognition, however shadowy, of Irish national unity in return for the acceptance of the Empire by Sinn Féin? ... The upshot of the whole talk was 'Will Mr Lloyd George help us to get peace?'

To a negotiator as tough and ingenious as Lloyd George, Griffith's appeal was a confession of weakness. So was his further plea that Lloyd George should see Collins secretly. 'This is our first attempt', Griffith pensively told Jones, 'at "secret diplomacy". I wish the P.M. would have a heart to heart talk with Collins.' Jones agreed to arrange a meeting at 9.15 a.m. and Griffith went out at one o'clock in the morning looking for Collins, who slept in the delegation's house at 15 Cadogan Gardens. Jones concluded his dramatic account with a plea of his own. 'I think Craig should be sent for. Peace with Ireland is worth that effort with Craig. War is failure at home and at Washington.' At 7 a.m. that morning Lionel Curtis left a draft statement[74] for Lloyd George with the watchman at 10 Downing Street explaining why the British government felt no purpose could be served by continuing the conference.

But the midnight tête-à-tête sent an unmistakable signal that Griffith, like Lloyd George, wanted a settlement. Collins was more ambivalent. His explanation for not attending the

Sunday evening conference was that he had already 'argued fully all points' and it was not until Monday morning that he yielded to the entreaties of Griffith, who led him to believe that Lloyd George 'desired to see [him]', whereas in fact it was Griffith himself who had set up the meeting. Lloyd George began by saying that his cabinet was meeting at twelve and he would tell them that the negotiations had broken down 'on the question of "within or without" the Empire'. Collins's response, like Griffith's the night before, focused on his dissatisfaction 'as regards the North East'. When Lloyd George remarked that Collins himself had 'pointed out on a previous occasion that the North would be forced economically to come in', Collins said he wanted 'a definite reply from Craig and . . . was as agreeable to a reply rejecting as accepting' because rejection would mean that, through the establishment of a boundary commission, they 'would save Tyrone, and Fermanagh, parts of Derry, Armagh and Down'. Lloyd George also expressed a willingness to 'discuss the form of Oath' provided that 'a definite understanding' had been reached on articles 1 and 2 (the Dominion articles); in that event 'he would be in a position to hold up any action until we had, if we desired to do so, submitted the matter to Dáil Éireann'. He also suggested a further meeting of the two delegations that afternoon at two o'clock; a still hesitant Collins would not commit himself, agreeing only to let 'the appointment stand tentatively'.[75]

But the conversation strengthened Lloyd George's hand because Collins had never challenged the predominance the British attached to articles 1 and 2. Although he queried the wording of the articles relating to the oath of allegiance, to defence, and to trade, these were not insuperable difficulties from a British perspective. What also encouraged Lloyd

George was that Collins never referred either to the nomen-
clature or to the constitutional status of the Irish Free State;
nor did he offer any objection to dominion status, still less
make any mention of external association. This enabled Lloyd
George to act on the assumption that Collins, like Griffith,
would not break on the issue of empire. There remained the
issue of Ulster and here Collins seemed poised to interpret the
establishment of a boundary commission as providing for the
essential unity of Ireland.

These were the considerations that shaped Lloyd George's
strategy in the final phase of the negotiations when, accompanied by Chamberlain, Birkenhead and Churchill, he met
Griffith, Collins and Barton at three o'clock that afternoon.
Lloyd George immediately confronted Griffith, saying that he
had already agreed to the Ulster clauses. There followed the
dramatic scene, recorded in Robert Barton's notes of the meeting,[76] when Lloyd George became, or pretended to become,
'excited. He shook his papers in the air, declared that we were
trying deliberately to bring about a break on Ulster because
our people in Ireland had refused to come within the Empire
and that Arthur Griffith was letting him down where he had
promised not to do so.' Then, with the air of a conjuror
pulling a rabbit out of a hat before a mystified Collins and
Barton, he produced Tom Jones's memorandum summarising
his luncheon conversation with Griffith on 12 November. A
disconcerted Griffith, having 'declared his adhesion to his
undertaking' also said that 'it was not unreasonable for us to
require that Craig should reply before we refused or accepted
the proposals'; he then switched the discussion to the wording of the oath. Here Birkenhead immediately gave ground
and accepted, with minor alterations, a new form of oath that
'Collins had handed in to him that morning'. Churchill, too,

accepted some small amendments on the defence clauses. Then Lloyd George pulled another rabbit out of his hat by suddenly abandoning free trade, one of the restrictive reservations in the proposals of 20 July. He instead promised to 'agree provisionally that there should be freedom on both sides to impose any tariffs either liked' subject to the acceptance of the document as a whole. This offer of fiscal autonomy out of the blue was especially welcome to Griffith as the author of Sinn Féin's protectionist economic programme and might have been designed to soften his resentment at the accusations of his having behaved dishonourably.

In any event, when the discussion 'went back to Ulster', Arthur Griffith was seduced into the monumental mistake that shattered the residual cohesion of the Irish delegation and transformed the chemistry of the negotiations: 'He agreed that he personally would sign the Treaty whether Craig accepted or not.' For the head of the delegation in a two-party negotiation suddenly to announce during the negotiations that he intends to sign the document under negotiation because his honour was allegedly impugned, regardless of whether the other members of his delegation did so, was as vain as it was naive. Despite his insistence 'that his colleagues were in a different position from himself in that they were not party to the promise not to let Lloyd George down' and his repeated efforts 'to avoid the question being put' to Collins and Barton, Griffith's personal pledge to sign the treaty meant that he was effectively siding with Lloyd George and forcing his colleagues to choose between disappointing him or breaking their pledge to de Valera. It also gave Lloyd George a blank cheque for Bonar Law's strategy of 'bullying the Sinn Féiners'. Assured of Griffith's signature and with reason to assume after their conversation that morning that Collins was disposed to follow suit, 'Lloyd George stated that he had always assumed that Arthur Griffith spoke for the Delegation'; that they 'were all plenipotentiaries and that it was now a matter of peace or war'. Every delegate must 'sign the document and recommend it, or there was no agreement'. He then produced two letters. The first was a covering letter to go with the treaty, stating that the Irish delegates were recommending its acceptance by Dáil Éireann; the second letter said the negotiations had collapsed and 'he had no proposals to send to Craig'. Lloyd George demanded acceptance or rejection of the treaty by 10 p.m. that evening as 'a special train and destroyer were ready to carry one letter or the other to Belfast'. There was one last concession: the British delegates agreed to reduce the twelve-month transition period within which Northern Ireland could opt in or out of the Irish Free State from twelve months to one month. The Irish delegation then withdrew to 22 Hans Place to make its decision and, on returning to 10 Downing Street, signed the treaty at ten minutes past two on the morning of 6 December.

The theatricality and melodrama of Lloyd George's behaviour – his affected rage, his waving of papers in the air, his threats of war, his talk of Belfast deadlines and of trains and destroyers – occasioned much subsequent but essentially meaningless debate on whether he was bluffing. Such debate was irrelevant from the perspective of the British delegation for whom all that mattered was that, bluff or not, it worked.

One British official, Lionel Curtis, described 'Lloyd George negotiating with the Irish [as] like Augustus John drawing. Every stroke was made with precision and mastery, and never needed correction.'[77] 'It was a wonderful day,' reported Tom Jones to Maurice Hankey, the cabinet secretary in Washington; 'the P.M. starting at 5.00 a.m. and snatching 25 minutes sleep just after 8.00 p.m. His patience and alertness have been extraordinary, even for him.' He then summarised the magnitude of Lloyd George's achievement in a single sentence: 'In essentials we have given nothing that was not in the July proposals.'[78]

12

1922: Escape from the Irish Bog

The parliamentary debate on the treaty, on 14–15 December 1921, was a major triumph for Lloyd George. Ireland 'quite suddenly became the government's badge of honour and respectability, its major asset'.[1] But that badge was soon tarnished by developments in Dublin where the treaty provoked a deep and bitter split and where de Valera led the republican campaign to reject it. The Dáil finally approved the treaty by 64 votes to 57 on 10 January 1922.

This paved the way for Arthur Griffith, as the leader of the treaty delegation, to summon the meeting on 14 January demanded by article 17 of 'members of Parliament elected by constituencies in Southern Ireland'. The meeting, attended only by the pro-treaty deputies and by four members elected for Trinity College Dublin, achieved within an hour its sole task of establishing a provisional government to constitute a parliament and government for the Irish Free State by 6 December 1922.

On Sunday evening, 4 December 1921, with the negotiations seeming on the brink of failure, the British government had promised that, if the Irish signed the treaty, 'they would hand . . . over Dublin Castle and withdraw their troops from the country'.[2] Lloyd George had already appointed Winston Churchill, the colonial secretary, to chair a cabinet committee to transfer power to the provisional government. It first met on 21 December and the need to sustain the embattled pro-treaty majority led by Griffith and Collins made it imperative for the British to keep their promise. They did so with alacrity. The Lord Lieutenant formally transferred power to Michael Collins at a ceremony in Dublin Castle on 16 January, the day after the Dáil had formally approved his appointment as chairman of the provisional government.

Churchill's appointment signalled that, having secured the treaty settlement, Lloyd George was content to take a back seat. In effect, Churchill became minister for Irish affairs, South and North; Lloyd George intervened only when he feared his settlement was in jeopardy. But Churchill's support of the treaty was unwavering. 'Our position is a vy strong one, *so long* as we adhere to the Treaty,' he told his wife. 'We must not get ourselves back into that hideous bog of reprisals, from which we have saved ourselves.'[3] He used the same metaphor in the House of Commons when he introduced the second reading of the Irish Free State Bill on 16 February: 'for generations we have been wandering and floundering in the Irish bog; but at last we think that in this Treaty we have set our feet upon a pathway, which has already become a cause-way – narrow, but firm and far-reaching. Let us march along this causeway with determination and circumspection, with-out losing heart and without losing faith.'

The treaty negotiations of October–December 1921 had offered the only opportunity for amending the terms of the partition of Ireland for generations to come. Indeed fifty years passed before British and Irish government delegations next met, at Sunningdale outside London in 1973, formally to confer on the terms on which Northern Ireland should be governed. But there was no likelihood that the partitionist tide that had been flowing since 1914 would be reversed because the imperatives of coalition government remained unaltered. The Ulster issue, from the perspective of the British delegation, had been resolved and was on the agenda only because the British knew that the Irish would otherwise refuse to negotiate.

Neither the treaty split, nor moreover the civil war it ultimately provoked, had anything to do with partition. The bitter fifteen-day debate in the Dáil had hinged not on the size or the shape but on 'the status of the new Ireland'.[4] It set the agenda for the first three decades of party politics in independent Ireland when the burning issue was sovereignty, not unity, and when what mattered above all was Dublin's relations with London, not Dublin's relations with Belfast. Nicholas Mansergh has demonstrated how 'the struggle had been waged for status – for the republic – and partition, subordinate to nothing else, was none the less subordinate to that . . . It was when republican status was attained that partition became *the* principal preoccupation.'[5] De Valera, in particular, made no bones about his priorities. The Northern provisions of his 'Document No. 2', his personal alternative to the treaty unveiled before the Dáil on 15 December, mirror the relevant articles of the treaty. 'The difficulty is not the Ulster question,' he then insisted. 'As far as we are concerned this is a fight between Ireland and England. I want to eliminate the Ulster question out of it . . . We will take the same things as agreed on there.'[6]

The reality was that articles 11 and 12 of the treaty were but fig leaves to cover the Irish negotiators' impotence to end partition. Article 11 provided that, until a month had expired after the treaty had been ratified by act of parliament,

... the powers of the Parliament and Government of the Irish Free State shall not be exercisable as respects Northern Ireland, and the provisions of the Government of Ireland Act, 1920, shall, so far as they relate to Northern Ireland, remain in full force and effect.

And article 12 provided that:

If before the expiration of the said month, an address is presented to His Majesty by both Houses of the Parliament of Northern Ireland to that effect, the powers of the Parliament and the Government of the Irish Free State shall no longer extend to Northern Ireland, and the provisions of the Government of Ireland Act, 1920 (including those relating to the Council of Ireland) shall so far as they relate to Northern Ireland, continue to be of full force and effect, and this instrument shall have effect subject to the necessary modifications.

Provided that if such an address is so presented a Commission consisting of three persons, one to be appointed by the Government of the Irish Free State, one to be appointed by the Government of Northern Ireland, and one who shall be Chairman to be appointed by the British Government shall determine in accordance with the wishes of the inhabitants, so far as may be compatible with economic and geographic conditions, the boundaries between Northern Ireland and the rest of Ireland, and for the purposes of the Government of Ireland Act, 1920, and of this instrument, the boundary of Northern Ireland shall be such as may be determined by such Commission.

In theory, the articles paid lip service to the Irish negotiators' principle of essential unity: they could not be construed as an endorsement of partition by the treaty's signatories and they allowed for the exercise of the Irish Free State's powers throughout the island of Ireland once what became known as the 'Ulster month' had expired. Like Pontius Pilate, the signatories washed their hands of any responsibility for the continuance of partition, for which the Northern Irish parliament was given exclusive responsibility.

In practice, essential unity was no more than a polite fiction because the British negotiating principle that Ulster could not be coerced also remained intact. No one, not even the Irish signatories of the treaty, pretended that the Northern Irish parliament would not consolidate partition by immediately opting out of the Irish Free State. The inevitability of its opting out was duly hammered home less than seventy-two hours after the treaty was signed when a joint meeting of the members of both houses of the Northern Irish parliament and of the Ulster Unionist MPs at Westminster 'decided that on no consideration would Ulster go into a Free State'.[7]

The provision for the appointment of a boundary commission was a different matter because it posed a threat to the territorial integrity of Northern Ireland. Although it could not impair the powers of the Northern Irish government, it could reduce the size of that government's jurisdiction. From the outset, however, two aspects of article 12 vitiated the commission as an anti-partitionist instrument. First, the inherent ambiguity about how 'the wishes of the inhabitants' in those areas of Northern Ireland in which there were nationalist majorities would be reconciled with 'economic and geographic conditions' in any adjustment of the boundary. Second, that the terms under which the commission was to be appointed assumed the Northern Irish government's acceptance of a provision in a treaty that they had not signed: 'that the implementation of the articles relating to Northern Ireland depended on the co-operation of the Northern Ireland government, which was not a party to the agreement'.[8]

Nationalists neither in the North nor the South construed the pregnant phrase 'economic and geographic conditions' as bearing on areas with nationalist majorities contiguous to the border. Nationalist enclaves deep within Northern Ireland were another matter and it was 'impossible to expect that either the glens of Antrim or parts of Belfast could be separated from their surrounding areas'.[9] What, then, of Lloyd George's encouraging Collins's expectations that 'the North would be forced economically to come in' at their crucial tête-à-tête on the morning of 5 December when the next day, within hours of his signing the treaty, he boasted to his cabinet that 'a boundary commission might even give the north more than she would lose'.[10] It was a classic example of what Lord Riddell, Lloyd George's confidant of many years, meant when he warned that 'you cannot rely on what L.G. says . . . He may not actually tell a lie, but he will lead you to believe what he considers will induce you to do what he wants.'[11]

The uncertainties inherent in articles 11 and 12 prompted anger and dismay among Ulster Unionists and Northern Ireland's prime minister, James Craig, reviewed strategy on the boundary commission on 10 January 1922, the day the Dáil narrowly approved the treaty. He feared that such a slender majority would make Griffith and Collins 'insist upon every single item of the Treaty' to deflect de Valera's criticism. The Northern Irish government's first option, argued Craig, was to state that, since they were not party to the treaty, they would refuse to take part in the commission and would not be bound by its decisions. The alternative was to participate in the commission while seeking safeguards in the terms of reference. Craig advised that the 'best course would be not to show our hand at the present time but to consider the matter very carefully during the few months that must elapse before the Boundary Commission would be established' and his cabinet 'agreed that no immediate decision should be given'.[12]

Again, Churchill responded swiftly and the first Craig–Collins meeting took place at the colonial office in London under his auspices on 21 January 1922. Although both men 'glowered magnificently'[13] when introduced by Churchill, the upshot of their three-hour meeting was the first Craig–Collins pact. It provided that 'the Boundary Commission as outlined in the Treaty . . . be altered'. The governments of the Irish Free State and of Northern Ireland would appoint one representative each to report to Collins and Craig, 'who will mutually agree on behalf of their respective Governments on the future boundaries between the two'.[14]

Such seeming harmony rested on the quaking foundations of diametrically different interpretations of the boundary commission and it collapsed within a week. Craig never contemplated anything more than tinkering with the border between North and South and publicly told a meeting of the Ulster Unionist Council in Belfast on 27 January that he would 'never give in to any arrangement of the boundary which leaves our Ulster area smaller than it is'. Collins, conscious that the publication of the pact had alarmed Northern nationalists, was meanwhile reassuring the Catholic Bishop of Dromore that 'no action or desire of the northern parliament could take' such places as Newry, South and East Down, and 'a great portion' of Armagh 'away from the Irish government'.[15]

When Collins next met Craig, in Dublin on 2 February, they publicly acknowledged that 'no further agreement was reached, and a very serious situation has consequently arisen' due to 'the Irish delegation's agreement with Mr Lloyd George that large territories were involved in the Commission, and not merely a boundary line, as Sir James Craig was given to understand privately'.[16] The joint statement was bad enough, but their individual interpretations, noted Tom Jones, made matters worse: 'Craig went and spoke about "no inch of Ulster's soil being surrendered" and Collins talked of the whole of Tyrone and Fermanagh coming to the South.'[17]

North–South tension heightened on 4 February when Collins issued a press statement declaring that 'majorities must rule, and . . . on that principle we secure immense anti-partition areas'; he called for a meeting of 'all the Parliamentary representatives of the whole of Ireland . . . to adopt a policy and frame a constitution for our common country'. The alternative, he added ominously, was 'a resumption of the old disturbances, the old conflicts, the old animosities'.[18]

Craig moved quickly to secure his London flank in a letter to Lloyd George: he had 'striven for peace but in view of the fact that the response of the leaders of the South to me is to threaten Ulster and to express the desire to rob her of territory guaranteed to her by Great Britain, my response to them is that what Ulster has she will hold, and that I and my colleagues now absolutely decline to enter into further conferences on the subject'. Craig's letter, with a threatening peroration calling for support from the 'great Conservative party',[19] prompted an immediate summons to 10 Downing Street where he confirmed its terms.

Violence erupted along the border within days. On 8 February, the Monaghan IRA kidnapped 43 Unionists in a series of cross-border raids into Tyrone and Fermanagh designed to force the Northern Irish government to reprieve three IRA volunteers under sentence of death and to release other recently arrested Monaghan volunteers. On 11 February, they attacked a party of Ulster special constables while they were changing trains at Clones, en route to Enniskillen from their training camp at Newtownards; the IRA leader and four constables were killed and five others were taken prisoner. The incident triggered sectarian attacks on Catholics in Belfast where there were 31 violent deaths between 13 and 15 February; by the end of the month, there were 43 dead, 25 of whom were Catholics. Although Collins secured the release of the Unionist hostages and Craig responded by releasing the Monaghan IRA prisoners, undeclared war simmered along the border.

On 14 February, Field-Marshall Sir Henry Wilson, on the point of retirement as chief of the Imperial General Staff, told Churchill's cabinet committee that protecting the border was not enough. Nothing could solve the Irish problem 'except reconquest' which could 'only be done if England is wholeheartedly in favour of it'.[20] Churchill jibbed; he also vetoed Craig's proposals to send a punitive expedition of 5,000 special constables south across the border and to requisition massive military supplies from the RIC depot in Dublin. But Churchill did agree to send three more battalions of British troops for border duty in Northern Ireland and promised another six if necessary. On 15 February he also conferred with Michael Collins at the colonial office about reducing border tensions.

On 16 February, Churchill, conscious of the 'formidable' support for Craig on the Tory back benches, introduced the second reading of the Irish Free State Bill in the House of

Commons. Although an amendment refusing assent to the boundary commission and declaring that Northern Ireland would use force to resist any change in the border moved by Charles Craig, the Northern Irish premier's brother, was defeated by 302 votes to 60, Churchill freely admitted that the boundary commission was 'the weak point' in the assurances given to Ulster. 'It affects the existing frontiers of Ulster and may conceivably affect them prejudicially'; but he also expressed the government's determination to 'defend every inch of Ulster soil under the Treaty as if it were Kent'.[21] None of Lloyd George's ministers 'would stand more than mere rectification of boundaries', he promised James Craig's wife at dinner on 9 March before assuring the Northern Ireland prime minister that 'Ulster would come out on top',[22] assurances he repeated to Craig when they met again next day.

The Northern Irish government continued to focus its energies not on adjusting but on defending the border; to holding what it had. On 13 March, it reaffirmed its determination to opt out of the Irish Free State at the first available opportunity. Craig told his cabinet that Henry Wilson, who had won a seat in the House of Commons in the North Down by-election on 21 February, had accepted an invitation to act as the Northern Irish government's military adviser 'in regard to the steps which should be taken for restoring law and order'.[23] Wilson made an immediate impression, Maurice Cowling has written, 'as a well-informed critic of Lloyd George, an irreconcilable enemy of Sinn Féin and a formidable accession of strength to the Die Hards'.[24]

The political asset of the treaty had by now become a threat to the survival of Lloyd George's government as the Tories chafed restlessly in the harness of coalition. On 13 February, a deputation of 35 diehard MPs rehearsed their grievances for their party leader, Austen Chamberlain; and Chamberlain's speech on 20 February, asserting the continued need for a coalition government, was publicly contradicted two days later by the Conservative Party chairman, George Younger. On 27 February, a beleaguered Lloyd George tried the ploy of offering his resignation as prime minister to Chamberlain if he could not be guaranteed Tory support. No guarantee was forthcoming and rumours of Lloyd George's retirement abounded during his recuperation from neuralgia at Criccieth[25] from 10 to 27 March.

Churchill's role was pivotal. Ireland was only one of a range of issues on which he now identified with the diehards in cultivating his image as the strongman of a government staggering into its death throes. He had used the Ulster issue to court radical support among the Liberals at the height of the Curragh crisis of 1914; now he used it to bolster his popularity among the Tories. The ever malleable Chamberlain, unnerved by the attacks on his party leadership and 'not prepared to take any action that might be construed by the diehards as being anti-Ulster',[26] bobbed along in Churchill's wake. Government policy on Ireland became almost as Ulster-centric in the spring of 1922 as it had been throughout 1920.

On 17 March, Tom Jones complained to Lloyd George that he and Lionel Curtis were 'very disquieted at the position we are moving into in relation to Ulster' because of the abandonment of 'the essence' of his 'bargain' with the Irish signatories of the treaty: 'that Northern Ireland was to remain a part of the United Kingdom with a Provisional Government but with powers no greater and no less than under the 1920 Act'. It would be another 'breach of faith', argued Jones,

... if we continue in the present policy of (a) paying for the Special Constables, (b) making other grants to Ulster, (c) cloaking a military force under the guise of a police force, (d) allowing Henry Wilson to proceed unchallenged to prepare his 'scheme' for which the Northern Parliament is voting £2,000,000 ... and bringing us back to the position we were in 1914 [during the Curragh mutiny] with the advantage that the Field-Marshall is making his preparations legally with the money of the British Government and without protest.

Is it not the duty of the British Government to undertake the control of the Border and to remove all justification from the Northern Government for these swollen police forces?[27]

But Jones's liberal pleadings ran up against both the brick wall of parliamentary arithmetic and the inexorable drift towards violence, North and South.

Sectarian atrocities against Catholics in Belfast included the gruesome murder of Owen McMahon and four other members of his family on 24 March. McMahon had no Sinn Féin or IRA connections and seems to have been singled out as a prominent Catholic – he was an affluent publican and a personal friend of Joe Devlin; the perpetrators were allegedly members of the Ulster special constabulary intent on a reprisal for the IRA's murdering two special constables on the previous day. The murders spurred Churchill into renewing pressure on Craig and Collins once more to confer, and they did so, again under his aegis at the colonial office, on 29 March. The outcome was the second Craig–Collins pact of 30 March. 'Peace is today declared', its first provision sonorously intoned and the Belfast and Dublin governments undertook 'to co-operate in every way in their power with a view to the restoration of peaceful conditions in the unsettled areas'. Other provisions included a special 'mixed' (Protestant and Catholic) force to police mixed areas of Belfast and a renewed aspiration to resolve the border issue without reference to the boundary commission. But the second pact, like the first, did nothing to arrest the accelerating spiral of violence. Defence and security continued to preoccupy the Northern Irish cabinet and, on 19 April, Craig reported that, when he had seen Churchill on the previous day, he 'had made it clear that Ulster could not afford to postpone her organisation for defence',[28] although he had agreed to avoid unnecessary or provocative demonstrations of force along the border.

In Dublin, the provisional government was similarly preoccupied with internal security as the mounting aggression of the anti-treaty elements in the IRA culminated in their occupation of the Four Courts in Dublin on 14 April. The provisional government's territorial claims within the six counties seemed increasingly irrelevant as it struggled to retain control within the twenty-six counties and one Northern Sinn Féin leader, Cahir Healy, complained that they 'had almost given up speaking of the Boundary Commission. This was a mistake. The Orangemen took this to mean that we had forgotten about it, or, at least, did not take it seriously, that in other words we would be quite content with the status quo.'

But the boundary commission inevitably lapsed deeper into the background[29] as the momentum towards civil war in the South accelerated. Both the British and Northern Irish governments remained apprehensive about the provisional government's Northern policy. On 12 May, Craig reported to his cabinet colleagues that 'the British Government were quite clear in their assurances that they would see Ulster through against any attack from the South, and were bringing five more Battalions into Ulster, making the total number 22'.[30] A council of war took place at the colonial office on the same day when Churchill and his Irish advisers, the pre-treaty Dublin Castle team of Fitzalan, Greenwood, Macready and Cope, conferred with war-office officials. Discussion hinged on the wisdom, first, of issuing further arms to the provisional government without proof that they intended to move against the insurgents in the Four Courts; and, second, of evacuating all remaining British troops from the twenty-six counties, especially from Dublin where there was an obvious danger of their getting sucked into the fighting that might begin between pro- and anti-treaty forces at any moment.[31] If the mood in Dublin and Belfast was tense, the mood in London, with the ever-bellicose Churchill at the helm in Lloyd George's absence (he was in Cannes from Christmas until mid-January, at Criccieth for most of March and at the Genoa conference from 8 April until late May), was so febrile that Tom Jones, the self-appointed guardian angel of the treaty, wrote to Austen Chamberlain, the acting prime minister,

. . . to make the somewhat startling suggestion that the right course is to withdraw the six or seven thousand British troops now in Dublin. It is impossible to confine so large a body of troops to barracks. 'Incidents' may occur at any moment. It is the deliberate aim of Rory O'Connor [the leader of the IRA in the Four Courts] to provoke such incidents and embroil British troops . . . It is absolutely necessary to remove every chance of this so that what fighting there is shall be between Irishmen.[32]

Churchill was further incensed when he got wind of the electoral pact Collins had negotiated with de Valera. The pact provided that a panel of Sinn Féin candidates, to be drawn from the pro- and anti-treaty factions in Sinn Féin in proportion to their relative strength in the existing Dáil, would stand jointly in the approaching election to the third Dáil or provisional parliament; it also provided that four of the nine seats on the executive to be appointed after the election would be allocated to the Republicans. On 15 May, Churchill fired off a pugnacious letter to Collins, denouncing the pact as 'an outrage upon democratic principles' which 'would not invest the Provisional Government with any title to sit in the name of the Irish nation'.[33] The general Whitehall reaction was more phlegmatic and officials at the colonial office, fearful that their increasingly excitable secretary of state 'would 'pull the whole plant out of the ground', tried in vain to get him sent on holiday; meanwhile Tom Jones set about getting Lloyd George back from Genoa.

The next day, however, an unrepentant Churchill briefed the cabinet in apocalyptic terms, warning that, if British troops were withdrawn from Dublin, 'he believed a Republic would be declared there. We must contemplate having to retain what he called the "English capital" and perhaps converting it into a "pale" once more.'[34] Austen Chamberlain, notionally in charge as leader of the Conservative Party in Lloyd George's absence, was so agitated that he communicated the government's 'grave anxieties . . . about the course of events in Ireland' to the ill and ageing Walter Long, now Lord Long of Wraxall, and for so many years the Tories' bellwether on Irish policy. Although Chamberlain believed Collins and Griffith were 'playing straight', 'we have had a Committee carefully examining the coercive measures which we might take if it became necessary, including the possibility of blockade as well as military action . . . [General] Macready has orders if the Republic were proclaimed in Dublin itself to act at once.'[35]

The publication of the Collins–de Valera pact the next day, 20 May, set Churchill's nerves further on edge and he invited Collins, Griffith and Duggan to confer in London on 24 May. The invitation was accepted but Craig immediately seized the opportunity presented by the mounting tension between Dublin and London to harden his government's stance on the boundary commission. 'We, as a united Cabinet, now state that we will not have any Boundary Commission under any circumstances whatever,'[36] he told the Northern Ireland parliament on 23 May. Even Churchill was constrained to protest against such a ringing 'declaration, made without any reference to this Government, that in no circumstances would you accept any rectification of the frontier or any Boundary Commission as provided for in the Treaty'. It made it 'far more difficult' for the British government to comply with Craig's simultaneous requests for 'enormous financial aid and heavy issues of arms' and it also 'robs the Ministers who will meet the Provisional Government representatives of any effective reproach against Mr Collins for the contemptuous manner in which he has spoken of the Treaty'. The effect had been to harden public opinion 'in favour of a policy of Britain disinteresting herself entirely in Irish affairs, leaving them "to stew in their own juice and fight it out among themselves"'.[37]

Craig's immediate response of 26 May to what he loftily dismissed as Churchill's 'private and confidential scold of yesterday' set out his strategy for aborting the boundary commission with remarkable frankness:

This recent pact between Collins and de Valera alters the whole circumstances. Hitherto, you and I have been anticipating the Free Staters holding out against de Valera, sweeping the country at the forthcoming Election and placing themselves in a strong position to maintain law and order in a Free State within the ambit of the British Empire. Now we are confronted with a combination, as 4 is to 5, of out and out Republicans and Free Staters who, through Collins, reiterate that this Treaty is merely a stepping stone to a Republic . . .

I believe it would have been impossible to have found a more appropriate moment to jettison this preposterous proposal and you yourself, will, later on, thank God that we got it out of the way so cleverly because, if matters go from bad to worse, you will be exonerated from having done this on our account, and, on the other hand, if matters go from bad to better and the atmosphere calms down, the imposition of the Border Commission would only once more start the vicious circle of trouble and recrimination with the consequent sad loss of life and devastation. You and we, therefore, have it both ways. If, as I am sure you will be yourself shrewd enough to take full advantage of this escape from an impossible position, it will clear the air for the defence of Ulster against the Republic.[38]

Craig's *cri de coeur* was impeccably timed: it coincided with the delivery of the provisional government's draft constitution of the Irish Free State designed, like the election pact, to avert civil war but which British ministers regarded, in Austen Chamberlain's phrase, as 'a republic scarcely covered by the thinnest monarchical varnish'.[39]

The price of Collins's stratagem of reconciliation with de Valera was a breach with Lloyd George, now back from Genoa and intervening personally in the direction of Irish policy for the first time since his triumphant conclusion of the treaty negotiations. Although Lloyd George pooh-poohed Churchillian apprehensions about the pact at a hastily summoned ministerial conference on 27 May, he led the denunciations of the draft constitution as 'a complete evasion of the Treaty and a setting up of a republic with a thin veneer'.[40] The upshot was an ultimatum from Lloyd George to Arthur Griffith with a series of specific questions designed to establish that the Irish Free State constitution would conform with the treaty. A subcommittee of the Committee of Imperial Defence, chaired by Churchill, meanwhile made contingency plans for British troops, who had by then evacuated the twenty-six counties except for Dublin and Queenstown (Cork Harbour), to occupy the waterline of lakes and rivers running from Dundalk to Letterkenny to defend the North against invasion.[41]

The crisis was compounded by the IRA's incursions at the end of May into the Pettigo–Belleek triangle, a small area in County Fermanagh cut off from the rest of Northern Ireland by Lough Erne and the River Erne. The border runs through Pettigo and, although Belleek is wholly in County Fermanagh, it was overlooked by an old fort on a hill across the border in County Donegal from where the IRA could dominate the village. After skirmishes between the IRA and the Ulster special constabulary, British troops moved into the triangle on 3 June and, when they were fired on from Donegal, crossed the border in pursuit of the IRA. Churchill, ever eager to indulge his martial instincts, was in his element. 'I don't think Winston takes any interest in public affairs unless they involve the possibility of bloodshed,'[42] a Conservative contemporary,

Lord Robert Cecil, later remarked. A furious Lloyd George compared Churchill 'to a chauffeur who apparently is perfectly sane and drives with great skill for months, then suddenly he takes you over a precipice', but he relaxed at the news that there had been few casualties and there followed a mock celebration in Chequers of 'the great bloodless Battle of Belleek' with the prime minister leading the singing of '"Scots wha hae" . . . putting in Winston's name wherever he could'.[43]

Although the battle of Belleek ended in merriment in Chequers, Lloyd George's sensitivity to its potential for disaster moved him to rebuke Churchill in a letter which he copied to the king. While he could not say 'whether Henry Wilson and de Valera are behind this . . . they both want a break and they both want to fight a battle on this ground'. He then described Britain's 'Ulster case [as] not a good one', pointing out that, despite the presence of 9,000 British troops in Ulster and 'half maintaining and wholly equipping another force of 48,000 Specials', in two years '400 Catholics had been killed and 1,200 have been wounded without a single person being brought to justice'. He urged Churchill to keep 'on the high ground of the Treaty – the Crown, the Empire. There we are unassailable. But if you come down from that height and fight in the swamps of Lough Erne you will be overwhelmed.'[44]

Lloyd George might accuse Churchill of disloyalty and of 'fancying himself as a leader of a Tory revolt', but, as Churchill had reminded Tom Jones, 'he had to watch our Parliamentary position'[45] and that meant sustaining the government's majority by holding diehards and disaffected Tories at bay. It was the Irish question that had first united the diehards into an organised group when, on 31 October 1921, 32 diehard MPs had backed a motion of no confidence in the government's negotiating with Sinn Féin, and five of the eight divisions forced by the diehards in the next nine months were on Irish issues. The most dangerous diehard was the fourth Marquess of Salisbury, son of the former prime minister, Bonar Law's intimate, Balfour's cousin and a relation of many other powerful peers. The Irish question is a 'moral question and not a political question', his brother, Hugh Cecil, had told the Commons during the debate on the treaty; 'asking Ulstermen to come under a Government which is dominated by murder [was] asking them to take a step down in civilisation' and Salisbury himself boasted to Bonar Law of having inherited the 'Cecil tradition of contempt for the Irish as a Celtic Catholic race'.[46]

The Pettigo–Belleek incursions inflamed diehard sentiment and fostered sympathy for Ulster. What was happening 'in the swamps of Lough Erne', *pace* Lloyd George, enabled Craig to seize the high ground. Thus Craig rebuffed a telegram from Churchill asking him to come immediately to London to talk to the cabinet about Michael Collins's complaints about the latest spate of sectarian murders of Catholics in Belfast – 'it looks as if Provisional Government might try and get out of their difficulties by throwing blame on Ulster' – because of the situation arising out of the occupation of the Belleek triangle. Craig's formal reply expressed his willingness to go to London to convey 'the real facts of the situation within our area on the distinct understanding that we are not asked to meet the delegates from Southern Ireland'. Collins and his colleagues, argued Craig, were 'evading the real issue by directing your attention to the troubles in Northern Ireland of which they are the original authors and for which they are mainly responsible . . . De Valera and Collins desire to accomplish the fall of Ulster.'[47]

Although it was nonsense to suggest that Collins was in cahoots with de Valera, slogans such as 'the fall of Ulster' had a powerful political resonance among Tories. Events in Northern Ireland coupled with the provisional government's derogations from the treaty, implicit in the Collins–de Valera pact and explicit in the first draft of the Irish Free State constitution, threatened to undermine Lloyd George's twin Irish settlements: the 1920 act and the treaty. 'Belfast remains a scandal,' wrote Austen Chamberlain on 10 June to his sister. 'The rabble whether Catholic or Orange is utterly out of hand, murders and burns indiscriminately.'[48] But, despite their distaste for Craig's failure 'to deal with the murderers in Belfast',[49] British ministers were at one with their Northern Irish counterparts in their determination to defend the 1920 settlement. Craig accordingly persuaded a meeting of British signatories to the treaty not to hold a judicial enquiry into the Belfast pogrom on the grounds that it would 'discourage the police, disconcert their plans and encourage the criminals'. Craig's suggestion 'to suspend judgement' pending the results of a private enquiry by a 'trustworthy agent' of the British government – Stephen Tallents, private secretary to the Irish viceroy, Lord Fitzalan – was accepted and Lloyd George and his colleagues were content piously to record that 'the duty of the British government was to observe the strictest impartiality as between all creeds and sections. No ground ought to be given for the charge that whilst in the recent negotiations with the Southern Irish the British Government had been prepared to take extreme measures, they took no care to protect Catholics in the North.'[50]

On the same day, 16 June 1922, the publication of the Irish Free State's constitution which, in its revised form, had been approved by Lloyd George and his colleagues as conforming with the Treaty, resolved the crisis between London and Dublin. That date was also polling day in the elections to the third Dáil (the provisional parliament of the Irish Free State) and the decisive defeat of the republicans (who won only 36 seats compared with the 58 seats won by pro-treaty Sinn Féin candidates) further reassured the British government.

A new crisis blew up on 22 June, however, when Henry Wilson, who had just been elected as an Ulster Unionist MP, was assassinated by two members of the London unit of the IRA. 'It was the first assassination of a Member of Parliament in London since Spencer Perceval was shot dead in the lobby of the House of Commons in 1812.'[51] Belfast reacted much as London had reacted to the assassination of the Lord Lieutenant, Frederick Cavendish, in Dublin's Phoenix Park forty years before. 'He was ours,' thundered the *Belfast News-Letter*; 'ours by blood, ours by sympathy and ours by service. He died a martyr to the cause of the freedom and liberties of Northern Ireland.'[52] Lloyd George himself was 'very upset' not least because his notorious physical cowardice – he 'went in terror of his life' at the hands of the IRA in 1920–21 – had been recently exacerbated by warnings from the home secretary, Edward Shortt, not to go to Chequers because 'there were dangerous Irishmen in London'.[53] But there were some in Downing Street who felt Wilson had received his just deserts. 'I fear Henry Wilson brought this on himself by his very bitter attitude towards the Irish policy of the Govt.', wrote the cabinet secretary, Maurice Hankey, to his wife, 'and he was suspected by the extremists of having caused the anti-Sinn Féin pogroms in Belfast.'[54] Yet the impact of such a sensational murder, in broad daylight on the doorstep of his house in Eaton Place, of a Conservative MP and former chief of the Imperial General Staff, so outraged the Tories that it imperilled the government's majority in the Commons and demanded a dramatic response. Lloyd George got Churchill to draft a letter, despatched by special messenger to Michael Collins, urging immediate action against the IRA occupants of the Four Courts.

On 24 June, impatient with the provisional government's failure to respond and incensed by an inaccurate special branch intelligence report that the occupants of the Four Courts were responsible for Wilson's assassination and were planning further assassinations as part of an intensified campaign of violence against British interests, Lloyd George's government ordered Macready, as general officer commanding the remaining British troops in Dublin, to move against the Four Courts the next day. Macready, unimpressed after a meeting in Downing Street where he had found 'the Prime Minister and certain members of the Government in a state of suppressed agitation in which considerations of personal safety seemed to contend with the desire to do something dramatic' and scornful of Churchill's 'feverish impetuosity',[55] delayed.

'The only way . . . the Irish question will ever be settled', Macready had written to Frances Stevenson in February 1922, 'is to let the two parties fight it out together.' So he now sent his staff officer, Colonel Brind, to London; Brind, having cast doubt on the intelligence report, explained why a British attack on the Four Courts would have disastrous consequences. 'It would prompt violent retaliation against loyalists and British troops in Ireland, cause a complete rupture in relations between Britain and the Provisional Government, and "draw the two wings of the IRA together."'[56] The order was duly countermanded and Churchill later tried to destroy the evidence of how close he had come to engineering just such a catastrophe. When Lloyd George's government collapsed in

October 1922, Churchill's secretary telephoned the cabinet secretary, Hankey, and asked him to burn the draft proclamation to be issued when British troops occupied the Four Courts. Hankey did not 'feel justified in burning it',[57] but handed it over to Lionel Curtis, the then secretary of the cabinet committee on Ireland.

Churchill instead told an angry House of Commons on 26 June, within hours of Wilson's state funeral at St Paul's Cathedral, that it was for the provisional government, strengthened by its new electoral mandate, to assert its authority over the occupants of the Four Courts. But he warned that, if it did not do so speedily, 'His Majesty's Government . . . shall regard the Treaty as having been formally violated . . . shall take no steps to carry out or to legalise its further stages, and . . . shall resume full liberty of action.'[58] His speech well illustrated why the secretary to the colonial office, James Masterton Smith, 'was fond of saying that [Churchill] could talk to the diehards in their own language and . . . was for this reason able to effect the most dangerous operation of launching the Treaty'.[59] Although the diehard censure motion was easily defeated (by 342 votes to 75), Churchill's description of Bonar Law's approaching himself and Lloyd George later that evening in the lobby of the House of Commons eloquently reveals the impact of Wilson's assassination. 'Although always holding himself in strict restraint, he manifested an intense passion . . . "You have disarmed us today. If you act up to your words, well and good, but if not — !!" Here by an obvious effort he pulled himself up and walked away from us abruptly.'[60]

On 28 June Collins finally ordered his troops to open fire on the Four Courts with artillery obtained from Macready; unsurprisingly, the sighting rounds fired by inexperienced gunners flew over the Four Courts and Macready found himself being momentarily shelled by his own guns in his headquarters in the Royal Hospital at Kilmainham. The opening salvo in the civil war signalled an immediate remarriage of convenience between the Irish and British signatories of the treaty and paved the way for sealing the settlements, both South and North.

'Now that the Provisional Government have committed themselves to definite action with the rebels', wrote Lionel Curtis from the colonial office, Churchill's policy was 'to give them every possible assistance and avoid troubling them with details while the fighting goes on'.[61] The enormous scale of British support ensured that once the war began there was no doubt who would win. By 26 June, even before the first shots were fired, the provisional government had already been supplied with 11,900 rifles, 79 Lewis guns, 1.7 million rounds of rifle ammunition, six armoured cars and a large number of trucks, against which the IRA could pit little more than 3,000 rifles with 120 rounds apiece. A series of conferences in Whitehall on 28 and 29 June authorised the immediate transfer to Dublin of the additional high-explosive shells necessary for taking the Four Courts and Macready was 'told to give the Irish government whatever support it requested, including troops'.[62] But so lavish were the supplies of arms and ammunition that the politically perilous use of British troops never arose. The Royal Navy also 'quietly assisted Provisional Government forces by providing transportation, wireless communication, ammunition, fuel and the use of searchlights. Its most important duty was patrolling Irish waters in order to prevent gun-running to the republicans.'[63] Provisional government troops took Cork by sea on 8 August and by 11 August, the day before Arthur Griffith died of a stroke, the IRA had lost control of every town in the country. From then until the IRA ceasefire in May 1923 the war became a guerrilla war, which the Irish government, bolstered by the Catholic Church's unequivocal support, successfully waged with much more draconian methods than the British had ever used in 1919–21.

The civil war also had the dramatic, albeit indirect, effect of stabilising the Northern Ireland settlement. Ten critical meetings of the Northern Irish cabinet, devoted to discussions of defence and internal security, had taken place between 12 May and 20 June. Once civil war effectively eradicated both internal and external threats to Northern Ireland's security – Northern-based units of the IRA were sucked into the fighting in the South and cross-border raids came to an end – James Craig and his cabinet colleagues saw no need to meet again until 27 July. This new, leisurely pace remained much the same throughout the second half of 1922 and thereafter.[64]

The disappearance of any immediate security threat also emboldened Craig to face down British ministers on whether Northern Ireland would be governed exclusively in the Unionist interest. The issue arose from the Local Government Bill (Northern Ireland) which was designed further to reduce the already minimal political power of Northern Ireland's nationalist minority. The bill abolished proportional representation in local government elections and required declarations of allegiance from persons elected to, or employed by, local authorities and was enacted on 11 September 1922 despite opposition from the British and Irish governments. But British opposition was never more than muted. Although both Lloyd George and Churchill went through the motions of protesting that the bill was in 'breach of the spirit of the Treaty', Churchill had 'pledged himself to Craig to ratify the Bill' and a meeting of the British treaty signatories on

7 September reached the timorous conclusion 'that appeal should be made to Sir James Craig's patriotism and good sense with a view to the suspension of the Bill for the present'. When Craig joined the meeting, he stressed that the bill was within the Northern Irish parliament's powers. The Lord Chancellor, Birkenhead, concurred and Craig's threat that his government must resign if the bill was not enacted was enough to bring British ministers to heel.[65]

The death of Michael Collins in an ambush at Béal na mBláth in a remote valley in his native west Cork on 22 August further ensured the stability of the Northern Irish settlement. Eamon Phoenix has shown how 'more than any other Sinn Féin leader between 1917 and 1922 Michael Collins was passionately concerned about both Irish unity and the plight of the beleaguered northern nationalist minority'; he was the architect of the avowed policy of non-recognition of Northern Ireland and also of the secret 'decision in May 1922 to launch a major IRA offensive designed to make the north unworkable'.[66] There had been rumblings among his colleagues in the provisional government against his free-lance, hawkish Northern policy in early August and the succession of W. T. Cosgrave as chairman of the provisional government removed the last obstacle to the abandonment of non-recognition. It brought an end, too, to the policy of secretly supporting the Northern Divisions of the IRA; 'the breaking up of this organisation', complained the commanding officer of the 3rd Northern Division which operated in Belfast, was 'the first step to making partition permanent'.[67] Lionel Curtis, secretary to Churchill's cabinet committee on Ireland, even argued that 'Collins' early death alone saved the Treaty.[68] Cosgrave in substance reverted [sic] his policy.' Craig felt the same: 'We got on very well together,'[69] he wrote to his schoolgirl daughter after he had met Cosgrave for the first time on 10 November 1922.

Tory diehards might have hoped that the fall of the Lloyd George coalition in October 1922 would trigger the collapse of the treaty settlement, but it did nothing of the kind. On 18 October, the day before the famous meeting of the Conservative Party at the Carlton Club that forced Lloyd George's resignation, Craig and his colleagues were already planning their strategy for the general election, which could not be long delayed: 'to ensure that as many persons as possible were returned who were Ulster's friends' and to send delegates to see the chairmen of all the Conservative Party constituency associations to press for the selection of candidates 'favourable to Ulster's interests'.[70] No one seemed to be more 'favourable to Ulster's interests' than Andrew Bonar Law, who succeeded Lloyd George as prime minister on 23 October 1922.

How the impending change of government would influence Irish policy had preoccupied Tom Jones, whose concern, as ever, was 'the safeguarding of the Irish Treaty'. This meant that parliament must ratify the Irish constitution before it dissolved in order to give final legislative effect to the treaty and bring the Irish Free State into existence on the due date of 6 December 1922. With Churchill laid low with appendicitis, one of Lloyd George's last acts in 10 Downing Street was to exchange published telegrams with Cosgrave assuring him that the treaty would not be compromised.[71]

Nor was it. Although Lloyd George resigned on 19 October, Bonar Law did not kiss hands as prime minister until 23 October because he insisted on being re-elected as leader of the Conservative Party before he agreed to form a government. But the passage of the Irish Free State Constitution Act was assured even before he became prime minister when, at his first audience with the king on 19 October, he immediately relieved royal anxieties that the treaty settlement might be jeopardised by the change of government.[72]

Whatever the vagaries of Britain's Irish policy since 1916, the Irish settlements of 1920–21 were too valuable to be jeopardised. The success of Bonar Law's career rested on the bipartisan foundations of his political partnership and personal friendship with Lloyd George and he had no appetite for reopening old wounds. His 'first major decision' as prime minister was to hold a special parliamentary session to pass the necessary legislation before 6 December 1922. On 16 November, the day after the Conservative triumph at the polls, he agreed with a relieved Tom Jones 'that if the Treaty and the Constitution must be put through it was better to do it handsomely than in any niggardly spirit'. Nor did he block the combined efforts of Jones, Curtis and Cope to ensure the appointment of Tim Healy, Parnell's arch-antagonist in the Irish Parliamentary Party split and a kinsman of Kevin O'Higgins, the strong man of the Cosgrave government, as the Irish Free State's first governor general, notwithstanding his own reservations that Healy was 'impulsive and . . . drank too much whisky at night'. It helped that the Duke of Devonshire was Churchill's successor as secretary of state for the colonies, for he told Tom Jones of his 'great regard' for Healy because he put flowers on the grave of his uncle, Lord Frederick Cavendish, every year on the anniversary of his assassination.[73] Healy was Devonshire's 'sole nominee'[74] and it was he who persuaded Bonar Law to send his name forward to the king.

Bonar Law's unenthusiastic but statesmanlike speech introducing the Irish Free State Bill on 27 November damped down party passions. He stressed that the treaty had already been approved by the previous parliament and no political party or candidate at the election had taken 'any other view than that this Treaty must be given a chance and everyone desires that this should be done'. It was a measure of the consensus that Ireland should not again become a cause of party political contention that the bill was passed without a division, 'though not without many mournful groans and gloomy jeremiads from the Ulster and Die-hard members'.[75] Even Salisbury, now Lord President of the Council and the only diehard member of the cabinet, admitted to Bonar Law 'that the Provisional Government must be treated with liberal patience so long as they are doing their best to carry out the Treaty'.[76]

Nevertheless, the formation of the first exclusively Conservative government since 1905 was a godsend to Craig and his colleagues in Belfast. Once the Tories were in office, as Paul Canning has observed, 'British policy was directed almost solely to maintaining the status quo in Ireland'[77] and that meant maintaining the border. Northern Irish ministers and their officials assumed, moreover, that the new government was 'not necessarily committed to the full policy of their predecessors'[78] and they immediately tried to undermine Lloyd George's closest Irish advisers, Tom Jones and Lionel Curtis, with Bonar Law and Devonshire.

Craig also set about ensuring that, once Northern Ireland had opted out of the Irish Free State, the home office, rather than the colonial office, would 'subsequently be the ordinary channel for communicating with the British Government'. He took 'the strongest exception' to the suggestion 'to set up a branch of the Colonial Office under Sir Mark Sturgis to deal with the affairs of "All Ireland"' and a proposal in January 1923 'to establish at the Irish Office a Free State and Ulster

Department working jointly' under the home office and the colonial office was also fiercely and successfully resisted.[79]

On 7 December 1922, the day after the Irish Free State came into existence and sealed the treaty settlement, resolutions were duly passed simultaneously in both houses of the Northern Irish parliament 'for the express purpose of opting out of the Free State'.[80] On the same day a relaxed Craig told his cabinet that he intended taking a month's holiday from 18 December;[81] in the event, he spent much of 1923 at Cleeve Court, his English home at Streatley-on-Thames.[82] There could be no clearer signal of his confidence that the Northern Ireland settlement embodied in the Government of Ireland Act of 1920 was also secure.

Epilogue: The Boundary Commission

The inauguration of the Irish Free State on 6 December 1922 and the Northern Ireland government's inevitable exercise of its veto on reunification by opting out of that state the next day sealed the British government's Irish settlements of 1920 and 1921. Only one loose end remained: the boundary commission.

The ambiguities in the wording of article 12 of the treaty, the tension between reconciling 'the wishes of the inhabitants' and 'economic and geographic considerations', have already been discussed. We have seen, too, how Lloyd George and Churchill had always favoured an interpretation that would curtail Northern Ireland's loss of territory and minimise the risk of disruption to their twin settlements. The violence of 1922 – the sectarian slaughter in Belfast, the fighting along the border, Henry Wilson's assassination and the Irish civil war – made it still more likely that the minimalist interpretation would prevail.

Even those in London who were as fervently committed to the implementation of the treaty as Tom Jones and Lionel Curtis and who were sympathetic to the Irish Free State government, overly sympathetic according to Northern Irish ministers and Tory diehards, never endorsed the extravagantly optimistic nationalist interpretation of article 12 propagated by Griffith and Collins. When the treaty was signed, as Tom

Jones observed shortly before the commission began its work, 'no one foresaw the deplorable events that followed in Ireland'.[1]

The Dublin government also recognised the civil war's impact on the prospects of the boundary commission: it could scarcely press its claim for more territory in the six counties while its authority was still challenged within the twenty-six counties. 'What a ridiculous figure we would cut – both nationally and universally,' argued Kevin O'Shiel, the head of their north-eastern boundary bureau, in February 1923, 'were we to argue our claim at the Commission for population and territory when, at our backs, in our own jurisdiction, is the perpetual racket of war.' There would be no answer to the response, 'What do you want with more territory and more population when you cannot maintain order in the territory you have or protect the lives and property of the population who declare their allegiance to you?' More galling still was that civil war had enabled 'Tories to say, "We told you so. Once Home Rule is granted to the Irish they will fight amongst themselves. They do not belong to that type of population which is ripe for self-government."'[2]

The instability of British politics in 1922–25 further reduced the chance of any British government reopening the Irish can of worms. There had been no change of government in nearly six years, between December 1916 (when Lloyd George became prime minister) and October 1922 (when he was succeeded by Bonar Law). There followed three changes of government in two years. In May 1923 the terminally ill Bonar Law made way for another Conservative prime minister, Stanley Baldwin. In January 1924 Baldwin was replaced by Ramsay MacDonald, the first Labour prime minister. In November 1924 Baldwin again became prime minister and it was his second government that concluded the boundary commission agreement of December 1925.

So marked was Stanley Baldwin's lack of interest in Ireland that he resented the drama of the last night of the treaty negotiations denying him the opportunity to enjoy dinner and a night in the master's lodge[3] at his alma mater, Trinity College, Cambridge. But he remained sensitive to the dangers of pursuing any Irish policy that might displease the diehards. On 10 June 1922 the dying Bonar Law predicted that, although 'Baldwin had begun well', 'the real trouble would be over the Boundary Commission – it was a very dangerous topic'. The response of the unswervingly liberal Tom Jones was even more significant: 'I agreed that we ought to play for its indefinite postponement.'[4] The new prime minister concurred and ensured continuity with Bonar Law's stance by reappointing the Duke of Devonshire as his colonial secretary. 'The issue was quarantined in the Colonial Office by Devonshire and his subordinates', and, as Kevin Matthews has observed, 'never, during Baldwin's first government, was the boundary question discussed in Cabinet'.[5]

The consensus between the British and Northern Irish governments on maintaining the status quo meant that the Irish government had to make all the running when it came to setting up the boundary commission. But, although their inhibitions diminished after the end of the civil war in the spring of 1923, Irish ministers noted that they now had to deal with 'a strong Tory Government' which was implementing the treaty only 'because *it has to*, because the Treaty is more than a mere statute, because it is in fact an international contract'.[6] The Irish government, despite British objections, duly registered the treaty as an international treaty with the League of Nations in Geneva on 11 July 1924.

When Bonar Law resigned the premiership, the Irish government held its peace in the vain hope that some of the Conservative signatories to the treaty, Chamberlain or Birkenhead, might become members of the new government. Cosgrave was almost apologetic when Lionel Curtis of the colonial office came to see him in Dublin on 26 May 1923 in explaining why he now felt 'absolutely bound to press for the Boundary Commission'.[7] Curtis gave him cold comfort, emphasising that he 'had no reason whatever to think that Mr Baldwin's attitude differed in any respect or in any degree'[8] from Bonar Law's or Devonshire's and when Cosgrave finally wrote to Baldwin, on 9 June, he gave only 'a very preliminary friendly informal warning that the ball is going to be thrown in very soon'.[9] He finally threw in the ball on the singularly inauspicious date of 12 July (the day when Orangemen annually celebrate their triumph at the battle of the Boyne) by appointing Eoin MacNeill, his then minister for education, who had been born in Antrim and educated in Belfast, as the Irish Free State's boundary commissioner. 'Although Cosgrave referred personally to the Boundary Commission', when he met Craig in London on 16 July 1923, 'there was little discussion between them on the subject';[10] they talked instead about Irish railways and political prisoners in Northern Ireland.[11]

Where the imminence of an Irish autumn election had demanded that Cosgrave do something, British electoral imperatives persuaded Baldwin to do nothing. In the throes of embracing a deeply divisive protectionist economic policy, he had no stomach for the Irish game and kicked the ball into touch, where it remained for the duration of his first government, by merely referring Cosgrave's letter to Devonshire. Although Baldwin went through the motions of issuing invitations to a tripartite conference to explore how article 12 might be implemented in September 1923, James Craig enigmatically reassured the Northern Ireland cabinet on 1 October that Baldwin 'did not want a very immediate reply owing to certain special reasons'.[12] The British general election in November 1923, called by Baldwin on the tariff issue on which the Conservative Party sustained a crushing defeat, then intervened. But the prospect of losing office made no difference to Baldwin's determination to steer clear of Ireland: 'I do not want the Irish conflict revived in the House of Commons in any shape or form if it can be justly avoided,'[13] he wrote to Craig in January 1924, the month Ramsay MacDonald succeeded him as prime minister.

MacDonald's precarious hold on office as the leader of Labour's minority government was another powerful incentive for not kicking the sleeping Irish dog. Like many Scottish Protestants, moreover, MacDonald, as Kevin Matthews has pointed out, 'disliked Catholics, particularly Irish Catholics'. The first Labour government's ties to the trade union movement compounded its sympathy for Ulster Protestants. If any members of the House of Commons were Ulster's natural allies, the new home secretary, Arthur Henderson, told the House of Commons, 'it was those of us who are and have been for so long officially connected with trade unions . . . [which] have large numbers of members in the North of Ireland'.[14]

Stanley Baldwin shared MacDonald's anti-Catholic prejudices. Back in January 1918, for example, after one of Lloyd George's Derby House breakfasts with Unionist ministers when Carson's resignation from the war cabinet had heralded the collapse of the Irish Convention, he wrote of how events 'are bringing home to some of us the attitude of our rude forefathers to the Church of Rome'. The convention's failure, he even argued, 'will be owing to the Roman Bishop at the

Vatican . . . The Vatican influence has been against us in Europe all the time.'[15]

The deliberations of the boundary commission need not detain us because their outcome merely affirmed the treaty settlement. Suffice it to say that the Northern Ireland government's persistent refusal to appoint a commissioner persuaded the British to pay lip-service to their obligations under the treaty by enacting legislation empowering them to appoint a commissioner acting for Northern Ireland: J. R. Fisher, a prominent Unionist journalist from Belfast and former member of the Ulster Unionist Council, who was friendly with James Craig. The British government's nominee as the third member and chairman of the commission was Richard Feetham, then a South African judge. Feetham, an Oxford-educated Welshman, owed his appointment to his old friend Lionel Curtis, who had prompted and nurtured his successful legal career in South Africa where he had become a justice of the supreme court in 1923. Feetham, Curtis confided in Churchill, was chosen 'because he was a man "of conservative temperament" who could be counted on to reject the sort of "preposterous and extravagant claims" being made by the Free State . . . On hearing of Feetham's appointment, Curtis sent his old friend a pregnant two-word telegram: "England expects".'[16]

The commission first met in November 1924 and, although its deliberations were shrouded in secrecy even from government ministers, Feetham duly delivered what England, or, more precisely, Baldwin expected: a report on the boundary commission that would not threaten the precarious stability embodied in the settlements of 1920 and 1921. Baldwin was always confident that 'Feetham will do what is right' and, if not, he would have ridden to the rescue. 'If the Com[missio]n should give away counties,' he wrote in September 1924, 'then of course Ulster couldn't accept it and we should back her.'[17] The commission's report, Tom Jones urged Baldwin on 28 October 1925, before he knew anything of its contents, 'ought to be applied automatically whatever it is . . . Once you begin to discuss, and negotiate and adjust you are in the Irish bog again.'[18]

On 7 November 1925, the shroud of secrecy was rudely ripped away when the *Morning Post*, London's most staunchly conservative daily newspaper, published what it claimed was a summary of the report. The summary, which proved uncannily accurate, predicted only minor adjustments in the border, transferring small parts of south Fermanagh and south Armagh to the Irish Free State and parts of east Donegal, where Protestants were in a majority, to Northern Ireland. Although the Free State gained much more than it lost – some 180,000 acres as against 50,000, and 31,000 inhabitants as opposed to 7,500 – the small scale of the proposed transfers and Northern Ireland's retention of Newry and south Down shattered nationalist hopes. The Free State government, moreover, had always rejected the prospect of losing *any* territory: 'The commission has no authority under the Treaty', wrote Cosgrave, 'to transfer any part of our territory to Northern Ireland.'[19]

The *Morning Post* story caused a political crisis in Dublin and a U-turn on the part of Cosgrave's government, which swiftly decided that it would be better if the commission had never reported than that it should report unfavourably. Eoin MacNeill resigned from the commission and Cosgrave's government, no longer represented on a commission in which it had lost all trust, demanded an immediate inter-governmental conference. With Cosgrave now singing from the same hymn sheet as Craig and Baldwin in wanting no change in the border, the path to agreement was clear. 'It is a pity the question was not allowed to sleep,'[20] remarked Baldwin, when he met ministers from the Dublin and Belfast governments at Chequers on 28 November. Now the question was consigned not just to sleep but to a hibernation of over four decades under the terms of the tripartite agreement signed in London on 3 December 1925. This provided for the suppression of the commission's report; it was not released until 1968 and then only as a historical document. The agreement further provided that the powers of the Council of Ireland relating to Northern Ireland under the 1920 Government of Ireland Act be transferred to the Northern Ireland government; and that the Irish Free State's liability for part of the British war debt under article 5 of the treaty be waived as a sop to soften the Dublin government's disappointment.

No longer could nationalists, North or South, claim that the treaty would serve as an instrument for Ireland's reunification. No longer need unionists fear a threat to Northern Ireland's territorial integrity. Maureen Wall's assessment has not been bettered: 'Ambiguities were now at an end. This time the unionists had got all they wanted, and the agreement bore the signatures not only of British and Free State representatives, but, for the first time, the signatures also of the representatives of Northern Ireland.'[21]

Conclusion

'There is no greater defect in statesmanship', Andrew Bonar Law told the House of Commons in his speech commending the treaty, 'than to propose something which in the nature of the fact is impossible.'[1] There is no better explanation of why the Irish policy of Asquith's government failed utterly. Indeed the policy embodied in the third Home Rule Bill was not just impossible but was acknowledged by its proponents to be impossible. As early as 1911, Augustine Birrell, the chief secretary with cabinet responsibility for Ireland; Lloyd George, the architect of the 1920 and 1921 settlements; and Winston Churchill, who presided over the bedding down of those settlements in 1922, all privately admitted the impossibility of a unitary solution to the Irish problem.

Why did John Redmond, and Irish nationalists in general, refuse to acknowledge this impossibility? Because, from 1910 to 1913, the Liberal government – and the prime minister in particular – allowed them to evade it by colluding in the pretence that the third Home Rule Bill could be enacted in the form in which it was introduced. Indeed British Conservatives and Irish Unionists were also tacit collaborators in this collusion because of their reluctance to abandon the advantages of the entrenched battlelines that first emerged when Gladstone introduced his Home Rule Bill in 1886. The Conservative and

Unionist Party had no appetite for campaigning for Ulster Unionists' right to self-determination when they had achieved such electoral success in opposing home rule root and branch and when, after three defeats at the polls between 1906 and 1910, they saw the Orange card as their best chance of regaining power; hence Balfour's rejection of the Irish compromise in Lloyd George's national government proposals of 1910 and Bonar Law's rejection of the Agar-Robartes amendment in 1912. The Irish, as opposed to Ulster Unionist leaders, personified by Walter Long and Edward Carson in the House of Commons and by Lansdowne in the House of Lords, sought not separate treatment for Ulster but to prevent Irish home rule being enacted in any form. The irresistible obstacle to home rule until 1911 of the in-built Tory majority in the House of Lords, moreover, was another deterrent to a recognition of the reality that the treatment of Unionist Ulster lay at the heart of the Irish crisis.

So, as we have seen, Asquith's prime ministerial procrastination prevailed over Lloyd George's and Churchill's preference for tackling the issue of Ulster. From 1912 to 1914, from 1918 to 1921, parliamentary arithmetic in the House of Commons was the key determinant of policy. Just as Lloyd George needed the Conservative Party for his majority in the House of Commons after 1918, so Asquith needed the Irish Parliamentary Party for his majority after 1910. The bottom line in British high politics throughout the twentieth century is crystal clear: prime ministers refused to embrace policies that might result in their losing office. So Augustine Birrell, despite his own conviction that Ulster Unionist resistance could not be ignored, played Sancho Panza to Asquith's Don Quixote as he tilted disingenuously at the windmill of the third Home Rule Bill during the parliamentary sessions of 1912 and 1913.

The provision of the Parliament Act enabling the House of Lords to reject the bill for two years created the perfect climate for this pantomime. It also bestowed on Ulster Unionists the gift of three years to plot revolution. Their planning of that revolution, like the planning of the republican revolution of 1916–21, falls outside the scope of this book. But the Ulster Unionists used that time well. The recruitment and arming of their paramilitary army, the Ulster Volunteer Force, the arrangements for the immediate establishment of a provisional government in the event of the bill's enactment, the funding and financing of these and of other institutions, all were in place in ample time for a revolution that never happened because it never had to happen. The Unionist revolutionaries achieved their objective without firing a shot when Asquith's government capitulated.

Their remarkable success was attributable largely to the unswerving support of the leadership of the British Conservative Party, well captured in the title of Alan Parkinson's account of Ulster's resistance to the third Home Rule Bill: *Friends in High Places*. Dr Parkinson understandably focuses on British Unionists and diehards of varying hues. But even more important in ensuring that the bill could not be enacted without the exclusion of Ulster were their friends in high places in Windsor and Whitehall and around the cabinet table. They ranged, to take but a few examples from these pages, from the king and his liaison with ministers, Lord Esher; to Arthur Nicolson, the permanent under-secretary at the foreign office; to Henry Wilson and the cabal of officers at the war office, and to the Gough brothers, at Aldershot and the Curragh, all intent on subverting the legislative policy of the democratically elected government – not for nothing did the Ulster Volunteer Force choose 'Gough' as the password for its gun-running operation.[2] Most influential of all was the tacit alliance between the radical pragmatists, Lloyd George and Churchill, and the hard core of Liberal imperialists in Asquith's cabinet.

Partition was probably unavoidable once Lloyd George and Churchill formally proposed the exclusion of Ulster to their cabinet colleagues on 6 February 1912; it was inevitable once Asquith, in moving the bill's second reading for the third time, offered temporary exclusion on 9 March 1914. On 20 March, moreover, the threatened mutiny at the Curragh exposed the Liberal government's impotence: thereafter, even in the unlikely event of its summoning the will to impose the democratic verdict of the House of Commons on Ulster, it had no means to do so.

The Great War then enabled Asquith to do what he had always wanted to do about Ireland: nothing. The enactment of the Home Rule Bill, on 18 September 1914, was another charade because it was accompanied, first, by a suspensory act that prevented its coming into force before the end of 1919 and, second, by Asquith's renewed and explicit assurance that the use of 'any kind of force' to coerce Ulster was 'absolutely unthinkable'.

The differences between government and opposition on the third Home Rule Bill, as F. E. Smith had explicitly admitted to Lloyd George in September 1913, were 'very artificial' and did not 'reach the realities'. The reality that Ulster was the key to the impasse held centre stage only between January and July 1914. The compromise of September 1914 swept it offstage once more because, notwithstanding Asquith's assurances that Ulster would never be coerced, the bill was enacted in the form in which it had been introduced. Hence the outrage of the Unionists who withdrew from the House of

Commons en bloc rather than witness the announcement that the bill had received the royal assent. Hence the jubilant triumphalism of Liberal and nationalist members who, shattering all parliamentary precedents, set the seal on their celebrations by singing the national anthem in unison. The scene signalled a return to the parliamentary pretence of 1912–13 that Ulster could be forgotten and partition avoided.

Nationalist jubilation proved to be even more misplaced than Unionist indignation because by the time the suspensory act ceased to have effect, in 1919, the party of Parnell and of Redmond had been swept into oblivion. The republican objectives of Sinn Féin, their successors as the elected representatives of Irish nationalists, again pushed the Ulster Unionists' demand for self-determination into the background and refocused attention on the demand for a unitary solution, albeit in a republican guise.

The prolongation of the Great War turned the Government of Ireland Act of 1914 into a cosmetic exercise that sowed the seeds for the downfall of the constitutional nationalists who claimed to have achieved their millennial goal yet had nothing to show for it. The emergence of coalition government in 1915 further undermined them. Coalition meant that compromise, not confrontation, became the order of the day and compromise copper-fastened the impulse towards partition because compromise meant that the British government's Irish policy must incorporate the Conservative Party's Ulster policy. The continuation of coalition government until 1922, moreover, denied Irish nationalist MPs any prospect of exerting leverage in the Westminster parliament.

Once the window of opportunity presented by Lloyd George's negotiations with Redmond and Carson in the aftermath of the 1916 rebellion slammed shut, Lloyd George himself, as the new prime minister appointed to win the war, ignored Ireland until the peace treaties had been ratified in the autumn of 1919. By then the 1918 election had transformed both the British and Irish political landscapes.

In Britain, there were two predominant circumstances. First, the coalition government's election manifesto had categorically ruled out any settlement involving the coercion of Ulster. Second, the election results had reduced Lloyd George to a condition of absolute dependence on the Conservative Party's Commons majority for his survival as prime minister.

In Ireland, Sinn Féin had displaced the Irish Parliamentary Party as the elected representatives of Irish nationalism, had refused to take its seats in the Westminster parliament, and had instead established its own one-party parliament, Dáil Éireann, in Dublin. There were, again, two consequences. First, the likelihood of Sinn Féin's achieving a larger measure of Irish independence than had been contemplated under home rule was enhanced once the British government recognised that it could not defeat the IRA without a politically unacceptable escalation of the war of 1919–21. Second, Sinn Féin's abandonment of Westminster effectively surrendered whatever influence Ireland's nationalist elected representatives might have exerted on the dimensions of partition. '"Sinn Féin", "Ourselves alone", that was the cry and by an act of self-abnegation, remarkable even when born of hatred, they cut themselves off for ever from an inheritance in the House of Commons which, though invidious, was in a worldly sense inestimable,' wrote Churchill of 'their merciful boycott';[3] Tim Healy less grandiloquently recognised that Sinn Féin

. . . could, without taking any oath, infest Parliament, its seats under the clock, its galleries and lobbies . . .

Ministers are men first and the crashing protests that could have been made even in Lobbies and Dining Rooms by an organised force, acting as a unit . . . could not have been ignored . . . The Shins were mostly ignorant of conditions at Westminster . . . and their absence gave Carson his chance.[4]

Partition was inevitable, perhaps in 1912, certainly by 1914, but the shape of the partitionist settlement remained an open question until 1920. Churchillian rhetoric apart, Sinn Féin unquestionably cut itself off from participating in any decision on the boundary between the Northern Ireland created under the 1920 act and what became the Irish Free State. The painstaking if ultimately futile discussions between Redmond and Carson at the Buckingham Palace conference of July 1914 as to where the line might best be drawn in Fermanagh, Tyrone and south Armagh now went for nothing; so, too, did Lloyd George's exchanges with Carson and Redmond in the summer of 1916 and the finer nuances of the first report of Walter Long's cabinet committee in November 1919 proposing a nine-county Northern Ireland. Instead when the line was drawn in what became the Government of Ireland Act of 1920 Ireland had no nationalist representatives at Westminster who would have to have been consulted by the British government. Instead Ulster's Unionists got precisely what they wanted: the crude cut of six counties in which they had an assured and decisive majority.

In regard to partition, Sinn Féin's calculated act of disinheritance was thus destructive of its own aspirations. In 1919–21 republican unilateralism proved a powerful weapon in advancing the case for independence, but it could do nothing to prevent partition or, later, to promote reunification.

Although the resistance of the Dáil and the IRA prevented the Government of Ireland Act of 1920 ever coming into effect outside Northern Ireland and although the treaty settlement of December 1921 conferred a much greater measure of independence on what became the Irish Free State than was envisaged under the terms of the 1920 act, Sinn Féin could do nothing to prevent the act's application to Northern Ireland; nor could it do anything subsequently to moderate the Unionist domination of the elected representation in Northern Ireland.

These circumstances explain why the Government of Ireland Act of 1920, with its provisions for a home-rule parliament in Dublin as well as in Belfast, was yet another charade. There was no prospect that Sinn Féin would accept it but, from Lloyd George's perspective, that did not signify: its purpose was to get the Ulster monkey off his back. Ulster's Unionists, apprehensive of the growing power of the British Labour Party, knew they would never get a better deal than a bill designed by Walter Long, their leader in the Commons until 1910, guided through cabinet by Bonar Law and their other Conservative ministerial allies, and duly amended as they wished.

Their military reverses in November 1920, Bloody Sunday and the Kilmichael ambush, triggered a British willingness to explore the possibility of negotiating with Sinn Féin but Lloyd George's dependence on the Conservatives meant that the Ulster settlement must be put in place before such negotiations could begin. The formal opening of the Northern Ireland parliament on 22 June 1921 met that requirement. In the meantime the retirement of the hardline Tory triumvirate (Bonar Law, Carson and Long), confident that its Ulster settlement was secure, and the appointment of the malleable

Austen Chamberlain as leader of the Conservative Party gave Lloyd George more room to manoeuvre. The war ended within three weeks and the way was clear for talking to the IRA in the guise of Sinn Féin.

The essence of the British negotiating position in regard to what became independent Ireland, as reported by Tom Jones to Bonar Law, was dominion status with 'no Navy, no hostile tariffs, and no coercion of Ulster'. As always, Ulster was the key. Provided the integrity of the Northern Ireland settlement remained intact and short of an independent republic, Tory and Liberal ministers alike were relatively indifferent to the details of the settlement with Sinn Féin. 'I would give the South anything or almost anything,' responded Bonar Law, 'but I would not attempt to force anything on Ulster.'[5]

Once the constraints of the British offer were hammered out in cabinet, the conduct of the negotiations with Sinn Féin presented no inherent difficulty. What mattered to the British government was the fact of a settlement, not its minutiae. 'The politician who thinks he can deal out abstract justice without reference to forces around him cannot govern,' Lloyd George had explained to Arthur Griffith during their exchange on Ulster on 14 October. His ultimate triumph was rooted in what Roy Hattersley has identified as his

. . . defining political characteristic. He set about his task uninhibited by either prejudice or principle. He was neither a Unionist nor a Home Ruler. All he wanted was a deal – any deal – which, at least for a time, removed Ireland from the political agenda. He had succeeded . . . where Pitt, Peel and Gladstone had failed. They had struggled to achieve what they thought was right. He had achieved what he judged to be possible.[6]

The recognition of that achievement explains why Lloyd George's successors in 10 Downing Street shrank from any action that might destabilise his settlements of 1920 and 1921. 'The Irish Treaty is the big event since the Great War,' wrote Beatrice Webb, the social reformer and Labour Party activist, in her diary on 7 December 1921. 'The amazing skill with which Lloyd George has carried through the negotiations with his own Cabinet and with Sinn Féin has revolutionised the situation . . . No other leader could have whipped the Tories to heel and compelled them to recognise the inevitability of Irish independence.'[7] Lloyd George's successors were likewise determined to contain the impact of the boundary commission. Above all, they wanted to ensure that the boundary commission report did not trigger a recrudescence of violence. When Baldwin decided to seek out Richard Feetham, the chairman of the boundary commission, at the end of October 1925, he had no interest in 'the details of the Report'; all he wanted was 'his opinion on the chances of bloodshed on the border when the Report comes out'.[8]

This understandable obsession with stability also explains why British ministers were so indifferent to the treatment of minorities in Ireland North and South; what happened in both jurisdictions, they argued, was henceforth a matter for the governments in Belfast and Dublin and no longer a British concern. Minorities, in Churchill's words of 24 May 1922, must be left 'to stew in their own juice'.[9] Hence the ruling that what happened in Northern Ireland was a matter for the Northern Ireland parliament and could not be discussed in the Westminster parliament, notwithstanding Northern Ireland's status as a part of the United Kingdom of Great Britain and Northern Ireland. The result was fifty years of persistent discriminatory repression against Northern Ireland's nationalist and Catholic minority. In the South, the repression of the Protestant minority, although it did suffer discrimination, for example in regard to legislation on marriage and on sexual morality, was never remotely of the same magnitude.

If a week, in Harold Wilson's phrase, is a long time in politics, fifty years is a political eternity. Although the treaty settlement proved fatal within a year to Lloyd George's prospects of remaining, or ever again becoming, prime minister, his excision of the Irish cancer from the British body politic endured for almost half a century. 'It does not rest with one individual, with one government', said Arthur Balfour in 1890, 'completely to solve so ancient a controversy, so old an historic difficulty as . . . the Irish Question.'[10] Maybe not, but David Lloyd George solved the Irish question in the form in which it had bedevilled British politics since 1886.

References

KEY TO ACRONYMS AND ABBREVIATIONS

ACP   Austen Chamberlain papers, Birmingham University Library

Asquith Letters   Michael and Eleanor Brock (eds), *H. H. Asquith Letters to Venetia Stanley* (Oxford, 1982)

BL   British Library

Blunt Diaries   Wilfrid Scawen Blunt, *My Diaries* (London, 1920)

BMH   Bureau of Military History 1913–21, Military Archives, Dublin

Bodl.   Bodleian Library

BP   Balfour papers, British Library

CAC   Churchill Archives Centre

C.P.   Cabinet memoranda (C.P. series 1919–39)

CUL   Cambridge University Library

Crawford Papers   John Vincent (ed.), *The Crawford Papers: The Journals of David Lindsay twenty-seventh Earl of Crawford and tenth Earl of Balcarres 1892–1940* (Manchester, 1984)

Dáil debs   Parliamentary debates, Dáil Éireann

DIFP   Ronan Fanning et al., *Documents on Irish Foreign Policy*, vol. 1: *1919–1922* (Dublin, 1998)

Esher Journals   Viscount Esher, *Journals and Letters of Reginald Viscount Esher*, vol. 3: *1910–1915* (London, 1938)

Fitzroy Memoirs   Almeric Fitzroy, *Memoirs*, 2 vols (London, 1925)

H. C. Deb.   House of Commons debates

HLRO	House of Lords Record Office
Hobhouse Diaries	Edward David (ed.), *Inside Asquith's Cabinet: From the Diaries of Charles Hobhouse* (London, 1977)
Lee Papers	Alan Clark (ed.), *'A Good Innings': The Private Papers of Viscount Lee of Fareham* (London, 1974)
LGP	Lloyd George papers (House of Lords Record Office)
NAI	National Archives of Ireland
NLI	National Library of Ireland
NLW	National Library of Wales
PFI	Chamberlain, Austen, *Politics From Inside* (London, 1936)
PRONI	Public Record Office of Northern Ireland
RA	Royal Archives, Windsor Castle
Riddell Diary	Lord Riddell, *Intimate Diary of the Peace Conference and After 1918–23* (London, 1933); *More Pages from My Diary 1908–1914* (London, 1934)
Scott Diaries	Trevor Wilson (ed.), *The Political Diaries of C. P. Scott 1911–1928* (London, 1970)
SRO	Scottish Record Office
Stevenson Diary	A. J. P. Taylor (ed.), *Lloyd George: A Diary by Frances Stevenson* (London, 1971)
Sturgis Diary	Michael Hopkinson (ed.), *The Last Days of Dublin Castle: The Mark Sturgis Diaries* (Dublin, 1999)
TCD	Trinity College Dublin
TJD	Keith Middlemas (ed.), *Thomas Jones: Whitehall Diary*, vol. I: *1916–1925* (London, 1969); vol. III: *Ireland 1918–1925* (London, 1971)
TJP	Tom Jones's papers, National Library of Wales
TNA	The National Archives of the United Kingdom
UCDA	University College Dublin, Archives Department
WdeB	HLRO, Willoughby de Broke papers

INTRODUCTION

1   Roy Foster, *The Irish Review*, no. 1 (1986), 1.
2   Lewis, 55.
3   Ibid., 53.
4   Foster (1988), 506.
5   Townshend (1975), 206.

1   GLADSTONE'S LEGACY

1   Cooke and Vincent, 402.
2   Lubenow, 9.
3   Mansergh (1965), 133.
4   Ibid., 118.
5   A. Jackson (2003), 63–4.
6   W. S. Churchill (1907), 474.
7   Curtis (1963), 33.
8   Pearce, 79.
9   Ibid., 91.
10 A. Jackson (1989), 322.
11 Jay, 327–8.
12 Mansergh (1965), 194.
13 Morley, III, 327.
14 Jenkins (1964), 70.
15 Mansergh (1965), 147.
16 Rhodes James (1963), 337–8.
17 Mansergh (1965), 172.
18 J. Wilson, 108–9.
19 McCracken, 159–60.
20 Ibid., 111.
21 McCready, 318–22.
22 Robbins, 94–5.
23 Lyons, 275.
24 Townshend (1988), 174.
25 Jenkins (1964), 132.
26 Rhodes James (1963), 453–4.
27 Gwynn (1932), 115.
28 J. Wilson, 109.

29 Cooke and Vincent, 17.

30 Willoughby de Broke, 249.

31 Mansergh (1965), 170–71.

32 Jenkins (1964), 62.

33 H. H. Asquith (1926), II, 181–2.

34 Lyons, 284.

35 O'Halpin (1987), 83.

36 Birrell (1937), 193–5.

37 *Hobhouse Diaries*, 72.

38 Lyons, 291.

39 Ibid., 294.

40 174 *H. C. Deb.* 4s, cols. 78, 103.

41 Townshend (1988), 176.

42 Gwynn (1932), 147–8.

43 175 *H. C. Deb.* 4s, col. 323.

44 R. S. Churchill (1969), 734.

45 Gwynn (1932), 130–32.

46 Cooke and Vincent, 66–7.

47 D. M. Jackson, 44.

48 Jenkins (1964), 189–93, and *Annual Register 1908*, 195–7.

49 Bodl. MS Asquith 46 f. 169.

50 174 *H. C. Deb.* 4s, cols. 317–18.

51 *Scott Diaries*, 53.

2 THE CONSTITUTIONAL CRISIS OF 1910–11

1   Blewett, 47.

2   Gwynn (1932), 159.

3   Ibid., 166–7.

4   Ibid., 168–9.

5   Ibid., 172.

6   HLRO LGP, C/6/10/3.

7   TNA CAB 37/102/1.

8   TNA CAB 41/32/45.

9   Robbins, 213.

10 Ibid., 215.

11 Hazlehurst, I, 99–100.

12 18 February 1910, HLRO LGP I/2/1/9/f.

13   Frances Lloyd George, 59–60.
14   Grigg (1978), 109–110.
15   Morgan (1989), 84–6.
16   Morgan (1973), 7.
17   Hattersley, 341.
18   NLW TJ A/2/24/1–2, Adams to Tom Jones, 31 January 1948.
19   Morgan (1989), 87–8.
20   Foster (1981), 378.
21   R. S. Churchill (1967), II, 343–5.
22   Ibid., 445.
23   Ibid., 450.
24   R. S. Churchill (1969), part 2, 787.
25   Ibid., part 1, xxvii.
26   Ibid., part 2, 1089.
27   Rhodes James (1970), 35.
28   R. S. Churchill (1967), II, 453.
29   Ibid., 363–5.
30   Masterman (1939), 159.
31   Austen Chamberlain to Mary Chamberlain, 31 March 1910, ACP 4/1/256.
32   *Blunt Diaries*, II, 301.
33   Ensor, 454.
34   *Hobhouse Diaries*, 88–9.
35   Bodl. MS Asquith 1 f. 279.
36   Masterman (1959), 164–6.
37   A. Murray, 45–6.
38   Blake, 63.
39   14 *H. C. Deb.* 5s, cols. 55–6.
40   Ensor, 454.
41   Peatling, 42.
42   Nicolson, 129–30.
43   Gwynn (1932), 182.
44   Fair, 91.
45   *PFI*, 190.
46   Note passed to Balfour by Chamberlain at meeting of 28 July 1910, ACP 10/2/47.
47   HLRO LGP C/16/9/1.
48   Bonham Carter, 203.

49 Masterman (1939), 163–4.

50 Bodl. MS 23, f. 136.

51 TNA CAB 37/104/60.

52 ACP 6/1/80.

53 BP, Carson to Balfour, 25 October 1910.

54 A. Jackson (1989), 315–16.

55 BP, Salisbury to Balfour, 7 March 1911.

56 *PFI*, 293.

57 Searle, 179.

58 Robbins, 219.

59 Jenkins, 216–17.

60 Grigg (1978), 109.

61 NLI MS 15215 (2).

62 28 *H. C. Deb. 5s,* cols. 1470–73.

63 Ervine, 185.

64 WdeB, 21 August [1911].

65 Ervine, 191.

66 A. Jackson (1989), 318–19.

67 Ervine, 192–3.

3 A 'PRICKLY HEDGE': THE CHARADES OF 1912–13

1   D. M. Jackson, 248.

2   C. P. Scott's diary, 2 February 1911, BL Add. MS 50901, f. 2.

3   Grigg (1978), 17–18.

4   Ibid., 437.

5   Fair, 103–4.

6   Blake, 95–6.

7   HLRO BLP 107/1/83.

8   Blake, 22.

9   Ibid., 97.

10 Ibid., 125.

11 Koss, 8.

12 Blake, 98.

13 PRONI D 2846/1/4/6.

14 Winston Churchill (1939) 240.

15 *The Times,* 27 January 1912.

16 Jalland (1976), 435.

17 Jalland (1980), 58–9.
18 Birrell, 212.
19 Jalland (1980), 59.
20 Ibid., 61.
21 *Hobhouse Diaries*, 11.
22 *Asquith Letters*, 452.
23 Jalland (1980), 64–5.
24 *Hobhouse Diaries*, 120.
25 Jenkins, 276–7.
26 Jalland (1980), 73–5.
27 O'Halpin, 101.
28 Jalland (1980), 137.
29 R. S. Churchill (1969), part 3, 1400.
30 Jenkins, 279.
31 Stewart, 54–5.
32 Morgan (1973), 161.
33 Riddell (1934), 52.
34 Ibid., 30.
35 37 *H. C. Deb.* 5s, col. 1707–9, 1718, 2096.
36 *Crawford Papers*, 274.
37 39 *H. C. Deb.* 5s, col. 734.
38 Jalland (1980), 97.
39 39 H. C. *Deb.* 5s, cols. 1126.
40 Ibid., 1129.
41 Blake, 130.
42 Stewart, 61–7.
43 R. S. Churchill (1969), part 3, 1396.
44 *Hobhouse Diaries*, 126–7.
45 Riddell (1934), 26–7.
46 Grigg (1985), 73.

4 REACHING THE REALITIES

1 Nicolson, 220–21.
2 RA PS/PSO/GV/C/K/2553/1/57.
3 Blake, 150–53.
4 Nicolson, 223–4.
5 Morgan (1973), 165.

6 *Hobhouse Diaries*, 145–6.

7 Jenkins, 282.

8 Jalland (1980), 138–9.

9 Gwynn (1932), 227–8.

10 *Hobhouse Diaries*, 147.

11 Jenkins, 543–9.

12 R. S. Churchill (1969), part 3, 1399.

13 Jalland (1980), 146.

14 Bonar Law to Balfour, 16 September 1913, BL Add. MS 49693 ff. 38–9.

15 Adams, 125.

16 Colvin, II, 203–5.

17 Shannon, 183.

18 Hyde, 339.

19 Jalland (1980), 146.

20 Balfour to Bonar Law, 23 September 1913, BL Add. MS 49693 ff. 48–54.

21 Colvin, II, 206–10; Stewart, 73–8; Jalland (1980), 133–4.

22 Campbell (1983), 341.

23 Jalland (1980), 149.

24 R. S. Churchill (1969), part 3, 1400.

25 Esher to George V, 29 September 1913, *Esher Journals*, 140.

26 Jalland (1980), 145.

27 Nicolson, 231.

28 Riddell (1934), 178.

29 RA PS/PSO/GV/C/K/2553/2/60.

30 Jenkins, 287–8.

31 Jalland (1980), 152.

32 *Hobhouse Diaries*, 146–7.

33 Mansergh (1991), 56.

34 Gwynn (1932), 232.

35 Riddell (1934), 181.

36 Blake, 161–3.

37 Jenkins, 291–2.

38 Blake, 165.

39 Rowland, 370–71.

40 Blake, 165.

41 Callwell, I, 131.

42 Shannon, 187–8.

43 RA PS/PSO/GV/C/K/2553/2/77.

44 Riddell (1934), 188.

45 Jalland (1980), 167.

46 Jenkins, 293.

47 Ó Broin (1969), 86.

48 Gwynn (1932), 224–6.

49 Lyons, 338–9.

50 NLI MS 15165 (3) 3.

51 *Hobhouse Diaries*, 151–2.

52 NLI MS 15165 (3) 5.

53 Bonham Carter, 274–9.

54 *PFI*, 572–7.

55 RA PS/PSO/GV/C/K/2553/2/94.

56 *Hobhouse Diaries*, 152.

57 RA PS/PSO/GV/C/K/2553/3/6.

58 Martin (1963), 57, 23–5, 65, 113–14, 81–2.

59 Gwynn (1932), 245–6.

60 Blake, 166.

61 Bodl. MS Selborne 77/64.

62 RA PS/PSO/GV/C/K/2553/3/31.

63 Colvin, II, 259–71.

64 Riddell (1934), 189–91.

65 Bonham Carter, 270–73.

66 R. S. Churchill (1967), 666; *Asquith Letters*, 40–41.

67 *Scott Diaries*, 76.

68 *Hobhouse Diaries*, 156–7.

69 *Scott Diaries*, 78.

70 NLI MS 15165 (4).

71 *Asquith Letters*, 44.

72 *Hobhouse Diaries*, 161.

73 NLI MS 15165 (4).

74 *Asquith Letters*, 44.

75 NLI MS 15169 (4).

76 *PFI*, 610.

77 *Hobhouse Diaries*, 161–2.

78 Riddell (1934), 202.

79 Gwynn (1932), 263–9.

80 NLI MS 15165 (4).

81 Jenkins, 303–5.

82 Gwynn (1932), 272–3.

83 Jalland (1980), 200.

5 1914: BRITAIN'S IRISH CRISIS

1 59 *H. C. Deb.* 5s, cols. 907–8, 920–21, 933–6.

2 Campbell (1983), 343.

3 Jalland (1980), 222.

4 George, 248.

5 Riddell (1934), 203–4, 14 March 1914.

6 R. S. Churchill (1967), 489.

7 George, 248.

8 Ryan, 120.

9 *Asquith Letters*, 55.

10 Ryan, 96–7.

11 Beckett, 59–60.

12 Esher to George V, 29 September 1913, *Esher Journals*, 140.

13 N. Macready, 1, 171, 175–6.

14 Jeffery, 116.

15 Callwell, 1, 138–9.

16 Jeffery, 123.

17 PRONI D2846/1/2/18.

18 59 *H. C. Deb.* 5s, cols. 2273–7.

19 Fergusson, 65–70.

20 Beckett, 79–80.

21 Ibid., 12.

22 Jeffery, 124.

23 Beckett, 16.

24 Ibid., 197.

25 Ibid., 200–201.

26 Stewart, 159.

27 *Asquith Letters*, 58–9.

28 Nicolson, 238.

29 Fergusson, 129, 136.

30 *Asquith Letters*, 59–60.

31 Beckett, 217–18.

32 Jalland (1980), 233.
33 Robbins, 282.
34 George, 248; *Hobhouse Diaries*, 165–73.
35 Ibid., 167.
36 Beckett, 186–8.
37 *Asquith Letters*, 62.
38 Mottistone, 130.
39 Ensor, 479.
40 *Hobhouse Diaries*, 171.
41 Gollin, 172.
42 Jalland (1980), 36–7.
43 Jenkins, 281–2.
44 Gwynn (1932), 301–2.
45 *Hobhouse Diaries*, 169.
46 Blake, 207–8.
47 Curtis (1968); see especially 50–51.
48 BL Add. MS 49725, 30 April 1914.
49 *Esher Journals*, 165–6.
50 D. M. Jackson, 247.
51 Lyons, 350–51.
52 *Asquith Letters*, 70.
53 Blake, 210–11.
54 Jalland (1980), 251.
55 *Esher Journals*, 167–9.
56 Ó Broin (1969), 100.
57 *Scott Diaries*, 88.
58 Jenkins, 318.
59 *Asquith Letters*, 291.
60 Ibid., 97.
61 Gwynn (1932), 329.
62 *Asquith Letters*, 105.
63 Gwynn (1932), 334.
64 Blake, 214.
65 Jenkins, 318–19.
66 *Asquith Letters*, 101.
67 Loughlin, 295.
68 *Asquith Letters*, 125.
69 Mansergh (1991), 74–5.

70 Nicolson, 241–2.
71 *Asquith Letters*, 105–6.
72 Ibid., 109.
73 Gwynn (1950), 119.
74 Laffan, 45.
75 Martin (1964), 168.
76 *Asquith Letters*, 127–8.

6 'CUTTING OFF ONE'S HEAD TO GET RID OF A HEADACHE'

1   Blake, 121.
2   *Asquith Letters*, 3.
3   Ibid., 126.
4   Ibid., 129.
5   Ibid., 485–6.
6   Ibid., 471.
7   Ibid., 112.
8   Ibid., 135–6.
9   Ibid., 240.
10 Mansergh (1991), 85.
11 Ibid., 86.
12 Callanan, 510.
13 Gwynn (1932), 423–5.
14 A. Jackson (2003), 149.
15 Jenkins, 393.
16 Townshend (2005), 80.
17 Ó Broin (1969), 115.
18 Townshend (2005), 207–8.
19 Dangerfield, 216–17.
20 O'Halpin, 118.
21 Turner (1992), 91.
22 Townshend (2005), 147.
23 Jenkins, 396.
24 Asquith to Bonar Law, 1 May 1916, HLRO BLP 53/2/1.
25 Roskill, I, 269.
26 Jenkins, 397.
27 Ó Broin (1969), 134.
28 Ibid., 133.

29 Dangerfield, 217.

30 Asquith to Lloyd George, 22 May 1916, HLRO LGP D/14/1/5.

31 HLRO LGP D/14/1/7.

32 Grigg (1985), 350–51.

33 *Crawford Papers*, 356–7.

34 Campbell (2006), 236.

35 Searle, 191.

36 HLRO LGP D/14/3/21.

37 F. W. Pennefather to Lord Tennyson, 28 September 1916, NLI MS 3429/7.

38 For example, HLRO BLP 53/3/8.

39 Lyons, 391.

40 Grigg (1985), 350.

41 *Lee Papers*, 152–3.

42 *Parliamentary Papers*, 1916 (Cmd. 8303), xxii, 415–16.

43 Alison Phillips, 112.

44 Gwynn (1932), 522–3.

45 Gwynn (1950), 166.

46 Gwynn (1932), 522–3.

47 D. M. Jackson, 169.

48 C. Asquith, 223.

49 Ibid., 127.

50 O'Halpin, 125–6.

51 Turner (1992), 153.

52 Petrie, II, 114–17.

53 88 *H. C. Deb.* 5s, cols. 1353–4.

54 HLRO LGP F/37/4/2–3.

55 Ward, 131.

7 'BLOOD IN THEIR EYES': THE AMERICAN DIMENSION

1 Fanning (2003), 185–220.

2 HLRO LGP D/14/3/8.

3 Ward, 112.

4 Hartley, 7–10.

5 BL Add. MS 49758 f. 307.

6 BL Add. MS 49777 ff. 175–8.

7 Hartley, 79–95.

8   Ward, 123; Hendrick, II, 169.

9   Ward, 123.

10 Roskill, I, 335–7.

11 Hendrick, II, 251.

12 NLW TJ W/1/20.

13 Turner (1980), 87, 1–22.

14 HLRO LGP F/63/1/1.

15 Colvin, III, 239.

16 Turner (1980), 88.

17 Sloan, 160, n. 40.

18 Ward, 146–7.

19 *Stevenson Diary*, 155.

20 Shannon, 232; Turner (1992), 183.

21 *Scott Diaries*, 282–3.

22 Worthington-Evans Papers, Bodl. MS Eng. hist. c.903, ff. 112–13.

23 Gwynn (1932), 546–50).

24 Turner (1992), 184.

25 Turner (1980), 93–4.

26 *Stevenson Diary*, 158.

27 Hartley, 161.

28 McDowell, vii.

29 Boyce (1971), 137.

30 Hattersley, 530.

31 Dangerfield, 257.

32 Lyons, 421.

33 127 *H. C. Deb.* 5 s 1326.

34 Mansergh (1991), 107.

35 Ibid., 104.

36 McDowell, 81.

37 Ibid., 89, 82.

38 Roskill, I, 406–7.

39 O'Halpin, 134.

40 TNA CAB 23/13/117–22.

41 HLRO LGP F/37/4/40.

42 HLRO LGP F/37/4/8–10.

43 *Crawford Papers*, 383.

44 Colvin III, 301.

45 Lothian papers, SRO GD 40/17/573.

46 *TJD*, I, 45.

47 HLRO LGP F/82/8/4.

48 Colvin, III, 306–7.

49 Turner (1980), 106.

50 Colvin, III, 308.

51 Carson to Lloyd George, n.d. [21 January 1918], HLRO LGP F/6/3/3.

52 *Crawford Papers*, 385–6.

53 H. A. L. Fisher's diary, 23 January 1918, Bodl. MS Fisher 10/25–6.

54 HLRO LGP F/6/3/6.

55 Bodl. MS Fisher 10/34.

56 Balfour papers, BL Add. MS 49709.

57 Roskill, I, 512; Turner (1992), 287.

58 War cabinet minutes, TNA CAB 23/14/8–12.

59 CAC MS Hankey 1/3/180.

60 Callwell, II, 80.

61 War cabinet minutes, TNA CAB 23/14/15–27; Bodl. MS Fisher 10/59.

62 War cabinet minutes, TNA CAB 23/14/18–23.

63 Colvin, III, 337.

64 CAC MS Hankey 1/3/185.

65 HLRO BLP 83/2/11.

66 *TJD*, III, 3.

67 Bridgeman diary, 'April 1918'; I owe this reference to the late Maurice Cowling.

68 Kendle, 147-8.

69 HLRO LGP F/7/2/8–10.

70 TJP, NLW Z/Diary 1918, p. 82.

71 Kendle, 148–9.

72 HLRO LGP F/48/6/7.

73 Bodl. MS Fisher 10/61.

74 16 April 1918, HLRO LGP F/37/4/51.

75 Miller, 413–14.

76 Lyons, 435.

77 Callwell, II, 94.

78 Fisher's diary, 16 April 1918, Bodl. MS Fisher 10/61.

79 HLRO LGP F/48/6/8.
80 *Scott Diaries*, 341–3.
81 Kendle, 153.
82 HLRO BLP 83/2/32.
83 HLRO BLP 83/2/33.
84 HLRO BLP 84/7/25.
85 Bodl. MS Fisher 10/73–4.
86 HLRO LGP F44/9/2 – 'Précis of information of German help to Sinn Féin rebels', 2 May 1918.
87 HLRO BLP 84/7/25.
88 Morgan (1973), 188.
89 HLRO LGP F/7/2/11.
90 HLRO LGP F/32/5/31.
91 *Fitzroy Memoirs*, II, 674.
92 HLRO LGP F/32/5/34.
93 O'Halpin, 157.
94 NLW TJP Z/Diary 1918, p. 91.
95 *TJD*, III, 9.
96 War cabinet minutes, 10 May 1918, TNA CAB 23/14/69–76.
97 Shortt to Lloyd George, 20 May 1918, HLRO LGP F/45/6/3.
98 War cabinet minutes, 22 May 1918, TNA CAB 23/14/94–100.
99 Balfour papers, BL Add. MS 49741/178–95.
100 TNA CAB 27/46/3–5.
101 TNA CAB 23/6/188.
102 12 October 1918, NLS MS 5914/91–2.

8 1919: FRENCH LEAVE

1 HLRO BLP 83/3/11.
2 *Crawford Papers*, 398.
3 *Irish Times*, 18 November 1918.
4 Waley, 183.
5 Beaverbrook, 9.
6 HLRO LGP F/48/6/24.
7 HLRO LGP F/33/1/35.
8 Adams, 281.
9 *Stevenson Diary*, 170, 5 March 1919.
10 Roskill, II, 39.

11 Ó Broin (1982), 76.

12 NLI MS 11016/9.

13 Bartlett, 403.

14 Bodl. MS Fisher 10/125.

15 Campbell (2006), 149–51.

16 Holmes, 348.

17 Kendle, 144–5.

18 O'Halpin, 163–4.

19 HLRO LGP F/46/1/2.

20 *Riddell Diary*, 77, 11 May 1918.

21 Carroll, 3–10.

22 Callwell, II, 192.

23 HLRO LGP F/46/1/3.

24 TNA CAB 23/15/65–8.

25 Strathcarron papers, Bodl. MS Eng. hist. c. 490/97–9.

26 HLRO LGP F/180/3/2.

27 HLRO LGP F/30/3/6.

28 HLRO LGP F/33/2/45.

29 Holmes, 340.

30 Strathcarron papers, Bodl. MS Eng. hist. c. 490 f. 100 et seq.

31 HLRO LGP F/23/4/69.

32 HLRO LGP F/23/4/81–2.

33 Childers papers, TCD MS 7811/7.

34 *Stevenson Diary*, 187–8.

35 Balfour papers, BL Add. MS 49741/1–2 and HLRO LGP
    F/46/1/9.

36 Townshend (1975), 27.

37 NLI MS 2269/32.

38 Blake, 418.

39 TJP W/9/140.

40 NLI MS 2269/36.

41 French's diary, NLI MS 2269/34–8.

42 LGP F/33/2/73.

43 Murphy, 83–4.

44 Morgan (1979), 112.

45 TNA CAB 27/68/63.

46 Conclusions of Committee on Ireland, 15 October 1919,
    Worthington–Evans papers, Bodl. MS Eng. hist. c. 905/11.

47 TNA CAB 27/68/4–10.

48 TNA CAB 27/69 (C. I. 21), 30 October 1919.

49 TNA, CAB 27/68/11, 11 November 1919.

50 TNA CAB 27/68/11.

51 Pearce, 99.

52 French's diary, 14 October 1919, NLI MS 2269/46–7.

53 TNA CAB 23/18/36.

54 TNA CAB 27/69 (C. I. 1).

55 TNA CAB 27/68/73; LGP F/108.

56 TNA CAB 27/68/73.

57 TNA CAB 24/93/374–8, 25 November 1919.

58 TNA CAB 23/18/109–19.

59 TNA CAB 23/18/155.

60 Midleton to Southborough, 10 August 1937, recalling an
    interview with Balfour 'about 1920', Bodl. MS Southborough
    6/2.

61 Boyce (1970), 100.

62 TNA CAB 23/18/204.

63 TNA CAB 23/18/247.

64 French's diary, 19 December 1919, NLI MS 2269/62.

65 Bodl. MS Eng. hist. c. 490 ff. 180–81.

66 *Scott Diaries*, 380.

67 123 *H. C. Deb.* 5s., col. 1186.

68 Grigg (1985), 216.

69 123 *H. C. Deb.* 5s., cols. 1202–3.

9 1920: ULSTER – THE 'FUNDAMENTAL ISSUE'

1   *TJD*, I, 104; TNA CAB 27/68/45.

2   TNA CAB 27/68/46–7, 82–5.

3   Kendle, 186.

4   TNA CAB 24/98/291–3.

5   TNA CAB 23/20/211.

6   Gwynn (1950), 188–90.

7   Lothian papers, SRO GD 40/17/79/139–40.

8   *Scott Diaries*, 382.

9   127 *H. C. Deb.* 5s. 1132.

10 29 March 1920, 127 *H. C. Deb.* 5s., cols. 986–90.

11 HLRO LGP F/33/2/90.

12 HLRO LGP F/34/1/27.

13 NLI MS 2269/73–4.

14 TNA CAB 24/104/142.

15 *Riddell Diary*, 150–51.

16 Townshend (1975), 74.

17 Strathcarron papers, Bodl. MS Eng. hist. c. 490/70.

18 N. Macready, II, 425.

19 HLRO LGP F/36/2/14 and N. Macready, I, 171–98.

20 HLRO LGP F34/1/19.

21 N. Macready, II, 430.

22 RA PS/PSO/GV/C/K/1593A/1.

23 Townshend (1975), 76.

24 O'Halpin, 201.

25 TNA CAB 23/21/62.

26 HLRO LGP F/36/2/13.

27 Stephen Gwynn to Philip Kerr, 5 April [1920], SRO
    GD 40/17/78/1–2.

28 Townshend (1975), 98.

29 HLRO LGP F/31/1/27.

30 HLRO LGP F/31/1/28.

31 TNA CAB 23/21/141–2.

32 HLRO LGP F/31/1/30.

33 HLRO, LGP F/31/1/32.

34 *Sturgis Diary*, 7.

35 HLRO, LGP F/31/1/33.

36 McColgan, 9.

37 *TJD*, III, 16–23.

38 *Sturgis Diary*, 13.

39 *TJD*, III, 25–31.

40 *TJD*, III, 31–2.

41 Lothian papers, SRO, GD 40/17/620/2/1–5.

42 Walsh, 144.

43 HLRO BLP 102/10/3.

44 Lothian papers, SRO GD 40/17/410.

45 TNA CAB 23/22/235–40.

46 HLRO BLP 102/10/6.

47 *Sturgis Diary*, 35.

48 Buckland (1973), 445–6.

49 TNA CAB 23/22/245.

50 Colvin, III, 391.

51 McColgan, 26–31.

52 Barton, 35.

53 McColgan, 32.

54 CAC Hankey papers, HNKY 1/5/154.

55 Morgan (1973), 192–3.

56 TNA CAB 27/70/234–6.

57 Bonar Law to Long, 30 September 1920, HLRO BLP 103/5/9.

58 TNA CAB 23/23/38-41; *TJD*, III, 39–41.

59 Townshend (1975), 116.

60 HLRO LGP F/180/5/16.

61 Callwell, II, 265.

62 TNA CAB 23/23/83–4.

63 Walsh, 91.

64 TNA CAB 27/108/138–9.

65 TNA CAB 27/108/180.

66 HLRO BLP 103/3/24.

67 Foy, 143.

68 For example, S.I.C. 55, TNA CAB 27/108/275.

69 *Sturgis Diary*, 69.

70 McMahon, 33–41.

71 CAC Hankey papers, HNKY 1/5/170.

72 *TJD*, III, 41.

73 Bodl. MS Fisher 10/125, Fisher's diary 16 October 1918.

74 Gilbert, 453, n. 1.

75 C. J. Phillips's note on 'Sinn Féin's proposals for peace',
    19 November 1920, TNA CAB 21/277; Lothian papers,
    SRO GD 40/17/622/3.

76 BMH W. S. 767, witness statement by Patrick Moylett,
    16 December 1952, 50–76.

77 R. Taylor, 106.

78 Forester, 172.

79 RA PS/PSO/G V/C/K1514/9; cf. extract from Steele's diary,
    22 November 1920, NAI DE 2/251.

80 BMH W. S. 767, 69–70.

81 TJD, III, 46, 20 December 1920.

82 *Sturgis Diary*, 89, 87–8.

83 TNA CAB 23/23/319 et seq.

84 TNA CAB 23/23/345.

85 TNA CAB 23/23/368–9.

86 CAC Hankey papers, HNKY 1/5/182.

87 TNA CAB 23/23/221; also Griffith to Collins, 17 December 1920, NAI DE 2/234B.

88 Lothian papers, SRO GD 40/17/627/2.

89 TNA WO 35/90/2.

90 Phoenix (1994), 104.

91 Bowman, 44.

10 FROM PARTITION TO PEACE

1   W. A. Phillips, chapter x, 'The Counter-Terror'.

2   *Sturgis Diary*, 123.

3   *TJD*, III, 49–50.

4   Ibid., 53.

5   Canning, 5.

6   *Stevenson Diary*, 236–7.

7   Colvin, III, 400.

8   Kendle, 195–7.

9   Townshend (1975), 174.

10 *TJD*, III, 98–9.

11 *Stevenson Diary*, 215–16.

12 Dutton, 164.

13 HLRO LGP F/36/2/18.

14 *Sturgis Diary*, 144.

15 Boyce (1972), 133–4.

16 HLRO, LGP F/19/3/17 and 12.

17 W. A. Phillips, 197–202.

18 *TJD*, III, 55.

19 TNA CAB 23/25/154–8; also C.P. 2829 and C.P. 2840.

20 *TJD*, III, 59.

21 HLRO LGP F/6/3/31.

22 *Sturgis Diaries*, 125.

23 HLRO LGP F/19/4/5.

24 Bew, 413.

25 TNA CAB 23/25/265.

26 HLRO BLP 107/3/4.

27 *TJD*, III, 63–70.

28 *Sturgis Diary*, 167.

29 HLRO BLP 107/1/33.

30 Bodl. MS Eng. hist. c. 209/65–8.

31 *Sturgis Diary*, 183.

32 TNA CAB 23/26/14–15.

33 *Sturgis Diary*, 185.

34 BMH W.S. 767, 85–8.

35 HLRO LGP F/86/1/5.

36 *Stevenson Diary*, 220–21.

37 *TJD*, III, 74–5, 247.

38 HLRO LGP F/86/1/7–8.

39 HLRO LGP F/25/1/42.

40 HLRO LGP F/36/2/19.

41 *TJD*, III, 77–9, 91–2; Nicolson, 351–4.

42 TNA CAB 23/26/85–6; *TJD*, III, 79–81; *Sturgis Diaries*, 192–3.

43 HLRO LGP F/11/3/9.

44 HLRO LGP F/18/2/3.

45 *TJD*, III, 82–5.

46 NAI D/E 2/262.

47 Fisher, 130.

48 *Stevenson Diary*, 227–8.

49 HLRO LGP F/29/4/57; *TJD*, III, 87.

50 *Stevenson Diary*, 231.

51 *Sturgis Diary*, 202.

52 *TJD*, III, 90–91.

53 HLRO BLP 107/1/32 and 40.

54 *TJD*, III, 91–2.

55 Nicolson, 357; *Stevenson Diary*, 230–31.

56 NLI MS 8427.

57 *Sturgis Diary*, 208–9.

58 PRONI CAB 4/1/12/6.

59 A. J. P. Taylor (1965), 131.

60 Beaverbrook, 72.

61 HLRO LGP F/25/2/2.

62 BL Add. MS 49704.
63 *TJD*, III, 97.
64 *Sturgis Diary*, 14 August 1921, TNA 30/59/5/21.
65 Adams, 299–300.
66 D. M. Jackson (2009), 185.
67 Campbell (2006), 214–19.
68 Self, 167.
69 *TJD*, III, 106, 112.
70 *Riddell Diary*, 318.
71 *TJD*, III, 108–11.
72 TNA CAB 23/27/1–5; *Official Correspondence Relating to the Peace Negotiations*, 17–18.
73 NAI DE 1/3/118A.
74 *Official Correspondence Relating to the Peace Negotiations*, 19.
75 Cowling, 120.
76 TNA CAB 23/27/19–23.
77 Beaverbrook, 93, n. 1.
78 HLRO LGP F/17/2/17.
79 HLRO LGP F/17/2/19.
80 *Private Sessions of Second Dáil*, 90, 14 September 1921.
81 Bodl. MS Curtis 89 f. 64.
82 Matthews, 39.
83 P. Murray, 50–51.

11 THE TREATY NEGOTIATIONS: 'WE ARE AFTER A SETTLEMENT'

1   *TJD*, III, 160–61.
2   *TJD*, III, 164.
3   Mansergh (1991), 178.
4   Longford, 128.
5   *TJD*, III, 129–30.
6   Printed in Bowman, 339.
7   Longford, 134.
8   *TJD*, III, 135–7.
9   UCDA P150/1913/637.
10 UCDA P150/1914/770.
11 *TJD*, III, 145.

12 UCDA P150/1906/108, Erskine Childers ('for A. G.')
   to de Valera, 25 October 1921.

13 *TJD*, III, 146–7.

14 *Stevenson Diary*, 234, 28 October 1921.

15 *Scott Diaries*, 402–3, 28–29 October 1921.

16 *Stevenson Diary*, 234, 28 October 1921.

17 *TJD*, III, 147–80.

18 TCD, Childers papers, 7790/47.

19 UCDA P150/1906/108.

20 *Scott Diaries*, 404–5.

21 *TJD*, III, 149.

22 Greenwood to Lloyd George, 29 October 1921, HLRO
   LGP F/14–5/36. Greenwood wrote to Lloyd George (who was
   at Chequers for the weekend) at the suggestion of Tom Jones,
   who enclosed his letter with the Irish note – *TJD*, III, 149.

23 *TJD*, III, 149.

24 *TJD*, III, 150.

25 *TJD*, III, 151.

26 UCDA, P150/ 906/110.

27 Memorandum of conversation between Griffith and
   Lloyd George, 30 October 1921, UCDA, P150/1906/109.

28 McColgan, 69.

29 Cowling, 139.

30 Morgan (1979), 247.

31 UCDA P150/1906/112, Griffith to de Valera, 1 November 1921.

32 Balfour to Lloyd George, 2 November 1921, HLRO
   LGP F/3/5/17.

33 UCDA P150/1914/783.

34 UCDA, P150/1906/117, Griffith's minutes of sub-conference
   on 3 November 1921.

35 UCDA, P150/1906/118.

36 *Stevenson Diary*, 234–5, 6 November 1921.

37 Worthington-Evans papers, 7 November 1921, Bodl. MS
   Eng. hist. c. 910 ff. 180–81.

38 *TJD*, III, 154–5.

39 Worthington-Evans papers, 8 November 1921, Bodl. MS
   Eng. hist. c. 910 ff. 184–5.

40 *TJD*, III, 155–6.

41 UCDA P150/1914/786.

42 *TJD*, III, 103.

43 *TJD*, III, 156-7.

44 HLRO LGP F/10/1/40, 9 November 1921.

45 *Stevenson Diary*, 236, 11 November 1921.

46 *TJD*, III, 159-60.

47 Lavin, 191.

48 *TJD*, III, 160-62.

49 TNA CAB 23/27/180-81.

50 *TJD*, III, 163.

51 *DIFP*, 307-8.

52 UCDA P150/1377.

53 TCD MS 7814/53, Childers diary, 12 November 1921.

54 HLRO BLP 107/1/83.

55 Self, 170.

56 HLRO BLP 107/1/71.

57 Chamberlain to Worthington-Evans, 23 November 1921, Bodl. MS Eng. hist. c. 910 ff. 211-12.

58 *DIFP*, 309-11.

59 *DIFP*, 311.

60 *DIFP*, 311-13.

61 *TJD*, III, 170.

62 Morgan (1973), 194-5.

63 *TJD*, III, 171-2.

64 *TJD*, III, 175.

65 *TJD*, III, 173.

66 *DIFP*, 317-18.

67 *TJD*, III, 176-7.

68 *DIFP*, 319-20.

69 *TJD*, III, 177.

70 *DIFP*, 344-6.

71 *TJD*, III, 180.

72 *DIFP*, 348-9.

73 *TJD*, III, 180-81; see HLRO LGP F/25/2/51 and TJP G/2/62/1-4 for the original memorandum.

74 *TJD*, III, 181.

75 *DIFP*, 350-51.

76 *DIFP*, 351-6.

77 NLW TJP W/3/121/1–2.
78 *TJD*, III, 184.

12 1922: ESCAPE FROM THE IRISH BOG

1 Morgan (1979), 24.
2 *DIFP*, 349.
3 Canning, 31–2.
4 Laffan, 88.
5 Mansergh (1991), 200.
6 *Dáil debs*, private sessions, 153.
7 PRONI D 1327/10/1.
8 Wall, 86.
9 Gwynn (1950), 214.
10 Laffan, 90.
11 Campbell (2006), 236.
12 PRONI CAB 4/29/15.
13 W. Churchill (1929), 333.
14 NAI T/D S 1801/A.
15 Phoenix (1994), 175.
16 Ibid., 180.
17 *TJD*, III, 197.
18 *DIFP*, 397–8.
19 PRONI CAB 4/31/23, 23A.
20 Gilbert, 689.
21 Ibid., 688, 692–4.
22 Matthews, 78.
23 PRONI CAB 4/35/16.
24 Cowling, 186.
25 Morgan (1979), 335–6, Cowling, 144, 154–6.
26 Canning, 59–60.
27 *TJD*, III, 194–5.
28 PRONI CAB 4/40/12.
29 15 May 1922, NAI T/D, S 1011.
30 PRONI CAB 4/41/19.
31 *TJD*, III, 200.
32 TJP Z 1922, 36–7.
33 W. Churchill (1929), 348–9.

34 *TJD*, III, 201.

35 Long papers, BL Add. MS 62405/102.

36 Kennedy, 111.

37 W. Churchill (1929), 350–51.

38 PRONI CAB 4/45/6; appendices A and B.

39 Self, 190.

40 TJP G/3/15/1.

41 Curran, 294.

42 Canning, 50.

43 *TJD*, III, 212.

44 Gilbert, 729–30.

45 *TJD*, III, 210.

46 Canning, 20–22.

47 PRONI CAB 4/46/2–4.

48 Self, 192.

49 *TJD*, III, 210.

50 TNA CAB 43/1/101–2.

51 Jeffery, 286.

52 Kennedy, 82.

53 Campbell (2006), 191, 239.

54 Roskill, II, 265.

55 Macready, II, 650–54.

56 McMahon, 79.

57 Roskill, I, 301–2.

58 Gilbert, 735–8.

59 Bodl. MS Curtis 89, f. 76.

60 W. Churchill (1929), 362–3.

61 Canning, 47.

62 Curran, 234–5, 327 (n. 51).

63 McMahon, 85.

64 PRONI CAB 4/37–59.

65 TNA CAB 43/1/103–8.

66 Phoenix (1998), 92, 116.

67 NAI T/D S 1801A.

68 Bodl. MS Curtis 89, f. 82.

69 Ervine, 480.

70 PRONI CAB 4/56/11.

71 *TJD*, III, 216–17.

72 Adams, 329.
73 *TJD*, III, 218.
74 CUL Baldwin MS 101/177.
75 Blake, 476.
76 Canning, 70.
77 Ibid., 73.
78 PRONI CAB 6/16.
79 PRONI CAB 4/68/8.
80 PRONI D. 1295/23A.
81 PRONI CAB 4/59/24.
82 Follis, 157.

EPILOGUE: THE BOUNDARY COMMISSION

1   *TJD*, III, 234.
2   UCDA P4/V/18.
3   Middlemas and Barnes, 101.
4   *TJD*, III, 221.
5   Matthews, 115.
6   UCDA P4/V/18.
7   *TJD*, III, 222.
8   TJP, P/2/13/7.
9   NAI T/D S 1801 C.
10 PRONI CAB 4/84/4.
11 NAI T/D G2/2/140.
12 PRONI CAB 4/87/12.
13 CUL Baldwin MS 101/197.
14 Matthews, 137.
15 Middlemas and Barnes, 67.
16 Matthews, 155.
17 Ibid., 167.
18 *TJD*, III, 236.
19 NAI S 1801L, 18 February 1925.
20 CUL Baldwin MS 99/169.
21 Wall, 89.

CONCLUSION

1 Mansergh (1991), 198.
2 Parkinson, 241.
3 W. Churchill (1929), 296.
4 Callanan, 552.
5 *TJD*, III, 91–2.
6 Hattersley, 546.
7 Webb, 220.
8 *TJD*, I, 331.
9 W. Churchill (1929), 351.
10 Shannon, 75.

Bibliography of Sources Cited

UNPUBLISHED SOURCES

Official Records

British Cabinet records | Public Record Office
(now the National Archives), London
Records of Dáil Cabinet | National Archives of Ireland
Records of Northern Ireland Cabinet | Public Record Office of Northern Ireland

Private Papers

Asquith papers | Bodleian Library, Oxford
Baldwin papers | Cambridge University Library
Balfour papers | British Library
Bonar Law papers | Beaverbrook Library, now House of Lords Record Office
Carson papers | Public Record Office of Northern Ireland
Austen Chamberlain papers | Birmingham University Library
Childers papers | Trinity College, Dublin
Curtis papers | Bodleian Library, Oxford
De Valera papers | Archives Department, University College Dublin
Fisher papers | Bodleian Library, Oxford
French diary | National Library of Ireland
Haldane papers | National Library of Scotland

Hankey papers	Churchill College, Cambridge
Tom Jones papers	National Library of Wales
Hugh Kennedy papers	Archives Department, University College Dublin
Lloyd George papers	Beaverbrook Library, now House of Lords Record Office
Long papers	British Library
Lothian (Philip Kerr) papers	Scottish Public Record Office
Moylett, Patrick (witness statement)	Bureau of Military History, Military Archives, Dublin
Art Ó Briain [O'Brien] papers	National Library of Ireland
Redmond papers	National Library of Ireland
C. P. Scott, diary	British Library
Selborne papers	Bodleian Library, Oxford
Strathcarron (Ian Macpherson) papers	Bodleian Library, Oxford
Southborough (F.J.S. Hopwood) papers	Bodleian Library, Oxford
Worthington-Evans papers	Bodleian Library, Oxford

PUBLISHED SOURCES

Parliamentary debates
Parliamentary debates, Dáil Éireann, 1919–21
Parliamentary debates, 4th and 5th series, House of Commons
Parliamentary debates, Northern Ireland, 1921–2

BOOKS AND ARTICLES

Adams, R. J. Q., *Bonar Law* (London, 1999)
Asquith, Cynthia, *Diaries 1915–18* (London, 1968)
Asquith, Herbert Henry, Earl of Oxford and Asquith, *Fifty Years of British Parliament*, 2 vols (Toronto, 1926)
Bartlett, Thomas, *Ireland: A History* (Cambridge, 2010)

Barton, Brian, *Brookeborough: The Making of a Prime Minister* (Belfast, 1988)

Beaverbrook, Lord, *The Decline and Fall of Lloyd George* (London, 1963)

Beckett, Ian F. W., *The Army and the Curragh Incident 1914* (London, 1986)

Bew, Paul, *Ireland: The Politics of Enmity 1789–2006* (Oxford, 2007)

Birrell, Augustine, *Things Past Redress* (London, 1937)

Blake, Robert, *The Unknown Prime Minister: The Life and Times of Andrew Bonar Law* (London, 1955)

Blewett, Neal, *The Peers, the Parties and the People: The General Elections of 1910* (London, 1972)

Blunt, Wilfrid Scawen, *My Diaries* (London, 1920)

Bonham Carter, Violet, *Winston Churchill As I Knew Him* (London, 1967 edn)

Bowman, John, *De Valera and the Ulster Question, 1917–1973* (Oxford, 1982)

Boyce, D. G., 'British Conservative opinion, the Ulster question and the partition of Ireland, 1912–21', *Irish Historical Studies*, XVII/65 (1970), 89–112

— 'How to Settle the Irish Question: Lloyd George and Ireland 1916–21', in A. J. P. Taylor (ed.), *Lloyd George: Twelve Essays* (London, 1971)

— *Englishmen and Irish Troubles: British Public Opinion and the Making of Irish Policy 1918–22* (London, 1972)

Brock, Michael and Eleanor (eds), *H. H. Asquith Letters to Venetia Stanley* (Oxford, 1982)

Buckland, Patrick, *Irish Unionism 1885–1922: A Documentary History* (Belfast, 1973)

— *James Craig* (Dublin, 1980)

Callanan, Frank, *T. M. Healy* (Cork, 1996)

Callwell, C. E., *Field-Marshal Sir Henry Wilson: His Life and Diaries*, 2 vols (London, 1927)

Campbell, John, *F. E. Smith First Earl of Birkenhead* (London, 1983)

— *If Love Were All . . . The Story of Frances Stevenson and Lloyd George* (London, 2006)

Canning, Paul, *British Policy towards Ireland 1921–1941* (Oxford, 1985)

Carroll, F. M. (ed.), *The American Commission on Irish Independence 1919: The Diary, Correspondence and Report* (Dublin, 1985)

Chamberlain, Austen, *Politics From Inside* (London, 1936)

Churchill, Randolph S., *Winston S. Churchill*, vol. II (London, 1967)

— *Winston S. Churchill: Companion to Volume II*, 3 parts (London, 1969)

Churchill, W. S., *Lord Randolph Churchill* (London, 1907)

Churchill, Winston, *The Aftermath* (New York edn, 1929)

— *Great Contemporaries* (London, 1939 edn)

Clark, Alan (ed.), *'A Good Innings': The Private Papers of Viscount Lee of Fareham* (London, 1974)

Colvin, Ian, *The Life of Lord Carson*, 3 vols (London, 1934)

Cooke, A. B., and Vincent, John, *The Governing Passion: Cabinet Government and Party Politics in Britain* (Brighton, 1974)

Cowling, Maurice, *The Impact of Labour 1920–1924: The Beginning of Modern British Politics* (Cambridge, 1971)

Curran, Joseph M., *The Birth of the Irish Free State 1921–1923* (Alabama, 1980)

Curtis, L. P., *Coercion and Conciliation in Ireland, 1880–92: A Study in Conservative Unionism* (Princeton, New Jersey, 1963)

— *Anglo-Saxons and Celts: A Study of Anti-Irish Prejudice in Victorian England* (Bridgeport, Connecticut, 1968)

Dangerfield, George, *The Damnable Question: A Study in Anglo-Irish Relations* (London, 1977)

David, Edward (ed.), *Inside Asquith's Cabinet: From the Diaries of Charles Hobhouse* (London, 1977)

de Broke, Willoughby, Richard Greville Verney, Baron, *The Passing Years* (London, 1924)

Dutton, David, *Austen Chamberlain: Gentleman in Politics* (Bolton, 1985)

Ensor, R. C. K. , *England 1870–1914* (Oxford, 1936)

Ervine, St John, *Craigavon: Ulsterman* (London, 1949)

Esher, Viscount, *Journals and Letters of Reginald Viscount Esher*, vol. 3: *1910–1915* (London, 1938)

Fair, John D., *British Interparty Conferences: A Study of the*

Procedure of Conciliation in British Politics, 1867–1921
(Oxford, 1980)

Fanning, Ronan, '"Rats" versus "Ditchers": the Die-Hard Revolt and
the Parliament Bill of 1911', in Art Cosgrove and J. I. McGuire
(eds), *Parliament and Community* (Belfast, 1983), 191–210

— 'The Anglo-American Alliance and the Irish Question in the
Twentieth Century', in Judith Devlin and Howard B. Clarke
(eds), *European Encounters* (Dublin, 2003), 185–220

— et al., *Documents on Irish Foreign Policy*, vol. 1: *1919–1922*
(Dublin, 1998)

Fergusson, James, *The Curragh Incident* (London, 1964)

Fisher, H. A. L., *An Unfinished Autobiography* (London, 1940)

Fitzroy, Almeric, *Memoirs*, 2 vols (London, 1925)

Follis, Bryan A., *A State Under Siege: The Establishment of Northern
Ireland, 1920–25* (Oxford, 1995)

Forester, Margery, *Michael Collins* (London, 1971)

Foster, R. F., *Lord Randolph Churchill: A Political Life* (Oxford,
1981)

— *Modern Ireland 1600–1972* (London, 1988)

Foy, Michael T., *Michael Collins's Intelligence War* (Stroud, 2006)

George, William, *My Brother and I* (London, 1958)

Gilbert, Martin, *Winston S. Churchill*, vol. 4: *World in Torment
1917–22* (London, 1975)

Gollin, A. M., *Proconsul in Politics: A Study of Lord Milner in
Opposition and in Power* (London, 1964)

Grigg, John, *Lloyd George: The People's Champion 1902–1911*
(London, 1978)

— *Lloyd George: From Peace to War 1912–1916* (London, 1985)

Gwynn, Denis, *The Life of John Redmond* (London, 1932)

— *The History of Partition 1912–1925* (Dublin, 1950)

Hartley, Stephen, *The Irish Question as a Problem in British Foreign
Policy, 1914–18* (London, 1987)

Hattersley, Roy, *David Lloyd George: The Great Outsider* (London,
2010)

Hazlehurst, Cameron, 'Herbert Henry Asquith', in John P. Mackintosh
(ed.), *British Prime Ministers in the Twentieth Century* (London,
1977)

Hendrick, Burton J., *The Life and Letters of Walter H. Page* (London, 1930)

Holmes, Richard, *The Little Field-Marshal: Sir John French* (London, 1981)

Hopkinson, Michael (ed.), *The Last Days of Dublin Castle: The Mark Sturgis Diaries* (Dublin, 1999)

Hyde, H. Montgomery, *Carson, the Life of Sir Edward Carson* (London, 1953)

Jackson, Alvin, *The Ulster Party: Irish Unionists in the House of Commons, 1884–1911* (Oxford, 1989)

— *Home Rule: An Irish History, 1800–2000* (London, 2003)

Jackson, Daniel M., *Popular Opposition to Irish Home Rule in Edwardian Britain* (Liverpool, 2009)

Jalland, Patricia, 'A Liberal Chief Secretary and the Irish Question: Augustine Birrell, 1907–1914', in *The Historical Journal*, 19 (1976), 421–51

— *The Liberals and Ireland: The Ulster Question in British Politics to 1914* (Brighton, 1980)

Jay, Richard, *Joseph Chamberlain: A Political Study* (Oxford, 1981)

Jeffery, Keith, *Field Marshal Sir Henry Wilson: A Political Soldier* (Oxford, 2006)

Jenkins, Roy, *Asquith* (London, 1964)

Kendle, John, *Walter Long, Ireland, and the Union, 1905–1920* (Dublin, 1992)

Kennedy, Dennis, *The Widening Gulf: Northern Attitudes to the Independent Irish State 1919–49* (Belfast, 1988)

Koss, Stephen, *Asquith* (London, 1976)

Laffan, Michael, *The Partition of Ireland 1911–25* (Dundalk, 1983)

Lavin, Deborah, *From Empire to International Commonwealth: A Biography of Lionel Curtis* (Oxford, 1995)

Lewis, Bernard, *History – remembered, recovered, invented* (Princeton, 1975)

Lloyd George, Frances, *The Years That Are Past* (London, 1967)

Longford, Lord (Frank Pakenham), *Peace by Ordeal* (London, rev. pbk edn, 1967)

Loughlin, James, *The British Monarchy and Ireland – 1800 to the Present* (Cambridge, 2007)

Lubenow, W. C., *Parliamentary Politics and the Home Rule Crisis: the British House of Commons in 1886* (Oxford, 1988)

Lyons, F. S. L., *John Dillon* (London, 1968)

McColgan, John, *British Policy and the Irish Administration 1920–22* (London, 1983)

McCracken, Donal P., *The Irish Pro-Boers 1877–1902* (Cape Town, 1989)

McCready, H. W., 'Home Rule and the Liberal Party, 1899–1906' in *Irish Historical Studies*, vol. XIII (September 1963), 318–22

Macready, Nevil, *Annals of an Active Life*, 2 vols (London, 1924)

McDowell, R. B., *The Irish Convention* (London, 1970)

McMahon, Paul, *British Spies and Irish Rebels: British Intelligence and Ireland, 1916–1945* (London, 2008)

Mansergh, Nicholas, *The Irish Question 1840–1921* (rev. edn, London, 1965)

— *The Unresolved Question: the Anglo-Irish Settlement and its Undoing 1912–72* (New Haven and London, 1991)

Martin, F. X. (ed.), *The Irish Volunteers 1913–1915: Recollections and Documents* (Dublin, 1963)

— *The Howth Gun-Running 1914* (Dublin, 1964)

Masterman, Lucy, *C. F. G. Masterman* (London, 1939)

— 'Recollections of David Lloyd George', in *History Today*, IX, 3 March 1959, 160–69

Matthews, Kevin, *Fatal Influence: The Impact of Ireland on British Politics, 1920–1925* (Dublin, 2004)

Middlemas, Keith (ed.), *Thomas Jones: Whitehall Diary*, vol. I: *1916–1925* (London, 1969)

— *Thomas Jones: Whitehall Diary*, vol. III: *Ireland 1918–1925* (London, 1971)

Middlemas, Keith, and John Barnes, *Baldwin: A Biography* (London, 1969)

Miller, David W., *Church, State and Nation in Ireland, 1898–1921* (Dublin, 1973)

Morgan, Kenneth, *Consensus and Disunity: the Lloyd George Coalition Government 1918–22* (Oxford, 1979)

— 'Lloyd George and the Irish', in *Ireland after the Union: Proceedings of the Second Joint Meeting of the Royal Irish*

Academy and the British Academy (London, 1989), 105–20

— (ed.), *Lloyd George: Family Letters 1885–1936* (Cardiff and London, 1973)

Morley, John, *The Life of William Ewart Gladstone*, 3 vols (London, 1903)

Mottistone, Lord (J. E. B. Seely), *Adventure* (London, 1930)

Murphy, Richard, 'Walter Long and the making of the Government of Ireland Act, 1919–20', *Irish Historical Studies*, xxv/97 (May 1986), 82–96

Murray, Arthur, *Master and Brother: Murrays of Elibank* (London, 1945)

Murray, Patrick, 'Obsessive historian: Éamon de Valera and the policing of his reputation', *Proceedings of the Royal Irish Academy*, vol. 101C, 37–65 (2001)

Nicolson, Harold, *King George V* (London, 1952)

Ó Broin, Leon, *The Chief Secretary: Augustine Birrell in Ireland* (London, 1969)

— *No Man's Man: A Biographical Memoir of Joseph Brennan* (Dublin, 1982)

O'Halpin, Eunan, *The Decline of the Union: British Government in Ireland 1892–1920* (Dublin, 1987)

Parkinson, Alan E., *Friends in High Places: Ulster's Resistance to Irish Home Rule 1912–14* (Belfast, 2012)

Pearce, Edward, *Lines of Most Resistance: The Lords, the Tories and Ireland* (London, 1999)

Peatling, G. K., *British Opinion and Irish Self-Government, 1865–1925* (Dublin, 2001)

Petrie, Charles, *The Life and Letters of Austen Chamberlain*, 2 vols (London, 1939–40)

Phillips, Gregory D., *The Die-hards: Aristocratic Society and Politics in Edwardian England* (London, 1979)

Phillips, W. Alison, *The Revolution in Ireland 1906–1923* (London, 1923)

Phoenix, Eamon, *Northern Nationalism: Nationalist Politics, Partition and the Catholic Minority in Northern Ireland, 1890–1940* (Belfast, 1994)

— 'Michael Collins: The Northern Question 1916–1922', in

Gabriel Doherty and Dermot Keogh (eds), *Michael Collins and the Making of the Irish State* (Cork, 1998)

Rhodes James, Robert, *Rosebery* (London, 1963)

— *Churchill: A Study in Failure, 1900–1939* (London, 1970)

Riddell, Lord, *Intimate Diary of the Peace Conference and After 1918–23* (London, 1933)

— *More Pages from My Diary 1908–1914* (London, 1934)

Robbins, Keith, *Sir Edward Grey* (London, 1971)

Roskill, Stephen, *Hankey: Man of Secrets*, 3 vols (London, 1970)

Rowland, Peter, *The Last Liberal Governments: Unfinished Business 1911–1914* (London, 1971)

Ryan, A. P., *Mutiny at the Curragh* (London, 1956)

Searle, G. R., *The Quest for National Efficiency* (London, 1971)

Self, Robert C. (ed.), *The Austen Chamberlain Diary Letters: The Correspondence of Sir Austen Chamberlain with His Sisters Hilda and Ida 1916–37* (Cambridge, 1995)

Shannon, Catherine B., *Arthur J. Balfour and Ireland 1874–1922* (Washington DC, 1988)

Sloan, G. R., *The Geo-politics of Anglo-Irish Relations in the 20th Century* (London, 1997)

Stewart, A. T. Q., *The Ulster Crisis: Resistance to Home Rule 1912–14* (London, 1967)

Taylor, A. J. P., *English History 1914–45* (Oxford, 1965)

— (ed.), *Lloyd George: A Diary by Frances Stevenson* (London, 1971)

Taylor, Rex, *Michael Collins* (London, pbk edn, 1961)

Townshend, Charles, *The British Campaign in Ireland, 1919–21* (Oxford, 1975)

— 'British Policy in Ireland, 1906–1921', in D. G. Boyce (ed.), *The Revolution in Ireland, 1879–1923* (Dublin, 1988)

— *Easter 1916: The Easter Rebellion* (London, 2005)

Turner, John, *Lloyd George's Secretariat* (Cambridge, 1980)

— *British Politics and the Great War: Coalition and Conflict 1915–18* (New Haven and London, 1992)

Vincent, John (ed.), *The Crawford Papers: The Journals of David Lindsay twenty-seventh Earl of Crawford and tenth Earl of Balcarres 1892–1940* (Manchester, 1984)

Waley, S. D., *Edwin Montagu* (London, 1964)

Wall, Maureen, 'Partition: The Ulster question (1916–26)', in Desmond Williams (ed.), *The Irish Struggle 1916–26* (London, 1966), 79–93

Walsh, Maurice, *The News from Ireland: Foreign Correspondents and the Irish Revolution* (London, 2008)

Ward, Alan J., *Ireland and Anglo-American Relations 1899–1921* (London, 1969)

Webb, Beatrice, *Diaries 1912–24* (London, 1952)

Wilson, John, *CB: A Life of Sir Henry Campbell-Bannerman* (London, 1973)

Wilson, Trevor (ed.), *The Political Diaries of C. P. Scott 1911–1928* (London, 1970)

Acknowledgements

The opening chapters of this book are based on my doctoral dissertation 'Arthur Balfour and the leadership of the Unionist Party in opposition, 1906–1911' (Cambridge, 1968). Chapters 3 and 4 draw on material in 'The Home Rule Crisis of 1912–14 and the Failure of British Democracy in Ireland' (Maurice J. Bric and John Coakley (eds), *From Political Violence to Negotiated Settlement* (Dublin, 2004), 32–48; chapter 7 on 'The Anglo-American Alliance and the Irish Question in the Twentieth Century' in Howard Clarke and Judith Devlin (eds), *Encounters with Europe: Essays in Honour of Albert Lovett* (Dublin, 2003), 185–220; and chapter 9 on 'Britain, Ireland and the end of the Union' in *Ireland after the Union* (Oxford, 1989), 105–20.

I am indebted to the Michael Collins Memorial Foundation Award for research into the Bonar Law and Lloyd George papers (both collections were then in the Beaverbrook Library and are now in the House of Lords Record Office) and the records of the Cabinet Office (then in the Public Record Office in Chancery Lane and now in the National Archives at Kew); the Institute of Irish Studies at Queen's University, Belfast, for appointing me as a Senior Research Fellow in 1995–96; and Peterhouse, Cambridge, for a Visiting Fellowship in 2004 when this book assumed its final form.

I gratefully acknowledge the permission of Her Majesty Queen Elizabeth II to make use of material from the Royal Archives at Windsor Castle. I am also indebted to the staff of the Archives Department, University College Dublin; the Beaverbrook Library; Birmingham University Library; the Bodleian Library, Oxford; the British Library; Cambridge University Library; the Archives Centre at Churchill College, Cambridge; the National Archives of Ireland; the

ACKNOWLEDGEMENTS

National Archives for the United Kingdom; the National Libraries of Ireland, of Scotland and of Wales; the Library of Trinity College Dublin; the Public Record Office of Northern Ireland; and the Scottish Record Office.

I am especially grateful to my agent, Jonathan Williams, and to Neil Belton, Editorial Director at Faber and Faber; their early enthusiasm and encouragement meant more to me than I can easily say. I am also grateful to Kate Murray-Browne and Rebecca Pearson of Faber and Faber and to Mark Duncan who found most of the illustrations. But the greatest debt I incurred as this book took shape is to Jill Burrows: her copy-editing and typesetting of both the text and of the illustrations was as sensitive as it was magisterial; so, too, was her preparation of the index.

I want also to thank all those who read this book in typescript, whether in whole or in part, and those who otherwise offered support and advice. They include Art Cosgrove, Catriona Crowe, Adrian Fanning, Tim Fanning, David Goodall, Adrian Hardiman, Michael Lillis, James McGuire, Jonathan Powell and Richard Ryan.

Finally, I owe a great debt to my children, Judith, Gareth and Tim, for their unwavering personal support and, above all, to Virginia, an Irish woman born in England, to whom this book is dedicated not least because she has had to live with it for as long as she has lived with me.

Index